Changing Minds Changing Tools

Changing Minds Changing Tools

From Learning Theory to Language Acquisition to Language Change

Vsevolod Kapatsinski

The MIT Press
Cambridge, Massachusetts
London, England

This book was set in ITC Stone Sans Std by ITC Stone Serif Std.

Library of Congress Cataloging-in-Publication Data

Names: Kapatsinski, Vsevolod, author.
Title: Changing minds changing tools : from learning theory to language
    acquisition to language change / Vsevolod M. Kapatsinski.
Description: Cambridge, MA : The MIT Press, [2018] | Includes bibliographical
    references and index.
Identifiers: LCCN 2017047700 | ISBN 9780262037860 (hardcover : alk. paper)
Subjects: LCSH: Language acquisition--Psychological aspects. | Linguistic change--
    Psychological aspects. | Language and languages--Psychological aspects.
Classification: LCC P142.K26 2018 | DDC 401/.9--dc23 LC record available at
https://lccn.loc.gov/2017047700

Contents

Acknowledgments

This book would not have happened without the contributions of many people. My biggest debt of gratitude is to my mentors, particularly Joan Bybee, who shaped my thinking on these issues when I was an MA student at the University of New Mexico. Joan has led the revolutionary "quantitative turn" in theoretical linguistics, turning it from a field in which "those who count don't count" into a field where probabilistic patterns are a primary topic of investigation and quantitative factors such as frequency of use (in particular contexts) are seen as driving language change and shaping language structure. I am also very grateful to David Pisoni, who provided me with excellent training in experimental methods and a very supportive environment at the Speech Research Laboratory at Indiana University during my PhD years. Being at Indiana in the second half of the aughts exposed me to a great deal of research that forms the foundation of this book. Of others at Indiana, I am particularly grateful to my coadvisor, Ken de Jong, who showed me how interesting phonetics could be if one approaches it from the perspective of learning, and to John Kruschke for giving me an early education in Bayesian methods. I am also in debt to Harald Baayen for teaching me much about the operation of the Rescorla-Wagner model and for generously sharing code implementing the model. My two visits to Tübingen and subsequent conversations with Harald have greatly increased my understanding of what error-driven models can and cannot do.

This book would also not be possible without my graduate students, Zara Harmon, Paul Olejarczuk, Amy Smolek, and Hideko Teruya. Without their insights and hard work, I would have nothing to write. Zara was the one who came up with the "associative triangle" framework and the insight that frequency might need to be logarithmically scaled to explain the puzzling results on skewed distribution learning (chapter 5). She is primarily responsible for the research on probability matching summarized in chapter 2, the study on effecting attention shifts via distributional learning in chapter 5, and the work on entrenchment vs. extension in word learning (chapter 6). She has also taken my research program on the role of automatization in disfluencies and extended it in ways I did not think possible, only some of which are reported in chapter 9. Paul is primarily responsible for the work on distributional learning from skewed categories in chapter 5 and for the biased belief updating data and model in chapter 4. His skill in experimental phonetics and speech synthesis has made it possible for us to branch out into the "low-level" mappings between acoustic cues and phonetic categories. Amy is responsible for documenting the inductive and channel biases that constrain the acquisition of paradigmatic mappings, bringing experimental rigor to this line of research (chapter 7). Finally, Hideko's ingenious demonstration that we would all say *schemar* if we did not know the word well enough, though it did not make it into this book, has instilled in me the belief that sublexical and lexical schemas compete in production (chapter 7). This book would be very short indeed without the team.

Finally, this book would also not be possible without my mother, Varvara Kapatsinskaya, and my grandfather, Mikhail Fuks, who are responsible for both biological and environmental contributions to everything I have ever learned.

Introduction

By the time you were just a year old, you had learned which sound distinctions matter and which do not. From the constant streams of acoustic and visual input, you had extracted a few acoustic forms and linked them to meanings—your first words. The muscles of your tongue, jaw, and larynx (and a few others) had been shaped into producing intricate, precisely coordinated patterns that would reproduce some of these complex patterns of sound closely enough to evoke the adept at producing words and sentences you had never heard before, planning and executing a novel sequence of muscle movements to convey a novel meaning. These feats appear miraculous, impossible for mere animals to accomplish. And indeed, they have led many researchers of language acquisition to posit that we are born knowing much about what human languages are like (Universal Grammar) and equipped with specialized learning mechanisms, tailored to the acquisition of language, mechanisms not subject to the laws that govern learning in the rest of the biological world (the Language Acquisition Device). The aim of this book is to convince you that this conclusion is—if not wrong—then at least premature. Language acquisition is simply learning. This book is one illustration of how accepting this proposition gets us much closer to explaining why languages are the way they are—the ultimate goal of linguistic theory—than does accepting innate knowledge of language universals and the Language Acquisition Device. Learning changes minds, and changing minds change the tools they use to accomplish their communicative goals to fit.

Explaining Language by Explaining Language Change

All theoretical linguists are primarily interested in explaining why languages are the way they are. *Usage-based* theoretical linguists like myself approach this question in what may seem like a roundabout manner, by explaining why languages change in the ways they do. As emphasized by Bybee (2001), languages are highly diverse, yet they change in predictable ways. Linguistic diversity has often frustrated the search for synchronic linguistic universals to enshrine in a Universal Grammar. Yet, it is fully compatible with *diachronic* universals, recurrent pathways of language change. According to usage-based linguistics, these pathways arise from the way languages are used and learned, from processes that happen in the individual moments of perception and production.

In phonology, the search for Universal Grammar culminated in a highly influential approach to linguistics called Optimality Theory, first developed in a 1993 manuscript published as Prince and Smolensky (2008). Optimality Theory proposed that the grammars of all languages consist of the same finite set of constraints, and the only way languages differ is in how they rank these constraints. In phonology, where this theory took hold, the constraints were prohibitions against particular structures (markedness constraints) and against particular changes (faithfulness constraints). For example, consider words like *prince*. The [ns] sequence at the end of that word is crosslinguistically rare, and indeed is changing into [nts] in English, so that the word comes to sound the same as *prints*. An Optimality Theorist would therefore be tempted to propose a markedness constraint against this offensive structure, say, *NS. In languages that do have [ns], this constraint would be ranked higher than the faithfulness constraints prohibiting various repairs to the sequence. In other languages, one of these constraints could be ranked lower than *NS, resulting in elimination of the structure. How could it be eliminated? One possibility is violating the universal constraint Max, which prohibits deletion. Demoting Max would turn *prince* into *prin* or *priss*. Another possibility is turning [s] into [t], resulting in *print*. What is chosen instead is violating Dep, which bans insertion. Why was that option chosen, and why was the inserted consonant [t] and not any other consonant, or perhaps a vowel that would break up the [ns] cluster, turning *prince* into *priness*? The theory does not answer.

In a diachronic account, this is not a mystery at all (Browman & L. Goldstein, 1989). Consider how *prince* is pronounced. To transition from a voiced nasal stop [n] into a voiceless oral fricative [s], three things need to happen at exactly the same time. The airflow into the nose needs to be stopped by raising the velum. The voicing needs to cease, which is accomplished by pulling the vocal folds apart to prevent them from vibrating. The tongue needs to be slightly lowered to allow for turbulent airflow between the top of the tongue blade and the hard palate. The first two actions can be done rapidly: no matter how far apart the vocal folds go, voicing will cease; no matter how fast you raise the velum, the airflow will cease. In contrast, the last action of lowering the tongue needs to be quite precise and carefully executed: lower the tongue too much, and you will end up with too much airflow and no frication. Think about jerking a door open or slamming it shut vs. opening it just a crack, just enough for your cat to come in: this last action requires quite a bit more time and premeditation. Now consider what happens if slamming the velum shut and jerking the vocal folds open happen too fast, before the tongue is lowered. What would result is a period of time during which there is no airflow from the mouth or nose and the voicing has ceased; in other words, a [t]. No other repair would just as easily result from a simple articulatory mistiming (see chapter 9 for a fuller account).

In English, almost all fricatives are allowed in the coda. The sole exception is [h], the fricative that lacks any oral articulation; thus we are allowed *kiss* but not **kih*. In some other languages (e.g., Slave, an Aboriginal language in Canada), [h] is the *only* consonant allowed in the coda; *kih* is fine but **kiss* is not. Synchronically, there seems to be no pattern here at all. In contrast, diachronically, we can say that oral fricatives in the coda position tend to lose their oral articulations, becoming [h], and that [h] itself is likely to be lost, reducing to zero. Thus, both languages that have [h] in the coda and lack other fricatives, and those that allow only [h] in this position, can result from the same diachronic pathway, {f;s;x} > [h] > 0 (Bybee, 2001, p. 221). If an old [h] is lost before newer fricatives have reduced to [h], we get languages like English. If coda fricatives have reduced to [h] but no further, we get a language like Slave. In this case, as in many others, much stronger generalizations can be made about the dynamic patterns of language change than about the static patterns of language structure.

In some cases, a strong generalization about synchronic systems *can* be made but appears mysterious without considering language change. For example, across languages, adjectives and determiners tend to be on the same side of a noun they modify: *the big cat* vs. **the cat big* or **big cat the*. (There are exceptions, like Spanish.) Like many universals (or near-universals), this one has been promoted to a principle of Universal Grammar, a piece of innate knowledge all human infants inexplicably share (Culbertson et al., 2012). Yet, diachronically, there is no mystery here either. Determiners are not coined by speakers de novo. Rather, they gradually develop out of adjectives through the process of semantic extension/bleaching inherent in reuse of a frequent form (see chapter 6). As the meanings of adjectives change, their position in the sentence does not: words tend to grammaticalize "in situ," rather than hopping around the sentence

(Givón, 1979). Eventually, we start calling the frequent, highly bleached adjectives determiners and are puzzled by the synchronic similarity between them and "true" adjectives. The synchronic similarity in behavior is the result of diachronic similarity in function. Adjectives and determiners stay close because they come from the same place. Like the synchronic patterns of phonology, the synchronic patterns of syntax are explicable only by considering where they come from.

Since there are so few true universals shared by all languages, an important advantage of the diachronic approach is that it explains both the prevalent patterns and the typological rarities. A sequence of perfectly natural changes can result in a system that synchronically looks utterly unnatural. For example, in Russian, [k] and [g] become [tʃ] and [ʒ] respectively before the suffix -ok, a palatalization process. Synchronically, this is inexplicable: palatalization usually happens when velars or alveolars assimilate to front vowels or glides; cf. the [d] in *would you*. The back vowel [o] shares little with [tʃ] and [ʒ]. However, diachronically, this is a simple case of assimilation followed by deletion: the suffix used to be -jok, and it is this [j] that caused palatalization before disappearing. Indeed, the English [dj] in *would you* and other frequent phrases is entering the same pathway (Bush, 2001). As part of acquiring one's native language, one has to learn many things that do not "make sense," that lack a synchronic motivation. It is by looking at how languages are reshaped by the processes of language learning and use that we can explain why the patterns we have to learn are the way they are.

On Innateness, Learning, and Learning Mechanisms

The primary aim of this book is to integrate usage-based linguistic theory with domain-general learning theory, to bring the body of knowledge on how we learn to bear on why languages change in the ways they do. However, much of this work is not based on learning *language*. One may therefore wonder whether it is at all useful for gaining insights into language acquisition. Indeed, Chomsky (1959 et seq.) has argued forcefully that language acquisition has to be considered on its own terms, as a unique, species-specific ability governed by its own laws and undergirded by a body of domain-specific innate knowledge.

There is no question that language is both specific to the human species and universal within it. However, a species-specific system of behavior need not require innate knowledge of the behavior. It is also uncontroversial that all organisms have specialized learning systems in the sense of distinct neural networks localized to specific parts of the brain and innately pre-pared to form certain kinds of associations rather than others. However, distinct learning systems need not operate according to unique principles. Distinct neural networks connect different representations, and so embody different systems of belief and conditional behavior. However, the same principles—*laws* or *mechanisms of learning*—can describe how the connection weights constituting the knowledge of a neural network change on the basis of experience. Laws of learning are constrained by two things: what the system *needs* to learn, and what it *can* learn given its biological makeup. Since distinct learning systems are built out of the same "stuff" (neurons) and need to accomplish the same basic task (learn contingencies between stimuli or between stimuli and behaviors), they have little choice but to obey the same laws. Throughout this book, we will see how these laws turn out to be helpful for explaining recurrent patterns in language change.

There are many cases of species-specific behaviors that are acquired by some species fairly rapidly and by others very slowly or not at all. For example, consider song acquisition in male cowbirds (*Molothrus ater*), extensively studied by Andrew King, Meredith West, and their colleagues. Cowbird songs are not sung by other bird species, and all male cowbirds end up acquiring a distinctively cowbird song. Importantly, cowbirds are not raised by cowbirds: like cuckoos, cowbirds place their eggs in other birds' nests. Unsurprisingly, this has initially led to claims of innate song knowledge— much like the claims of innate grammatical knowledge in linguistics (e.g., Mayr, 1974). However, it turns out that cowbird songs are shaped by the females, who prefer the kinds of songs adult males in their community sing (West & King, 2008). Most times a male cowbird sings, he sings to a female. The female does not sing, but indicates her attraction to a male by giving a little twitch of the wing—a good song gives her the shivers, so to speak. The closer the male's song is to the songs of the adult males in the female's community, the more likely she is to twitch in appreciation (West et al., 2003). In a novice performer, there is always much random variation in performance—a novice does not hit the target on every try. In the young cowbird, this variation produces a range of variants, some closer to the adult song than others. The closer variants are more likely to be reinforced by the females. In this way, the range of song variants shifts ever closer to the adult song, a process called *shaping* (King et al., 2005) as well as *reinforcement learning* and *selection by consequences* (Skinner, 1984). Shaping leads the male cowbird to converge on the type of song preferred by the females he is housed with. Indeed, male cowbirds reared with female canaries incorporate canary elements into their songs—and prefer to court unfamiliar canaries over unfamiliar females of their own species, despite the canaries never reciprocating their advances (King et al., 1996). While much could still be innate about this process, innate song knowledge is not required to explain it.

Like birdsong, speech is a species-specific behavior that develops in all neurotypical members of the species in typical social environments. Also like cowbird song, speech develops in part by imitating *the right* models. When placed in their normal social environment, male cowbirds are shaped to imitate only adult males rather than (continuing) to reproduce songs of the birds that raised them when they were little chicks (West & King, 2008). Similarly, children learn to speak like their peers rather than like their caregivers (e.g., Kerswill, 1996). The parallels are quite striking.

It is uncontroversial that we are prepared to produce speech: all infants babble, both vocally and manually. Like immature birdsong, early babble is highly variable. Whereas adults find it much easier to produce vocal or manual gestures that are part of their native language—to the extent that other sorts of gestures seldom surface even in error—early gestures do not closely resemble the gestures of the ambient language and are far less differentiated. Over time, gestures that approximate ambient language sounds (and especially words!) are reinforced, making the child more likely to attempt them in the future. With repeated attempts, the reinforced gestures become easier and easier to produce, while the unreinforced gestures become harder. As this process continues, reinforced targets are reached with increasing precision. Furthermore, mothers become increasingly selective: the better one's vocalizations are on average, the harder it is to impress mom with one's vocal skill to elicit reinforcement (M. Goldstein & West, 1999). In this way, mothers lead children closer and closer to the adult articulatory targets. Indeed, when mothers' behavior is experimentally decoupled from infant behavior, vocalization development slows down considerably (M. Goldstein et al., 2003). As with cowbird song, a domain-general learning mechanism results in the acquisition of species-specific behavior.

Not every behavior is learned in this way. Indeed, some behaviors may be innate and even innately linked to classes of stimuli. For example, many mammal species appear to be prepared to associate symptoms of poisoning with tastes rather than sights (Garcia & Koelling, 1966; Seligman, 1970). Members of these species rapidly acquire taste-nausea associations and find it difficult or impossible to acquire color-nausea associations or taste-footshock associations. Many species also come prepared to associate particular kinds of stimuli with specific behaviors (Breland & Breland,

1961; Seligman, 1970). For example, different stimuli naturally elicit different food-searching behaviors in the rat. When food is signaled by a light, the rat rears up on its hind paws. When it is signaled by a sound, the rat instead jerks its head around in an excited manner (Ross & Holland, 1981). Nonetheless, updating the weights of associations one is prepared to update appears to be governed by the same laws as updating associations one is less willing to change, and can be described by the same associative learning models. For example, cue-competition effects hold for learned taste aversions in rats, sound-food associations in dogs, and associations between fictitious diseases and their symptoms in humans. If two equally strong stimuli redundantly cue the same outcome (whether nausea, food, or a novel name for a fictitious disease), only one of them tends to become associated with the outcome (see chapter 3). The fact that some associations are learned more readily than others does not challenge associationist learning mechanisms: theories of associative learning are not about *what* is learned but *how*.

The Structure of This Book

Writing is linear. Thoughts are not. In choosing to linearize one's thoughts in a certain way, one is therefore faced with a number of competing motivations. For me, one main motivation has been starting simple and introducing complications when they become relevant. Thus, in chapter 1, I introduce the basic concepts of learning theory. Chapter 2 discusses what is to be learned, outlines the aspects of language structure I focus on in this book, and describes some ways gradient, associative knowledge can give rise to systematic, categorical grammatical behavior. Chapter 3 focuses on properties of nodes, salience and associability, and discusses chunking processes that fuse co-occurring units together into larger units and selective attention that breaks them apart. It also introduces the notions of mediation and conditional mappings. Chapter 4 introduces the ideas of Bayesian learning theory, the most serious challenger to associationism. Chapters 5–9 then showcase associationist approaches to various problems in language acquisition and point out the implications for language change.

A second way of viewing the structure of the book is to follow the "speech chain" from comprehension to planning and then executing a production plan. Chapters 3–5 are focused on comprehension; chapters 6 and 7 discuss the relationship between comprehension and production. Chapter 8 takes on planning, particularly planning a novel, morphologically complex word. Finally, chapter 9 deals with execution of the plan.

A third way to view the chapters is with respect to the kinds of issues learning models face in these various domains. Much of this book will deal with what Zara Harmon (p.c.) has called the (associative) *triangle*, illustrated in figure 0.1. The triangle can be seen as the basic constituent of the language network, though the full picture is more complicated because the flow of activation down each of the connections in figure 0.1 is partially blocked by a leaky gate. These gates can be activated (opened) or inhibited (closed) by various contextual cues. The conditioning of the mappings on the context can be quite intricate and comes up again and again throughout the book, but especially in chapters 3 and 6.

In figure 0.1, there are two forms that occur in a fixed order, $Form_2$ following $Form_1$, and are both linked to the same meaning (though each form may also be linked to other meanings, and the meaning could be linked to other forms). All of the links shown in the triangle have been argued to be used in the tasks facing the speaker/listener, and the existence of almost all of them can be questioned. For example, much associative learning theory is concerned with the circumstances under which one would learn both the $Form_1 \rightarrow Meaning$ association and the $Form_2 \rightarrow Meaning$ association (the issue of cue competition). Debates on the role of bidirectionality in leaning focus on the relationship between $Form \rightarrow Meaning$ and $Meaning \rightarrow Form$ links, and the extent to which learners develop and use backward connections, $Form_2 \rightarrow Form_1$. The first two have also been a focus of debates on the role of feedback in comprehension and production. The existence of parallel $Meaning \rightarrow Form$ connections is questioned by many morphologists and syntacticians but usually assumed in theories of speech planning and execution.

We have assumed so far that the relationship between the two forms in figure 0.1 is a syntagmatic one: $Form_2$ follows $Form_1$ in time. The processing

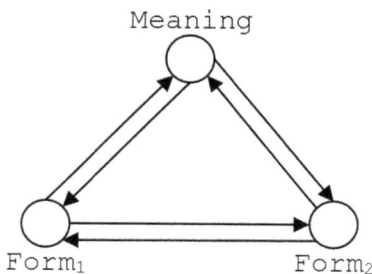

Figure 0.1
The associative triangle

of linearly ordered forms is a big issue in comprehension (chapter 3)—where the forms are encountered by the listener in the order the speaker produced them. It is also a big issue in execution—where forms need to be produced in a preplanned order (chapter 9). However, the biggest issue in generating a plan is resolving competition for selection between alternative forms. In that case, only one of Form$_1$ or Form$_2$ needs to be selected for inclusion in the plan to express the desired meaning, and the connections between them are no longer about temporal precedence (or are they? see chapter 7).

Competing forms first appear in chapter 5, where the forms are alternative values on an apparently continuous phonetic dimension. There, I show that—despite their seemingly infinite number—such values (or rather intervals) can still be treated as cues in the associative triangle and that this has certain advantages (see also chapter 9 for production). In chapter 6, I focus on the relationship between Meaning→Form connections and Form→Meaning connections, an issue that makes brief appearances throughout the book. Finally, chapters 8 and 9 discuss paradigmatic Form→Form connections. Chapter 10 brings together what we've learned throughout the book and tries to connect the strands that permeate the book into a cohesive canvas covering all aspects of language, from acquisition and processing to structure and change.

1   The Web in the Spider: Associative Learning Theory

In language, we have developed a bad habit. Many problems in language appear too complicated for simple processes to solve, and consequently, domain-general processes have been ruled out altogether.

—McMurray et al. (2013, pp. 49–50)

This book is about the learning mechanisms that allow humans to acquire language. But what are these mechanisms? In this chapter, we will review three basic kinds of learning: Hebbian learning, summarized by Hebb's (1949) dictum that "neurons that fire together wire together," chunking, and error-driven predictive learning, an approach that has dominated learning theory since the early 1970s (Rescorla & Wagner, 1972). I finish this chapter by discussing what a learning mechanism is, and why associationism is a promising approach to learning theory.

Despite Chomsky's (1959) rejection of the term *language learning*, learning mechanisms have been the focus of work in linguistic theory for decades. Chomsky and Halle (1965) spoke of an *acquisition model* (later, the *language acquisition device*) that induces grammars on the basis of linguistic experience. Chomsky (1965) proposed that a theory of grammar has explanatory adequacy only insofar as it can predict what grammar would be acquired on exposure to a particular language.

In rejecting the term *language learning*, Chomsky rejected the learning mechanisms of associationist learning theory, built on research on classic and operant conditioning in nonhuman animals (Pavlov, 1927; Skinner, 1957). Rejection of standard learning theory initiated work on what *domain-specific* learning mechanisms have evolved to learn language (culminating in the Principles and Parameters framework in syntax (Chomsky & Lasnik, 1993) and Optimality Theory in phonology (Prince & Smolensky, 1993/2008)). More recently, even generative linguists have started to explore the possibility that domain-general learning mechanisms might be able to do the job of acquiring language, at least if they are allowed to operate on domain-specific representations (Chomsky, 1995; Hayes & Wilson, 2008; C. Yang, 2004). This change of heart has been spurred on by the rise of connectionist and Bayesian approaches in psychology and cognitive science.

Instead of rejecting the associationist approach to learning, the present book embraces it. By taking associationist learning theory seriously, we can determine where it proves insufficient and how it can be modified to achieve a full(er) account of language acquisition. I begin with the simplest possible learning mechanisms, forming the foundation of elemental associationist learning theory. In subsequent chapters, I introduce and evaluate complications, including selective attention (chapters 3–5), configural/holistic representations (chapter 3), and confidence in belief (chapter 4). After reviewing the toolkit of biologically grounded and experimentally supported learning mechanisms, I apply it to problems of learning speech sound categories (chapter 5), form-meaning mappings (chapter 6), planning novel, creative productions by generating never experienced speech plans (chapters 7 and 8), and fluent yet accurate execution of planned action (chapter 9).

1.1 Associationist Learning Mechanisms: Hebbian and Error-Driven Learning

Classic associationist learning theory (e.g., Hebb, 1949; Pavlov, 1927; Rescorla & Wagner, 1972) views the mind as a network of simple interconnected representations (nodes). Nodes are connected to each other by links (also known as connections or associations), which encode the co-occurrence structure among the nodes. For example, consider the link A→B. This is a directed link from node A (the *cue*) to node B (the *outcome*). The fact that it is a directed link means that the weight of A→B does not have to be equal to the weight of B→A.

Associationist learning theory deals with the updating of link weights on the basis of experience. All information contained in a link is its weight, so link weights constitute most if not all of what the network knows. The weight could be positive, making the link excitatory, negative, making the link inhibitory, or zero. In most learning models, there is no inherent difference between excitatory and inhibitory links, so that a link's weight can cross zero under pressure from experience. If the A→B link is *excitatory*, activation of A drives the activation of B up; if the link is *inhibitory*, activation of A drives the activation of B down. The absolute value of the weight is the strength of the link, encoding the strength of the relationship between A and B.

A link represents a relationship that the learner keeps track of. For example, the existence of A→B means that the learner is trying to learn whether the occurrence/activation of B does, or should, depend on the occurrence/activation of A. While there are a variety of network architectures that bias the learner to pay attention only to certain relationships between the units s/he represent, the simplest assumption is that every node is connected to every other node, so the learner keeps track of all relationships between the represented units. Argumentation from learnability and/or neuroscience is then necessary to argue for specific deviations from full connectivity (e.g., Kapatsinski, 2011; Warker & Dell, 2006).

Updating of connection weights can proceed in at least two ways, which constitute distinct *learning mechanisms*. In *Hebbian learning*, association weights are updated on the basis of simple co-occurrence: representations of events that tend to occur at the same time are wired together (just as neurons that fire together wire together; Hebb, 1949). Co-occurrence of the connected units drives the connection weight up. Non-co-occurrence drives it down. In *error-driven learning* (Rescorla & Wagner, 1972), association weights are instead updated on the basis of prediction error: the weight of the connection is updated if the node at the end of the connection is activated when it should not be or not activated when it should be. Connection weights are updated in the direction that minimizes the error. For example, if the connection is excitatory, and the node it leads to is excited too easily, the connection weight decreases and may eventually become negative, turning the connection inhibitory.

Specifically, Rescorla and Wagner (1972) proposed that weights are updated following the equations in (1) and (2). The weight from a cue C to a present outcome O at time $t + 1$ is increased via equation (1), while the weight from a cue C to an absent outcome is decreased using equation (2). The learning rate Λ is intended to reflect cue and outcome salience. If all outcomes that occur on a trial have activations equal to 1 and all absent outcomes have activations equal to 0, the model learns nothing. Otherwise, weights are adjusted so that the activation of the present outcomes given the same cue set would be closer to 1, and activations of absent outcomes would be closer to 0. The fact that the learning rate on a trial is weighted by error (the difference between the current activation of an outcome and the correct activation, here 0 or 1) is what makes the model *error-driven* rather than Hebbian.

$$w_{t+1}^{C \to O} = w_t^{C \to O} + \left(1 - a_t^O\right) \times \Lambda \tag{1}$$

$$w_{t+1}^{C \to O} = w_t^{C \to O} + \left(0 - a_t^O\right) \times \Lambda \tag{2}$$

Until Kamin's (1969) demonstration of cue competition, learning theory was dominated by Hebbian learning models (Bush & Mosteller, 1951; Estes, 1950; Hebb, 1949). Kamin (1969) showed that forming an A→X association prevented formation of a B→X association if B was always encountered together with A—that is, exposure to A→X followed by exposure to AB→X did not seem to result in a B→X association. The influence of A→X on the strength of B→X is called the *blocking effect*. The RW model accounts for the blocking effect by setting the learning rate in Stage I high enough for the activation of X after encountering A at the end of Stage I to be close to 1. This means that the model then learns nothing on AB→X trials in Stage II: X is already fully expected on the basis of A, so B has nothing to explain.[1]

Arnon and Ramscar (2012) have argued that the difficulty often exhibited by second language learners in learning to use determiners may also be due to blocking. They reason that a learner who experiences a noun without an article first can directly associate the form of a noun with the meaning of the noun and the determiner (e.g., cat→CAT.DEF). When later presented with determiner phrases like *the cat*, the learned association blocks the determiner from associating with the meaning DEF.

The blocking effect provided the primary motivation for Rescorla and Wagner's (1972) error-driven learning model of associative learning: since X is expected in the presence of A, exposure to AB (which contains A) results in no error and therefore no learning, hence nothing is learned about B. Thus, the existence of blocking effects in language provides prima facie evidence for the same error-driven mechanisms playing a role in language acquisition (Arnon & Ramscar, 2012).

However, the Rescorla-Wagner model is not the only way to account for blocking. Other explanations of the blocking effect—which do not rely on the assumption that we only learn from errors—suggest that something *is* learned about B. In particular, Ralph Miller and colleagues argue that B is actually associated with X after AB→X trials (Matzel et al., 1985; Miller & Matzel, 1988; Stout & Miller, 2007). Several studies provide support for this hypothesis by showing that exposure to A alone following AB→X trials reduces or eliminates blocking, so that B alone comes to reliably activate X despite no additional training on B→X (e.g., Blaisdell et al., 1999). Based on this kind of data, Miller and colleagues have suggested that learning is actually based on simple Hebbian contiguity and all co-occurring stimuli are associated together in a noncompetitive manner: B is associated with X in AB→X trials but A→X interferes with retrieval of this association.[2] Blocking effects do not provide a knockout argument against simple Hebbian learning models that preceded Rescorla and Wagner (1972), provided that learning results in a knowledge base that can be queried in different ways.

Human learning, unlike animal learning, has most often been studied experimentally within a *causal learning* or *contingency learning* paradigm. In a typical version of this task, participants are presented with diseases and their symptoms and learn to either predict diseases from symptoms or symptoms from diseases (e.g., Gluck & Bower, 1988). Their acquired knowledge is then explicitly tested by asking them questions like "Is B a symptom of X?" or "Is X a disease caused by B?" Blocking can be observed in this paradigm when participants deny that B causes X after AB→X trials. Matute et al. (1996) showed that blocking is observed with some test questions but not others, suggesting that either different questions tap into different stores of associations, or the same memory store is flexibly used in different ways depending on the question (e.g., whether the question is about which cue is *most* predictive of an outcome or about which cues are predictive of an outcome *at all*). Other recent work has suggested that blocking can also be reduced or even reversed in human causal learning, by putting participants under time pressure or having them perform a demanding secondary task during training (e.g., DeHouwer & Beckers, 2003; Sternberg & McClelland, 2009; Vadillo & Matute, 2010).

While this work has often been framed as speaking to the nature of *the* learning mechanism, it may be more productive to interpret it from the perspective that humans utilize both Hebbian learning and error-driven learning. This interpretation is supported by neuroscientific findings that both types of learning exist at the level of individual synapses, which are the neural analogs to connections. Hebbian learning modifies connection weights in the cortex, while error-driven learning modifies connection weights in subcortical, striatal structures (Ashby et al., 2007; Doya, 1999; see also the discussion in Conway & Pisoni, 2008, and Lim et al., 2014).

Ashby et al. note that error-driven learning requires rapid release and re-uptake of the neurotransmitter dopamine. Dopamine is crucial to error-driven learning because dopamine levels are increased by unexpected rewards and reduced by unexpected punishments or unexpected absence of reward. The rewards do not have to be overt ones like money or food. Instead, any kind of "correct response" feedback can serve as a reward, and "error" feedback can serve as punishment. This feedback can be provided by an external feature, or can be generated internally (e.g., when the learner expects to hear a certain word but then actually hears a different one).

Synapses that have a dopamine projection are strengthened whenever the presynapse neuron is excited enough to activate the postsynapse neuron, *and* the dopamine level is above baseline. For the weight of a connection to change, the connection must have been *used*, transmitting activation across the gap between the neurons, just before dopamine is released. In contrast, Hebbian learning causes synapse strengthening whenever the two neurons bordering the synapse are active simultaneously. Error-driven learning therefore requires dopamine to be rapidly released in response to a reward, strengthening connections responsible for the reward.

Ashby et al. (2007) argue that synapses in the cortex learn in a Hebbian fashion. Several populations of patients with subcortical dysfunction have been observed to show deficits in error-driven learning, including patients suffering from Parkinson's or Huntington's disease, who have reduced dopamine levels in the striatum (Ashby et al., 2007), as well as amnesiacs, who have damage to the hippocampus (McClelland, 2001). The argument for Hebbian learning in the cortex is clearcut for posterior areas, where synapses do not have a dopamine projection. It is less clear for anterior areas, particularly prefrontal areas implicated in the learning of co-occurrences between noncontiguous stimuli (Eghbalzad et al., 2017; see also section 1.3). Synapses in these areas do have a dopamine projection but differ from subcortical synapses in that dopamine, once released, persists in the synapse, rather than being rapidly reabsorbed. Ashby et al. argue that this rapid reabsorption is crucial for error-driven learning because otherwise connections that are active *after* the correct response is produced will benefit from the accuracy of a response for which they are not responsible. While this may be true, the net effect would appear to be an increase in cue competition rather than the absence of cue competition predicted by Hebbian models.

Ashby et al. (2007) proposed that nonautomatic behavior is under the control of subcortical structures, while automatic behavior is accomplished via direct cortical connections. For example, in a categorization task, nonautomatic behavior is mediated by the striatum, while automatic behavior involves direct connections from the sensory cortex to the motor cortex. Subcortical areas learn quickly, allowing the organism to rapidly adapt to changes in the environment, while cortical areas learn slowly, maintaining stable long-term knowledge (McClelland et al., 1995). However, direct cortical-cortical connections allow for faster processing. Therefore, when learners are under time pressure or have to perform a secondary task, they may not be able to use the slow-processing cortical-subcortical-cortical loops, forcing all learning to happen in the cortex. The cortex learns more slowly. Interestingly, error-driven learning models such as Rescorla and Wagner (1972) show very attenuated (and therefore possibly undetectable) cue-competition effects when the learning rate is slow, because a slow learning rate means that outcome activations do not approach the limiting values (0 and 1 in equations 1 and 2) before the end of training. The differences in neurophysiology suggest that Hebbian and error-driven learning mechanisms are both implemented in the brain, and both need to be taken into account in explaining language learning (Ashby et al., 2007; Lim et al., 2014; McClelland, 2001; O'Reilly, 1996). However, Hebbian learning can often be indistinguishable from slow error-driven learning at the behavioral level. In particular, cue-competition effects may be absent in both (see also chapters 6 and 8).

1.2 Associative Symmetry and Chunking

Error-driven learning is inherently directional: the cue should precede the outcome for the organism to use the cue in order to *predict* the outcome (e.g., Rescorla & Wagner, 1972; Ramscar et al., 2010)[3] Nonetheless, following Asch and Ebenholtz (1962), many studies of paired associate learning have supported the *Principle of Associative Symmetry*, which states that encountering A followed, in short order, by B strengthens A→B as much as it strengthens B→A (e.g., Arcediano et al., 2005; Barr et al., 2002; Kahana, 2002; Lionello-DeNolf, 2009; Stout & Miller, 2007).

In paired associate learning, much research indicates that the strength of an A→B association is usually equal to the strength of a B→A association. For example, Kahana (2002) showed that a studied word pair like *cat-eagle* is recalled, by the same participant, equally well regardless of whether the first or second word is used as a cue. However, Caplan et al. (2014, p. 1169) and Rizzuto and Kahana (2001) argue that these cases involve a distinct *nonassociative* learning mechanism: rapid formation of a *unitized, configural* representation of the word pair AB in hippocampal episodic memory (McClelland et al., 1995), which can be retrieved equally well given either cue. The proposal that associative symmetry arises from hippocampal learning is also directly supported by findings that rats appear to require an intact hippocampus to learn B→A (odor-odor) associations from A→B training (Bunsey & Eichenbaum, 1995).

Note that associative symmetry does not mean that the representation is necessarily directionless—clearly, participants do know whether they heard *cat-eagle* or *eagle-cat*—or that learning in the hippocampal chunking system is not error-driven. Rather, bidirectionality may arise because the chunk representation allows for the retrieval of the whole chunk given any part of it, which can be captured by rapid formation of part-whole associations. Kahana (2002) argues that the primary function of this kind of hippocampal learning is in fact *pattern completion*—that is, retrieving the whole representation based on degraded, partial perceptual input. Pattern completion is an extremely important process for spoken word recognition and speech perception in general (e.g., McClelland & Elman, 1986; Salasoo & Pisoni, 1985), since any part of a spoken word may be missing from the auditory signal due to environmental noise or a momentary lapse in attention on the part of the listener. Thus, even though speech is normally perceived incrementally, the listener must be able to fill in the missing parts based on context, even if the missing parts *precede* the contextual information, like a reader inferring that what is hiding behind the symbols in #####potamus is probably a hippo. Fortunately, human speech perception does appear to be robust in this way: even noninitial parts of a word can act as retrieval cues to the word (Salasoo & Pisoni, 1985). Recently, McMurray et al. (2009) found that a sound ambiguous between [b] and [p] was perceived as [b] when followed by the [ærəked] of *barricade* but as [p] when followed by the [ærəkit] of *parakeet*. Gwilliams et al. (2016) presented ERP evidence showing that place of articulation of the ambiguous initial consonant could be recovered from the EEG signal shortly after the consonant was heard but then disappeared *until the disambiguating final vowel was perceived*, as if the consonant is retrieved from memory at this later point when its identity is retrodicted. It may well be that intact hippocampal function is required to fill in missing beginnings of recently learned words via this storage and retrieval process, just as it appears to be required for learning to predict the beginning of a recently learned stimulus sequence from its end. McClelland and Elman's (1986) influential TRACE model suggests that the way this retrodiction works is through the use of part-whole connections, where the whole is activated from its parts (in this case noninitial) and activates its missing parts in turn. Mirman et al. (2006) argue that the way such part-whole connections are formed is through Hebbian learning, although others have also suggested an important role for prediction error in hippocampal chunking (Schapiro et al., 2017).

1.3   Setting Up the Problem: A Role for Cognitive Control

Another way one can attempt to predict the past from the future and learn from one's mistakes is through deploying *cognitive control*. Suppose you participate in a word learning experiment where you see pictures of objects and then hear the words or phrases referring to these objects. L. B. Smith et al. (2011) put cameras on the heads of children acquiring English and found that this order of presentation is very representative of their experience with learning words. Parents spend much time labeling objects for their children, and the objects they label are usually the ones the child is already looking at. In this situation, an error-driven associative child would predict the word from the cues comprising the picture and discover what aspects of the picture are particularly predictive of the word (e.g., that the shape of the picture is predictive of whether you hear *dog* or *cat*). However, ideally, the child would also want to predict the picture from the following utterance, learning what cues in the utterance are particularly predictive of a particular picture. Interestingly, children don't seem to routinely do this kind of backward prediction when words and objects are presented asynchronously in an experimental situation (Ramscar et al., 2010). When pictures are presented before labels, nonpredictive features of the picture (like number of legs for predicting whether you hear *cat* or *dog*) are not associated with the label. On the other hand, when labels are presented before pictures, the label is associated with all features of the co-occurring picture. Adults, in contrast, do engage in bidirectional prediction, showing cue competition in both directions (see also Arcediano et al., 2005). However, they too can be prevented from predicting the past from the present if a secondary task is used to load their working memory between trials. Thus, an adult can predict the label from a picture in a picture-before-label experiment after seeing the picture, unless they have to do something else at that time (e.g., a math problem in Ramscar et al., 2010). Interference from a secondary task suggests that backward prediction is something that requires top-down application of cognitive control (Broadbent, 1958).

How does cognitive control allow for backward prediction? My take is that, in order to treat the present as a cue for retrodiction of the past, cognitive control needs to set up the learning problem. The learner naturally attempts to predict the future. Predicting the past involves bringing it up in working memory. Following Cowan (2001), I take *working memory* to be a "spotlight" of conscious attention that activates a subset (subnetwork) of memories stored in long-term memory. Similarly, predicting the present from a hypothetical cause is likely to also involve activating the cause in working memory. Both are therefore expected to involve frontal lobe activity, in addition to striatal basal ganglia activity implicated in automatic associative learning (e.g., Ashby et al., 2007) and hippocampal activity involved in unitization (Kahana, 2002).

Evidence for cognitive control throwing a spotlight of attention on some cues and outcomes that would not otherwise be associated so strongly is reviewed by Ramscar and Gitcho (2007). These researchers suggest that the cognitive control area of the prefrontal cortex is disadvantageous for language learning because it makes learning less flexible, by making the learner ignore potentially relevant information. They suggest that maturation of the prefrontal cortex makes the learner worse at acquiring languages by imposing the learner's prior beliefs on the evidence, resulting in confirmation bias. In the view outlined here, cognitive control does highlight some cues over others but this can lead to increased flexibility as well, whenever those cues would not otherwise be used for prediction. This may be important for acquiring long-distance dependencies, whose successful acquisition appears to correlate strongly with activity in cognitive control areas of the cortex (Eghbalzad et al., 2017). It may be particularly important for paradigmatic relations, which are not robustly mastered by young children (e.g., Kuo & R. Anderson, 2006). Finally, cognitive control may also be required for something as simple as learning sequential dependencies between stimuli from different modalities. Keele et al. (2003) review evidence suggesting that whereas tracking sequential dependencies within a modality is robust to interference, tracking cross-modality dependencies is easily disrupted by a momentary lapse of attention. Furthermore, only attended stimuli appear to wire together cross-modally. These results follow if keeping track of such cross-modal sequences requires the learner to keep both in the focus of attention.

Transcending time in this way is effortful and sensitive to other demands tugging on one's conscious attention. It is not going on at all times. Nonetheless, it is likely routinely attempted by language learners (and increasingly so with maturation of the prefrontal cortex). Proficient language learners know that the order in which representations are activated by current experience will not be the order in which they will need to activate the same representations when trying to reproduce the same experience for somebody else.

Once cognitive control has set up the problem, *bringing into contiguity* otherwise noncontiguous cues and outcomes (e.g., bringing to mind the singular form of a noun when the learner perceives the plural form), associative learning can update the links between them. Importantly, the *learning mechanisms* involved in modifying the weights of the cue-outcome connections can be the same as when cognitive control is not involved in determining what is to be predicted from what (Keele et al., 2003; see also Ervin, 1961; McNeill, 1963). The same principles for updating the weights, such as those specified in equations (1) and (2), can be used whether the task is predicting upcoming stimuli from current stimuli (as when a rat expects a food pellet having just heard a bell), or predicting what other constructions a verb you've just heard can occur in. The difference is in what is being associated with what, not in how association formation works.

1.4   Node Properties: Attention, Associability, Accessibility

In standard associative learning theory, activation of an outcome given a set of cues depends entirely on the sum of cue→outcome connection weights. However, there are good arguments for additional weights associated with nodes. In particular, it appears that learning A→B is at least facilitated by, and may require, attention to A and B (Ellis, 2006; Kruschke, 1992).

We learn to attend to the cues that have been informative in the past and to ignore uninformative ones (Kruschke 1992, 1996). Particularly clear evidence of such learning is demonstrated by experiments exposing learners to different, conflicting regularities in different stages of an experiment. These experiments often find that *reversal shifts*, in which the cue-outcome mappings are reversed, are easier than *extradimensional shifts*, in which previously irrelevant cues become relevant. What seems to matter is that the extradimensional shift is a shift toward associating cues that have been experienced as irrelevant. When the extradimensional shift is toward using cues that were not previously experienced—for example, yellow vs. blue objects after experiencing only red and green objects varying in size—it can be easier than a reversal shift (Kruschke, 1996). Kruschke argues that the difficulty of an extradimensional shift to previously irrelevant cues comes from the participants having learned that the irrelevant cues are not worth paying attention to (*learned irrelevance*). Other work in associative learning suggests that cues learned to be irrelevant are also hard to associate with *novel*, not previously experienced outcomes (Kruschke & Blair, 2000; Mackintosh & Turner, 1971). As a result of attention being limited, cues learned to be useless can lose their *associability*, the ability to be associated with other units (Mackintosh, 1975). Ramscar et al. (2013) have demonstrated the same effect in word learning, where a word present on every trial is not only left unassociated at the end of training but is also not considered a possible name for newly introduced referents. According to the hypothesis that loss of associability is due to lack of attention (Kruschke, 1992), the learner generalizes the cues' irrelevance beyond the current context by no longer paying attention to these cues when they are present. In support of this hypothesis, Kruschke et al. (2005) show that visual cues learned to be irrelevant no longer draw eye fixations.[4]

In the literature on lexical processing, word frequency is said to increase the word's *accessibility* (in both perception and production; e.g., Howes & Solomon, 1951, and Oldfield & Wingfield, 1965), which makes frequent words easier to recognize, easier to produce, and harder to inhibit (Kapatsinski, 2010a; Logan, 1982). But what is accessibility? One approach is to reduce accessibility to connection strength. In perception, we can think of accessibility as the strengths of connections from low-level perceptual features to the semantics of the word (Allopenna et al., 1998). In production, accessibility can likewise be thought of as meaning→form connection strengths (Kapatsinski, 2010a). On the other hand, accessibility can also be thought of as a property of nodes. For example, more accessible forms or meanings might have higher *resting activation levels*, requiring less activation from elsewhere (the signal or the context) to "fire; that is, to be recognized or produced (Morton, 1969).

Allowing frequency to influence resting activation levels of nodes means that frequency directly biases the *decision* about which node—out of a set of mutually exclusive possibilities—should "fire" (Broadbent, 1967). Without information about what the right answer is, we choose the answer that's been right more often. Without having a strong sense of which tool is most appropriate for a job, we reach for the tool we use the most (Zipf, 1949). As noted by Norris (2006), the inherent danger is that the bias would be too strong: the learner needs to balance relying on information from the signal with the bias to respond with the a priori more likely response. You would not want to be the listener who always guesses that the word they've just heard was *the*, the most frequent word in English, no matter what sound waves are hitting the ears. Norris argues that human readers and listeners use the bias optimally, relying on it to the extent that the signal is uninformative. Indeed, the effect of word frequency on word recognition appears to increase at higher noise levels (Howes, 1957). Nonetheless, whether frequency is always used in a normatively optimal fashion remains an open question across domains (e.g., Hertwig et al., 2004; Hudson Kam & Newport, 2005; Kahneman, 2011), and one we will return to in chapters 4–6.

1.5   What Is a Domain-General Learning Mechanism Anyway?

This review of learning mechanisms brings us to the questions of what a learning mechanism *is*, and what it means to claim (as I do) that language is learned using domain-general learning mechanisms. Following Chomsky (e.g., Chomsky & Halle, 1965; Chomsky, 1981), many researchers in language acquisition speak of the *language acquisition device* as a specific module in the brain that has evolved to acquire language (e.g., Lidz & Gagliardi, 2015; Moreton, 2008). In their view, there is a discrete "inference engine" that makes contact with a body of innate knowledge about language structure (*Universal Grammar*) and operates on a distinct class of preprocessed perceptual representations stripped of extralinguistic information. No learning, or at least no learning relevant to the acquisition of language, appears to happen inside the production system. The biases of the learner module (*analytic* or *inductive bias*) are discretely separated from, and have no inherent connection to, the biases of the production and perception systems (*channel bias*) that filter and distort the input to and output of the learner.

Ignoring production-internal learning reduces one's ability to explain crosslinguistic patterns. Consider the most basic difference between production and perception, which is the direction of information flow. In production, the meaning is available and the form remains to be constructed. In perception, the form is available and it is the meaning that one wants to predict. Gagliardi and Lidz (2014) examined noun class learning in an endangered Nakh-Daghestanian language, Tsez. Noun classes (also known as declensions or genders) are partially arbitrary sets of nouns that exhibit similar (or identical) morphological behavior (e.g., taking the same sets of affixes). There are usually both semantic and phonological cues to a noun class. Gagliardi and colleagues have noted an apparent paradox. They found that children presented with noun forms and noun meanings determine the class of a noun on the basis of the phonology and largely ignore the semantics. At the same time, the semantic cues to noun class are stronger than the phonological ones in Tsez, and they tend to be stronger across languages. The children's behavior initially makes it puzzling that languages do not organize their noun classes in a more learnable way, on the basis of phonological characteristics of the nouns. To resolve the paradox, Gagliardi et al. argue that children possess a bias to pay more attention to phonological predictors than to semantic ones, and that the bias flips sometime before adulthood. Nonetheless, even adults in their experiments appear to pay more attention to phonological cues than to semantic ones.

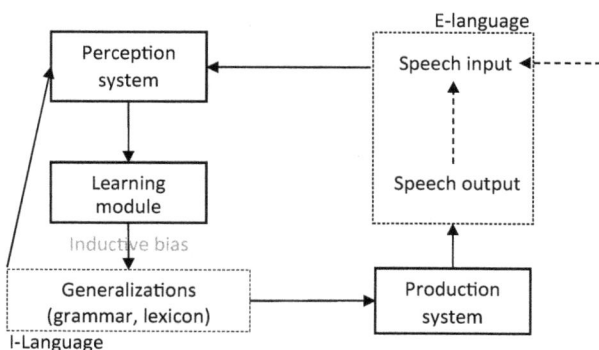

Figure 1.1
A modular view of learning (based on a synthesis of diagrams in Moreton, 2008, and Lidz & Gagliardi, 2015). The learning module takes in perceptual input and produces generalizations (which comprise *I-Language*, language as represented in the mind), and feeds a production system, which produces *E-Language*, language as it exists outside of the head. In Moreton's terminology, the learning module has an *inductive bias*, which favors some generalizations over others, given the same perceptual input. All other arrows are subject to *channel bias*.

Of course, this is only a puzzle if one ignores learning within the production system. When one wishes to produce speech, the semantic information is available and could easily be used to select a noun suffix. In contrast, phonological information may not be available until later even if the form is retrieved or constructed incrementally. Production is also where noun classes are most useful. A noun class tells you what affixes a noun can take, beyond the ones you *know* it can take. There is no point to guessing what suffixes other than the one actually heard a noun takes during perception (see also Taatgen & Anderson, 2002). In contrast, producing novel forms of known words is a very common problem in morphologically rich languages that have noun classes (Ackerman et al. 2009), and noun class is often essential to this process.

It is therefore no wonder that noun classes in all languages are based on semantics more than on phonology. While children (and less so adults) are more likely to attend to the phonology when *presented with* the phonology and a pictorial representation of the semantics, this has little bearing on how noun classes come about or are maintained because the phonology is unavailable until late in the process of normal production, and most noun class learning happens in production. Throughout this book, we will see examples in which production-internal and perception-internal learning both need to be modeled to explain language change. The general point is that learning does not happen in a box. It happens throughout the brain.

If one were to fit a domain-general learning mechanism into the kind of system shown in figure 1.1, where would it go? Presumably it would be yet another box, perhaps one that takes in many different kinds of inputs, linguistic and nonlinguistic, and does not make contact with any body of knowledge specific to language, though it might make contact with a body of knowledge about *all* environmental patterns. It is easy to see how one would conclude that a domain-general learning mechanism is extremely unlikely if this is one's view of what a learning mechanism is.

While Bayesian approaches to the mind have contributed real insights to cognitive science (as we discuss in chapter 4), they appear to encourage this kind of thinking insofar as Bayesian theorists often follow the research strategy of decomposing the mind into an ideal learner (tellingly called an *ideal observer*, as if all learning is observational; Anderson, 1991) and performance limitations that explain why biological organisms are imperfect. Positing a "learning box," a learner within and distinct from the biological organism, allows one to embed a perfectly *rational* Bayesian learner in a globally nonrational, biological system (see also Kruschke, 2006; Courville et al., 2006). The output of the learner is close to Chomsky's Platonist conception of *competence*, messed up by our imperfect perception and production systems.

I see this view of learning as fundamentally misguided. Learning happens throughout the brain, including (crucially) the production system. There is no one learning box that does language learning. Language learning is accomplished by a number of brain areas acting in tandem. Each of these brain areas can be seen as a network of nodes and connections. The weights of the connections are updated on the basis of experience. The principles (or "rules") behind this updating, including Hebbian learning and error-driven learning, are the true domain-general learning mechanisms. They determine what is learned throughout the brain, largely regardless of the type of input a brain area deals with. Christiansen and Chater (2016) call this principle that the same neural circuits can be used to deal with the same kinds of learning problems across brain areas *neural recycling*.

The point that different brain areas may learn according to the same principles, which are the true learning mechanisms, has implications for the kinds of evidence that can disconfirm a general learning mechanism. In particular, because distinct brain areas can be damaged or developed somewhat independently, dissociations between learning abilities in different domains have to be interpreted carefully. For example, dissociations between learning abilities with visual and auditory inputs provide evidence of modality-specific representations (Conway & Christiansen, 2006). However, to the extent that beliefs about both types of representation may nonetheless be updated according to the same principles, these results do not provide evidence against a domain-general *learning mechanism*. To show that two types of inputs are processed using different mechanisms, one needs to show that changing the input changes the principles of belief updating, ideally in a way not captured by differences in how the input is encoded.

Connection weights in the cortex are not updated in the same way as connection weights in the hippocampus or the basal ganglia (Ashby et al., 2007; McClelland et al., 1995). In this sense, then, there are *more* learning mechanisms than a strict Bayesian would believe in, and some of them can be fairly localized to particular brain areas (e.g., rapid, one-shot learning is largely subcortical), which justifies thinking of these areas themselves as distinct learning systems. However, the areas that learn in distinct ways are *complementary learning systems* (McClelland et al., 1995), acting in concert to allow the organism to acquire and perform complex behavior. At a higher level, then, the whole organism is a single box that receives experience and, through competitive dynamics not unlike those by which specializations develop within a society, ends up representing the useful structure of that experience in the subnetwork best suited to learning that kind of structure and carrying out the behavior (Bates et al., 2001; Karmiloff-Smith, 1995; Mareschal et al., 2007).

1.6   Why Associationism?

Learning theorists are not unified behind the associationist approach to learning. Many possible difficulties for associationism have been identified in the last twenty or thirty years, some of which we will encounter later in the book (see chapter 4 in particular). On the broadest level, there is an ongoing debate between associationist approaches and cognitive approaches, including causal theory (Waldmann, 2000; Waldmann & Holyoak, 1992), the closely related Bayesian network approach (Courville et al., 2006; Gopnik et al., 2004; Kruschke, 2008; Shanks, 2006), and even the proposal that associative learning is propositional in nature (Mitchell et al., 2009). Of these, the Bayesian approach is currently the strongest competitor to associationism, as causal theory can be seen as a limited precursor, while propositional theory is clearly limited in its range of applications. My choice of the associationist approach as the foundation of language learning is largely motivated by (1) the relatively effortless way in which the "brain-style" computations of this approach (Rumelhart, 1990) allow for integrating description at the level of behavior and the level of neural activity, (2) the ability of this approach to account for learning across species in a unified fashion, suggesting that the proposed principles are basic to all neural systems, and (3) the fact that mechanistic theories of trial-to-trial learning predict specific ways behavior will depart from the Platonic ideal observer. In contrast, the Bayesian approach makes no predictions regarding deviations from the ideal beyond stating that the learner's behavior should approximate it. Since my focus in this book is providing learning-theoretic explanations of language change, the third advantage is particularly important for my purposes.

It may be surprising to some readers that I would fault Bayesian models for not fully describing the biases of the learner, given the explicit focus of many Bayesian theorists of language acquisition on the contents of the prior beliefs the learner brings to the task (e.g., Chater et al., 2015; Lidz & Gagliardi, 2015; Moreton, 2008; C. Yang, 2004). However, describing the prior is important but insufficient for explaining the biases of the learner: an adequate description of the prior takes care of only one kind of bias, what Moreton (2008) called *analytic bias*. As shown in figure 1.1, analytic bias resides inside the learner module modeled by Bayesian learning theory, forming the learner's *prior* (the set of beliefs about hypothesis probabilities the learner brings to the task). The locus of channel bias is outside of the learner module and beyond the domain of Bayesian learning theory. Channel bias filters the input to the learner so that examples supporting some hypotheses are harder to perceive than others, or some inferences of the learner are harder than others to implement in behavior.

A simple example of channel bias is presented by cue salience: hard-to-perceive cues to a meaning may be underutilized (ignored) by the learner given how reliably they cue the meaning in question (see MacWhinney et al., 1985; Wanrooij et al., 2013, for linguistic examples from morpho-syntax and phonetics respectively). For the hypothetical learner module that acquires phonology, channel bias is "the effect of systematic errors in transmission between speaker and hearer" (Moreton, 2008, p. 83). As noted by Moreton (2008) and Moreton and Pater (2012b), it has been difficult to find any substantive knowledge to place into the prior of the phonological learner, beyond a preference for generalizations involving single features, which falls out of the domain-general principle that attention is selective (chapter 3). Analytic bias is rather limited in scope (see also Chater et al., 2015).

Channel bias must be explained mechanistically, through describing the mechanisms underlying learning. Associationism is well suited to this task because the associationist mind is much like the brain, making it easy to translate cognitive processes into neural ones. In particular, because the to-be-associated representations map onto places in the brain, our ability to learn a correlation between the represented events, stimuli, or actions should depend directly on how plastic the relevant neural connections are and how much the brain needs to change to match the environmental statistics.

This prediction is supported by the finding that associations between dissimilar stimuli are harder to learn than associations between similar ones (Rescorla & Furrow, 1977; see also Keele et al., 2003). In language learning, it has long been noted that dependencies between different instances of the same feature are easier to learn than dependencies between different features (e.g., Chomsky & Halle, 1968; see Moreton & Pater, 2012a, 2012b, for review, and Keele et al., 2003, for a nonlinguistic example). For example, Moreton (2008) reports that agreement in voicing between nonadjacent consonants is easier to learn than a correlation between the height of a vowel and the voicing of the following consonant. Warker and Dell (2006) suggest that dependencies between phonological and indexical features of the speech signal are harder to learn than dependencies among phonological features. Recent work in my lab has suggested that paradigmatic relationships between dissimilar segments such as "p→tʃ" are harder to learn than paradigmatic relationships between similar segments such as "k→tʃ" (Stave et al., 2013; see chapter 8). Note that dissimilar stimuli are likely to be represented in distinct parts of the brain. Thus, forming an association between two similar stimuli will usually involve a smaller change to the brain than forming an association between two dissimilar stimuli, making associations between dissimilar stimuli harder to learn (Kapatsinski, 2011; Warker & Dell, 2006). The bias against associating dissimilar units follows straightforwardly from the structure of the brain.

From this perspective, one of the main biological adaptations that allows humans to learn language is our ability to rapidly form associations between forms and referents, despite their perceptual dissimilarity (Deacon, 1997; Landauer & Dumais, 1997; Tomasello, 2003). One of the main functions of the neocortex appears to be multimodal, multisensory integration, often seen to be essential for the development of complex, multidimensional concepts (e.g., Binder et al., 2009; Fernandino et al., 2015; Ghazanfar & Schroeder, 2006). Evolution may have "prepared" us to rapidly associate vision and audition in the same way as it prepared many species to rapidly associate taste with illness (Garcia & Koelling, 1966; Gemberling & Domjan, 1982; Seligman, 1970) or certain motor actions with obtaining food or avoiding danger (Bolles, 1970; Breland & Breland, 1961). Multimodal integration areas may be evolution's way of preparing humans for rapidly acquiring a large lexicon.[5]

1.7 Sources of Bias

There are deep parallels between Bayesian approaches to learning and the generative tradition in linguistics, just as there are important parallels between associative learning and linguistic functionalism (which are the focus of this book). Like generative grammar (Chomsky, 1966), Bayesian approaches to learning fall squarely within the rationalist approach (Anderson, 1991; Gallistel, 2012). The Bayesian learner comes to the task of learning something with a set of prior beliefs, which can be as strong as an innate Universal Grammar à la Chomsky (1981) or could be quite rudimentary (à la Chomsky, 1995, and the classic empiricist/functionalist position). In either case, the prior beliefs are explicitly described by the researcher and therefore form much of the subject matter of Bayesian theorizing, just as the contents of Universal Grammar form the core of generative grammatical theory. These prior beliefs are one source of bias in learning, called *inductive bias*.

The foundational hypothesis of Bayesian learning theory is that, whatever the learners' beliefs, they update these beliefs in a *normative, rational* fashion, making optimal use of the information available. In other words, belief updating must obey Bayes's theorem, as described below. Therefore, to the extent that a learner's beliefs after exposure to some environment fail to match the structure of that environment, this discrepancy must be attributed to either the learner's prior beliefs (inductive bias) or to imperfections in the intake of information: information available in the environment may not be available to the learner. For example, in figure 1.1, the input to the learner is filtered and possibly distorted by the perception system. The biases inherent in the translation from input to intake have been called *channel biases*, as have the biases inherent in the production system and in the physical environment (Moreton, 2008).

1.7.1   Inductive Bias

We begin with inductive bias, the kind of bias that is well captured by Bayesian models. Bayesian models are called Bayesian because they update beliefs in accordance with *Bayes's theorem* (Bayes, 1763; Laplace, 1812), shown in (3). The Bayesian learner comes to the learning task with a set of hypotheses she is willing to entertain. The learner wants to estimate the probabilities of these hypotheses given the data, $p(H|D)$: given the data at hand, how much should the learner believe in each hypothesis?

$$p(H|D) = \frac{p(D \mid H)\, p(H)}{p(D)} \tag{3}$$

What makes Bayesian learning normative is that Bayes's theorem is true: mathematically, $p(D|H)$ is equal to $p(D|H)p(H)/p(D)$. By definition of conditional probability, $p(H|D)=p(H,D)/p(D)$, and $p(D|H)=p(H,D)/p(H)$. Substituting these terms into (3), we get (4). $p(H)$ cancels out, yielding an obviously true equality. Any other way of updating beliefs is not normative and a departure from rationality.

$$\frac{p(H, D)}{p(D)} = \frac{p(H, D)\, p(H)}{p(D)\, p(H)} \tag{4}$$

Inductive bias is directly encoded in the model, forming its prior beliefs. Specifically, each hypothesis the learner is willing to consider has a prior probability, $p(H)$, which encodes the learner's belief in the hypothesis prior to learning. Some hypotheses may be a priori more plausible than others, and therefore would have a higher $p(H)$. The higher $p(H)$, the more evidence is required for the learner to be convinced that the hypothesis is false.

Strength of evidence is quantified by $p(D|H)$, the probability of the data given the hypothesis. The strongest evidence against a hypothesis are data that would never occur if the hypothesis were true. The $p(D)$ in the denominator is the sum of the numerator terms across all the hypotheses, $\Sigma_H p(D|H)p(H)$, which is usually thought of as simply a normalizing term that ensures that $p(H|D)$ values sum to 1 and are therefore true probabilities. However, it is also useful to think of $p(D)$ as a measure of how surprising the data are, given the learner's current set of beliefs. If $p(D)$ is low, the data are unexpected. The log-transformed $p(D)$ is the amount of information in the data, or *surprisal*.

A good illustration of Bayesian inference applies it to the September 11 attacks in the United States (Silver, 2011), which is useful for showing the influence of inductive bias and its limits. On 9/11/2001, two planes collided with two skyscrapers in New York, killing thousands. Suppose that you were watching TV that day and were trying to determine whether what is happening is a terrible aviation accident or an intentional act of terror. Suppose that prior to this event, your estimate of the likelihood of an aviation accident were much higher than your estimate of the likelihood of a terrorist attack involving a plane; say, you might believe that there are 99 plane accidents for every one intentional attack involving a plane. This difference would be encoded in the prior probabilities of the alternative hypotheses in (5) and forms your inductive bias.

Prior: $p(\text{Attack}) = .01$, $p(\text{Accident}) = .99$ (5)

However, the probability of a plane crashing into a skyscraper in an aviation accident is quite low, as the pilot will try to do everything possible to avoid this outcome and most airspace is not covered by skyscrapers. In contrast, the probability of a plane crashing into a skyscraper given an intentional attack is quite high, because the pilot will do everything possible to achieve this outcome. Nonetheless, the probability of the pilot failing to achieve his objective seems much higher in the case of an attack, perhaps as high as 40%. Suppose the probabilities of hitting skyscrapers given an attack vs. an accident are

$p(\text{Hit.Skyscraper}|\text{Attack}) = .6$, $p(\text{Hit.Skyscraper}|\text{Accident}) = .01$ (6)

Then, $p(D)=.01^*.6+.99^*.01=1.6\%$ and $p(\text{Attack}|D)=.01^*.6/.016=38\%$. Because your prior beliefs made you think that an attack involving a plane is so unlikely, the evidence did not convince you that an attack is in fact happening. However, prior beliefs can be overridden by overwhelming evidence. Now, consider what happens when the second plane hits. The posterior probabilities (.38 and .62) are now our prior probabilities. Assuming the crashes are treated as independent, $p(D)$ of the second crash is $.38^*.6+.62^*.01=23\%$, and $p(\text{Attack}|D)=.38^*.6/.23=97\%$. At this point, you should be almost certain that you have witnessed an attack, a highly unexpected event prior to this experience. The data have overcome your inductive bias.

In general, the prior biases of a Bayesian learner are quickly overridden if the events it observes are really inconsistent with the beliefs it holds. This makes Bayesian learning very powerful. For example, F. Xu and Tenenbaum (2007) argue that the rapidity of Bayesian learning makes it a good mechanism for learning words (though cf. Yu & L. B. Smith, 2012). At the same time, however, it also makes it difficult to capture persistent unwillingness to give up on a patently incorrect belief (e.g., Wilson, 2006, for phonological learning). On perceiving clear counterevidence to an incorrect belief, a rational Bayesian learner should give it up. To the extent that a learner does not do so, they must not be perceiving the counterevidence correctly (and are therefore subject to channel bias) or they are not making rational use of it (the belief updating itself is biased).

1.7.2   Channel Bias

Channel biases are the only class of biases in the Bayesian framework that cannot be ascribed to the prior. One class of cases is due to the fact that learning is biased by the "performance limitations" of biological learners. Try as you may, you will not detect a tone too high or low to be detected by the human ear. Likewise, when multiple stimuli impinge on your sensory organs at the same time, you cannot pay attention to all of them simultaneously. An interesting case of this kind is reported by Ferdinand et al. (2013), who presented human learners with either one bag of marbles or six differently colored bags. Differently colored marbles were drawn from each bag with a certain frequency ratio. For example, with a 1/9 ratio, a bag would generate one blue marble for every 9 orange marbles. In the one-bag condition, a participant would experience 10 draws from one bag. In the six-bag condition, a participant would experience 10 draws from *each* bag, with each bag having a different color frequency ratio. Participants were then asked to predict a sequence of 10 marble draws, either from the one experienced bag in the one-bag condition, or from each of the six experienced bags in the six-bag condition. Participants in the one-bag condition exhibited *probability matching*, replicating the frequency ratios in the input. Participants in the six-bag condition often *regularized* the distribution, so they would consistently draw the same marble from a particular bag.

Ferdinand et al. (2013) fit a Bayesian model to each condition and found that the two conditions required different priors: modeling the six-bag condition required a prior strongly committed to all marbles in a bag being the same color, while modeling the one-bag condition required a rather noncommittal, liberal prior easily swayed by the learning data. As they note, participants were assigned to conditions randomly. Therefore, it is virtually impossible that participants in the two conditions *actually* had significantly different prior beliefs about how likely bags are to contain marbles of more than one color (cf. Perfors, 2011). Instead, participants in the six-bag condition must have had a hard time keeping track of the exact probabilities associated with each bag, a channel bias rooted in the participants' biological limitations:

Strictly speaking, the prior represents the inductive bias of the learner, and participants should come to a marble-drawing task with a particular expectation about the ratios of marbles in containers, regardless of the difficulty of the task. The fact that we find different best-fit priors according to different task demands means that we are not revealing the inductive bias of our participants, per se, but a composite picture that characterizes more than one cognitive constraint. At least one constraint that is sensitive to task demands should be added to the model. (Ferdinand et al., 2013, p. 440)

Learning must be near-Bayesian to be adaptive: it is not of much use for the organism to learn if learning will not pick up on environmental statistics (e.g., Anderson, 1991; Kruschke & Johansen, 1999; Shanks, 1995). Even in a system that is constantly recreated by its users, like language, a learner needs to match the system in use fairly closely if one wants to communicate with older users, who are usually rather attached to their ways of saying things and are in a position of power over the learner and consequently the learner's linguistic behavior. Because of this need for accuracy, Bayesian analyses of environmental statistics provide a valuable source of explanations for characteristics of behavior. However, they do not provide a full explanation for the biases of the system—that is, the ways it departs from optimality, ascribing them all to the prior. If we are interested in answering the question of "why languages are the way they are" (e.g., Chomsky & Halle, 1965), the answer "they are this way because of the prior" is as unsatisfactory as the answer "they are this way because of Universal Grammar" (and is indeed very nearly the same answer). What we need to do is explain where the prior comes from. Mechanistic accounts provided by neural networks and associationist learning theory help us start addressing this question.

1.7.3   Bayesian vs. Biased Belief Updating

Note how $p(D)$ has increased over time in the September 11 example. The first plane crash was highly unexpected, but the second crash was less so. By increasing your estimate of the probability of an attack, you have increased the probability of the data. As learning proceeds, the probability of the data grows. In a constant environment, as we learn more and more, we are surprised less and less. Conversely, the more surprising the data you have observed, the more evidence they provide that your current beliefs are incorrect.

Error-driven learning models assume that surprise matters, and that minimization of surprise is the goal of learning. However, they differ in the role they assign to surprise. In particular, the use of surprise can be normative—described by Bayes's theorem—or can be subject to a *confirmation* or *disconfirmation bias*. Confirmation bias has been proposed as early as Bacon (1630/1939) and extensively studied in psychology (see Nickerson, 1998, for a review). Wilson (2006) has more recently applied it to language acquisition. Learners that have a confirmation bias ignore or underutilize evidence inconsistent with their beliefs and overutilize evidence that confirms their beliefs. Confirmation bias is the name for persistent unwillingness to revise one's beliefs in the face of veridically perceived counterevidence. In other words, surprising observations shift beliefs of a learner who has a confirmation bias less than Bayes's theorem would predict, while unsurprising observations matter more than expected.

Conversely, learners with a disconfirmation or *novelty* bias ignore evidence that is consistent with their beliefs and overemphasize evidence that is inconsistent (C. Chang, 2013; Johnston & Kapatsinski, 2011). Learners that have either a confirmation or a disconfirmation bias are not rational; they do not make optimal use of the available data. Like ignoring the unexpected, paying special attention to the unexpected generally reduces belief accuracy. However, it may be essential for a biological learner, because what is unexpected is likely to be particularly dangerous or particularly rewarding. One does not want to miss a tasty mushroom that has sprung up overnight by one's house. Nor does one want to be eaten by a tiger that is sitting on one's porch (cf. Lieder et al., 2014).

Why should there be confirmation and disconfirmation biases? *Complementary learning systems theory* (McClelland et al., 1995) notes that there is a danger that comes with rapid learning, which is that new learning will overwrite old knowledge (*catastrophic interference*). For this not to occur, newly learned beliefs must be context-specific, and therefore somewhat "episodic." Storage of episodic memories is a well-known function of the hippocampus: damage to the hippocampus results in amnesia. The hippocampus is also implicated in many aspects of rapid learning, including statistical word learning (Schapiro et al., 2017). A plausible hypothesis is therefore that disconfirmation bias is a characteristic of hippocampal learning. One also sometimes wants to update long-term beliefs based on recent experience. This is the function of slow cortical learning, which makes use of highly distributed representations. These representations allow for broad generalization but are also subject to catastrophic interference if learning is too fast. Slow cortical learning may be subject to confirmation bias. Again, different areas of the brain may learn in different ways, neither of which is quite Bayesian.

I return to this issue in section 4.1, where I present a case of a disconfirmation bias in language learning, speculate on the circumstances under which confirmation and disconfirmation biases arise, and suggest how the assumptions of Bayesian learning can be relaxed to incorporate biased belief updating.

1.8   Conclusion and Preview

What is a domain-general learning mechanism? In this chapter, I have argued that a learning mechanism determines how the brain changes as a result of a given experience. In keeping with the connectionist tradition, I view the mind as much like the brain, a network of interconnected nodes. In the case of the brain, the nodes are neurons. In the case of the mind, they are representations that correspond to entire patterns of activation over populations of neurons. Viewing the mind as a network means that learning mechanisms can be seen as affecting either connection weights or properties of nodes. In this chapter, I have focused on mechanisms for updating connection weights and have only briefly touched on the properties of nodes—salience (how much attention should be paid to the node's firing), resting activation level (how easy it is for the node to fire), and associability (how easy it is for the node to associate with other nodes)—and the mechanisms that affect them. In chapter 2, we examine what the nodes and connections need to represent and the linguistic structure learners need to comprehend and produce. In chapter 3, we then take a closer look at the possible learning mechanisms for forming nodes and updating node weights. In particular, I focus on the function of learned selective attention, which in chapters 4 and 5 will play a prominent role in explaining the ways in which human learning departs from that of optimal statistical learners.

An important consequence of viewing the mind as a network is that experience-driven changes have to be describable as changes to connection or node weights. The mind is nothing *but* a network. This constrains one's theorizing in certain ways. For example, in chapter 4, we will see that learners often seem to have different levels of *confidence* in their various beliefs. The beliefs of a network are straightforward: they are encompassed by the connection and node weights. However, there is no clear way to encode confidence in a weight that is independent of the weight itself. In chapter 4, I argue that this limitation might be a feature and not a bug in that it captures ways human behavior is not that of optimal learners.

Viewing the mind as a network means that continuous dimensions pose a challenge, as these dimensions must be discretized into a set of nodes. In chapter 5, I describe ways to convert continuous dimensions into sets of discrete cues and discuss evidence for discretization. Continuing the theme from chapter 4, human learning of distributions over continuous dimensions departs from optimal statistical learning, in ways that are captured by selective attention to the unexpected.

The view of the mind as a network of gradually changing associations that capture, in predictably limited ways, the statistical structure of the environment is challenged by two kinds of data. First, under certain conditions, some learners appear not to track frequencies or co-occurrence probabilities. Second, there appear to be rapid changes in behavior as a result of only one or two additional exposures to a stimulus, often preceded and followed by long periods in which additional exposures to the same stimulus result in no behavioral change. In other words, learning within an individual often looks like a step function. In chapter 2, I describe how these kinds of counterevidence can be attributed to decision-making processes, which turn continuous knowledge of co-occurrences into categorical behavior.

In this chapter, we reviewed three different learning mechanisms localized to specific parts of the brain, all of which are expected to contribute to our ability to acquire language. Slow, gradual Hebbian learning acquires knowledge of co-occurrences between temporally adjacent or near-adjacent units. It is complemented by chunking, which rapidly forms local representations for recently encountered configural patterns or perceptual episodes. The chunking process appears to happen in multiple areas, including the hippocampus. Error-driven striatal learning makes predictions and adjusts beliefs when those predictions are disconfirmed. Error-driven learning may also adjust selective attention, particularly in early perceptual processing areas within the cortex. It is important to realize that while localizable to specific areas of the brain, and particularly suited to certain tasks, all of these learning mechanisms are domain-general in that they are not specific to linguistic inputs, or indeed to any particular kind of input. To the extent that we can tell, they also affect both perception/comprehension and production (action planning). In the rest of this book, we will take a step toward a theory of how the various mechanisms work in concert to allow us to learn the structure we encounter in the linguistic environment.

2 From Associative Learning to Language Structure

> A linguist who could not devise a better grammar than is present in any speaker's brain ought to try another trade.
> —Householder (1966, p. 100)

Having reviewed two ways of learning, we now turn to a description of what one must learn to be considered a competent language user: in other words, language structure. But before diving into what structure is out there in languages, we briefly consider where that structure comes from and why it refuses to go away. As foreshadowed in the preface, I adopt a dynamic usage-based approach to explain language structure (Bybee, 2001). According to this perspective, to explain language structure we need to explain language change: languages are the way they are because they change in the ways they do. While there are few strict synchronic universals—statements that are true of all languages at a point in time—there are many recurrent pathways of language change (see Bybee, 2015, for a review). Given the current state of the language, the language's future is somewhat predictable. The reason for this predictability is that language change is effected by people using language, and speakers of different languages have similar neural and motor hardware as well as similar goals, abilities, and limitations. As language is learned and used by humans, it changes. Because all humans are humans, it changes in somewhat predictable ways. A major aim of the present book is to examine how a language changes when it is passed through the filter of associative learning.

I should note at the outset that the focus on learning does not mean that I am blaming all language change on children (cf. Crain et al., 2006). Rather, I assume that any instance of language use results in learning. This could be learning about what is out there in the world, or learning how to (better) accomplish an intended goal. It could also be learning that doing something is hard and should be avoided in the future (Martin, 2007).

While more is learned from a single experience early in life (when the brain is plastic, and there is little relevant prior knowledge stabilizing the system), learning continues throughout one's lifespan. For example, vocabulary continues to grow (Keuleers et al., 2015), as does knowledge of constructions induced from the vocabulary (Bates & Goodman, 1997), pronunciation of vowels changes throughout life as one interacts with speakers with different language varieties (Harrington et al., 2000), and pronunciation of specific words becomes more and more automatic as they are reused (Baayen et al., 2017; Bybee, 2002b; Goldinger, 1998; Kapatsinski, 2010a; Ryalls & Pisoni, 1997; Tomaschek et al., 2013). Language change can come from imperfections of biological learners but it can also come from streamlining goal-directed behavior. For example, to the extent that much sound change is driven by automatizing articulation (Bybee, 2002b, 2015), sound change should be explained by lifelong learning within the production system (see chapter 9).

2.1   What We Can vs. What We Want

All theories of language change identify directions in which the language *may* develop. The major problem with all such theories (including the present one) is that the language may *not* change, remaining stable. It is unlikely to change in an unexpected direction (e.g., undoing a previously accomplished sound change). However, even variable patterns—such as the choice between alveolar and velar-final pronunciations of -*ing* in English— can remain stable for many generations (Labov, 1994). This is known as the actuation problem (Weinreich et al., 1968). The present book provides predictions about possible directions of change but says little about whether these changes will be actuated (though see chapter 9 for some glimmers of hope). The reason is that, in my view, the actuation problem has more to do with community pressure *on* the learner than with predispositions *of* the learner.

Whether through learning or evolution, an organism adapts to the tasks that it needs to accomplish in its ecological niche. What we want/need to do determines what we learn as much as (if not more than) what is easy to learn. Languages retain structures that are not at all easy to learn. The Russian palatalized trill, the Polish consonant clusters, the English interdental fricatives, the Zulu clicks, the Xhosa labial palatalization, the nearly arbitrary noun classes of Hausa or German are all learned by children despite their apparent difficulty. Thus, any account of language change must take into account not only what is easy for learners, but also what is important for learners to learn in order to do what they want to do with language. This includes not only transmitting information but also fitting into the community. If a pattern is difficult to learn, it may nonetheless be retained because of being a salient marker of social identity and its mastery a mark of accomplishment, a shibboleth indicating that the speaker belongs to the in-group of those for whom the language is a mother tongue (Boyd & Richerson, 1987). The community usually shapes the learner into conformity. This is as true of a human trying to fit in with a peer group as of a male cowbird trying to become an attractive mate by singing the kinds of songs preferred by females in his community (M. Goldstein et al., 2003).

We assume that learners want to replicate all the patterns in the input (particularly of the speakers they want to sound like), and that nonreplication of a pattern upon exposure in the lab is a sign of learning difficulty. However, learning difficulty in the lab provides only a motivation for change and nonreplication "in the wild." Despite having a good motivation, the change may nonetheless not be actuated in the speech community if learners of the language are forced to learn the original pattern by social pressure.

When social pressure not to change the language is strong, as it is in many societies, the language may not change even if it is hard to learn. Rapid changes in the direction of easy-to-learn structures tend to occur when community speech norms are relatively weak. Examples include homesigners brought together into a community for the first time, slaves speaking multiple languages brought together to work on a plantation, speakers of multiple dialects moving to one area when a new town is formed in a previously low-population locale around a new source of employment, children learning a language from nonnative speakers, or a community experiencing an influx of high-status second language learners due to an invasion (DeLancey, 2014; Hudson Kam & Newport, 2005; Kerswill & Williams, 2000; Singleton & Newport, 2004; Trudgill, 2011). When there are no entrenched norms, or these norms cannot be effectively enforced, change can happen quickly.

2.2 When Hell Freezes Over

As implied by the Householder (1966) quote in the epigraph, there is a tension between the apparent messiness of the brain, a tangle of neural spaghetti, which is well captured by associatiative models, and the clean regularity of a grammar. There are some ways in which this regularity is only apparent. For example, it is readily revealed by elicited production tasks, called "wug tests" after Berko's (1958) famous original stimulus (*This is a wug. Now there are two. There are two* ____). When subjected to the wug test, many rules that look perfectly regular and productive from examining a corpus of existing utterances turn out to be only partially productive when the speaker is asked to extend them to novel inputs (e.g., Kapatsinski, 2010b, 2010c). Sentence comprehension is far from a purely syntactic computation and is instead continuously affected by extragrammatical and extralinguistic sources of information, even down to the visual context (Tanenhaus et al., 1995). Grammatical and extragrammatical information fight it out in parallel until interpretation emerges from the chaos of competing cues (Bates & MacWhinney, 1989). Behavior is the outcome of a competition between struggling cues, each clamoring for its favored outcome(s). No wonder Selfridge (1959) called his early connectionist model of this struggling mass of competing cues "pandemonium."

Behavior is produced only after the mind has settled on a decision to produce it. The process of settling is often described using the metaphor of cooling a liquid to produce crystalline structure (Kirkpatrick et al., 1983). Early during both processing and learning, the mind is in a high-temperature state. Like a liquid flowing down a complex surface, or a ball in the pinball machine, the mind can settle into a large number of possible beliefs or decisions depending on subtle nudges from the environment. Gradually, the temperature lowers down to the freezing point. At this point, the liquid is frozen in place, and the mind has crystallized into a decision. The pandemonium of competing cues has frozen over and can no longer affect the choice of behavior.

2.2.1   Regularization, Positive Feedback, And Rich-Get-Richer Loops

Like many other communities of struggling individuals, the pandemonium is subject to a *rich-get-richer loop*. Just as demons can be thought of as tools for accomplishing devilry, language can be thought of as a set of tools for accomplishing communicative goals (see Zipf, 1949, for many examples). When multiple tools could be used to achieve a goal, one must choose among them. It stands to reason that one chooses the tool that is easiest to use. Importantly, using a tool makes it even easier to use it the next time around. A tool with which one is well practiced is easier to use than a tool with which one is unfamiliar. The easier a tool is to use, the more likely it is to be selected for use. In this way, use increases the probability of reuse. This is an example of *positive feedback*. Positive feedback is the force that pushes languages toward regularization.

For example, Zipf (1929) suggests that

the proto-Indo-European felt free to accent that part of the word—the root, stem, or ending—which he chose ... to make more conspicuous to his hearers. ... But in proto-Indo-European times, as in modern, though the option as to the position of the accent remained, one particular order of accent, in a given case, was in fact more frequent in occurrence than any other. In time this more usual or more frequent manner of accenting the elements of an inflected word became the customary way of accenting that word, until finally, through frequent usage, it petrified into the regular and obligatory accent. (pp. 5–6)

If you plot word frequency vs. the number of distinct words that have that frequency in log-log coordinates, you see a straight line (Zipf, 1935), a fact known as *Zipf's law*. In any corpus, there are a few words like *the* that are very frequent, while most words occur only once (Baayen, 2001). The most frequent word is about twice as frequent as the next most frequent one. Zipf's law is a telltale sign of a rich-get-richer loop. The same curve is seen over and over in every domain with positive feedback. In free-market economies, there are a few billionaires, while most have next to nothing. The richest person has much more money than the next-richest one. Again, there is a positive feedback loop: the richer you are, the easier it is for you to make more money. Most websites are rarely visited, while a small number are enormously popular. Again, the most popular site is *way* more popular than the second most popular one. The more popular a site is, the more likely new people are to click on it.

Recent research has confirmed the existence of a positive feedback loop spiraling toward regularization in experiments with miniature artificial languages presented to human learners as well as in newly evolved sign languages. For example, Sandler et al. (2005) show that Al-Sayyid Bedouin sign language has converged on a fixed SVO word order within a few generations. In the lab, Hudson Kam and Newport (2005) showed that children exposed to a language with two randomly alternating determiners tended to produce the more frequent determiner 100% of the time, regularizing the language. Interestingly, adults did not, instead *matching* the probabilities of the determiners in their production, suggesting that it is children who create regularity in language. However, K. Smith and Wonnacott (2010) and Reali and Griffiths (2009) found that *chains* of adults do regularize unpredictable variation. Thus, if the output of a probability matcher serves as the input to another probability matcher, imperfections in probability matching add up, over time, to regularization. This kind of *iterated learning*, an experimental game of broken telephone in which the output of one learner serves as input to another, clearly demonstrates how even weak biases can, over time, lead to significant language change through *imperfect transmission*. Languages that are hard to learn/use change to become more learnable/usable (see Christiansen & Chater, 2016, for an extensive review).

K. Smith et al. (2013) showed that the bias toward regularization is not only a learning bias but also operates at the level of interpersonal interaction. In their iterated learning experiments, participants were first trained and tested on a language with variable singular marking individually, and then were paired up and asked to use the language to communicate. When communicating, participants who would use both competing forms on their own *accommodated* their nonvariable interlocutors, coming to always use the preferred form of their nonvariable partners. In contrast, categorical speakers did not accommodate, continuing to use their preferred forms, resulting in rapid elimination of unpredictable variation in favor of regularity. This kind of accommodation by those who can use two forms to those who can only use one is constantly performed in real life by skilled bilinguals, who have two entirely different ways of speaking that they use to communicate to different monolingual interlocutors. Positive feedback loops push languages toward regularization at both the level of the individual and the level of a speech community.

2.2.2   Decision Rules: Maximizing vs. Probability Matching

If one wants to *maximize* one's probability of choosing the right form on a particular trial, one should always choose the most likely form given the current cues. Thus, regularization observed by Hudson Kam and Newport (2005) need not imply that the children in their study failed to learn that they heard two different determiners, or even that they underestimated the frequency of the less frequent determiner. If a speaker knows which form is more probable, they should choose the more probable form every time they are given the choice, if they want to maximize their accuracy. The more probable response is more probable on every trial.

Unless there are some occasions on which the more frequent form *will not do*, we should all *maximize*, choosing the more frequent form every time, rather than choosing the forms in proportion to their probabilities (*probability matching*). The fact that, as adults, we often do not maximize therefore suggests that we think there is some reason to use the less frequent form or at least that we *should* use it on occasion, even if we don't know why (Perfors, 2016).

Having not discovered what the reason for using a form is, we may try and use it to explore the consequences (Gittins, 1979; Lea, 1979). The choice between frequent and rare forms with equivalent functions is usefully thought of as an instance of the *exploration/exploitation dilemma* in decision making, where exploitation (choosing the easy, familiar, safe option) maximizes rewards while exploration (choosing the hard, unfamiliar, high-risk option) maximizes information/surprise. Of course, as something becomes familiar, we habituate to its consequences and it becomes boring. A reward easily obtained is hardly rewarding (see Zentall, 2016, for a review). In a safe but boring environment, surprise is rewarding, and choosing the potentially inferior option does not lead to anything particularly undesirable, which is why such environments favor exploration. Think of a sleepy college town vs. a war zone, an experiment with "no wrong answers" vs. a graded test vs. giving a password to armed guards at a secure facility (see also Christian & Griffiths, 2016, p. 55; Gopnik et al., 1999; Oudeyer & L. B. Smith, 2016). To take an extreme example, consider Judges (12:6):

> The Gileadites captured the fords of the Jordan opposite Ephraim. And it happened when any of the fugitives of Ephraim said, "Let me cross over," the men of Gilead would say to him, "Are you an Ephraimite?" If he said, "No," then they would say to him, "Say now, 'Shibboleth.'" But he said, "Sibboleth," for he could not pronounce it correctly. Then they seized him and slew him at the fords of the Jordan. Thus there fell at that time 42,000 of Ephraim.

Suppose you have to cross the fords of the Jordan River. You know both dialects, so you *can* pronounce the word either way. You don't know for sure if the men you confront are Gileadite or Ephramite, but you think there is a 75% chance they are Gileadite. I sure hope that there is a less than 25% chance you would say "Sibboleth" when you come to the crossing!

2.2.3 The Prevalence of Probability Matching

Tests of pattern productivity in adults tend to show probability matching (Hayes et al., 2009). This result appears to be problematic for the idea that maximization in decision making can save us from the ubiquity of random variation. Interestingly, participants in tests of productivity appear to be actively trying to match probabilities.

For example, Zara Harmon and I have asked participants to imagine themselves in a fords-of-the-Jordan situation. In a series of training trials, the participants encountered an alien that would greet them with either *bes osto* or *osto zon* on each trial. The greeting was random, except one of the greetings occurred 75% of the time while the other occurred 25% of the time. Participants were then told that they will meet the alien ten more times, every time greeting the alien by clicking on either *bes osto* or *osto zon*, depending on what they think is most likely to be correct. If they made too many mistakes, the alien would shoot them, they were told—an event that of course never happened. The vast majority of participants showed probability matching, choosing the more frequent greeting ~75%. When queried about why they behaved this way, most replied that they *tried* to match the experienced greeting probabilities, which they reported back very accurately, indicating that probability matching in this task was not due to any performance limitations.

However, Azab et al. (2016) noted that probability matching is usually found in tasks with multiple test trials, while maximizing is usually found in tasks with a single test trial. Azab et al. show that maximizing can also be found on the first trial of a multitrial test that, in the aggregate, demonstrates probability matching. (This means that one's first crossing of the fords of the Jordan would be far less dangerous than subsequent crossings.) Based on this finding, Azab et al. argued that probability matching arises from making sure that the sequence of responses one has produced is representative of training (see also Kahneman & Tversky, 1972).[1]

To ensure that a sequence of responses matches the probabilities encountered in training, the participant must remember the response sequence they have just produced. This raises the intriguing possibility that children maximize because their memory is underdeveloped (Hudson Kam & Newport, 2005).[2] This explanation is supported by Ferdinand et al.'s (2013) finding that adults also maximize when their memory is overloaded.

Interestingly, if this explanation is accurate, then adults should also be more likely to maximize in real life than in multitrial experiments testing pattern productivity ("wug tests"). Participants do overwhelmingly match pattern probabilities in wug tests (Hayes et al., 2009; see also chapter 8). However, a multitrial wug test makes it easy to remember one's prior form choices, a task that may be much more difficult in real life. Thus, the same probabilistic knowledge may give rise to probability matching in wug tests and maximizing in everyday language use, making the grammar look much more regular in a corpus than in a productivity test, where participants are able to remember their previous responses to ensure that their productions reflect pattern probabilities. Indeed, C. Yang (2016) has recently argued that children's spontaneous production data make the grammar look far more categorical than data from multi-trial elicited production tests in the laboratory.[3]

In addition, real production involves accessing or constructing a production plan and executing an intricate sequence of motor movements it calls for. Producing something one has not produced (in a while) is often difficult. Compare this to a wug task, in which one is required to—at most—produce a single word, and often chooses among alternative productions by pressing a button or clicking on an icon. With such responses, the difficulty of the response is no longer strongly affected by its probability or frequency. The more room there is for frequency to influence response difficulty, the more likely one should be to maximize, choosing the easier response option every time.

For example, young children—for whom many motor responses adults consider trivial are difficult—are much more likely to repeat responses they have just performed even when they know that these responses are inappropriate (L. B. Smith et al., 1999). In the A-not-B task, children are asked to retrieve objects from locations such as buckets. An experimenter would repeatedly hide a toy under one bucket, letting the child retrieve it every time, and then hide it under the other bucket. Young children tend to reach for the old location. At the same time, their eyegaze indicates that they know where the toy really is. The articulatorily easier eyegaze response is less influenced by the difficulty of doing something new and therefore reflects the child's beliefs about the toy's location more faithfully. In contrast, the child becomes entrenched in previously performed reaches. The more difficult responses are, the more room there is for frequent use to alleviate the difficulty of a response. Therefore, frequency should influence response choice the most when responses are difficult to perform without practice. Indeed, forced-choice tasks—where the alternative responses are made maximally easy to plan and perform—are often less subject to frequency effects. When frequent and infrequent responses are equally easy, participants may not even match probabilities but equalize them (see Harmon & Kapatsinski, 2017, and chapter 6 for examples).

The pressures toward regularity, toward elimination of the rare in production, are important to keep in mind. In an associative framework, an individual's mental grammar is variable, uncertain, conflicted. Associations compete, tugging the speaker in different directions, rooting for different outputs. The mind looks much messier than the behavior it generates. The Zipfian rich-get-richer dynamics are the key to why this messiness is not to be feared: positive feedback loops turn too much choice into no choice at all.[4]

2.2.4 Exploration/Exploitation and S Curves

We have seen that maximizing in decision making can make the use of gradient, probabilistic knowledge look like the use of a categorical, nonprobabilistic system. In addition, it can also make gradient learning look like a sudden flash of insight. In 2004, Gallistel and colleagues pointed out that previous analyses of the timecourse of learning in simple conditioning paradigms have all relied on averaged data. Whereas averaged data show a smooth rise in probability of producing the response associated with reinforcement or avoidance of punishment, "the learning curves for individual subjects show an abrupt, often step-like increase from the untrained level of responding to the level seen in the well-trained subject," suggesting that "the appearance of conditioned behavior is mediated by an evidence-based decision process" (Gallistel et al., 2004, p. 13124). In other words, participants may gradually accumulate evidence that a certain behavior leads to reinforcement but do not commit to performing that behavior until the evidence becomes overwhelming, with individuals varying in how easily the inertial tendency to continue doing whatever they had been doing before training is overwhelmed by the evidence. In this way, gradient increases in association strength can lead to an abrupt, categorical change in behavior that at first glance seems inconsistent with associative learning.

Rehder and Hoffman (2005) used eyetracking to examine the emergence of selective attention in learning categories that required attending to one, two, or three dimensions of the same visual stimuli. Rehder and Hoffman found that learners attended to all dimensions early in training, and that "the restriction of eye movements to only relevant dimensions tended to occur only after errors were largely (or completely) eliminated" (p. 1). As in Gallistel's study, Rehder and Hoffman's participants showed initial reluctance to commit to an optimal behavior but rapidly shifted their behavior, restricting gaze to the single relevant dimension, after enough evidence has been accumulated. Interestingly, after making the decision, they "stuck with it," continuing to attend to a chosen stimulus dimension after it became irrelevant to the task, and failing to switch attention to other dimensions when they suddenly became relevant (see also Kruschke, 1996; Lawrence, 1949, 1950). It is hard to explain these kinds of bursts and lulls in behavioral change over the course of learning without appeal to making and "sticking with" decisions on the basis of accumulated evidence. The representation of accumulated evidence must be continuous to be updated, but it can be used to drive categorical and persistent behavioral choices.

Once a choice is made, the system is frozen in its current location in the space of possible cue-outcome mappings. For it to move out of that location, it must be "reheated." Recent work in our lab (section 4.1.2) demonstrates precisely this kind of reheating effected by surprising events. To the extent that they manage to capture attention, surprising events do not simply shift the organism's beliefs but also increase the temperature, leaving the learner more malleable and more willing to learn again, which temporarily boosts the learning rate. The overall result is a series of "frozen" equilibria punctuated by periods of rapid change (see Gould, 2007, for punctuated equilibria in other domains).

2.2.5 Categorization: Making the World Discrete

Associative learning involves gradient updating of continuous association weights, giving rise to continuous probabilistic knowledge.[5] However, because associations need to connect nodes, there is another way the representations built up by associative learning are surprisingly discrete. While sounds seem to live in a continuous multidimensional acoustic space, the continuous dimensions that define this space must be discretized into *categories*, which can then be associated with other categories. Although category learning is traditionally assumed to be part of language learning, this assumption is challenged by distributed connectionist models of the mind, which eschew category nodes (Rogers & McClelland, 2004). I do not wish to dispute that category nodes may be represented in the brain only approximately, with a sparse but nonetheless distributed code. What I wish to emphasize, however, is that localist (or near-localist) nodes have useful properties for language learning and use, and are therefore worth approximating for a distributed system.

First, discretization of the sound signal allows for access to statistics like frequencies of segments and transitional probabilities between them (Aslin et al., 1998; Maye et al., 2002, 2008; Saffran et al., 1996) and co-occurrence probabilities between sounds and meanings (Yu & L. B. Smith, 2007). Once a new member of a category is recognized as belonging to the category, one can immediately generalize the associations shared by the known category members to this new stimulus, allowing for extrapolation. In their model of learning to map wordforms onto meanings with Hebbian associative learning, McMurray et al. (2013) show that learning of word-meaning associations is accelerated by prior emergence of semantic and phonetic categories. Emberson et al. (2013) show that participants track sequential dependencies between classes of sounds only when members of a class are similar enough to form a perceptual category.

Category nodes provide learners with the ability to learn dependencies between these nodes. For example, McMurray et al. (2012) point out that category nodes allow categories to compete with each other through mutual inhibition, resulting in rapid—and generally accurate—decisions even while the learners' knowledge is quite uncertain. Clustering of experienced exemplars through techniques such as unsupervised deep neural networks has also been argued to be essential for learning representations that are useful across tasks—that is, representations that can be associated with many different responses (e.g., Bengio et al., 2012; Zorzi et al., 2013). As I discuss in chapter 5, discretization of continuous space into categories also allows for selective attention to particular regions of this space (Kalish & Kruschke, 2000). In production, too, discrete units allow one to produce an infinite variety of unit combinations, subserving linguistic creativity (Bryan & Harter, 1899; Hockett, 1960; Nowak & Krakauer, 1999).

Category nodes are also useful for making decisions on whether something is not in any known category. Children and adults appear to differ in how willing they are to extend known categories to novel exemplars that are beyond the range of encountered category exemplars, with children being more accepting of deviations from previous experience than adults (Gibson & Gibson, 1955; Kapatsinski et al., 2017). It is easy to see how one would represent category *confusions* without category nodes: the perceived pattern would simply activate properties of other categories. However, it is not clear how (or why) one would decide that the stimulus must not belong to any of the categories experienced without some representation of the breadths of the known categories (see also Cohen et al., 2001; Hahn et al., 2005).

Categorization is also suggested by the available evidence from neuroscience: at least early in training, sensorimotor mappings are typically mediated by subcortical structures in which single cells respond to a wide variety of patterns in the sensory cortex, leveling the differences between them (Ashby et al., 2007). The most extreme leveling occurs in the striatum, whose cells are massively convergent. With its ability to allocate cells to respond to complex sensory patterns, the hippocampus allows for learning of more complex categories that require maintaining category-internal similarity structure (e.g., when the category comprises several distinct clusters of exemplars; Seger et al., 2011; Zeithamova et al., 2012). However, even hippocampal cells do not respond to single exemplars. For example, cells that preferentially respond to the Sydney Opera House respond to many different views of the building (Suthana & Fried, 2012).

2.2.6 Full Connectivity and Learning by Pruning

To a first approximation, the category-category network starts out fully connected: connections between any two categories are available for strengthening and subject to pruning. This means, in particular, that (contra Hockett, 1960) the present approach does not allow for duality of patterning. There is no qualitative difference between lexical and sublexical units, the meaningless and the meaning*ful*. Meaningfulness is a continuum, and even the smallest form units are available to be directly linked to meanings. The existence of phonaesthemes like #gl~LIGHT and *cran*berry morphemes makes this very clear (Aronoff, 1976; Baayen et al., 2011; Bergen, 2004; Endresen, 2015; Kapatsinski, 2005b; Kwon & Round, 2015). So does research on grammaticalization, which documents how very meaningful units become more and more bleached of their meaning with repetition (Bybee, 2003; Occhino, 2016). The meaningless units are meaningless simply because they have not had a history of reliably co-occurring with a specific meaning. For example, because they are so frequent, most phones occur in every imaginable semantic context, and are thereby rendered meaningless.

Full connectivity means that learning involves weakening connections between representations of things and events that *do not* co-occur as well as strengthening connections between those that do (Edelman, 1987; Rescorla, 1988; Skinner, 1981).[6] McMurray et al. (2012, 2013) show that this hypothesis makes it possible even for a simple Hebbian learner to acquire a sizable vocabulary. Suppose one encounters a speaker labeling something with a word in a cluttered visual environment (*"Look! A wug!"*). One may not be certain what object the word maps onto (Quine, 1960), and in fact may provisionally map it onto the wrong object. This error may nonetheless help one learn what the word means because by mapping it onto the wrong object the learner weakens a large number of other wrong associations, those pointing to referents absent from the current environment. Landauer and Dumais (1997) point out that to account for adult vocabulary sizes, we must assume that schoolchildren learn more words in a day than they encounter. This is only possible if children are zeroing in on many different word meanings in parallel, so that encountering a word constrains the meanings of other words. This assumption of parallel learning also explains the childhood vocabulary spurt, the remarkable increase in the speed of word learning that happens around a child's first birthday: as long as there is a small number of easy words and a large number of harder words, learning words in parallel is bound to accelerate (McMurray, 2007; McMurray et al., 2012). Parallel learning of simple associations between categories is surprisingly powerful.[7]

2.3 What Is to Be Learned?

Now that some of the qualms concerning associative learning have hopefully been addressed, we turn to the question of what a language learner needs to learn in order to be said to have acquired the language. In other words, what kinds of structure are (1) robustly attested in languages, and so likely to be present in the linguistic environment of a language learner; and yet (2) need to be learned and reproduced by language learners to remain in the language?

2.3.1 Syntagmatic Structure

The first kind of structure to be learned is *syntagmatic structure*. Syntagmatic structure involves dependencies between forms that often co-occur in a temporal sequence. Learning of syntagmatic structure allows learners to anticipate what is coming up, to extract perceptually robust chunks that can serve as cues to meanings, and to produce linguistic units intended to express a particular meaning in the right order.

Syntagmatic structure in language operates at multiple levels. In phonology, syntagmatic structure is called *phonotactics*, sequential dependencies between sounds that appear to be automatically acquired from either perceptual or production experience with meaningless sound sequences (e.g., Dell et al., 2000; Onishi et al., 2002). For example, making participants read lists of CVC syllables in which [s] is always in the onset while [f] is always in the coda (*sef*) makes them highly unlikely to produce coda [s] and onset [f] even when making a speech error. Reading lists in which [f] was always an onset and [s] was always a coda produces the opposite pattern (Dell et al., 2000).

According to the theory of *statistical word learning*, tracking dependencies between sounds and syllables allows the learner to segment words out of continuous speech: a word boundary is marked in part by the fact that the next sound is less predictable than the sounds that came before (e.g., in *pretty baby*, the probability of *tty* after *pre* is higher than the probability of *ba* after *tty*; Saffran et al., 1996). Saffran et al. presented infants with syllable sequences like … *badokugolapupadotigolapubadokupadotibadokupadotigolapu* … generated via random concatenation of three words, each consisting of three unique syllables. The sequences were synthesized, so there were no prosodic cues to word boundaries. In this toy language, the syllable transition probabilities within words are three times higher than probabilities at word boundaries: *do* always follows *ba* but *ku* can be followed by *ba*, *go*, or *pa*. When infants were subsequently presented with a word like *badoku* vs. a "partword" spanning a word boundary like *kugola*, they attended more to the partword, as it contained a surprising, low-probability syllable sequence (see Baayen et al., 2011). In natural language, phonotactics also provide cues to word boundaries. Some sound sequences are more likely to occur within words, while others provide good cues to word boundaries. For example, in languages with vowel harmony, a disharmonic sequence is a cue to a word boundary, and speakers of such languages learn and use this fact to identify words (Vroomen et al., 1998).

In morphology, syntagmatic structure corresponds to *morphotactics*, as some morphemes are more likely to follow others. Ryan (2010) finds that attested morphotactic patterns can be learned by tracking morpheme bigram statistics much like the syllable bigram statistics used in statistical word learning experiments. Finally, syntagmatic dependencies constitute the core of sentence processing. Sentence comprehenders are exquisitely sensitive to what the speaker is likely to say next, rapidly anticipating the likely continuations and being taken aback by unlikely ones (e.g., G. Altmann & Mirković, 2009; MacDonald, 1994; Reali & Christiansen, 2007; Trueswell et al., 1993).

Representation of temporal dependencies and temporal order is a challenge that extends well beyond language learning. Even in simple classical conditioning, one wants to remember whether food will follow or precede a click. A click that precedes food should elicit a salivation response while a click that follows food should not. Remarkably, Matzel et al. (1988) find that rats can integrate two temporal relationships into an overall temporal schema: if trained on a click followed by a tone, and then on the same tone preceded by food, they learn to salivate to the click as long as food precedes the tone by less time than the click did (as shown in (1)). Similarly, any sequence of actions requires temporal sequencing and memory for temporal order. Recurrent sequences of events are ubiquitous in the environment. Any organism must be able to learn to predict the future, alerting to signals of danger or reward and readying oneself with preparatory behaviors for what comes up next. Any organism must also learn to perform sequences of actions to obtain rewards and evade punishments. This means that all species must be able to accomplish sequence learning to survive. Sequence learning is neither domain- nor species-specific. Indeed, nonhuman animals have also been documented to show sensitivity to syllable co-occurrences in statistical word learning experiments (Hauser et al., 2001; Newport et al., 2004), although there is also evidence that humans are particularly adept at sequence learning (Broadbent, 1958, pp. 46–47). This generality does not mean that sequence learning is simple, but rather that it is highly useful for any learning system. I will argue that, in humans, it involves at least three domain-general mechanisms: (1) acquisition of predictive dependencies through error-driven learning, (2) chunking of co-occurring sounds (chapter 3), and (3) automatization of motor sequences with practice (chapter 9).

(1) Training:

Click	$\rightarrow$	Tone
Food $\rightarrow$		Tone

Learn:

Click	$\rightarrow$	Food ☺

Training:

	Click $\rightarrow$	Tone
Food	$\rightarrow$	Tone

Learn:

Click	$\rightarrow$	No Food ☹

2.3.2 Schematic Structure

As emphasized by Bryan and Harter (1899), Zipf (1949), and Bybee (2003), we do not learn syntagmatic structure for its own sake. The reason we want to predict what the speaker will say next is because what they say next is a good cue to a meaning they want to express. The reason we say things is to convey meaning to the listener (sometimes, ourselves). In learning language, complex, syntagmatically organized forms need to be associated with meanings. We call these meaning-linked forms *schemas* (Bybee, 1985; see also Head, 1920; Oldfield & Zangwill, 1942; Broadbent, 1958, pp. 63–65).[8] Words are one kind of schema, but both smaller and larger stored form units are also schemas. Some schemas are thought to include open slots where other schemas can be placed. According to Construction Grammar, it is largely these *open* schemas that allow for morphological and syntactic *creativity*, the ability to generate and understand an infinite number of novel words and sentences we've never heard or said before (Booij, 2010; Goldberg, 1995, 2006; see also Bryan & Harter, 1899, pp. 365–367).[9] Nonetheless, there is a continuum between *filled* schemas and open schemas that suggests that the openness of a slot is a matter of category breadth. Filled schemas like {cat;CAT;**cat**;cat}—{🐈🐈🐈🐈🐈} permit only a limited range of variants, while fully open schemas, pairings of sequences of abstract categories like NP VP ~ Agent Action, permit a much wider range. Partially open schemas like DIE ~ *kick(ed;s;ing) the (proverbial) bucket* are in between.[10] The system of form-meaning associations of a language constitutes its *schematic structure*. For syntagmatic structure to subserve schematic structure, stored temporal sequences need to evoke and be evocable by meanings.

As noted earlier, the ability to rapidly associate forms and meanings may be one of the major adaptations that allows for language acquisition to happen (Deacon, 1997; Tomasello, 2003; though cf. Broadbent, 1958, p. 46). However, preparedness for rapidly forming certain kinds of associations does not mean that these associations cannot be formed using domain-general associative learning mechanisms (see Bouton, 2016, chap. 6, on the similar example of preparedness in flavor aversion learning). Recent work on *cross-situational word learning* (introduced by Yu & L. B. Smith, 2007, and illustrated in figure 2.1) and computational modeling of word learning "in the wild" suggests that schematic structure is acquired by associative learning mechanisms. In particular, despite earlier claims of one-shot word learning, work in both domains shows that word learning involves gradual accumulation of word-referent co-occurrence statistics (Horst & Samuelson, 2008; Kachergis et al., 2012; McMurray, 2007; McMurray et al., 2012, 2013; J. Warren & Duff, 2014; Yurovsky et al., 2014). Like flavor aversion learning, another fast and supposedly domain-specific learning mechanism, word learning shows nonnormative cue-competition effects that have been observed in classic associative learning paradigms (Ramscar et al., 2013; Yoshida & Burling, 2012; Yoshida & Hanania, 2007; Yurovsky et al., 2013). Wasserman et al. (2015) show that pigeons trained using instrumental conditioning can also learn a sizable inventory of word-picture mappings in a cross-situational learning paradigm. Furthermore, the pigeons show the same cue-competition effects obtained in human word learning.

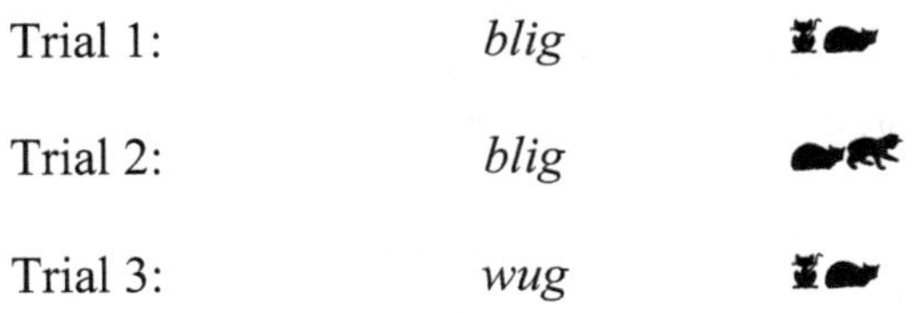

Trial 1:   *blig*

Trial 2:   *blig*

Trial 3:   *wug*

Figure 2.1
An illustration of cross-situational word learning. The paradigm was designed to simulate word learning in a situation of referential uncertainty aka Quine's (1960) *gavagai* problem. If we are looking at a complex visual scene and somebody says *gavagai*, how do we know which object (if any) *gavagai* refers to? There is no way to do this if one has never experienced *gavagai* or any of the objects before. However, one could solve this problem across multiple training trials. In this illustration, the learner might think—based on the first two trials—that *blig* means "●." On the third trial, they would then shift attention to "✶," mapping it onto *wug*.

2.3.3 Paradigmatic Structure

The last kind of structure is *paradigmatic structure*, form-form mappings that are used to generate a form when the other form is accessed but is not deemed appropriate to produce given the current context and the meaning the speaker wishes to express. Paradigmatic mappings have been proposed to link together (1) wordforms or affixes belonging to a morphological paradigm, (2) syntactic constructions related by a transformation, and (3) antonymous words. Given that paradigmatic mappings link together semantically similar forms that occur in complementary distribution, one could also argue for paradigmatic mappings linking allophones of a phoneme (*a~ă* as in *log/lock*), allomorphs of a morpheme (ɪk ~ ɪs as in *electric/electricity*), or even synonymous forms that occur in partially distinct contexts (*-ness* ~ *-ity*; *sofa~couch*). In fact, failing to form a paradigmatic connection between A and C on the basis of exposure to AB and BC ("associative inference") has been argued to be diagnostic of schizophrenia (Ragland et al., 2008) and other kinds of neurological abnormality (Zeithamova et al., 2012). Paradigmatic mappings differ from syntagmatic ones in that they link forms on the basis of *correspondence* or *context similarity* rather than direct co-occurrence. In fact, to be useful, a paradigmatic mapping should link forms that *do not* occur in the same contexts. Otherwise, there is no motivation to ever use the mapping: one could simply output whichever form one accesses first.

While everyone believes that acquiring a language involves acquiring syntagmatic and schematic structure, the need to acquire paradigmatic structure is more controversial. In morphology, paradigmatic structure is embraced by word-and-paradigm morphology (Matthews, 1972) but denied by item-and-arrangement theories in generative linguistics (Halle & Marantz, 1993) and, on occasion, by usage-based linguists as well (Bybee, 2001, p. 129).

According to the nonbelievers, forms are not derived from other forms. Rather, forms are activated by semantics and adjusted on the basis of the syntagmatic context. In syntax, paradigmatic mappings (aka transformations) were embraced by early generative grammar, which suggested that— to take one example—passive sentences are generated by transforming active sentences (Chomsky, 1957). While retaining the notion that sentences are generated by a series of transformations, subsequent work in generative linguistics abandoned the proposal that surface structures are derived from each other, instead suggesting that sentences are derived independently from underlying forms.

Rejecting the notion of transformations in favor of direct meaning-form mappings, Construction Grammarians have also emphasized the schematic dimension, with some arguing that paradigmatic structure plays no role in syntax (W. Croft, 2001, p. 46; Hilpert, 2008, p. 9, Assumption #1; Schöne-feld, 2012, p. 11). Others, however, have taken a more nuanced approach. For example, despite arguing for the importance of schematic structure, Goldberg (2002, p. 349) writes that "the arguments in this paper should not be taken to imply that possible paraphrase relations [paradigmatic mappings] play no role in the learning, processing or representation of language." Some recent work in Construction Grammar has reintroduced the notion of syntactic paradigms, arguing for the notion of *allostructions*, variants of a single construction that are in complementary distribution and linked by paradigmatic mappings (Cappelle, 2006; see also Perek, 2012; Uhrig, 2015). Nonetheless, it is unclear that the putative paradigmatic mappings play much of a role in normal sentence production. For example, it is conceivable that the double-object dative (*I gave him a book*) and the prepositional dative (*I gave a book to him*) are paradigmatically linked allostructions. But how often does a speaker formulate a sentence using one of these constructions first and then, unsatisfied, transform it into the other? Usually, there is little cost to producing the allostruction accessed first. Furthermore, rejecting it and producing the other allostruction may not require transforming the accessed allostruction. Instead, top-down inhibition of the selected allostruction could allow the shared meaning to activate its competitor without any need for form-to-form mappings. The same argument applies to allophony and allomorphy, which therefore also do not absolutely *require* paradigmatic mappings between members of a form category.

In the early 1960s, free association data was proposed to support the existence of paradigmatic mappings between semantically similar words within the lexicon (Brown & Berko, 1960; Deese, 1962; Ervin, 1961; McNeill, 1963). In the free association test, participants are given a word and asked to say the first word that comes to mind. Brown and Berko (1960) and Ervin (1961) noticed that children would often produce words that tend to follow the prompt word. Adults, on the other hand, would often produce antonyms of the prompts. Thus, in response to *shallow* a child might say *pool* while an adult might say *deep*. Ervin (1961) called this the *syntagmatic-to-paradigmatic shift*. McNeill (1966) explains why this is interesting:

> It is assumed that one factor critical to the formation of associative bonds [be-tween words] is the experience of words in contiguity. ... Words from the same

part of speech rarely appear together in sentences. They have a relation to one another different from co-occurrence. Words of the same grammatical class share privileges of occurrence, which means that they replace one another in speech. We might say *the hole is too deep*, or *the hole is too shallow*, but we never say *the hole is too deep and shallow*. Thus the opportunity for learning paradigmatic responses seems to be absent under ordinary circumstances of speaking or listening to speech. (pp. 548–549)

Of course, it is not true that "words from the same part of speech rarely appear together in sentences" and antonyms are even more likely to co-occur than unrelated words from the same form class. We do in fact often say things like *the hole is neither too deep nor too shallow* or *both deep and shallow holes can be dangerous to the unwary traveler*. While it took a quarter century before evidence of this fact began to emerge from quantitative corpus studies, it is by now indisputable that associations between antonymous adjectives can be explained by syntagmatic co-occurrence (Fellbaum, 1996; Jones et al., 2007; Justeson & Katz, 1991) due to the existence of a set of specialized constructions that utilize pairs of antonyms to emphasize or downplay contrast (Jones, 2002; Justeson & Katz, 1991; Murphy, 2006).

Adjectives do appear to form miniparadigms. Speakers of a language seem to have intuitions about which pairs of antonyms "belong together." For example, Justeson and Katz (1991) note that speakers of English intuit that *big* belongs with *little* while *small* belongs with *large*. However, Jones et al. (2007) show that such pairings can also be acquired from syntagmatic co-occurrence. This is an important point. If a paradigmatic mapping can be acquired from syntagmatic co-occurrence, then there is no need for a specialized learning mechanism designed to acquire paradigmatic structure.

While Jones et al. (2007) retain the notion of an antonym paradigm, this may not be necessary. As with other examples we discussed, it is difficult to imagine situations in which one would need to use paradigmatic mappings between antonyms. Suppose one accesses *shallow* while trying to express the meaning DEEP but recovers from this error, producing *deep*. As in the case of allostructions, the inappropriate accessed form can be simply suppressed so that *deep*, a stronger associate of the to-be-expressed semantics, wins the competition for production. There is no need for a paradigmatic *deep→shallow* association.

This leaves only one place in grammar where paradigmatic mappings are in fact needed and frequently used, and that is morphology. Morphology requires paradigmatic mappings because the shape of the to-be-produced form depends on what other forms of the same word are like. For example, in Russian a noun that ends in a nonpalatalized consonant in the nominative singular case like *kot* 'tomcat' forms its genitive plural by the addition of *-ov#*, thus *kot~kotov*. On the other hand, a noun that ends in *-a* in the nominative singular loses that *-a* in the genitive plural, sometimes gaining or losing a vowel inside the stem, thus *koʃka* '(female) cat' becomes *koʃek*. This system is easily captured by paradigmatic associations, where $C_1\#_{Nom.Sg}\sim C_1ov\#_{Gen.Pl}$ and $C_1a\#_{Nom.Sg}\sim C_1\#_{Gen.Pl}$. However, it cannot be captured by schematic or syntagmatic associations. There are two distinct Genitive Plural schemas, with the choice determined by characteristics of another, paradigmatically related form. The fact that the same consonants can occur at the ends of stems in both masculine and feminine genitives also precludes a syntagmatic account of schema choice in the Genitive Plural. Nominative-Genitive mappings are productive: Russian speakers are sensitive to the shape of the Nominative Singular when they are trying to produce a Genitive they have not produced or heard before, suggesting that the paradigmatic mappings above are learned from experience with Russian.

The Russian genitive is not an isolated case, a strange aberration on the face of morphology. For example, Łubowicz (2007) reports that in Polish the locative is marked by either *-e* or *-u*, and that *-e* triggers palatalization. However, palatalized nominatives take *-u* rather than *-e*. In this case, it is impossible to correctly select *-e* vs. *-u* without knowing what the nominative ends in: in the locative, both suffixes are preceded by the same consonants.

In some ways, then, morphology is the hardest part of language, as it has all three kinds of structure we have examined. There is substantial individual variability in the extent to which paradigmatic associations are learned, even by native speakers. For example, Dąbrowska (2012) shows that knowledge of the Polish inflectional system is quite variable among adult native Polish speakers. Similarly, many Russian speakers are famously unsure whether *pomidorov* or *pomidor* is the right Genitive Plural for the word "tomato." Paradigmatic associations are hard to learn and in fact may not be possessed by most speakers of most languages. Nonetheless, at least some speakers of some languages do acquire them as part of learning morphology. Thus, it should come as no surprise that this book will spend quite a bit of space on morphology (chapters 7 and 8), for it is there that we can examine interactions between syntagmatic, schematic, and paradigmatic structure in their full complexity.

2.4   Directionality

As noted in chapter 1, one of the most basic issues in both learning theory and linguistics is the issue of directionality. Suppose that you encounter stimulus A before stimulus B. While it is uncontroversial that you form an A→B association, do you also form a B→A association? And are these indeed two associations or a single bidirectional one (A←→B, or simply A-B)?

Kahana (2002) notes that bidirectionality is consistent with models of learning that take the goal to be developing the ability to perform *pattern completion*, retrieving a stored pattern given degraded input in which parts of the pattern are missing (e.g., to recognize a familiar stimulus when it is obscured by noise; McClelland & Elman, 1986). It is probably for this reason that learners in statistical word segmentation experiments appear to keep track of both forward and backward transitional probabilities (Pelucchi et al., 2009; Perruchet & DeSaulty, 2008). While backward transitional probabilities are useless for predicting the future, they are useful for filling in what one has just missed.

In contrast, predictive error-driven models of associative learning have assumed that associations are unidirectional, linking preceding events to following events but not vice versa (Mackintosh, 1975; Rescorla & Wagner, 1972). Directional associations are clearly useful for representing sequences of actions that need to be executed in a specific order, something essential for language production (chapter 9). However, backward associations may also be useful for constructing a production plan: it is conceivable that one will fill in one part of the plan before filling out the part that precedes it (chapter 8). In that case, backward syntagmatic associations may help select the filler appropriate for the context. For example, if a Russian speaker accessed a noun before an adjective they want to place before it, she would be well served by an association between the noun's gender and the appropriate adjectival suffix.

Backward syntagmatic associations are necessary for constructing a production plan if it is constructed flexibly, rather than in a strict left-to-right manner (cf. Baayen et al., 2011; Caballero & Inkelas, 2013). Such flexibility is suggested by work in the FishFilm paradigm (Tomlin, 1995), which asks participants to describe animations in which two fish swim toward each other. On each trial, the subject's attention is drawn to one of the fish by a flashing arrow. In addition, the fish with the arrow is a previously mentioned fish, making it more accessible for this reason as well. When the fish meet, the fish with the arrow either eats the other fish or gets eaten by it. English-speaking participants typically use the fish with the arrow as the subject of the sentence, rather than the object. Interestingly, Malagasy-speaking participants do too, despite the fact that the subject follows the object in Malagasy (Rasolofo, 2006). Thus, Malagasy speakers place the more accessible agent at the end of the speech plan. If plan construction begins as soon as possible, this means that the end of the utterance plan is filled in before the beginning in Malagasy. In general, it is likely that the parts of the plan that are easier to construct—that is, about whose content the speaker has less uncertainty—are constructed before the harder parts. If the plan is not constructed linearly, left to right, then backward associations will help the speaker fill in the harder parts once the easier parts are filled in (e.g., selecting the right prefix for an already-selected stem).

Kapatsinski (2009a) and Ramscar et al. (2010) noted that unidirectional associations are incompatible with the notion of a construction/schema as a Saussurean sign, a form-meaning *pairing* used to both comprehend and produce language. Of course, the plausibility of a bidirectional form-meaning mapping depends crucially on what we mean by form. Given the desire of construction grammarians to avoid intermediate representations intervening between form and meaning (e.g., Bybee, 2001; Goldberg, 1995; Langacker, 1987), one might be tempted to accept the (admittedly somewhat extreme) proposal that form representations are sensorimotor. In perception, the form representations would then be auditory exemplars not unlike a fuzzy spectrogram (Goldinger, 1998; Klatt, 1979; Port & Leary, 2005). In production, they would be sequences of commands to muscles (Mowrey & Pagliuca, 1995). Of course, with this level of detail at the form level, bidirectional form-meaning associations used for both comprehension and production are biologically impossible.

Retaining the notion of a sign therefore requires abstracting away from the details of form, and positing that the same abstract form level activates meaning in comprehension and is activated by meaning in production. There are many proposals for what this abstract level is like. The abstract forms may consist of phonological features (Chomsky & Halle, 1965), idealized gestures (Fowler, 1986; Liberman & Mattingly, 1985), or auditory category representations (Boersma, 1998, 2011; Guenther et al., 1998). It is not crucial for our purposes *what* the abstract form is, as long as there is some form that is used in both production and comprehension.

Some have argued that such a form may not always be defensible. For example, Labov et al. (1991) have argued that there are speakers who can produce a phonetic distinction (e.g., between *Mary and Murray*) but do not perceive it, suggesting that they have only one perceptual category but two production representations. However, one could argue that these speakers do have two form representations, and that they have learned that the acoustic cues they produce are uninformative about form identity when encountered in the environment; these speakers are usually surrounded by speakers who do not produce the distinction.

Can abstract forms save the sign hypothesis? In 2009, I argued not. My argument was based on the existence of asymmetries between production and perception in cases where the form-meaning mapping is not one to one (Kapatsinski, 2009a). For example, consider the competition between *but* and *however*. Each of the conjunctions can express both meanings illustrated in (2) and (3). When a conjunction is used to express the preventive meaning, the event described by the clause following the conjunction *prevents* the event described by the preconjunction clause from running to completion. In (2), the agent does not end up fleeing the country. When the conjunction is used in the denial-of-expectation (D-o-E) meaning in (3), the event described in the postconjunction clause is *unexpected* given the preconjunction event but does not prevent it from running to completion. The agent in (3) may have fled the country. Most instances of *however* are D-o-E uses, which makes *however* a good cue to the D-o-E meaning for the comprehender. A smaller proportion of *but* tokens express D-o-E. Nonetheless, because *but* is much more frequent than *however*, a speaker who wants to express D-o-E is much more likely to use *but* than *however*. This discrepancy can be described as follows: the D-o-E→*but* connection is stronger than the D-o-E→*however* connection, but the *but*→D-o-E connection is weaker than the *however*→D-o-E connection. Note that this account of the schematic structure of the adversative conjunction system would require unidirectional form→meaning and meaning→form connections.

(2) PREVENTIVE: *He was about to flee the country but was detained at the airport.*

(3) DENIAL-OF-EXPECTATION: *He was about to flee the country but didn't even think of saying "goodbye."*

However, note that the overuse of *no* in D-o-E contexts can also be attributed to the greater *accessibility* of *but*. Paraphrasing Maslow's (1966) "if all you have is a hammer, then everything looks like a nail," if all you can access is *no*, then D-o-E looks like just another adversative context (Zipf, 1949). Instead of the D-o-E→*but* connection being stronger than the D-o-E→*however* connection, we could then describe the preference for *but* in D-o-E contexts as coming from the *but* node having a higher resting activation level than the *however* node, making *but* easier to access from either meaning. The prediction of this account is that leveling form acceptability differences between *but* and *however*—for example, by forcing participants to choose between the two in a forced-choice test—should eliminate the preference for *but* in D-o-E contexts. In chapter 6, I discuss evidence for this prediction from an experimental paradigm where form-meaning co-occurrence statistics and form accessibility can be independently manipulated (Harmon & Kapatsinski, 2017). Together with the Abstract Form Hypothesis, the Accessibility Hypothesis saves the notion of the construction/schema as a Saussurean sign, a bidirectional form-meaning pairing. This, however, does not mean that the construction is a single bidirectional connection. Rather, form→meaning and meaning→form connections involving the same form and meaning tend to be of similar strength.

As noted above, unidirectionality is a feature of predictive learning. Given at least a modicum of experience with an environment, we know that there are things in this environment we want to predict. These are the important events. In a classical conditioning paradigm, they are unconditioned stimuli or—more precisely—their sensory consequences; likewise for a preverbal infant lying in his crib or even a fetus in its mother's womb. The learner seeks cues that will allow him to anticipate the important events in his environment. Some of the best cues are in the caretakers' utterances. Given that the mother is literally the environment of the fetus, her utterances are almost inevitably the most predictive cues regarding what will happen to the environment in the near future. For an infant in the crib, parental utterances likewise contain the best cues to important events, like whether they are about to be played with, ignored, fed, or doused with water. In fact, much of the literature on infant speech perception can be accounted for by the simple hypothesis that infants attend most to cues that are most informative in their environment. Is it any wonder that infants, including newborns, pay particular attention to speech over non-speech (Vouloumanos & Werker, 2007), their mother's voice over other people's voices (Mehler et al., 1978), and the cues that distinguish speakers and their affective states over phonemic distinctions (Houston & Jusczyk, 2003; Singh et al., 2004), or that the earliest-learned words tend to be the ones that are most predictive of times, places, and discourse topics (Roy et al., 2015)? While some of these preferences have been described as helpful innate biases and others as signs of immaturity, all of them follow from predictive cues drawing attention to themselves.

It makes perfect sense for the infant to use features of spoken utterances to predict "protomeanings," the events that follow them and require some behavioral preparation, such as feeding or washing. Trying to predict adults' utterances from events is of much less importance as utterances are not inherently reinforcing. However, as the infant grows up, bidirectionality becomes more important. As noted above, there are many cases where one may wish for the power of retrodiction. If one knows what stems follow *im-*, one may also want to learn to choose *im-* having accessed *possible*. Because every listener is also a speaker, whenever one learns that a form has a certain meaning by perceiving the form and then perceiving or inferring the meaning, one would also wish to be able to *produce* the form to express the meaning. If one knows how to form a plural form from a singular, one may also want to produce the singular when one accesses the corresponding plural first. Generally, one wants to be able to generate any form of a word given any other form or forms that one knows and happens to access in the moment of production. Thus, by the time one is an adult, one should generally want and try to form bidirectional mappings. Forming backward associations is hard and effortful. As shown by Ramscar et al. (2010), learners can be denied their wish for bidirectionality by overloading their brain. However, bidirectionality is something learners should strive for. A plausible learning scenario is as follows: (1) Perceiving A followed by B, the learner forms the A→B association as the stimuli are coming in; (2) then, having perceived B, the learner endeavors to form a B→A association. Under normal circumstances, for a proficient learner in a domain like language that calls for bidirectionality, this effort is likely to succeed.

In other words, associative mappings are bidirectional *by default*. Importantly, natural learning environments may provide plentiful opportunities for such bidirectional association formation, at least in the domain of learning word-meaning pairings. In experimental tasks, words and objects are often presented asynchronously, so that the object is no longer seen when the word is heard or vice versa (as in Ramscar et al., 2010). However, at least in many cultures, caregivers tell children the names of objects the children are already looking at, typically naming an object after the child has been looking at it for a few seconds. Furthermore, the child continues to look at the object for several seconds after the word is finished (Pereira et al., 2014). These kinds of interactions afford plenty of opportunities to first learn a meaning→form association and then a form→meaning association, and may scaffold other kinds of bidirectional learning.

2.5 Specificity

Another foundational issue is that of specification vs. generalization. In contrast to the generative view of grammar acquisition as setting a small number of parameters (Chomsky, 1981), usage-based approaches to language have emphasized the need to acquire a large number of fairly specific constructions like the *way* construction exemplified by *I verbed my way up the slope* and have hypothesized that acquisition involves memorizing specific utterances followed by gradual generalization, eventually culminating in abstract constructions like Subject-Verb-Object (Tomasello, 2003; see also Braine, 1963). This *item-based* approach thus posits a specific-to-general order of acquisition. The initial state consists of a few mappings between specific forms and meanings. This idea is supported by findings that, in any given context, inexperienced learners produce a smaller variety of forms than more experienced learners do (see Ambridge & Lieven, 2011, for a review).

On the other hand, connectionist models of language have proposed a largely general-to-specific acquisition order, starting from a state where every form-meaning mapping is possible and gradually pruning the mappings not supported by experience, narrowing down both the class of forms mapping onto a meaning and the class of meanings mapping onto a form (e.g., McMurray et al., 2012, 2013; Rogers & McClelland, 2004). In Kapatsinski (2013), I have likewise supported a general-to-specific acquisition order for morphological schemas, reasoning that the learner starts out thinking that, for example, PLURAL forms could sound like anything, and a word-final /z/ could *mean* anything. Only later does the learner zero in on the appropriate form-meaning mappings. This idea is supported by findings that perceptual categories become narrower with experience. When one knows little about a category, one is more willing to judge new examples that do not match one's previous experience with that category as nonetheless belonging to it. Thus, seeing one Dalmatian labeled *dax* leads one to consider that all kinds of dogs are *daxes* but seeing three Dalmatians labeled *dax* makes this less likely (F. Xu & Tenenbaum, 2007; see also Cohen et al., 2001, for visual categories not linked to wordforms). Children often think of all sorts of animals as being kitties (the superordinate-to-basic shift; Rogers & McClelland, 2004). Both children and adults can accept badly mispronounced words as being the same word—as long as the word is relatively unfamiliar (Fennell & Werker, 2003; K. White et al., 2013). Distinct structures are able to prime each other as if they were repetitions of the same thing—again, as long as they are relatively unfamiliar (Castles et al., 2007; Thothathiri & Snedeker, 2008). Paradigmatically, inexperienced learners of German map all sorts of singulars onto -*en*, while more experienced learners are much more selective about the kinds of singulars that correspond to -*n* plurals (Köpcke & Wecker, 2017).

The general-to-specific acquisition order is neurologically plausible because learning in the brain tends to involve more pruning of unused or error-generating synaptic connections than strengthening of ones that are frequently used or help prevent error (see Baayen et al., 2011; McMurray et al., 2012, 2013). Research on classic conditioning, starting with Pavlov (1927), likewise suggests a general-to-specific acquisition order—called *stimulus generalization* in that literature—and a functional explanation. An organism evolving in an environment where biologically relevant events are relatively rare should develop so as not to miss them. Falsely thinking that food will be there and checking in vain is less consequential than falsely thinking that the food will not be there and missing the opportunity to feed. Missing a hidden predator is more dangerous than falsely detecting one when it is absent. As a result, one should be fairly lenient regarding the match between the current stimulus and known cues to consequential outcomes. As Pavlov (1927) observed,

> if a tone of 1000 d.v. is established as a conditioned stimulus, many other tones spontaneously acquire similar properties, such properties diminishing proportionally to the intervals of those tones from the one of 1000 d.v. Similarly, if a tactile stimulation of a definite circumscribed area of skin is made into a conditioned stimulus, tactile stimulation of other skin areas will also elicit some conditioned reaction, the effect diminishing with increasing distance. ... This spontaneous ... generalization of stimuli can be interpreted from a biological point of view by reference to the fact that natural stimuli are in most cases not rigidly constant. ... For example, the hostile sound of any beast of prey serves as a conditioned stimulus to a defense reflex in the animals it hunts. The defense reflex is brought about independently of variations in pitch, strength and timbre of the sound produced by the animal according to its distance, the tension of its vocal cords and similar factors. (pp. 112–113)

In contrast, stimuli often trigger specific behavioral responses. For example, though both electric shock and nausea are aversive unconditional stimuli, they trigger different preparatory responses, which are themselves quite specific. Functionally, if a behavior has worked to avoid or diminish shock, one is best off practicing and automatizing that specific behavior, rather than thinking that a broad range of behaviors would serve just as well. Similarly, it is only functional to generalize over outcomes (unconditional stimuli) in a classical conditioning experiment if the responses they demand are similar or identical.

Consider taste aversion (Garcia & Koelling, 1966). Rats appear to be innately *prepared* to associate food cues—tastes and smells—with symptoms of gastrointestinal distress like nausea (Rudy & Cheatle, 1977). Rapid learning of food-poison associations is of course important for survival: one does not want to be repeatedly poisoned by foods one could have learned to avoid. However, this does not mean that other associations are innately ruled out. In fact, young rats are quite ready to *also* associate nausea with other things such as tactile stimuli or the boxes in which they experienced it, an "open-mindedness" that disappears by adulthood as the aging rat learns that these other cues are irrelevant (e.g., Molina et al., 1991; see also Gibson & Gibson, 1955; Gopnik et al., 2015; Kapatsinski et al., 2017, for impressionablity reducing with age in human development). As long as nausea is rapidly associated with the taste of the food recently consumed, it is not too detrimental if it *also* becomes associated with other aspects of the context in which the poisoning occurred. With a biologically signifi-cant outcome like poisoning, better safe than sorry. Importantly, Molina et al. (1991, p. 446) find no generalization over outcomes, a result they find puzzling: "[Cue] equivalence was established only if the unconditioned stimuli paired with the olfactory and visual events were identical. It was not sufficient that these unconditioned stimuli be equally aversive. Given the intermodal transfer observed in terms of the conditioned stimuli, why was there such resistance to intermodal transfer between the gustatory and tactile unconditioned stimuli?" I suggest that it is not puzzling at all: an aversive taste does not demand the same reaction as an aversive shock to the foot. One should not treat cues to shock as cues to a bad taste, even if both are "equally aversive."

Where we see specificity in language is in production, which is a specific kind of neuromotor behavior, a set of coordinated sequences of articulator movements not unlike sequences of muscle movements involved in detect-ing and obtaining food or fleeing from a predator. It may be that we are prepared to generalize over stimuli more than over behaviors. Thus in lan-guage comprehension, one starts out accepting a large variety of forms as cues to a given meaning: a form can be mispronounced and still be mapped onto the same meaning, especially so if it is relatively unfamiliar (e.g., Fen-nell & Werker, 2003; Kapatsinski et al., 2017). In contrast, forms produced by an inexperienced speaker are specific sequences of motor movements, albeit imperfectly executed: an adult's imitations of a child's mispronuncia-tions are not perceived by the child as correct productions. In production one starts out accepting a variety of meaning inputs as mapping onto a single form: a child may use *kitty* for all kinds of animals (Clark, 1973; Naigles & Gelman, 1995; Rogers & McClelland, 2004). An automatized, eas-ily accessible behavior known to work in transmitting at least the part of the meaning of *dog* it shares with *cat* is extended to *cat* as well (see chapter

6). In producing a new form of a known word, the speaker is cued by the meaning they want to express and the known forms of the word. Stimulus generalization therefore predicts that the form produced will become more and more strictly conditioned on what the other forms of the word are like (as is suggested by Köpcke & Wecker's, 2017, acquisition data), but the speaker will attempt to produce a specific form. Note that this should not be the case for judgment tasks: when judging whether, say, *wugs* is the right plural form for *wug*, both forms are stimuli—unless the participant simulates the production process and responds on the basis of this simulation. They may therefore accept a much wider range of plural forms than they would themselves produce. This is indeed the common finding in comparing judgment to production (e.g., Kapatsinski, 2012), outside of cases where the judged form is a strong cue to a dispreferred sociolinguistic identity (Labov, 1996).

If we believe in a form level that mediates the acoustic-semantic mapping in comprehension and the semantic-articulatory mapping in production, it is not immediately clear whether it should be treated as a stimulus, and so subject to stimulus generalization. Essentially, the issue comes down to how closely we think this level is tied to articulatory planning. If a form in fact *is* an articulatory plan (as one might expect under early versions of Motor Theory or Direct Realism), then forms should be fairly specific. In that case, the tolerance of form deviations in comprehension could be seen to reside in the acoustic-to-form mapping, affecting the breadths of acoustic categories. With specific form representations, the tolerance of deviations in form can be seen as decisional in nature. As proposed by Signal Detection Theory, whenever a category of perceptual stimuli is a category of useful cues, that usefulness is expected to reduce the degree to which the stimulus must match known category members in order to be considered part of the category (Blough, 1967). If forms are *not* articulatory plans, but are instead *cues* to articulatory plans, then they should be subject to stimulus generalization.[11] We will not be able to settle this question in the present book. My wish here is simply to note that comprehension-production asymmetries are compatible with a form level that is shared between production and comprehension.

2.6   Conclusion and Preview

While "all grammars leak" (Sapir, 1921, p. 39), grammar seems like a mostly regular, orderly symbolic system, more akin to math than to a tangle of neural spaghetti. How can squishy associative representations possibly do the job of representing knowledge of grammar? First, the knowledge any individual has of his or her language can be much less regular and systematic than the way that language looks from grammatical description. Maximizing decision-making processes operating within and between individuals allows individuals that have only an uncertain, gradient knowledge of the community grammar to behave much more systematically than one might expect in examining the squishy knowledge structures in their long-term memory (McMurray et al., 2013). Second, positive feedback loops operating within and across individuals turn gradient patterns and soft biases into ironclad regularities (K. Smith et al., 2013; Wedel, 2007). Even though individuals can represent gradient, irregular patterns, such patterns are inherently unstable and likely to be regularized as the language is learned and used.

We considered three kinds of structure that play a prominent role in language: syntagmatic structure, which specifies likely and unlikely form sequences; schematic structure, which specifies form-meaning co-occurrences; and paradigmatic structure, which involves mappings between forms that can be used to generate each other, largely by scraping material off an accessed form to generate a related form one could not access. We examined the evidence for each kind of structure and found that there is one domain of linguistics where all three kinds of structure are well attested, and that is morphology.

Finally, we discussed some controversial issues that any model of language learning must tackle, to which we return throughout the book. One of these issues is the issue of whether associations obey the flow of time, providing only a way to use the present and past to predict the future. I argued that competent learners also form present→past associations, in part to perform pattern completion / cued recall when environmental noise impinges on one's ability to perfectly perceive a stimulus or internal noise prevents one from perfectly retrieving what one knows. Nonetheless, despite our best efforts, our attempts at forming present→past associations can be thwarted, just like our attempts at recall. The final issue we examined is the issue of whether representations start out specific and become more general or start out more general and become more specific. Here, I noted that one wants to be tolerant of deviation from prior experience when one is dealing with a cue to an important outcome. On the other hand, there is little benefit to overgeneralizing outcomes. This led to the working hypothesis that associations link fairly specific cues and outcomes but, when considering whether a stimulus belongs to a known category of cues, one starts out fairly tolerant of mismatch between that stimulus and the category representation, narrowing the category down with experience.

In the next two chapters, we return to the question of learning mechanisms. In chapter 3, we examine the evidence for and implications of *attentional learning*, the idea that we learn what we should attend to when performing a particular task. Attentional learning is crucial for acquiring language but can also lead to difficulties in acquiring a second language when the cues one is used to attending to are no longer informative, and the cues one has learned to ignore are suddenly all-important (Ellis, 2006; Escudero, 2005; Francis & Nusbaum, 2002). In chapter 4, I introduce the ideas of Bayesian learning models, which view us as optimal learners maximizing belief accuracy and have been especially influential in the domain of distributional category learning, which is considered next in chapter 5. As I argued above, categories are the building blocks of associative learning, the objects connected by association lines. Thus, we tackle how continuous dimensions are discretized to make associative learning and selective attention possible. We then turn to acquisition of schematic structure, exemplified by mappings between meanings and suffixes. There, I argue that form accessibility plays a crucial role in semantic extension (Zipf, 1949). We then tackle morphological creativity, where schematic and syntagmatic structure come into contact—and sometimes conflict—with the mysterious paradigmatic structure as the speaker constructs a motor plan for a wordform they have never heard or produced before. Finally, we consider the process of automatization, which streamlines frequently executed meaning-linked motor plans and is argued to be responsible for much sound change.

3 What Are the Nodes? Unitization and Configural Learning vs. Selective Attention

He who defends everything defends nothing.
—Frederick the Great

If we believe that the mind is a network of interconnected nodes, we have to answer the question "What are these nodes?" What are the units that can be associated together by the associative learning mechanisms we have reviewed back in chapter 1? How big are they? In this chapter, I will argue for a fairly conventional answer to this question: the sizes vary. There are big units and small units, and the big units contain smaller units inside them. This answer, however, begs some really tough questions. What causes a unit to form or to split apart? What roles do the larger and smaller units play in learning and processing? This chapter will start addressing these questions, on both the timescale of learning and the timescale of processing, but they will continue to vex us throughout this book.

3.1 Elements and Configurations

Associative learning theory distinguishes between elemental and configural models of learning. In an *elemental model*, all associations form between elemental units: if a whole can be decomposed, it is. Rescorla and Wagner's (1972) model, often considered the standard model of associative learning, is elemental: there are no representations for combinations of cues or outcomes. Accordingly, in applying the model to language, Baayen et al. (2011, 2013) argue that much of the evidence in favor of storing complex linguistic units—morphemes, words, idioms, and so on—in memory can be accounted for without assuming separate representations for complex units (at least, complex units of form). For example, Baayen et al. argue that chains of letter bigrams suffice to capture the finding that frequent phrases such as *in the middle of* are processed faster than rare phrases such as *in the side of* (Arnon & Snider, 2010). Baayen et al.'s Naive Discriminative Learner model accounts for this result by learning associations between all letter bigrams comprising a phrase and the meaning of the phrase. At least some of these associations will be stronger for a frequent phrase than for a rare phrase, predicting that the meaning of the frequent phrase should be more easily accessible. Note that while letter bigrams are hardly the elements of visual perception, Baayen et al.'s (2011) model is elemental because there is only one level of chunking accessible to it: *for the model*, letter bigrams are elements, as are phrase meanings, because they are undecomposable.

In contrast, a *configural model* proposes that at least some of the time a whole and its parts are both available to be associated with other units (e.g., Atkinson & Estes, 1962; Friedman, 1966; Pearce, 1994; Rescorla, 1973). In its extreme version, a configural model claims that *only* the whole is represented, and the same response can only be transferred to the parts by generalization (Pearce, 1994; see Goldinger, 1998, for a wholes-only model in speech perception). In either case, the whole can have associations that its parts do not have (a finding demonstrated as early as Pavlov, 1927, and Woodbury, 1943).

The most common type of configural pattern in language is a *superadditive interaction*, illustrated in (1). Something special happens when all parts of a linguistic unit are "there" (i.e., inferred by the listener as having been intended to be produced by the speaker) but the individual parts of the unit are nonetheless associated with the response appropriate for the whole. A classic example of such an interaction is found in speech perception, where a video of a speaker's talking face results in very low intelligibility on its own but produces a large boost to intelligibility in the presence of congruent audio (Sumby & Pollack, 1954). Recent work has also shown that some brain areas are superadditively activated by temporally aligned audiovisual speech (Calvert et al., 2000). Single-cell recording studies of nonhuman animals also indicate that even single neurons can fire superadditively when presented with a combination of stimuli from different modalities (Avillac et al., 2007).

(1) Stimulus   Activity/response above baseline
         A   → |
         B   → |||
         AB   → ?

                        |||| Additive
                        |||||||||||||| Superadditive

Some of the earliest work on this issue was conducted by Yum (1931), who asked participants to learn associations for pairs of printed CVC words such as "see REB-QIM → respond WOLF," followed by a recall test in which participants were asked to recall the response after being cued with either the studied word pair or a misspelling thereof. A single misspelled letter at a syllable onset was sufficient to greatly diminish probability of recall and had as much of an effect on recall as two misspelled letters. Results were different when visual similarity between simple visual patterns or semantic similarity between studied and test cue words was varied. In both of these cases, effectiveness of the "mangled" cue varied as a continuous function of similarity to the original stimulus, rather than exhibiting a steep increase when the test stimulus matched the training stimulus exactly. Much more recently, Glezer et al. (2009) have presented evidence suggesting that neurons in the visual wordform area respond to specific words, firing as little when presented with one-letter-away neighbors of the words they represent as when presented with completely dissimilar words. These results suggest a superadditive interaction among the perceptual features of a visual wordform, where the whole is greater than the sum of its parts.

3.2 What Makes Units Fuse?

In Kapatsinski (2009c), I proposed that being associable is what it means to be a *unit*: a unit is allocated a node in the associative network, which can be readily associated with other nodes, either as cue or outcome. In particular, learners can associate a sequence of segments with a response that is not appropriate for any of its parts when that sequence is a preexisting unit in their language. This task is much more difficult when that sequence is not a preexisting linguistic unit. But what is it that makes something a unit? What makes something associable?

An error-driven answer to this question is that cues are induced when they are useful (Goldstone, 2003): we parse the stimuli we experience into the parts that are most predictive of things we want to predict. In contrast, a Hebbian answer is that cues fuse together into larger cues on the basis of pure co-occurrence. Some support for a Hebbian contribution to fusion comes from the fact that error-driven learning requires one to make a prediction before encountering the stimulus that confirms or disconfirms the prediction. It is not currently known how fast such predictions can be made. However, there is reason to believe that it may not be fast enough for all syntagmatic associative learning to rely on prediction error. For example, Baayen et al. (2011) model Saffran et al.'s (1996) finding that infants track statistical co-occurrences between adjacent syllables using Rescorla and Wagner's (1972) error-driven learning theory. This fits with Aslin et al.'s (1998) finding that learners pay attention to transitional probabilities between syllables rather than (only) frequencies of syllable bigrams. Error-driven predictive learning is also somewhat plausible for Saffran et al.'s synthesized syllables, which did not (by design) feature the extensive coarticulation that characterizes natural speech. However, in a natural speech stream acoustic cues to the upcoming syllable are available in the preceding syllable, and even several syllables in advance (Benguerel & Cowan, 1974; Daniloff & Moll, 1968; Grosvald, 2009; Recasens, 1989). As a result, the second syllable of an utterance can be identified simultaneously or near-simultaneously with the initial syllable. Furthermore, it is clear that language learners acquire subsyllabic co-occurrence knowledge. For example, English speakers know that syllable-initial [tl] and [sr] do not occur in English, rapidly deploying this knowledge in speech recognition. Thus a sound acoustically intermediate between [l] and [ɹ] is perceived as [ɹ] in the [t__i] context and as [l] in the [s__i] context (Massaro & Cohen, 1983). It appears impossible for the learner to acquire this knowledge by predicting whether the sound that follows, say [t], is [ɹ] or [l] and then confirming or disconfirming the prediction because the acoustic cues to whether the initial sound is [t], [p], or [k] are largely *in* the following sound. Thus, there is no time to make a prediction. The same argument applies, a fortiori, to knowledge of stop-vowel co-occurrences. At least some co-occurrence knowledge must involve chunking mechanisms that yield configural units, which can then be used as cues or outcomes in error-driven predictive learning.

Another problem for a purely predictive account of statistical learning is that statistical learning can proceed on the basis of *backward* transitional probabilities (Pelucchi et al., 2009; Perruchet & Desaulty, 2008). In fact, backward transitional probabilities are better than forward ones at identifying syntactic constituent boundaries in preposing languages (Kapatsinski, 2005a; Onnis & Thiessen, 2013). In *The linguist swallowed* [*the marmalade*], *p(the|__marmalade)* >> *p(swallowed|__the)*. A break in syntactic cohesion therefore corresponds to a bigram with low backward transitional probability. In contrast, *p(the|swallowed__)* >> *p(marmalade|the__)*, forward transitional probability suggesting a higher degree of cohesion in the former transition.

The conditioning literature likewise provides much evidence that associations do not always link preceding cues to following outcomes. Burkhardt and Ayres (1978) and Mahoney and Ayres (1976) showed that conditioning can occur with simultaneous presentation of the CS and US despite the CS not providing the learner with the ability to anticipate the US. As we saw in chapter 1, Matzel et al. (1988) showed that sensitivity to backward associations from a consequent to its antecedent is likewise not unique to language or humans.[1]

In an error-driven model, sensitivity to backward transitional probabilities requires retrodicting the past (given the current segment, what was the preceding one likely to be) and then bringing the past up in memory to test the retrodiction. This kind of backward learning is denied by Rescorla and Wagner (1972) and Ramscar et al. (2010) as inconsistent with the predictive nature of learning. In contrast, bidirectional association is a natural consequence of chunking models, which rely on rapid formation of representations for cohesive wholes in hippocampal episodic memory (French et al., 2011; Kahana, 2002; Perruchet & Vinter, 1998). It appears impossible to avoid the conclusion that the formation of configural cues involves, at least in part, the latter two mechanisms. Parsing the signal into relatively large cues is perhaps what makes predictive, error-driven learning over these cues particularly powerful.

Given these considerations, it is worth asking whether fusion between *non*contiguous units (Gómez, 2002; Newport & Aslin, 2004) involves the same process as fusion between contiguous units. In particular, it is quite possible that fusion between contiguous units is Hebbian ("units used together fuse together"; Bybee, 2002a)—there may not be enough time to predict the following unit from the preceding one, especially given that the preceding unit may already bear coarticulatory cues to the following unit, allowing for simultaneous recognition of the two. On the other hand, dependencies between noncontiguous units may result from error-driven prediction. Depending on how much time elapses between the two units, the prediction may also rely on maintenance of the predictor in its activated state, or retrieval of the predictor from long-term memory under the bidding of cognitive control.

If it is the case that adjacent and nonadjacent dependency learning relies on different mechanisms, and (uncontroversially) the mechanisms can vary in their efficacy across individuals, then some individuals may be really good at learning adjacent dependencies and others really good at nonadjacent ones. In accordance with this prediction, Siegelman and Frost (2015) found extremely low—and sometimes negative!—correlations between individual adjacent and nonadjacent statistical learning abilities. Misyak and Christiansen (2010, 2012) discovered that whether one excels at adjacent or nonadjacent dependency learning has consequences for sentence processing. They found that learners who were really good at learning adjacent dependencies between nonlinguistic stimuli were more susceptible to making and failing to detect errors like *The key to the cabinets were on the table, in which the verb is mistakenly made to agree with the adjacent noun rather than the nonadjacent head of the subject noun phrase. Those who excelled at nonlocal statistical learning were instead especially good at avoiding and detecting such errors. Nonadjacent syntactic dependencies therefore likely involve prediction and/or retrodiction, as do the paradigmatic dependencies of morphology (chapters 7 and 8).

3.3   Part-Whole Interactions in Learning: Hierarchical Inference

The existence of parts and wholes raises the question of how they interact. This question arises at both the timescale of learning (do they compete for associations?) and the timescale of processing (do they compete for processing resources or recognition?). A positive answer to the former question is assumed by all theories of configural learning and forms the basis for *hierarchical inference*, which has received much attention in the Bayesian literature. The answer to the latter question is unsettled, as we will see in the next section. To understand the notion of *hierarchy* in hierarchical inference, it is useful to realize that parts of units can also be thought of as *potential categories* of these same units. For example, an intervocalic /t/ in words like *butter* and *emitter* can give rise to the category "words containing an intervocalic /t/," of which *butter* and *emitter* are mere examples. One can therefore think of a hierarchy with the most general categories at the top, and increasingly specific categories lower down. So, in this case, the category "instances of the word *butter*" would be below (and part of) the category "words containing /VtV/," which may itself be part of the category "words containing /t/," etc.

It is possible for various levels of the hierarchy to be associated with different predictions. We saw this earlier in the case of blocking in morphology: "ACTION PAST" may be associated with -ed but "GO PAST" (a subtype of "ACTION PAST") would be associated with *went*. The case of words like *butter* presents another example of the same situation: an intervocalic /t/ preceding an unstressed vowel is usually realized as a flap in American English. Nonetheless, individual words may deviate from this overall rate of flapping, becoming associated with the flap or the stop realization of the consonant. While there are no words that fully block flapping, words that tend to occur in formal contexts like *emitter* are significantly less likely to be flapped than words that occur in colloquial contexts like *bullshitter*, even when both are placed in the same context for people to read (Kapatsinski, 2015). This appears to be a general process: words that tend to occur in contexts favoring a certain phonetic realization of a phoneme become associated with that phonetic realization, statistically favoring its production, even outside of its proper phonological and stylistic context (Bybee, 2002b; Raymond & Brown, 2012; Seyfarth, 2014; Sóskuthy & Hay, 2017). At the same time, segments that tend to occur in reduction-favoring contexts also favor deletion, even outside of the reduction-favoring context (Cohen Priva, 2015). When a reduction-favoring segment like /t/ occurs in a reduction-disfavoring word like *emitter*, or a reduction-disfavoring segment like /b/ occurs in a reduction-favoring word like *probably*, the predictions of the two levels can come into conflict, and blame can be reassigned. When blame is reassigned from the word to the phone, reduction is generalized, spreading through the lexicon. When it is reassigned from the phone to the word, lexicalization occurs.

The reassignment of blame from context to something that occurs in that context is not unique to phonetics. Semantic features can also be transferred from context onto a word that frequently occurs in that context. Bybee (2015) notes the example of the French *pas*, which used to only mean "step" but, as a result of frequently occurring in the context of *ne* 'not' in the construction *ne pas* 'not a step', has come to mean "not." Thus, now *pas* can be (and usually is) used without *ne* to mean "not." In this case, the diachronic trajectory suggests that the whole unit *ne pas* has come to mean "not," as *ne pas* grew in frequency relative to other emphatic *ne* N constructions due to a rich-get-richer loop in production. The more *ne pas* was used to express emphatic negation, the more accessible it became relative to synonymous *ne* N expressions, and the more likely it was to be reused to express emphatic negation. Subsequently, however, *pas* has become associated with "not" without the necessary presence of *ne*. Pavlov (1927) reports that when two tones differing in pitch and loudness are presented to a dog as redundant predictors of an unconditioned stimulus (food or shock), the more salient loud tone becomes associated with the unconditioned stimulus while the softer tone does not. The louder tone is said to *overshadow* the softer tone (see also Kruschke, 2006; Trabasso & Bower, 1968). Perhaps, in the same way, the low-salience unstressed *ne* has become overshadowed by the more salient *pas* (Harmon & Kapatsinski, 2016).

Such cases of blame reassignment or *reanalysis* can be explained by *imperfections* of hierarchical inference. The pronunciation of a sound or a perceived meaning can be blamed on the word or the context, or both to some degree. Hierarchical inference suggests that the learner assumes by default that the blame is shared, and tries to infer how much of the blame should be placed on the word. According to normative, Bayesian models of inference, how much the word is blamed for the sound and the meaning perceived in context should be a function of how often the word occurs in the context, how often it occurs outside of the context, and how many different words occur in the context. However, it may also depend on normatively irrelevant characteristics like the acoustic salience of the word relative to other parts of the context. For example, in sentence processing, MacWhinney et al. (1985) document that comprehenders may underutilize some highly reliable cues to the identity of the agent because of their low acoustic salience.

Even if blame is apportioned optimally by hierarchical inference, sharing of the blame between parts and wholes is likely impermanent, both because of selective attention and because of rich-get-richer loops in processing. For example, if a word is usually produced with a devoiced final stop, the devoiced pronunciation is easier to retrieve during production. It therefore is likely to outcompete the pronunciation with a voiced stop for selection. The more the devoiced pronunciation is used, the easier it is to use, and the more likely it is to be reused in the future (Zipf 1949; Martin 2007). Similarly, in perception, the more often a word ends with a devoiced sound, the more likely its voiced pronunciations are to be misperceived as voiceless (Ganong, 1980): the word context will bias the perception of the final sound, and will do so ever more as the proportion of devoiced pronunciations of the word grows. As a result, configural patterns in language are likely to be diachronically unstable.

3.4   Occasion Setting and Cue-Outcome Fusion

From a learning-theoretic perspective, it is useful to distinguish between configurations of cues, configurations of outcomes, and cue-outcome configurations. While selective attention argues against models that rely exclusively on configurations of *cues*, it does not argue against cue-outcome configurations. There is in fact extensive evidence for cues to cue-outcome or action-outcome configurations, often called *occasion setters* (Jenkins, 1985; J. W. Moore et al., 1969; Rescorla, 1985; Ross & Holland, 1981; Skinner, 1938; see also Bouton, 2016, pp. 178–187). In occasion setting during operant conditioning, Skinner (1938) noted that organisms can learn to only perform an action when a certain contextual stimulus indicates that the action will be reinforced. In the classic conditioning occasion-setting paradigm, there is a primary cue (e.g., a tone) that is occasionally followed by an unconditional stimulus (like food or electric shock). On these same special occasions, the cue is preceded by another, secondary cue that tells the learner that the primary cue will be followed by the unconditional stimulus. So, the organism exposed to the trials illustrated in (2) would eventually learn to look for a snack in response to tones only when the tone had been preceded by a light.

(2) Light as a positive occasion setter
   (time flows left to right):
   Reinforced trial: light   →   tone   → food
   Unreinforced trial: tone

Given the existence of blocking and overshadowing, you might have expected the light to block the formation of the tone→food association. Since light is the better cue to food in (1), the animals exposed to (2) could associate only the light with food and treat the tone as uninformative and to be ignored. This does happen if the light and the tone are presented simultaneously and are equally salient. However, when the light is harder to associate with the food than the tone is, occasion setting results. A functional analysis suggests itself: when the light is easily missed because of its dimness and/or easily forgotten by the time the unconditioned stimulus is perceived, the learning system better not let it block other cues that, though less reliable, are more easily utilized.

Ross and Holland (1981) showed that blocking of the tone→food association does not happen if the light precedes the tone by a significant amount of time. In a really ingenious experiment, they took advantage of the fact that different stimuli naturally elicit different food-searching behaviors in the rat. When food is signaled by a light, the rat rears up on its hind paws in response to the light. When food is signaled by a sound, the rat instead jerks its head around excitedly. Ross and Holland found that rats exposed to (2) performed head jerking rather than rearing when the light preceded the tone as if they were simply reacting to a tone. Rats exposed to light and tone simultaneously reared up without head jerking as if reacting to the light (see also Rescorla, 1985). In other words, the light overshadowed the tone when both were presented simultaneously but served as an occasion setter when preceding the tone. Later, Holland (1989) found that it is also possible to observe occasion setting with simultaneous light and tone stimuli if the light is made so dim that it develops only a weak direct association with food.

Pearce (1994) proposed that what is learned in occasion setting is a configural cue comprising the light and the tone. This can plausibly explain what happens when the occasion setter is a low-salience cue presented simultaneously with a stronger cue: the weak cue fuses with the more salient cue presented simultaneously because it is not easily parsed out of the background (see also Harmon & Kapatsinski, 2016). However, cue fusion is rather unlikely to happen in the case of two strong, salient cues, because here increasing the delay between the two increases occasion setting (Ross & Holland, 1981). Why would the light and the tone be chunked together more when they are more widely separated in time? (See also Holland, 1992, as well as Bouton & Nelson, 1994, for arguments against a configural tone-light unit being formed in this paradigm.)

Instead, it may be that the tone-food association acts as a unit, so that the light activates the tone-food compound (Bonardi, 1989; Holland, 1983). Bonardi and Jennings (2009) tested this hypothesis in an experiment summarized in (3). In their experiment, A, B, C, and D were occasion setters. Crucially, A predicted that X would be followed by food and Y would occur without food, while C predicted that X would not be followed by food while Y would. In the second stage, A was paired with shock, while C was paired with absence of shock. X, Y, and food never occurred in this stage. In Stage III, the animals were presented with X and Y with or without food. The participants acted as if expecting a shock when presented with cue-outcome combinations that were previously cued by A (X→+food and Y→-food). X alone, Y alone, or food alone were powerless to elicit expectation of shock. Thus, participants seemed to have fused primary cues with their outcomes in Stage I training.

(3) Bonardi and Jennings's (2009) experiment design:

Stage I	Stage II	Stage III		
{A;B}→X→+food	A→+shock	X→+food	→shock?	yes
{A;B}→Y→-food	C→-shock	X→-food	→shock?	no
{C;D}→Y→+food		Y→+food	→shock?	no
{C;D}→X→-food		Y→-food	→shock?	yes

Note that there is often a need to selectively attend to one of a multitude of cues, preventing cue-cue fusion. There is also often a need to selectively attend to one of many outcomes of an event (or cue) so that one can decide how to respond to the event (should you run because of expected shock, or stay because of expected food?). However, there is no functional motivation to selectively attend to a cue over the associated outcome or vice versa. Thus, it appears quite possible for cues to fuse with their outcomes. In language, this proposal is of course consistent with the notion of a construction as a form-meaning pairing that acts as a configural whole

(Goldberg, 1995). On the perception side, form-meaning associations may then be cued by other formal occasion setters (e.g., in a bilingual setting, cues to the language being spoken). On the production side, they may be cued by semantic occasion setters (e.g., stylistic ones).

3.5 Incremental Processing and Loss of Configurality

Configural patterns—where a whole demands a response that is different from the response associated with (one of) its parts—are inherently unstable whenever the organism cannot help but access the part(s) in accessing the whole. In language processing, this appears to be a typical problem in comprehension, which is largely *incremental*. Incremental processing in comprehension means that one does not wait until the end of a meaningful unit to begin processing the incoming signal and accessing meanings. At every moment, one accesses all the associations consistent with the input so far.

There is extensive evidence for incremental processing within words in speech perception—that is, one does not wait until the end of a word to start activating meanings. Rather, meanings are activated from partial input before the word is completely perceived, or even completely pronounced (Allopenna et al., 1998; Dahan, 2010; Grosjean, 1980). For example, hearing the word *beaker* elicits looks to the picture of a beak, until the listener hears cues to the final *-er* (Allopenna et al., 1998). Incremental processing appears to be necessary in speech perception because word boundaries are not clearly marked in the speech signal. So, if one waited until the end of the word, one would not know when to stop waiting.[2] In most cases, incremental processing also allows the listener to understand the speaker's intended meaning as soon as possible. Because language is redundant, the intended meaning is usually identifiable well before the word is complete, even when the word is presented out of context (Grosjean, 1980; Marslen-Wilson & Welsh, 1978). In context, even less of the word needs to be perceived for the meaning to be correctly recognized (e.g., Tanenhaus & Brown-Schmidt, 2008).

Pirog Revill et al. (2008) provided interesting converging evidence by exposing learners to an artificial lexicon while their brains were imaged with fMRI. Participants were exposed to novel motion and nonmotion words. Crucially, some of the nonmotion words shared the first syllable with a motion word. For example, if *piba* is a motion word, referring to moving up and down, *piri* might be a similar-sounding nonmotion word referring, say, to spiky objects. Pirog Revill et al. showed that the area of the visual cortex that processes motion (area MT) lights up not only to the novel motion words but also to similar-sounding nonmotion words, even when these words are correctly understood. Nonmotion words that did not share the first syllable with motion words (e.g., *zanu*) elicited no MT activation. The results can be explained by activation of semantics on the basis of the word-initial syllable. Thus, during recognition of *piri*, a nonmotion word, the semantics of motion are activated by *pi* (shared with the motion word *piba*) before *piri* is correctly recognized as a nonmotion word.

Incremental processing has also been well studied and well supported for sentence reading, where it leads participants to run into difficulties when reading *garden-path sentences* like *The old man the boats*. In such sentences, the beginning of the sentence is most consistent with an interpretation that later turns out to be incorrect. In this example, *man* is first erroneously interpreted as a noun. This later turns out to be an error, since the *man* is actually a verb (and *old* is a noun). Because *man* is usually a noun, *old* is usually an adjective, and *old man* is usually a noun phrase, the two words are initially interpreted incorrectly, and revising this initial interpretation is hard. Importantly, the correct interpretation is much more consistent with the sentence as a whole than the incorrect interpretation: the latter renders the sentence utterly ungrammatical. So, if participants waited until the end of the sentence before starting to interpret it, garden-path sentences would not have led to so much trouble. Consider how much easier *the old man the boats* would be to process if presented starting from the end as in (4) rather than from the beginning as in (5). By processing the sentence incrementally starting from the beginning, one is led down the wrong path that leads one to face the obstacle of reviving an interpretation that has been at least downgraded, if not rejected entirely.

(4) ... boats   →N
     ... the boats   →Det N
     ... man the boats   →V Det N
     ... old man the boats   →N V Det N
     The old man the boats   →Det N V Det N
(5) The ...   →Det
     The old ...   →Det Adj
     The old man ...   →Det Adj N
     The old man the ...   ????
     The old man the boats

Incremental processing is not the only source of difficulty with *The old man the boats*. Note that *The old man the boats* still gets difficult in (4), as soon as one gets to the *old* part. What this suggests is that one cannot help but activate *old man* the noun phrase even though it is not consistent with the sentence so far. Semantic access appears to be *nonselective*: we don't access just what we must, we access all we can, everything for which the signal provides even a shred of evidence (possibly because the signal is usually noisy; e.g., Dahan, 2010). This is also the message of a large number of studies of sentence processing beginning with Swinney (1979): frequent meanings of words can become activated even when they are not consistent with the context. For example, the "spying device" meaning of *bug* is initially activated by hearing *The man found several spiders, cockroaches, and other bugs in the corner of his room* so that the sentence primes recognition of spying-related words if these words are presented immediately after the word *bugs*. Contextual constraints need to be very strong to prevent a meaning from becoming activated altogether (Tabossi, 1988). Speakers do sometimes say unexpected things, and the perceptual system is somewhat robust to this variability.

In speech perception, work in the visual-world paradigm suggests that meanings of words sharing the *end* with the word being presented are also often activated, relatively late in the process of word recognition (Allopenna et al., 1998; Dahan, 2010). The fact that they are activated late suggests that this is not because the listener has failed to notice the beginning: as the beginning is heard, participants activate the meaning of the target word and any words sharing the beginning with the target (*cohort competitors*), looking more at pictures of these meanings than at the picture of the meaning of the word with which the target shares the end (*rime competitor*). Throughout the process, pictures that don't have names related to the target word (*distractors*) are ignored. However, later on, as looks to the picture of the cohort competitor decrease, the participants start looking at the depiction of the rime competitor's meaning. Again, this suggests nonselective access to semantics: the meaning of the rime competitor is accessed even though the rime competitor is not consistent with the context (the beginning of the word). While inconsistent with purely incremental processing (Marslen-Wilson & Welsh, 1978), these effects are a sensible way for the listener to behave: the beginning of the word could be mangled by the speaker, obscured by noise, or misperceived. Word recognition must be robust to the possibility of not correctly perceiving the beginning of the word (Salasoo & Pisoni, 1985; McMurray et al., 2009; Dahan, 2010).

To summarize the work reviewed in this section, the normal course of processing appears to be characterized by activation of everything for which there is even a shred of evidence followed by competition among the activated interpretations until (ideally) one of them emerges with a decisive victory. Perception is largely incremental and nonselective.

While functional in dealing with various sources of misperception, these properties of the perceptual system can be detrimental to configural learning. For example, in Kapatsinski (2007b, 2009c), participants were trained on a configural pattern in two stages. In the first stage, they learned to associate /CæC/ stems with the affix /mɪn/ and /CʌC/ stems with /num/ but /Cæʃ/ and /Cʌg/ were never presented. In the second stage, they experienced /Cæʃ/ paired with /num/ and /Cʌg/ paired with /mɪn/, while continuing to be exposed to the Stage I mappings but less often. Importantly, as the Stage II mappings improved, Stage I mappings declined. While participants knew the consonant-affix associations well after Stage I, they nearly lost them after Stage II (Kapatsinski, 2007b). If one learned the pattern perfectly, /æʃ/ and /ʌg/ would associate with the suffixes in Stage II but /ʃ/ and /g/ would maintain their associations. However, it appears that whenever one hears /æʃ/ one cannot help but hear /ʃ/, making /num/ associate with /ʃ/ whenever /æʃ/-/num/ is presented. By this process, a configural pattern inevitably becomes less configural, with parts becoming cues to the meaning of the whole, which then makes incremental nonselective recognition well suited to the task of maintaining the pattern. Accordingly, interactions between separable features in perception are usually at most *superadditive* (with each feature weakly activating the associates of the whole but the whole giving its associates an extra boost) rather than *crossover* (with individual features of a whole inhibiting the associates of the whole). Crossover interactions in perception result in a garden path, which is not a path that is easy (or desirable) to maintain.[3]

3.6   Elemental Comprehension

Even superadditive interactions among perceptual features appear to be the exception rather than the rule in perceptual category learning (Trabasso & Bower, 1968; Yum, 1931). For example, Durvasula and Liter (2016) exposed participants to a language of CVCV pseudowords in which the two consonants had to agree in both voicing and continuancy, so that for instance the participants would hear /pati/ and /gubo/ but never /bati/ (continuancy agreement only) or /pasi/ (voicing agreement only). They then presented participants with new CVCV pseudowords with consonants agreeing in only voicing (pasi), only continuancy (bati), neither (basi), or both (pasi). If participants learned a superadditive interaction between voicing agreement and continuancy agreement, they would have accepted stimuli with consonants agreeing in both (pati) much more than they accepted stimuli with consonants agreeing in either (bati or pasi). The latter may not have even been very different from stimuli agreeing in neither (basi)—that is, pati > bati = pasi = basi (cf. Yum, 1931). This is not what Durvasula and Liter found. Instead, voicing agreement increased ratings (pasi > basi), as did continunancy agreement (bati > basi), and agreement in both behaved like the sum of the two: (bati-basi)+(pasi-basi)=(pati-basi). Voicing and continuancy agreement contributed to goodness independently.

Not only are cues usually combined independently, many cues comprising a stimulus are likely to be ignored: attention is *selective*. This is dramatically illustrated by *change blindness* experiments. In these experiments, the visual scene presented to the participant changes but the participant does not notice. A common paradigm is to present the participant with a picture on a computer screen, then replace it first with a blank screen for a few milliseconds, and then display an almost identical picture. If the participant knows what to attend to, the difference between the two pictures is easily detected. However, if they do not, and do not accidentally attend to the location in which the two pictures are different, the difference is very unlikely to be found (Simons, 2000). I have personally stared for minutes at the online demonstrations of this effect without identifying the difference.

In phonotactic learning, Linzen and Gallagher (2014) also exposed participants to a set of words obeying a phonotactic constraint (vowel harmony; e.g., /basa/ and /pisi/ are in the language but /basi/ and /pisa/ are not). They found that early in training participants would not prefer words they have experienced over novel words obeying the phonotactic constraint, yet they preferred novel words obeying the constraint over ones that did not obey it. For example, having experienced /basa/, they would prefer both /basa/ and /kama/ over /bisa/ but would not prefer /basa/ over /kama/. If novel words were configural patterns, we would have expected the exact opposite.

Phonotactic learning can be seen as a kind of *category learning*: participants are learning what kinds of forms they are likely to encounter in the experiment. As noted earlier, these kinds of results are also typical of visual-category learning experiments (L. Thompson, 1994; Ward et al., 1990; Wills et al., 2013; see Kapatsinski et al., 2017, for a review) as well as of research on conditioning and contingency learning (Pavlov, 1927; Trabasso

& Bower, 1968). When multiple cues are equally usable and equally informative about category membership or the likely occurrence of an outcome,
participants usually pick one cue to focus on, ignoring others. In the first
report of overshadowing, Pavlov (1927) showed that dogs presented with
lights and sounds as redundant cues to food learned either the sound→food
association—salivating in response to the sound whether or not the light
was present—or the light→shock association, salivating to the light regardless of whether it was accompanied by the trained sound cue.

Linzen and Gallagher's (2014) results suggest that learning to treat stimuli configurally takes extended training: stimuli start out as sets of separable
cues to category membership and only gradually does the learner come
to make decisions on the basis of complex configurations of cues. Similar results are obtained in studies of conditioning, where *overtraining* participants on a discrimination or prediction problem with redundant cues
beyond the level of consistent 100% accuracy appears to be necessary for
participants to pick up on the less noticeable redundant cues, overcoming
the effects of selective attention (C. James & Greeno, 1967; Sutherland &
Holgate, 1966; Schover & Newsom, 1976; Trabasso & Bower, 1968). Mature
categories of linguistic forms tend to be defined by configurations of (near-)
necessary characteristics (Stockall & Marantz, 2006) forming the category
schema, but overcoming selective attention takes time and experience. For
example, Idemaru and Holt (2013) show that American children as old as
9 pay attention only to the primary acoustic cue for the English r/l distinction, F3, and ignore the weaker, secondary cue, F2. Adults, on the other
hand, rely on both cues, and are therefore able to distinguish [ɹ] and [l]
on the basis of F2 when F3 is unreliable. If it takes more than 9 years for
a native English speaker to learn of the secondary cue to the distinction
between *lice* and *rice*, selective attention is not easy to overcome.

3.7   Determinants of Attention

If selective attention pervades perception, then one of the most important
tasks in describing how we perceive speech and comprehend language is
describing what cues we pay attention to. Several properties of a cue have
been argued to draw attention (see Kruschke & Johansen, 1999; Lawrence,
1949, 1950; MacWhinney et al., 1985; Pavlov, 1927; Trabasso & Bower,
1968). First, we orient to what is *sensationally salient*: other things being
equal, loud sounds draw more attention than quiet ones, though quiet
sounds can be salient if their quietness contrasts with their loud surround-
ings. As discussed above, a possible example of overshadowing can be found

in the history of French (Bybee, 2015), where *pas* 'step' has come to be able to cue "not" on its own, having frequently occurred in the expression *ne 'pas* 'not a step'. Why would *ne* be omitted in *ne pas*? One reason could be that it is an unstressed, "little" sound that becomes overshadowed by the stressed *pas*, so that it is *pas* and not *ne* that emerges as the dominant cue to negation. Overshadowing of the nonsalient by the salient also provides a novel explanation for the finding that infants appear to posit "word boundaries" before stressed syllables, omitting them in production and tolerating such omissions in recognition (Cutler & Norris, 1988; E. Johnson & Jusczyk, 2001; Jusczyk et al., 1993): *banana* becomes *nana*, and *guitar* becomes *tar*. If salient, stressed syllables are linked to meaning in preference to unstressed syllables, which are then blocked by the stressed syllable from associating with the same meaning—at least for a while—then these results are entirely unsurprising. By saying *tar*, the child is in fact giving the adult the best cue to the meaning of GUITAR. Large-scale analyses of lexica show that stressed syllables bear more information about word identity than unstressed syllables across languages (Piantadosi et al., 2009). Overshadowing provides an account of how languages get to be this way: stressed syllables are preferentially associated with meanings.

With incrementally processed stimuli like words or sentences, cues that occur first may also overshadow subsequent cues because they are recognized earlier than other cues and therefore have more of an opportunity to influence understanding of the entire stimulus. Harmon and Kapatsinski (2016) demonstrated this effect by presenting participants with written sentences of the shape *bes* NOUN or NOUN *zon*, which were paired with pictures indicating that the referent of the noun is either above or below a table. Participants were then shown sentences like *bes* NOUN *zon*, which placed the cues in conflict. The participants overwhelmingly chose the meaning of the initial cue. Over time, the initial cue may overshadow subsequent cues. If the meaning of a word is available to wire with when or before the initial syllable is heard (which head-camera data suggest it often is; Pereira et al., 2014), then the early cue will get the semantic association. In languages—and words—with noninitial stress, stress and initial position are in conflict, which may explain why initial unstressed syllables in words like *banana* do not *always* disappear.

Salience of initial syllables may come from many sources. One important reason they may be salient is because they are relatively unpredictable when they occur, and we orient to the unexpected. In audition, salience of the unexpected was demonstrated early on by Poulton (1956), who presented listeners with noisy auditory signals occasionally emanating from various loudspeakers placed around the participant. He found that signals coming from previously quiet loudspeakers were comprehended better than those coming from loudspeakers that had been active before (see also Broadbent, 1958, pp. 84–85).

In speech production, prosodic prominence is often thought to be a conventionalized way to draw the listener's attention to a particular part of the utterance: *I want to adopt THIS kitten* (not THAT one) vs. *I want to ADOPT this kitten* (not BUY it). However, the prosodic cues to emphasis have been subject to debate, particularly with respect to pitch. Sometimes the emphasized word is high-pitched, but at other times it is low-pitched. Kakouros and Räsänen (2016) showed that either high-pitched or low-pitched utterance-final syllables could be perceived as emphasized, depending on whether the listeners had previously experienced sentences ending in a high pitch or a low pitch. Unexpected pitch draws attention and is perceived as prominent.

Sanders et al. (2002) showed that listeners presented with a stream of randomly ordered nonsense words without any prosodic cues to word boundaries—à la Saffran et al. (1996)—come to generate rapid electrophysiological responses to the onsets of the nonsense words (the N100, generated a mere 100 ms after the word onset). In their experiment, words were meaningless and word onsets were defined solely based on their relative unpredictability. Sanders and colleagues argued that the N100 indexes upregulation of attention at points of unpredictability, an *orienting response*. Astheimer and Sanders (2009) showed that the same ERP component occurs in response to onsets of real words in continuous speech, suggesting that the same mechanism may contribute to the salience of initial cues in word recognition.

Salience of the unexpected is of great importance to the present book and has been abundantly documented in psycholinguistics and beyond. In psycholinguistics, salience of the unexpected may be responsible for the fact that an additional exposure to a word matters more if that word had been experienced once before than if it had been experienced a thousand times before (figure 3.1; see Howes & Solomon, 1951, for perception; Oldfield & Wingfield, 1965, for production; Broadbent, 1967, for a review). Salience of the unexpected is also seen in priming tasks. Repetition priming refers to the finding that a word is easier to recognize or produce if it has just been recognized or produced. The more frequent a stimulus, the smaller the effect of repetition (see Forster & C. Davis, 1984, for words and Snider, 2008, for syntactic constructions).

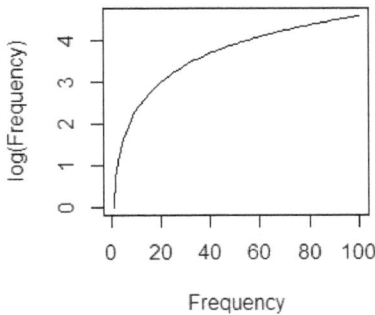

Figure 3.1
The relationship between frequency and log(frequency), the latter roughly corresponding to ease of processing or execution. A word experienced 20 times is much easier to recognize than a word experienced once. A word experienced 80 times is almost as easy to recognize as one experienced 100 times.

Salience of the unexpected—and resulting *associability* of the unexpected—has major consequences for language change. Zipf (1949) and, more recently, Gries (2005) and Szmrecsanyi (2005) have argued that speakers self-prime when generating continuous speech: producing a structure makes one more likely to produce the same structure thereafter. Christian Schwarz (2016) suggests that frequency attenuation is also observed with this kind of self-priming in production. Speakers of German, like those of other tongues, often command a regional pronunciation of a sound and a standard one. Speakers vary in how likely they are to produce the regional pronunciations. Interestingly, those speakers who produce more dialectal sound variants show less self-priming of the dialectal variants. As pointed out by Schwarz (2016), the salience of the unexpected can keep low-frequency dying variants alive, preventing their obsolescence and keeping the language from becoming completely regular. It may also allow low-frequency new variants to increase in frequency despite being in the minority.

In chapter 5, we will see that subphonemic frequency attenuation is also found in perceptual distributional learning: when learners are exposed to distributions of sounds along acoustic continua and then asked to rate the goodness of each sound, their ratings track log(frequency) rather than raw frequency (Olejarczuk et al., in press).

3.8   Learning to Attend

Finally, we orient to what has been *informative* and task-relevant in past experience. Attention can be learned. When one has experience with a task, one *learns* to attend to the parts of stimuli that are particularly useful, or predictive of how the stimulus should be treated in that particular task. For example, if one were presented with a series of pictures in a change blindness experiment but the change always occurred in the same place, one would eventually learn to attend to the right location. Learned selective attention has been demonstrated in many experiments on both classic conditioning and category learning. For example, in an eyetracking study we discussed in chapter 2, Rehder and Hoffman (2005) have demonstrated that visual features that a participant looks at the most are the features they rely on for deciding on category membership, and—once the categories are well learned—participants come to streamline their looking behavior by attending only to the features relevant for category identification.

How is selective attention learned? The dominant position in the field has been that it is learned via error-driven learning: when one makes a prediction, and that prediction is incorrect, attentional biases are adjusted (Kruschke, 1992; Kruschke & Johansen, 1999). However, work by Blair and colleagues (Blair et al., 2011) suggests a significant contribution of Hebbian learning. Error-driven learning predicts that attention should shift more after an error than after a correct response. By tracking eye movements, Blair et al. were able to show that attention shifts after these two types of trials are roughly equal, a pattern of results error-driven learning models have been unable to fit. These results have provided support for the idea that attention can shift to the relevant features because those features are associated with responses on the basis of simple co-occurrence. In other words, if a cue is relevant to the task, it must co-occur with *some* outcome, and this co-occurrence can drive attention to the cue.

Several studies in associative learning have shown that predictive cues are easier to associate with new outcomes than cues that have been uninformative in the learner's experience. For example, LePelley and McLaren (2003) exposed learners to cue-outcome pairings in (4), with two training stages followed by a test stage. In Stage 1, some cues (A, B, C, and D) were learned to be predictive and some nonpredictive. Thus, A and D perfectly predict o1; B and C perfectly predict o2. On the other hand, V, W, X, and Y are not predictive, occurring with o1 as often as with o2. In Stage 2, all cues were equally predictive. Thus, o3 could be attributed to either A or X and either C or V. At test, participants were presented with either pairs like AC (two predictive cues that have been paired with o3) or VX (two nonpredictive cues that have been paired with o3). The cues that had been predictive in Stage 1 were associated with o3 and o4 during Stage 2 much more strongly than cues that had been nonpredictive in Stage 1. Livesey and McLaren (2011) further showed that the changes in associability were linked to changes in attention (as proposed by Kruschke, 1992) by showing that participants looked less at nonpredictive visual cues than at predictive ones, in both Stage 1 and Stage 2. Thus, in Stage 1, participants learned to pay attention to A-D and ignore V-Y, and this difference in attention persisted into Stage 2 training, rendering nonpredictive cues less associable than predictive ones.

(6) AV→o1   AX→o3   AC→? (o3>>o4)
    AW→o1   BY→o4   BD→? (o4>>o3)
    BV→o2   CV→o3   VX→? (o3~o4)
    BW→o2   DW→o4   WY→? (o3~o4)
    CX→o2
    CY→o2
    DX→o1
    DY→o1

If a certain cue has been particularly useful in one's experience, attending to that cue becomes automatic, so that learners persevere in their attentional focus even when it ceases to be useful (Kruschke, 1992; Lawrence, 1949, 1950). Since selectively attended cues are more associable than others, they can overshadow other cues, or block them from associating with the same outcome by associating with the outcome first.

In many studies of category learning, participants have a much easier time learning categories defined by a single feature, where there is one perfect cue predicting category membership, than categories that can be learned only by attending to multiple features (e.g., Feldman, 2009; Goudbeek et al., 2009; Rehder & Hoffman, 2005). Furthermore, when exposed to categories in which multiple features are equally predictive of category membership, individual learners tend to settle on attending to only one dimension (L. Thompson, 1994; Trabasso & Bower, 1968; Ward et al., 1990). As mentioned earlier, children may persist in attending only to the primary cue to a phonetic contrast for many years (Idemaru & Holt, 2013), as can second language learners (Escudero, 2005; Francis & Nusbaum, 2002). Blocking and overshadowing are subject to positive feedback: the more one pays attention to a particular cue, the more that cue is able to block other cues, supplanting them.

Learned selective attention provides an explanation for many of the difficulties faced by learners of a second language (see Ellis, 2006; Escudero, 2005; and Francis & Nusbaum, 2002, for reviews), and indeed many researchers of second language acquisition have argued that instruction helps by drawing attention to features of the second language forms that the learner would otherwise miss or ignore (Ellis, 2006; Schmidt, 2001; Terrell, 1991). For example, temporal adverbials like *yesterday* may block tense inflections like -*ed* (lower-salience cues that are likely to not be attended to without attention being drawn to them) from becoming associated with temporal reference, causing naturalistic second language learners to omit them (Ellis, 2006; Terrell, 1991, p. 59). Similar results are observed with other redundant inflections. Pica (1983) reported that naturalistic L2 learners omit the plural -*s* on nouns that are premodified by quantifiers, while instructed L2 learners (whose attention was explicitly drawn to the -*s*) do not. Guion and Pederson (2007) show that drawing attention to low-salience cues helps with learning to distinguish similar sounds that map onto the same phoneme in L1. With the same exposure, participants instructed to attend to consonants learn nonnative consonant contrasts better than participants instructed to attend to vowels. Directing attention to subtle, easy-to-miss cues can help the learner discover that these cues are actually informative.

3.9   Learning to Ignore

Even when second language learners can usually distinguish two sounds, they often differ from native listeners in the cues they rely on. For example, native Japanese listeners unfamiliar with English tend to rely on both F2 and F3 to distinguish /ɹ/ from /l/, while native English listeners rely exclusively on F3 (Francis & Nusbaum, 2002, p. 351). Learning to distinguish the two sounds in this case involves learning that a cue thought to be reliably predictive is actually not. Idemaru and Holt (2011) found that this kind of *downweighting* of a cue can be learned implicitly from a short exposure in the laboratory. In natural speech, VOT and F0 are both cues to voicing, with VOT being the more reliable cue. Reversing the positive VOT/F0 correlation found in natural speech results in a rapid switch of attention away from F0, so that it is no longer relied on for deciding whether the consonant is voiced or voiceless. We can think of this kind of learning as *extinction* of F0 as a cue to voicing.

Importantly, Idemaru and Holt (2012) show that this training does not generalize to new speakers, new consonant pairs, or even new items: the downweighting of F0 is stimulus-specific unless the reversed F0/VOT correlation is experienced in several lexical items. A similar unwillingness to generalize downweighting is also reported by Apfelbaum and Sloutsky (2016). They show that asking learners to categorize instances of the pseudoword *du(:)bo* on the basis of the duration of the first vowel improves discrimination of subphonemic differences in vowel duration. This improvement generalizes to tokens of *du(:)bo* produced by another speaker. However, the training also causes reduced discriminability of *du(:)bo* exemplars differing in pitch contour on the second vowel, suggesting that selective attention to initial-vowel duration caused inattention to other aspects of the word. Whereas improved discrimination of vowel duration generalizes across speakers, inattention to pitch does not. Learned inattention appears to be highly context-specific. This conclusion is bolstered by Miyawaki et al. (1975). Native Japanese listeners are well known not to attend to F3 in a speech context, which leaves them unable to distinguish the English [ɹ] and [l]. Yet they are perfectly capable of hearing the difference in a nonspeech context—that is, when the same harmonics are borne by nonspeech sounds. Even when inattention is based on a lifetime of linguistic experience, it remains somewhat context-specific.

In the associative learning literature, Bouton and colleagues have argued that extinction does not involve eliminating an excitatory cue-outcome association but rather acquiring a parallel inhibitory association. Thus, after extinction the conditioned stimulus is connected to the unconditioned stimulus by two associations. However, unlike the excitatory association, the inhibitory association is *gated* by context as shown in figure 3.2 (Bouton & Nelson, 1994). As a result, extinction is context-specific. If a stimulus is associated with a reward, and then repeatedly presented without the reward, learners eventually act as if they do not expect a reward when

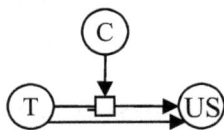

Figure 3.2
Bouton and Nelson's (1994) account of the context specificity of extinction. The unconditioned stimulus is both activated and inhibited by the conditioned stimulus that was the target of extinction (T), but the inhibitory link requires the extinction context (C) to be present for inhibition to flow through: it is gated by a propagation filter. Like contextual cues, occasion setters transmit activation or inhibition to this propagation filter.

presented with the stimulus. The stimulus-response association appears to be extinguished. However, when the same stimulus is presented in a novel context, the expectation of reward comes roaring back, as if extinction never happened. Context specificity of extinction has been very important for psychiatry. For example, treating a spider phobia in a treatment center is largely ineffective because the extinction does not generalize to other locations.

Bouton and Nelson's theory provides an interesting account for the finding that responses to stimuli that have been extinguished—as well as those that have served as targets in occasion-setting experiments—are more subject to being influenced by an occasion setter. As a result of undergoing extinction or being in an occasion-setting experiment, all such stimuli have a gated inhibitory connection to the unconditioned stimulus, which has a propagation filter (Sumida & Dyer, 1992). What defines an occasion setter is that it sends activation or inhibition to the propagation filter on the inhibitory CS-US connection, influencing CS-US relationships only for CS's that have this filter. This also explains how an occasion setter can have a negative connection to the US and yet signal a positive CS-US relationship: nothing precludes C in figure 3.2 from also having an inhibitory connection to the US (see Bouton, 2016, p. 183; Holland, 1984; Rescorla, 1986).

As one would expect from figure 3.2, context specificity turns out to be a general feature of inhibition (Bouton, 2016). For example, it is also true of *latent inhibition* (Lubow & A. Moore, 1959): a cue that is learned to be uninformative in one context can still be associated with outcomes in other contexts (Hall & Channell, 1985; Lovibond et al., 1984; Swartzentruber & Bouton, 1986). Context specificity is also true of *conditioned inhibition* (see Bouton, 2016, pp. 140–142, for a review). In these experiments, a CS (A) is paired with a US (shock) *except* in the presence of another CS (B). When A and B are presented together, nothing happens. Once conditioned inhibition is acquired, the learner fears A but not AB. However, if presented in a new context, AB does elicit fear.

Given the context specificity of inhibition, it is interesting to ask whether learned inattention presents major difficulties in language (especially *second* language) learning (Best et al., 2013). Most examples of first language interference in second language phonetics can be interpreted as a cue being blocked or overshadowed by another, partially redundant cue to which the speaker preferentially attends. Nonetheless, hints of learned inattention can be glimpsed as well. For example, Escudero and Boersma (2004) show that Spanish learners of English rely on duration in distinguishing the vowel in *beet* from the vowel in *bit*, whereas English speakers rely—in part or in whole—on spectral cues (F1 and F2). Duration is not a cue to vowel identity in Spanish. However, Spanish is a syllable-timed language with relatively short vowels. Therefore, values on the duration continuum that are associated with stressed English vowels are likely to be unfamiliar to a Spanish speaker. In contrast, spectral values characteristic of English *beet* and *bit* vowels are familiar and have been learned to belong to the same phonemic category, or to make no difference to the identity of the word. The finding that the unfamiliar durational cues are used by Spanish speakers in preference to the preexposed spectral cues is therefore consistent with the notion of learned irrelevance. If learned inattention is context-specific latent inhibition, these difficulties could likely be alleviated by learning the second language in a very different context than one's first language—especially if it is that context in which one wishes to use the second language.

Like all representational theories, Bouton and Nelson's (1994) account does not explain *why* conditioned inhibition should be more context-sensitive. For this, we must hew to the notion that it behooves the learner not to miss important, biologically relevant events (Pavlov, 1927). Thus, one is generally better off being too vigilant than not vigilant enough. If a cue has not been followed by food or shock in one environment, one is better off thinking that it might still be followed by food or shock when it unexpectedly pops up in a new context. As summarized by Bouton (2016, p. 171), "extinction does not destroy the original learning." Instead, the learner is conservative in retaining the meanings of cues: when a previously meaningful cue seems to become meaningless, the learner makes the generalization that it is only meaningless in that particular context, which could be a *temporal* context. The perceptual system has some inertia that prevents rapid across-the-board learning to ignore a cue on the basis of limited experience in a particular context. Meaning, once found, is hard to abandon (see also Skinner, 1948). If a subtle sound sometimes cues the presence of a dangerous predator, one does not want to forget about this even if one repeatedly encounters the sound in the absence of the predator. If a yellow spot in one's peripheral vision signals that one has come upon a delicious mushroom, one does not want to give up on that cue despite numerous false alarms to autumn leaves. The reward for attending to an important cue is usually higher than the cost of attending to an unimportant one. Therefore learning *not* to attend to a cue is often quite difficult, especially across the board.

With this functional explanation in mind, we may reconsider Bouton and Nelson's (1994) representational account. Excitatory connections may be more easily generalized in a new context simply because one is lenient at deciding whether the novel context is similar enough to the old context (Blough, 1967)—that is, whether the cues defining the new context match the cues defining the training context enough to be classified into the same category. Then, excitatory connections can have propagation filters too (i.e., excitation can also be context-specific). We will find uses for this notion in chapters 6 and 9.

3.10   Mediation: An Open Field

Occasion setting is one case in which the relationship between two stimuli is mediated by another. Thus, an occasion setter is not associated with the unconditioned stimulus itself. With respect to form-meaning mapping in speech comprehension, several structures have the potential for this kind of mediation. At the phonetic level, we often speak of primary cues and secondary cues to phonological features. For example, Voice Onset Time and F0 at the onset of the following vowel are both thought to be cues to voicing of an initial stop, with VOT being the much stronger cue (Lisker, 1986). In natural speech, the two cues are correlated, high VOT correlating with high F0. As mentioned above, Idemaru and Holt (2011) showed that reversing this correlation in a speech stream presented to an English speaker causes the learner to rapidly downweight F0. Thus, before training, listeners disambiguate stimuli with ambiguous VOT on the basis of F0 but they no longer do so after training. We can think of this training as extinction of the association between F0 and the outcome it signals, but what is that outcome? One can think of it as being the primary cue, VOT. Alternatively, it could be the contrast between the two words participants are actually asked to discriminate in the experiment, *beer* vs. *pier* or *deer* vs. *tear*, or it could be a phonological distinction (voiced vs. voiceless or /b/ vs. /p/). The first hypothesis suggests phonetic mediation of the F0/semantics relationship, while the others suggest that VOT and F0 are independent cues to a lexical or phonological contrast. As a result, they make different predictions regarding the use of F0 for lexical disambiguation when VOT is made an unreliable cue to the lexical contrast. If VOT varies randomly regardless of whether the intended word is *beer* or *pier* and F0 is held constant at an intermediate value throughout, what would happen to the use of F0 for *beer/pier* disambiguation? If F0 is a cue to VOT (e.g., Escudero & Boersma, 2004), then participants should learn that F0 differences are powerless to distinguish *beer* and *pier*. In contrast, if F0 directly cues the lexical contrast, then participants should come to rely on it more heavily now that its competitor, VOT, is out of the running.[4]

While mediation in learning is yet to be addressed, McMurray and colleagues have investigated phonetic-cue mediation in processing using the visual-world paradigm (McMurray et al., 2008; Toscano & McMurray, 2015; see also Reinisch & Sjerps, 2013). They discovered that some acoustic cues directly cue lexical or semantic contrasts while others appear to function like occasion setters, biasing the interpretation of an upcoming cue. Independence has been shown for VOT of a stop and duration of the following vowel. Because VOT is the stronger cue and becomes available to the listener before the duration of the following vowel, we would not expect occasion setting in this situation. As expected, McMurray et al.'s (2008) participants did not wait to interpret VOT until they knew vowel duration. Instead, looks to words like *pear* and *bear* were based on VOT first, as soon as it became available, with some adjustments based on vowel duration later. In other words, processing of the two cues was independent and incremental.

In contrast, speech rate preceding the stop—estimated in part on the basis of vowel durations in preceding words—does not appear to cue voicing of an upcoming stop directly. Toscano and McMurray (2015) reasoned that as one hears *I want you to click on the …* pronounced quickly, one might look at the *pear* over the *bear* because rapid speech rate expands the range of VOTs perceived as voiceless. This does not happen: looks to *pear* vs. *bear* do take into account the speech rate / VOT relationship but only after VOT is perceived (Reinisch & Sjerps, 2013; Toscano & McMurray, 2015). In this case, the preceding speech rate influences the interpretation of potentially ambiguous VOT values. Mapping the cues in question onto the diagram in figure 3.2, these VOT values (around 25 ms) act as T's whose mapping onto voiceless or voiced (US) is gated by input from perceived speech rate (C). As illustrated in figure 3.3, a fast speech rate may cause a 25 ms VOT to be mapped onto "voiceless"/*bear* while a slow speech rate would cause it to be mapped onto "voiced"/*bear*. While Toscano and McMurray (2015) conclude that the results are problematic for associative learning accounts of cue integration, this is not necessarily true: this is simply an example of cues cueing how other cues should be interpreted, akin to occasion setting.[5]

As also noted by Toscano and McMurray (2015), a similar distinction can be made with respect to indexical cues like characteristics of a speaker's voice that allow the listener to identify the person. According to speaker-normalization models of speech perception, such characteristics are not

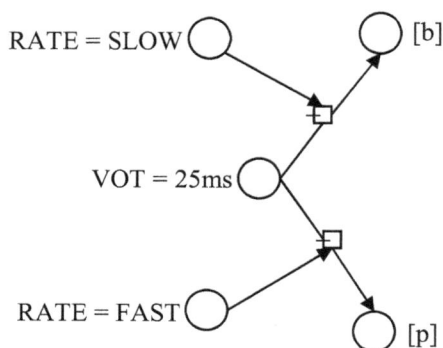

Figure 3.3
A partial specification of the network of cues contributing to classifying an intervocalic labial stop as a [p] or [b] in English. Speech rate gates the interpretation of the
ambiguous VOT value of 25 ms.

used to access the meaning of what the speaker is saying but rather to identify the relationship between acoustic cues the speaker produces and the
phonemes she is trying to produce. According to exemplar models and cue-
integration models, both indexical and linguistic features are used to access
meaning (see K. Johnson, 2005; Toscano & McMurray, 2015).

According to many morphologists, whenever there are multiple discrete exponents of a meaning, one of these exponents is the primary one,
directly linked to the meaning, while other exponents are linked to the
meaning only through the primary exponent (e.g., Booij, 1996; Halle &
Marantz, 1993). For example, Booij (1996) makes the distinction between
inherent and contextual inflection, where a case or gender marker on a
noun would be inherent and so directly linked to meaning, while a case
marker on an adjective or a gender marker on a verb is contextual, present
only to signal the case or gender of the noun. If one takes this distinction
as applicable to processing morphology in comprehension, then one might
expect that changing the relationship between a meaning and its primary
exponent would automatically change the relationship between the meaning and the secondary exponents but not vice versa. Thus, experiencing
a speaker marking case inconsistently on unmodified nouns would leave
one unable to interpret case markers on the same speaker's adjectives. On
the other hand, experiencing case being inconsistently marked on adjectives (say, with the agreeing nouns obscured by a cough) would have little
effect on one's interpretation of case markers on the speaker's nouns when
those are eventually presented. In contrast, the Competition Model (Bates

& MacWhinney, 1989; MacWhinney, 1987) treats all formal correlates of a meaning as cueing the meaning directly, and language comprehension is thought to proceed by utilizing all the available cues in parallel. Under this view, then, making one cue unreliable should cause learners to rely more on the other cues.

As few relevant experiments have been done yet, the extent to which form-meaning relationships are mediated by other forms is unresolved, presenting an interesting avenue for future research that would do much to clarify the architecture of the language system as well as elucidating the conditions for the emergence of occasion setting. For my part, I would usually bet on the form-meaning mappings being only partially mediated, providing multiple redundant, parallel routes from form to meaning (e.g., Baayen et al., 1997; Bates & MacWhinney, 1989). As long as a secondary cue is predictive of the outcome, I would expect it to be directly linked to the outcome because the primary cue is not perceived 100% of the time. In a typical occasion-setting experiment, the conditioned stimulus is seldom missed. In speech, the primary cue may be easily obscured by noise, forcing reliance on the secondary cue. Mediation is risky if the mediator is liable to be missed. It is likely precisely these occasions of missing the primary cue that provide the main motivation for developing direct mappings between meanings and secondary cues.

3.11   Conclusion

No organism wants to miss out on important cues, therefore failing to prepare for the outcomes they predict to be imminent. However, the attention of any organism is limited: at any time, you have to decide what to look at, and how much processing power to devote to vigilantly monitoring the acoustic stream. Trying to attend to everything amounts to attending to nothing. As a result, we learn—or at least try to learn!—which cues to attend to.

The need for selective attention is what generally prevents complex stimuli from being treated as undecomposable configurations. Nonetheless, sometimes cue configurations do emerge, particularly when it allows the learner to associate the whole with outcomes not predicted by its parts occurring alone. Cues can also fuse together as they are repeatedly encountered in the same order. Fusion likely involves both Hebbian and error-driven mechanisms.

The cues we attend to are sensationally salient: a salient cue is easy to recognize, affording faster decisions. They are unexpected: an unexpected cue indicates that one's beliefs about the world are in need of revision. They are also ones that have been informative in the past: what has been useful is likely to remain useful. This final point is in need of elaboration. We seek meaning in the sensory stream. When we find it, we are loath to abandon what we found: an informative cue that seems to have stopped being informative is not simply abandoned. Rather, we shift attention to another cue, learning why a reliable cue has betrayed our trust. In this way, attention can shift to cues that we know little about (Kruschke, 1996, 2009), which can take the blame for the unexpected outcome (*highlighting*), or for an unexpected cue-outcome relationship (*occasion setting*).[6]

With attention comes associability. Thus cues that we attend to during a learning experience are likely to benefit most from that experience. We learn about the sensationally salient, the unexpected, the informative, and the potentially informative more than our amount of exposure to these cues would predict. This link between learned selective attention and associability is one of the most important ideas in learning theory and solves many puzzles, some of which we will encounter in subsequent chapters.

4 Bayes, Rationality, and Rashionality

> We must not be hasty. I have become too hot. I must cool myself and think.
> —Fangorn/Treebeard, quoted in J. R. R. Tolkien, *The Lord of the Rings*

Until now, we have approached learning squarely within the associationist framework. However, that framework has not gone unchallenged. Currently, the strongest challenge to associationism (and its connectionist variant) is represented by Bayesian inference. In this chapter, we consider the phenomena that are thought to be challenging for associative learning mechanisms and that have formed the empirical basis for Bayesian approaches to learning theory.

Bayesian models have long been used in work on associative learning to describe *normatively correct* behavior: what a perfect or *ideal learner* would learn when exposed to the same data as the organism of interest (e.g., Beach & Scopp, 1968; Gluck & Bower, 1988; Medin & Edelson, 1988). Departures from the ideal (*"irrational behavior"*) have also long provided valuable insights about the nature and limitations of human and non-human learning and decision making (e.g., Hertwig et al., 2004; Kahneman & Tversky, 1972; Tversky & Kahneman, 1974; see Zentall, 2016, for a recent review). However, within the last two decades, work on Bayesian modeling of learning has exploded, driven at least in part by increases in computational power. Our computers can now perform optimal Bayesian learning in many domains. The question is whether we have been doing it all along.

Some of the new Bayesian models of learning can be seen as "Bayesifications" of traditional associative models of learning, extending these models with probabilistic prediction and augmenting association weights with a representation of uncertainty about the weight (e.g., the Kalman filter, Dayan et al., 2000, a Bayesian extension of Rescorla & Wagner, 1972). Others—particularly *generative* Bayesian models—propose a more radical break with the associative tradition (e.g., Courville et al., 2006). In this book, I take the position that the Bayesian revolution has offered important insights but biological learners are not Bayesian ideal learners. Bayesian insights should therefore be incorporated into a framework that is mindful of the limitations and goals of living, breathing, biological learners (see also Daw et al., 2008; Gigerenzer & Selten, 2002; Kahneman, 2011; Kruschke, 2006; Kruschke & Johansen, 1999; Lieder et al., 2014).

The ideal learner is traditionally thought to maximize the accuracy of its beliefs about the world (e.g., Anderson, 1991). However, to borrow a blend from Kruschke and Johansen (1999), biological learners are not rational, but *rashional*: we rush to judgment, we jump to conclusions, we are rash and impatient, because we have to be. Having evolved in an environment of constant danger, of fight and flight, of fleeting stimuli and transient opportunities, of salient distractions and hidden treasures, we are inextricably bound by time. Coming up with a true inference has to be balanced with deciding quickly and with a minimal expenditure of valuable resources. As Kruschke and Johansen (1999, p. 1115) put it,

> It would seem rational or optimal to learn about partial correlations between cues and outcomes as they actually exist in the world, but instead it is the case that humans and other animals exhibit nonnormative utilization of cues. Have all these species thrived despite having irrational, suboptimal learning? Have the selective pressures of all these species' evolutionary niches been so benign that inaccurate learning goes unpunished in reproductive success? We believe that the answer to these questions is "no". Instead, the learning behavior of these species is an evolutionary adaptive solution to a constraint on learning other than long-run accuracy: the need for speed.

Bayesian theorists emphasize that behavior is functional. By analyzing the task, one can identify the optimal way(s) to accomplish it, and evolution pressures organisms to arrive at near-optimal solutions to the problems that confront them (Anderson, 1991). However, for a biological organism, accuracy of belief is not the only thing one would wish to optimize (unless one is an immortal and nearly invulnerable ent). Learning and decision making need to be not only reasonably accurate but also reasonably speedy and efficient, both in terms of the resources required to decide on a behavior and the resources required to execute it. Departures from rationality (the way rationality is *bounded*, Gigerenzer & Selten, 2002; see also Lieder et al., 2014) have much to teach us about the adaptive pressures on the biological learner.

Importantly, there is more to learning than inference, whether rational or rashional. All too often, Bayesian models of learning are content to postulate a "learning module" that "does learning" on the basis of perceptual experience (chapter 1). However, learning happens throughout the brain, and perceptual inputs are only one kind of input on which learning operates. For example, automatization of motor control within the production system is a major source of constraints on language structure (chapter 9). An ideal Bayesian learner module embedded in a nonideal performance system makes little biological sense. There is no domain-general learning *module*. Instead, throughout the brain, neuronal learning obeys a small set of common principles underlying experience-based changes in connectivity (see also Christiansen & Chater, 2016). Given the biological facts, it appears more promising to incorporate Bayesian insights into imperfect local learners constrained by their biological embodiment, which together form the hodgepodge we are used to calling the "Language Acquisition Device" or (more simply) the human brain. The local learners can be thought of as functional modules, accomplishing specific evolutionarily useful tasks. However, all of them can be represented as networks of simple nodes, and all of these networks learn using common learning principles (see Kruschke, 2006, for a similar perspective). The task at hand is to incorporate the insights of Bayesian learning theory into this set of learning principles.

4.1 Confidence

Bayesian models have been hailed as "a revolutionary advance over traditional approaches" (Kruschke, 2008, p. 210), for one primary reason: associative learning theories, and the connectionist models that grew out of them, do not represent the *degree of uncertainty* about their various beliefs. They have, as Kruschke (2008) put it, "a punctate state of mind." In the associative approach, the weight of a link like A→B is a single number, a point estimate of the relationship between A and B. The model might know that the weight of A→B is .7 but that is all it knows: it has no representation of how *confident* it is in its belief. In other words, how likely is its belief to change as more instances of A and/or B are encountered? The link has no representation of the number of observations its estimated weight is based on, the strength of belief in the estimate, or the range of somewhat believable weight values.

In contrast, Bayesian approaches suggest that the learner always entertains all possible link weights: while some value might be more probable than others based on the learner's experience so far, it matters whether other values are nearly as probable, or not probable at all. In the Bayesian framework, the learner's knowledge about the strength of a link or the resting activation of a node is not a single number, but rather a *probability distribution* over the continuum of possible link weights. In many applications (e.g., Dayan et al., 2000), that distribution is assumed to be *normal* (on some scale). It can therefore be conveniently described by just two numbers: the *mean*, which represents the most likely link weight given the learner's experience so far, and the *variance*, which represents the learner's confidence in that belief and, therefore, its willingness to adjust it. Traditional associative models represent the mean but not the variance.

4.1.1 Confidence and Frequency Attenuation

Bayesian models suggest that the more experience one has had with A→B, the less one is willing to adjust one's beliefs about the A→B relationship on the basis of a single experience. Perhaps the best-studied example in language learning is presented by the *frequency attenuation effect* in repetition priming (Forster & C. Davis, 1984). An additional token of experience with a word helps recognition of a word less when the word is frequent than when it is rare. As a result, various measures of processing ease and familiarity are decelerating functions of word frequency (e.g., Broadbent, 1967; Goldiamond & Hawkins, 1958; Howes, 1957; Keuleers et al., 2015; Kreuz, 1987; Oldfield & Wingfield, 1965).

A crucial empirical question distinguishing Bayesian and non-Bayesian accounts of frequency attenuation in priming is whether target frequency also matters for *inhibitory* priming, which happens when a competitor to the target is primed (Goldinger et al., 1989; Marsolek, 2008). Like Bayesian learning, the error-driven associative learning approach predicts a deceleration of learning with experience in many circumstances. As a word is experienced, its occurrence is more and more expected. According to error-driven learning theory, learning happens only when the word is *unexpectedly* present (Rescorla & Wagner, 1972). Thus, error-driven learning can account for reduced *excitatory* priming with frequent target words (see chapter 5 for another example). It can also account for an effect of *prime* frequency on the magnitude of inhibitory priming observed by Goldinger et al. (1989). Inhibitory priming results from priming a competitor to the target: the prime trial teaches the learner to perceive or produce the prime rather than any of its competitors, including the target (Goldinger et al., 1989; Marsolek, 2008; see also Oppenheim et al., 2010). Presenting an infrequent, unexpected prime increases its competitiveness more than presenting a frequent prime. However, by the same logic, frequent targets should suffer more from priming a competitor than infrequent targets: the frequent target is more expected, hence its absence on the prime trial is more *un*expected, generating a larger error signal and a greater belief revision.

If, on the other hand, the magnitude of inhibitory priming is reduced with a high-frequency target, then there is a need for some mechanism that would make it harder to adjust the connection weights that are based on extensive experience. One way to do this would be to abandon the assumption that the weight of a link is a single number, adding a representation of the variance of believable values (Dayan et al., 2000). The variance of the distribution should steadily decrease as experience with A and B accumulates, reflecting increasing confidence that the weight of the link reflects the true/target relationship between A and B.

Unfortunately, there is no clear evidence for an effect of target frequency in inhibitory form priming. For example, Goldinger et al. (1989) find a robust prime frequency effect along with no significant target frequency effect. Radeau et al. (1995) find inhibitory priming only when the prime is a low-frequency word while the target is a high-frequency word, but target frequency was not manipulated independently of prime frequency in their study. Finally, Dufour and Frauenfelder (2016) found no significant effect of target (or prime) lexicality in inhibitory phonetic priming. Overall, the empirical issues remain unresolved, preventing any strong theoretical conclusions. Given the small magnitude of the inhibitory priming effect, definitive conclusions must await higher-powered experimentation.

4.1.2 Confidence-Shattering Surprise and Biased Updating

Paul Olejarczuk and I have recently argued that experience can adjust confidence in one's beliefs and that these adjustments may be the source of biased belief updating. In particular, as mentioned in chapter 1, learners sometimes exhibit a confirmation or disconfirmation bias. A learner with a confirmation bias ignores events that are inconsistent with their beliefs. A learner with a disconfirmation bias pays special attention to such events.

Our case of a disconfirmation bias comes from an experiment on phonological learning (Olejarczuk & Kapatsinski, 2015, 2017), a domain where confirmation biases have previously been posited (Wilson, 2006). We suspect that belief updating can be subject to both confirmation and disconfirmation biases. In particular, strong prior beliefs can cause the learner to misperceive unexpected events as more expected ones, provided that the expected and unexpected events are perceptually similar enough to be confused. For example, clicks located inside words can be perceived as occurring at nearby boundaries (Fodor & Bever, 1965). Entire segments can be replaced by coughs and nonetheless perceived as having occurred when they are expected based on the preceding or following context (R. Warren & Obusek, 1971). When an unexpected stimulus is similar enough to an expected one, a confirmation bias is likely to be found. In contrast, when an unexpected event is perceived, it can exert a disproportionate influence on beliefs, resulting in a disconfirmation bias. We argue that a disconfirmation bias can be implemented in a learning model by assuming that surprising events shatter the model's confidence in its current beliefs (see also Sakamoto et al., 2008). The notion of confidence is crucial to this proposal, but confidence may be updated in an "irrational," nonnormative way, leading to biased use of the available evidence.

We exposed English speakers to various stress patterns, varying in how surprising they were given English language experience. Our participants accurately reproduced the presented words during training, suggesting that they did not misperceive unexpected stress patterns as expected ones. Like other Germanic languages, English has an initial-stress pattern, exemplified by words like 'character and 'seminal. However, because of the influx of Latinate vocabulary, English also has a more complex variable-stress pattern borrowed from Latin, which is usually called *Latin Stress*. According to this pattern, stress falls on penultimate (second-from-the-end) syllables when they are heavy (ending in a consonant or containing a long vowel), and on the third syllable from the end otherwise. Thus, the heavy penult of *se.'man.tic* attracts stress away from its default initial position. The interaction of the two patterns means that words like 'se.mi.nal, with an unstressed light penult, are entirely unsurprising: they are favored by both Latin and Germanic stress. At the other extreme, words with a stressed light penult like *Se.'mi.tic* are really rare. Words with heavy penults are intermediate, as words like 'cha.rac.ter are favored by Germanic stress and words like *se.'man.tic* are favored by Latin stress.

We exposed adult native English speakers to one of two stress patterns, one of which was a categorical version of Latin stress—all words were like *semantic* and *seminal*—while the other was a categorical pattern in the opposite direction, *anti-Latin*, with words like *character* and *Semitic*. We first determined the participants' prior knowledge by testing for productivity of Latin stress without any training on Latin stress or its opposite. The participants read aloud novel trisyllabic words with light and heavy penults (alongside a set of filler words of shorter length where Latin and Germanic stress both support initial stress). The proportion of penult stress in words with heavy and light penults is shown by the "baseline" point in figure 4.1. This point represents the prior of the participants before training: as expected from the English lexicon, heavy penults are stressed about half the time, while light penults are stressed only 25% of the time. Since the participants' priors closely matched the statistics of the English lexicon,

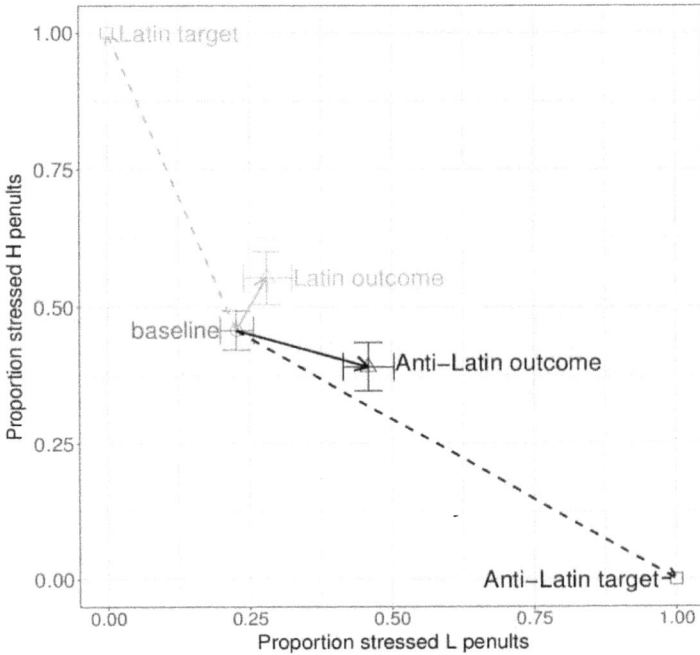

Figure 4.1
In research reported by Olejarczuk and Kapatsinski (2015; see also 2017 for a full description of the results), English speakers were trained either on a categorical version of an English stress pattern ("Latin stress") or on its opposite ("anti-Latin stress"). Overall, they learned more when exposed to the pattern that was less consistent with their native language and prior expectations, exhibiting a greater change from baseline after training in the anti-Latin condition.

we did not observe a strong inductive bias against one of the four attested stress patterns. These data therefore ruled out an inductive bias account of the remaining data.

We then exposed the participants to either a categorical Latin pattern or a categorical anti-Latin pattern. As shown in figure 4.1, participants exposed to the anti-Latin stress pattern learned more than those exposed to the Latin stress pattern. In particular, they learned to stress light penults more, whereas those exposed to the Latin pattern failed to learn to stress light penults less.

We fit the results using a Bayesian model built using the code for a Bayesian logistic regression from Kruschke (2015). The model estimated the rate of initial stress for words with light penults and an effect of a heavy penult on stress location. In associative terms, this corresponds to learning associations between an input layer containing a context cue and a "heavy-penult" cue and an output layer consisting of a "penult stress" node. The model was exposed to the same data as the participants, and the center of the prior distributions matched the participants' pretest data. The model was allowed to fit the variance of the prior to the data. This reflected the fact that the participants' pretest means are derived from an unknown amount of prior experience with English. It also gave the model the freedom to adjust the flexibility of its prior to match the experimental data. Nonetheless, the model performance was rather poor. In particular, the model underestimated how fast the learners could increase the rate of penult stress in words with light penults, like *Semitic*. In addition, the model thought that all participants should have learned to stress heavy penults in words like *semantic*, which was not true of the anti-Latin group. In the anti-Latin training, heavy penults are never stressed. However, because the rate of penult stress in both training groups was higher than it is in English, the model concluded that the training should lead participants to produce more penult stress across syllable structures.

We then modified the Bayesian model in two different ways. First, we implemented a channel bias in favor of ignoring expected events: the probability of using a word to update one's beliefs was made proportional to $p(D)^w$, where w was a free parameter estimated from the data. Unfortunately, the best-fitting values of w meant that participants in both training groups would have to ignore 90% of the words with heavy penults regardless of stress, 100% of unstressed light-penult words, and over half of stressed light penults. It is doubtful that participants are really that inattentive. In addition, even with the best-fitting values, the model was still underpredicting learning of the really unexpected light-penult stress.

Since our efforts to account for the data with channel bias had been thwarted, we had to resort to biased belief updating. The resulting model is not Bayesian, in that it is not making normative use of available evidence, but the Bayesian notion of confidence is crucial to its ability to model the data. As noted above, whereas an associative model would represent an association between, say, syllable structure and stress location by a single number, a Bayesian model also represents its confidence in this belief by another number, variance, or its inverse, *precision*. The higher the precision, the more confident the model is in its estimate of the association weight. The higher the model's confidence in its estimate, the less willing it is to change it on the basis of contradictory data. In our *Surprise-Weighted Intake Model* (SWIM), the precisions are multiplied by $p(D)^w$, with w again estimated from the human data. Values between 0 and 1 indicate confirmation bias, while values above 1 indicate a disconfirmation bias. For our data, the best-fitting values of *w* were well above 1, with values between 4.6 and 5.6 allowing the model to predict the amount of learning for all four combinations of syllable structure and stress position. These results suggest that surprising events shatter the learners' confidence in their beliefs, leaving them open to adjusting beliefs on the basis of ensuing experience (see also Stahl & Feigenson, 2015, 2017). To put it more positively, surprise leads to learning. The end result is a model that quickly adjusts beliefs when it finds that it has made a grievous prediction error. This does not maximize belief accuracy in an unchanging environment: it seems to make learners rashly abandon prior beliefs, at least within the context in which the beliefs have failed to make an accurate prediction (Kruschke & Johansen, 1999). However, this may be essential for living in the real world, which is in constant flux, so what was true of the world yesterday may no longer be true tomorrow (see also chapter 5).

Though it has only been tweaked in a minor way, a Bayesian model with a flexible *w* is no longer completely rational, which means that it does not quite fit with the rationalist orientation of the Bayesian framework. It is therefore important to note as well that *w* can also be a direct adjustment to the system's *temperature* or global learning rate, which would allow it a spot in the associative framework. Future work should determine whether surprising observations destroy one's confidence about the specific beliefs that make them surprising. If so, then the Bayesian notion of confidence as a property of a specific connection weight may be essential for capturing biased, not-strictly-Bayesian belief updating. If not, a global temperature adjustment at the level of an entire network may do. In other words, does surprise simply make you (or some part of you) more ready to learn? Or does it make you ready to revisit the assumptions that appear to be incorrect?[1]

4.2 Entrenchment and Suspicious Coincidence

As one keeps encountering AB, A→B grows strongly positive, and A→*notB* links become more and more negative. In other words, as one becomes more and more confident that B always occurs in the context of A, one grows more and more confident that A does not occur without B. This effect has been termed *entrenchment* (Braine & Brooks, 1995; Stefanowitsch, 2008) or the *suspicious coincidence effect* (F. Xu & Tenenbaum, 2007).

Entrenchment allows learners to avoid overgeneralization in the absence of explicit negative evidence. For example, if a child experiences cats labeled *kittie*, how does s/he eventually learn that *kitty* refers to "cat" and not a broader category like "animal"? After all, every cat is an animal, so every time *kitty* is experienced, it occurs in the context of an animal as well as a cat!

F. Xu and Tenenbaum (2007) report on an ingenious word learning experiment examining this process. Participants were shown one Dalmatian and told that it is called a *dax*. In a subsequent test, they were shown pictures of other Dalmatians, non-Dalmatian dogs, and nondog mammals, and asked if these too were daxes. Participants were quite likely to think that non-Dalmatian dogs were also daxes, mapping *dax* onto "dog," the more commonly used, basic-level category. They were then presented with two more pictures of Dalmatians and told that these too were daxes. Now, the participants were much less likely to think that non-Dalmatian dogs were also daxes. The term has become restricted to Dalmatians, despite every training instance pairing *dax* with a picture of a dog.

F. Xu and Tenenbaum (2007) called their finding the *suspicious coincidence effect*, based on their Bayesian explanation of the finding. The Bayesian learner assumes that daxes presented to her are random samples from the population of daxes (like raffle tickets being drawn from a hat). Even if the hat contained all kinds of dogs, it would not be too implausible for somebody to randomly draw a Dalmatian from it once. But it would be a suspicious coincidence for one to randomly draw three Dalmatians in a row out of a hat containing all sorts of dogs. In a non-Bayesian framework, one could also consider this a case of cue competition à la Rescorla and Wagner (1972): the more one encounters Dalmatian→*dax*, the weaker other cues to *dax* become, eroding one's belief that dogs of other colors, shapes, or sizes could also be called *dax*.

In phonology and morphosyntax, the same effect has been termed *entrenchment* (or sometimes negative entrenchment). For example, in syntax, frequent intransitive verbs placed in the transitive construction elicit more disgust than synonymous infrequent verbs (Theakston, 2004; see also Braine & Brooks, 1995; Brooks et al., 1999; Stefanowitsch, 2008; Ambridge et al., 2008). Thus, *He vanished it* is judged as being more acceptable than *He disappeared it*. The more frequent *disappear* has become restricted to the intransitive construction and generates a strong expectation against a direct object showing up next. The less frequent *vanish*, not so much. Again, as one encounters additional examples of a verb not being followed by a direct object, one grows more and more confident that direct objects will not (and should not) occur after that verb.

Like other kinds of learning, entrenchment happens throughout life. On the production side of things, continuing entrenchment is beneficial as it makes productions less and less variable as one ages: repeatedly used behaviors are automatized and infrequently deviated from. If we assume that the production target is the peak of the distribution of phonetic realizations of a speech unit (e.g., Buz et al., 2016), then the more one shoots for the target the peakier the distribution of realizations becomes (Pierrehumbert, 2001). Indeed, if one looks in detail, productions of speech sounds are less variable in adolescents compared to children, in younger adults compared to adolescents, and even in older adults compared to younger adults (Baayen et al., 2017). Other things being equal, entrenchment makes the entrenched item harder to associate with new things. Entrenchment makes you better at doing the things you do often, but it also makes you more set in your ways. Loss of plasticity is the price we pay for expertise. Thus, older adults are worse at learning new random word pairs such as *eagle-jury* (*paired associate learning*, Asch & Ebenholtz, 1962; Desrosiers & Ivison, 1986). After experiencing a couple of *eagle-jury* pairings, younger adults have an easier time than older adults trying to retrieve *jury* when probed with *eagle*. Declines in cued recall performance begin early, so that 40-year-olds are worse at it than 30-year-olds, a finding that suggested to many that the brain begins deteriorating after one hits 21 (see Ramscar et al., 2014, for review). However, as Ramscar et al. (2014) point out, cued recall may be more difficult for older adults because they know vastly more words than younger adults. On average, a 70-year-old knows twice as many words as a 20-year old (Keuleers et al., 2015). Therefore, any given cue activates a lot more words in the minds of older adults, preventing them from retrieving any single one.[2] Furthermore, older adults' word associations are stronger than those of younger adults: familiar words are more entrenched in their contexts. Learning new associations for familiar words becomes harder and harder as one ages (and learns!) because the randomly paired words already have strong associations that are difficult to undo or suppress. An older adult knows more than a younger adult, and has greater confidence in their knowledge.[3]

4.3 Learned Inattention

If the learner's environment is constant, then the learner must grow more and more confident in her knowledge with the passage of time, reducing the variances on association weights. In principle, variance can change independently of the mean. With experience, the probability distributions over link weights become more and more peaky. The learner becomes more and more certain about the strength of each link, whatever that strength might be. So, if A always co-occurs with B, the A→B link weight approaches 1, and the variance shrinks so that eventually 1's probability towers over the probabilities of its competitors. If A always co-occurs with the absence of B, the A→B link weight approaches -1. If A and B co-occur at chance levels, the weight of A→B approaches 0, the learner becoming more and more confident that there is no correlation between A and B.

This is where things get a bit tricky. If confidence in one's estimate of link strength is what determines how likely one is to change one's beliefs about the strength of the link, then one's current estimate of that link's strength should play no additional role. This, however, is not true. It is much more difficult to change near-zero weights than it is to change weights that are close to 1 or -1. The primary reason for this is *learned selective attention*: once we have learned that A is irrelevant for predicting whether B will occur, we stop attending to A when trying to predict the (non)occurrence of B (Kruschke, 1992, 2006; Kruschke & Johansen, 1999). As a result, it is difficult to revise the belief that A is nonpredictive.

For example, Kruschke (1996) and Lawrence (1949, 1950) found that learning to reverse cue-outcome mappings (a reversal shift, illustrated in the left column of [1]) was easier than learning to switch attention to a previously irrelevant cue (illustrated in the right column).

(1) A.C→X   A.C→X
     B.C→Y   A.D→Y
     A.D→X   B.C→X
     B.D→Y   B.D→Y

Thus, switching the weights of A→X and B→Y from 1 to -1 and A→Y to B→X from -1 to 1 appeared to be easier than switching the weights away from 0, despite the latter being a smaller change. Kruschke (1996) explains this finding by *attentional perseveration*: participants exposed to Stage I training in which A and B are nonpredictive learn not to attend to these cues, which makes it difficult to start attending to them in Stage II (see also Trabasso & Bower, 1968). As first proposed by Mackintosh (1975), cues learned to be irrelevant lose *associability*, the ability to be associated with outcomes. As we saw earlier, learned inattention is an obstacle often faced by those trying to acquire the phonology or syntax of a second language, where cues ignored in processing one's first language can suddenly become essential (Ellis, 2006; Escudero, 2005; Escudero & Boersma, 2004; Francis & Nusbaum, 2002; MacWhinney, 1987).[4]

4.4 Exoneration and Holmesian Inference

The Bayesian learner is Sherlock Holmes, an ideal detective. It keeps in mind all possible causes of an event and assigns blame for the event in an optimal manner. Any evidence favoring a particular cause of the event simultaneously provides evidence against all other causes of the same event. In other words, Bayesian models propose that *causes compete*. Kruschke (2006) calls this the *logic of exoneration*, also known as *explaining away*. If you are trying to find out whether your wool sweater was damaged by your cat or a moth, and you see a moth flitting about the closet, the cat is thereby exonerated. If you find a suspect's blood at a crime scene, other suspects are exonerated. Evidence supporting one cause automatically reduces the likelihood of other causes. Exoneration follows from the most fundamental claim of Bayesian models. According to Bayesian models, the mind deals in *probability*, not activation (see Norris, 2006, as well as Norris & McQueen, 2008, for an extensive discussion). Unlike the weights of links connecting cues to a single outcome, probabilities of all possible causes given an outcome must sum to 1. The more likely it is that A was caused by B, the less likely it is that it was caused by something else.

The converse of exoneration is sometimes called *Holmesian inference* or *argument by elimination*. "How often have I said to you that when you have eliminated the impossible, whatever remains, however improbable, must be the truth?," says Holmes to Watson in *The Sign of Four* (Doyle, 1890). Any evidence *against* a possible cause makes other causes of the same event more likely. If one cause is eliminated, others become more probable. Again this is a simple consequence of the fact that the probabilities of alternative causes given an outcome must sum to 1.

The Bayesian learner does not update links or even layers of links one by one. Rather, it evaluates hypotheses about what the full set of weights comprising the network is likely to be (though Kruschke, 2006, shows that it is sometimes useful to update some links before others). The global updating allows the Bayesian learner to maintain multiple very different hypotheses about the state of the world at any one time and then to quickly narrow down the set when disambiguating information becomes available.

Bayesian theorists wishing to show that learners automatically infer competition have emphasized a phenomenon called *backward blocking*. Recall that in forward blocking, learners experience A→X in Stage I, followed by exposure to AB→X in Stage II. After Stage II, the B→X association is often weak or nonexistent, compared to the condition in which learners are exposed to C→X in Stage I (Kamin, 1969). In backward blocking, the order of the two stages is reversed. So, B→X appears to weaken if AB→X training is followed by A→X training (Shanks, 1985). Bayesian models predict that blocking should happen regardless of the temporal order of the stages because B→X trials increase the likelihood of B being the cause of X, which automatically reduces the likelihood of A being the cause of X (e.g., Gopnik et al., 2004; Sobel et al., 2004).

The Rescorla-Wagner model does not capture backward blocking because, whenever a cue is absent from a certain trial, the model learns nothing about that cue (Rescorla & Wagner, 1972; cf. Tassoni, 1995; Danks, 2003). Bayesian models instead update the entire system of beliefs on every trial, which allows them to capture blocking in whatever direction. In language acquisition, learning about absent cues is suggested by the observation that the number of new words a school-age child learns to understand in a day greatly exceeds the number of new words to which she is exposed in a day (Landauer & Dumais, 1997).

While we do appear to learn about cues in absentia, and this should be captured by a model of learning, a Bayesian approach is not necessary to capture the effect. As several researchers have pointed out, all that is needed is for cue-outcome links to lose strength when the cue in question is unexpectedly absent (Dickinson, 1996; Ghirlanda, 2005; Markman, 1989; Tassoni, 1995; Van Hamme & Wasserman, 1994), implementing a kind of *bidirectional* prediction (see chapter 6). The debate thus comes down to the issue of whether the learning biological learners engage in can be described as optimal computation of Bayesian statistics.

If one examines the backward and forward blocking effects in greater detail, one notices that the backward blocking effect is weaker than forward blocking (Chapman, 1991; Kruschke, 2006). In other words, the B→X association is stronger (less blocked) at the end of training if AB→X trials precede A→X trials than if they follow them. *Trial order* matters, with earlier trials having a stronger influence, a kind of *primacy* effect. Bayesian models of trial-order effects suggest that the learner uses trial order to estimate how the world is changing (e.g., Courville et al., 2006; Navarro & Perfors, 2009). Thus, experiencing A→X trials in Stage II after B→X in Stage I could be interpreted as indicating that the world has changed, so it is A and *not* B that causes X now, though B had caused it in the past. However, note that this predicts, counterfactually, that backward blocking should be stronger than forward blocking and, generally, that recent training trials should matter the most for predicting current behavior: the more recent an experience, the more relevant it is for estimating what the world is like *now*.

The greater strength of forward blocking is not rational. It is *rashional*. The learner seems to make up her mind early on, jumping to a conclusion about how the world is and always will be. When you find some structure in the world, that belief is hard to give up. You stick with it, and it colors your future learning. This can happen even when the structure you've discovered is in fact spurious, imposed by you on the input. We stick with our beliefs for as long as we can—that is, for as long as those beliefs are not resulting in some kind of (costly) error. This is not unlike sticking with a behavior that "works" in operant conditioning. In a classic experiment, Skinner (1948) placed hungry pigeons in cages that delivered food at random intervals with no relation to the pigeon's behavior. The pigeons were found to associate the delivery of food with whatever behavior they happened to perform when first reinforced:

> One bird was conditioned to turn counter-clockwise about the cage, making two or three turns between reinforcements. Another repeatedly thrust its head into one of the upper corners of the cage. A third developed a "tossing" response, as if placing its head beneath an invisible bar and lifting it repeatedly. Two birds developed a pendulum motion of the head and body, in which the head was extended forward and swung from right to left with a sharp movement followed by a somewhat slower return. (Skinner, 1948, p. 168)

As the pigeons continued performing their superstitious behavior, they continued to be randomly reinforced, which led them to continue performing the behavior. It is easy to see the analogy with superstition in humans: an irrelevant behavior that happened to precede a salient reward like a good harvest or a lucky spin of the roulette wheel can be elevated to the status of ritual, unflaggingly performed every time before harvesting the crops or gambling one's savings away. Even when one's luck turns, the ritual—and the belief in its effectiveness—are not easily given up. Doll et al. (2009) suggest that a false belief—in their case, explicitly communicated to learners by a deceptive experimenter—can lead the executive control system in the prefrontal cortex to mislead the striatal implicit learning system by amplifying belief-consistent outcomes and inhibiting inconsistent ones.

The greater effectiveness of forward blocking compared to backward blocking is only one trial-order effect problematic for viewing biological learners as having achieved Bayesian optimality. Another such effect is *highlighting*, when implemented as a pure trial-order effect (in the so-called canonical highlighting design; Kruschke, 2009). In this design, there is an uninformative cue present throughout training (I) and two perfect predictors cueing different outcomes. One of these predominates in early trials (PE), while the other predominates in late trials (PL). At test, participants are presented with the familiar cue combinations I.PE and I.PL, but also with the novel combination of cues PE.PL and the uninformative cue I on its own. PE.PL tends to elicit the outcome that is more frequent in late training and associated with PL (L), while cue I elicits the outcome associated with PE, which dominates early training (E). The pattern of results in highlighting thus cannot be described as a simple primacy or recency effect. It also cannot be ascribed to a difference in how a priori likely E and L are, since they have equal frequency of occurrence.[5] Kruschke (1992, 1996, 2006) argues that, in Stage I, participants associate cues I and PE with E (the more common outcome in that stage). In other words, I acts as a *context cue* (Rescorla & Wagner, 1972; Kruschke & Johansen, 1999), associating with base rates of the outcomes in the experimental context during Stage I (75% E). For participants to respond with L when presented with I.PL, PL's association with L has to overcome cue I's association with E. In contrast, PE→E can remain relatively weak because cue I roots for the same outcome. For this reason, the PL→L association has to be stronger than PE→E. In addition, the learner comes not to pay attention to the misleading cue I when presented with I.PL. As a result of this attention shift, the model learns little about cue I in Stage II, and I's association with E persists.

(2) Stage I: I.PE→E x 3   I.PL→L x 1
     Stage II: I.PE→E x 1   I.PL→L x 3
     Test: PE.PL → ? (L)
                                 I → ? (E)

As we saw in chapter 2, associative learning models suggest that learning rates are faster early in training (Kirkpatrick et al., 1983). As a result, the learner may commit to a view of the world early, making Stage I experience in blocking and overshadowing designs more efficacious in changing connection weights than Stage II experience. This hypothesis is supported by findings that delayed introduction of an informative cue (A→X followed by A→X, AB→Y) leads to decreased reliance on the cue that persists even after hundreds and hundreds of training trials, with reliance on B decreasing as the delay before first exposure to B is increased (Edgell, 1983; Edgell & Morissey, 1987; Kruschke & Johansen, 1999). As few as 20 training-initial trials without a cue appear to result in persistent underutilization of that cue. After 400 trials, cues whose introduction was delayed by 20, 40, or

200 trials catch up with each other but they don't catch up with cues that were there from the start (Edgell, 1983; Edgell & Morrissey, 1987). Kruschke and Johansen (1999, p. 1105) argue that the learners in these experiments decide what to pay attention to very quickly, in an early "exploration" phase, followed by exploitation of cues detected to be informative (see also Trabasso & Bower, 1968). Unless cued that the world has changed, the learners then have no reason to shift attention away from these "tried-and-true" cues. (And even if the world has changed, as when one tries to learn a second language, attention may persist on the cues that are no longer useful; Kruschke, 1996; Lawrence, 1949, 1950.) An optimal Bayesian learner would not show these effects.

At a broader level, note that *cue* competition is not particularly optimal. Following earlier work in *causal learning* (Waldmann & Holyoak, 1992), Bayesian models propose competition between alternative *causes* rather than between alternative *cues*. For example, it makes sense to take evidence for the cat having torn your sweater as evidence against the holes being caused by a moth. But it seems illogical to take evidence for somebody having licked sour cream off your half-eaten dumplings as providing evidence against the window being open, even though both are cues to a cat having sneaked into the house.

Evidence for causal model building in human learning is provided by findings that cue competition is affected by whether cues are thought to be causes or effects of an outcome. For example, Waldmann (2000) presented learners with a set of simulated medical diagnosis trials in which substances in the blood of patients were predictive of various diseases. In one condition, participants were told that the substances were causes of the diseases. In another condition, they were told that the substances were caused *by* the diseases. Participants were asked to rate how well each cue predicted each disease. Some of the cues were redundant. When the substances were causes, participants tended to think that only one of the substances was the real cause for a given disease, giving redundant cues lower predictiveness ratings. When the cues were caused by the diseases, the predictiveness ratings for redundant cues were higher, suggesting reduced cue competition (though see Arcediano et al., 2003; Matute et al., 1996; Waldmann & Walker, 2005, for failures to replicate).

Cue competition only makes sense if one wants to minimize how much time or attention one wants to spend making the decision—that is, if the learner is optimizing criteria other than long-run accuracy (Kruschke & Johansen, 1999). Having seen that the sour cream is missing, one may decide to stop searching for cues to what happened and not check the window, preventing it from influencing your decision. By not checking the window, you forgo some information about what happened, reducing long-run accuracy. But a *rashional* learner has limited time and attention to waste on figuring out who made a hole in his sweater. Having explored enough, we move on.

To maximize accuracy, one should take into account all possible cues to the outcome, weighting each optimally based on how predictive of the outcome it has been. Nonetheless, many experiments show that each individual learner ignores at least some informative cues, weighting others more than they should (Kruschke & Johansen, 1999; L. Thompson, 1994; Trabasso & Bower, 1968, p. 78; Ward et al., 1990). It may be tempting to dismiss this as an artifact of the unnatural categories and tasks used in category learning experiments. However, Idemaru et al. (2012) find stable individual differences in the weighting of cues used to perceive the phonological categories of one's native language, with most listeners paying attention to a limited subset of informative cues. There seems to be too much cue competition for us to be ideal Bayesian learners. In effect conceding the point that human learners possess only limited rationality, Waldmann and Walker (2005, p. 211) retreat to the position that learners have the "competence" to distinguish between cause and effect but "this competence displays itself best in learning situations with few processing demands."

4.5   Outcome Competition as Covert Cue Competition

Arcediano et al. (2005) have reported that competition is not restricted to cues or causes but can also occur with outcomes and effects. This seems distinctly irrational. If I infer that a disease causes a fever, there does not appear to be ansy reason for this inference to reduce my belief in the same disease causing vomiting. (In contrast, if I infer that the fever was caused by the flu, it is rational to not also blame Zika for the same symptom.) While not necessarily rational, outcome competition makes a lot of sense for biological learners. We are not really after accurate beliefs but rather adaptive behavior, and in order to behave as the situation demands, we often need to allocate attention to some outcomes over others. If I infer that the disease causes fever, I should now pay attention to fever so that I can take measures to keep it in check. Because attention is limited, this necessarily involves taking attention away from controlling vomiting, even if I still believe that the disease causes both. The reason there is outcome competition is that, very often, the different outcomes demand different behavioral responses. Since one can do only one thing at a time, one must decide how much control over behavior each outcome should have. If a tone is followed by both shock and a tasty snack, one must decide whether to flee or stay in place. If a meaning can be expressed in two different ways, then on any given occasion, one must choose to produce one or the other.

Behavioral choices have consequences for future learning. No outcome is the final outcome. Running away after hearing the tone will prevent one from experiencing both the shock and the tasty snack. It will therefore prevent you from learning anything more about the tone's consequences. Staying would allow you to learn if the tone's consequences change. Choosing to produce the word *couch* rather than *sofa* to express their shared meaning deprives you of the opportunity to experience the consequences of this lexical choice. Learning feeds into behavior, which feeds into further learning.

4.6 Active Learning: What Do We Seek?

The discussion above highlights the importance of decision making for learning. Bayesian theorists have often criticized associative approaches to learning for viewing the learner as a passive recipient of information, rather than an active explorer who seeks out informative learning experiences (e.g., Kruschke, 2008). An *active learner* can explore the environment, choosing what to learn about next, and even intervening to change the environment to optimize learning opportunities. For example, instead of passively listening to his mother's speech and relying on her to name interesting objects, a child may instead ask her about the names of interesting but not-yet-named objects in his environment, eliciting information that is most useful for him at that stage of his development.

Active learning is clearly important in many learning situations. The learner often knows best, both what she does not yet know, and what she wants to experience next. However, what is it that the learner wants to experience? Under Bayesian conceptions of the ideal learner, the learner seeks information that will maximize the estimated reduction in uncertainty about what the world is like (e.g., Nelson, 2005). Is that really what we seek to sample?

There seem to be clear counterexamples that suggest that the drive to obtain the most informative learning experiences is at least balanced out by the drive to avoid punishments and seek rewards. In an old Soviet movie (*Due to Family Circumstances*, 1977), a speech pathologist repeatedly instructs a child to say the Russian word for "fish," /riba/. Like many

Russian children, the child is unable to properly trill her /r/. Instead of attempting to repeat the word, she therefore chooses to say /sel'otka/, the word for "herring," which lacks the hard-to-say sound. See Schwartz and Leonard (1982) for documentation of this tendency to avoid attempting hard-to-produce words in child speech. Word avoidance has important diachronic consequences, as it pushes hard-to-produce words out of the language (Berg, 1998; Martin, 2007).

Avoiding hard-to-produce words (at least in social contexts) makes perfect sense as a strategy to avoid punishment. However, it is not what an ideal learner would do. An ideal learner would push themselves to practice the sounds that are hard for them, so that they can improve their production. By avoiding hard tasks, one may never learn to accomplish them. For example, an athlete must push themselves hard to practice skills past pain and physical discomfort. Yet not all of us are athletes because it is difficult for somebody to start pushing themselves that hard on their own. Usually, a trainer or community support are required, at least early on. Later on, the trainer is internalized as the athlete's prefrontal executive control circuits flood the cortical-striatal-cortical learning system with blissful dopamine when they practice their skill (Silvetti & Verguts, 2012).

When a child asks her mother about the names of objects around her, does she ask about the names that she estimates will be particularly useful—that is, ones she is most likely to need to know? Perhaps, but how would the child estimate this? Presumably, on the basis of the objects that draw attention: a critter runs past, you ask what it is; a rock, in a field of rocks, does not draw attention and remains nameless. It so happens that the attention-grabbing referents are also ones that are likely to be talked about, so one may indeed end up asking about the most useful words, but that is not *why* one asks about them.

To the extent that we seek information that maximizes uncertainty reduction, this may fall out of the dynamics of attention. Our attention is drawn to novelty (e.g., Samuelson & L. B. Smith, 1998), so we are likely to ask about things we know little about. When something we should really learn about is not something that draws attention, it is learned about slowly. Attention gates knowledge acquisition, and attention is not so controlled as to be insensitive to the purely sensory characteristics of stimuli. Thus, short, easily missed morphemes are not relied on as cues to meaning even when they co-occur with it very reliably (MacWhinney et al., 1985). The inherent loudness of F1 compared to F2 may make listeners rely on the former over the latter as a primary cue to vowel identity (Wanrooij et al.,

2013). Like sensory salience, novelty may affect associability because novel sounds and sights attract attention.

While our active learning is unlikely to be optimally tuned to reducing uncertainty about the world, there is active learning, and it demands decision making. At the most basic level, one must often decide whether to explore the space of the possible, or to stick with what is known to be rewarding, exploiting the knowledge one has already acquired (cf. Aston-Jones & Cohen, 2005; Kaelbling et al., 1996). Ideally, one would also want to learn whether exploration is likely to pay off in the present environment. As noted in chapter 2, the decision to exploit what one has learned may ultimately be responsible for another property of learning that has been argued to undermine associative models, the finding that individual learning curves are often S-shaped (Gallistel et al., 2004): for a while, behavior does not improve with experience but then improves rapidly to a stable level of responding within a short period (less than 10 responses). The rapid shift from not manifesting the behavior to manifesting it is a hallmark of an exploitation decision being made: when a behavior is potentially costly, one waits to accumulate sufficient evidence for its benefits before committing to the behavior and "running with it."

4.7   Generative vs. Discriminative Models

Machine learning models are often divided into two broad classes: *discriminative* and *generative* (Efron, 1975). Most associationist models of learning are discriminative (e.g., Baayen et al., 2011; Rescorla & Wagner, 1972), while Bayesian models are largely generative (e.g., Hsu & Griffiths, 2009, 2010). A discriminative learner tries to directly infer probabilities of unobserved (or not-yet-observed but expected) outcomes given observed cues. The generative learner instead aims to build and update a *causal model* of the world, a representation of what causes the observed stimuli to occur (see also Waldmann, 2000; Waldmann & Holyoak, 1992).

For example, an associationist approach to classic conditioning assumes that the learner tries to predict the unconditioned stimulus (a *reinforcer*, like shock or food) from the conditioned stimulus (say, a tone). However, note that the conditioned stimulus is not the *cause* of the reinforcer. It is merely a *cue* to the reinforcer. If the learner were to turn off the tone, this would not spare him the shock. Ideally, the learner would realize this, although it is not clear how, assuming it is prevented from performing *interventions* (here, turning the tone on or off at will). From a Bayesian perspective, the learner may not always be successful in uncovering the causal structure of

the world but is constantly trying to do so. In the case of classic conditioning, Courville et al. (2006) proposed that the learner assumes that observable stimuli are generated by *latent* (not directly observable) causes. In their
model, the learner therefore tries to infer the set of latent causes generating
cue-reinforcer sequences, the probabilities with which each cause generates each cue-reinforcer sequence, and the probabilities of occurrence of the
various causes themselves.

Bayesian models of speech perception and word recognition (Norris,
2006; Norris & McQueen, 2008) are modern versions of *analysis-by-synthesis*
models (Stevens & Halle, 1967; Liberman et al., 1967; see Bever & Poeppel,
2010, for discussion), proposing that the listener tries to model the production process that has generated the perceived speech. For example, suppose
that the model hears someone pronouncing a word. If that someone is me,
the word would be pronounced in a Russian accent. To someone unfamiliar
with how I (or Russians in general) talk, the sound might be a better acoustic match to the word *kitchen*. The Bayesian perceiver would generate a list
of utterance hypotheses (words I could have said) along with their probabilities in the current context, and retrieve the stored distributions of possible acoustic/perceptual realizations for each. How likely am I to intend to
say "kitchen" vs. "kitten"? This gives you the prior probabilities of the two
hypotheses, "kitchen" and "kitten," $p(H)$. If I were to try to say "kitchen,"
how likely would the perceived sound be to come out? What if I were trying to say "kitten"? These give you the probabilities of the perceived data
given each of the two hypotheses, $p(D|H)$. The model can then decide on
whether I said "kitchen" or "kitten" given the perceived acoustics by applying Bayes's theorem. Learning then consists of learning $p(H)$—how likely
am I to say "kitten"?—and $p(D|H)$—when I intend to say "kitten," what is
likely to come out?—for every H.

Bayesian models of grammar acquisition assume that, upon perceiving
some utterance (sentence, word, etc.), the learner tries to recover the process by which the utterance was generated. For example, O'Donnell (2015)
proposes that upon perceiving a word, the learner tries to estimate the
likelihood of that word having been retrieved holistically from the lexicon
vs. generated from smaller parts using the grammar. If the frequency of a
word in experience is unexpectedly high given the frequencies of its parts
($p(\text{word}=\text{morph}_1,\text{morph}_2) > p(\text{morph}_1)^*p(\text{morph}_2)$), the learner obtains evidence against the hypothesis that the word is generated using the grammar
(by combining morphemes) and therefore evidence for the speaker having
retrieved the word from the lexicon.[6]

In category learning, generative Bayesian models treat categories as generators of members (in the same way that a probability distribution generates samples). The Bayesian category learner estimates the likelihood that the current percept would be generated by sampling from each of the categories stored in memory (Hsu & Griffiths, 2010; F. Xu & Tenenbaum, 2007). Random sampling is usually assumed. However, one can imagine other sampling assumptions. For example, if the category is a category of perceived instances of /i/ produced by a particular speaker, the listener may assume the speaker to preferentially sample instances of /i/ that are far from instances of other categories (see also Vong et al., 2013). As in other *adaptive clustering* approaches, a new category may be induced to fit an ill-fitting stimulus dissimilar from all previously experienced exemplars. In Bayesian models, this means a stimulus none of the known categories are particularly likely to have generated.

Non-Bayesian models can also be generative. For example, Sakamoto et al. (2008) developed a generative error-driven model of category learning, while emphatically rejecting Bayesian optimality (see also Zorzi et al., 2013). What makes their model generative is that it tries to predict upcoming *stimuli* given the current set of categories. Its generative nature allows it to capture the *category variability effect*: when a stimulus lies exactly halfway between the nearest exemplar from a high-variability category and a low-variability one, it tends to be classified into the high-variability category (figure 4.2; Cohen et al., 2001). But its response to this surprise is non-Bayesian, increasing the uncertainty of the generator too much (like that of the SWIM model above). The hypothesis that learners build generative

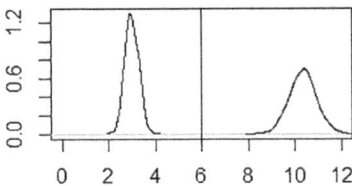

Figure 4.2
A broader category and a narrower category with a point equidistant between the two most confusable members of the two categories indicated by the vertical line. Note that the center of the narrow category is closer to the point indicated by the vertical line. Nonetheless, participants in Cohen et al. (2001) would likely assign the point to the broader category. Both categories contain 1,000 tokens randomly distributed around the mean. The standard deviation of the broad category is twice that of the narrow category.

models of the world to generate predictions and update the models on the basis of whether the predictions are confirmed must be distinguished from the hypothesis that they do so in a statistically normative way.

Generative Bayesian models inherently prefer generators that can only generate a small number of outputs, including restrictive grammars and small categories (Regier & Gahl, 2004). Suppose that you encounter the sentence 'I like cats', and you are considering a grammar that always generates 'I like cats' (Grammar$_1$) and one that can also generate 'Cats I like' (Grammar$_2$). The probability of encountering the observed data ('I like cats') under Grammar$_1$, p('I like cats'|Grammar$_1$), is as high as a probability can be, 100%. The probability of 'I like cats' under Grammar$_2$ is lower, since some of the probability mass is allocated to 'Cats I like'. The same logic applies to word meanings. If you are trying to decide whether *dax* means "Dalmatian" or "dog" upon seeing a picture of a Dalmatian paired with a picture of a Dalmatian dog, the *dax*=Dalmatian hypothesis benefits from its restrictiveness: p(picture of a Dalmatian dog|*dax*, *dax*=Dalmatian)= 100% > p(picture of a Dalmatian dog|*dax*, *dax*=dog). Thus, any examples consistent with two hypotheses differing in restrictiveness provide support for the more restrictive hypothesis, the one that predicts fewer possible data patterns. This is the basis for entrenchment in a Bayesian model.

The bias in favor of the more restrictive hypotheses is a very tempting idea. However, the bias cannot be allowed to run unchecked, as it has a dark side. In particular, the hypothesis that maximizes $p(D|H)$ is always the one that states that all that can happen has already happened. Any generalization beyond what has been experienced is unexpected. As a result, Bayesian models assume that the prior $p(H)$ favors more general hypotheses, the so-called *natural prior* (Rissanen, 1983). The same job is accomplished by corrections for preventing overfitting in standard statistical models, the Akaike and Bayes Information Criteria (AIC and BIC). Like these criteria, the prior is assumed to be sensitive to the number of parameters needed for specifying the model or bits needed to describe the model, disadvantaging more complex models (see Chater et al., 2015; O'Donnell, 2015):

Whether human learners optimally balance fit to the experienced data and model complexity, remains controversial. However, it is likely that selective attention can interfere with this aspect of Bayesian learning as well. By paying attention to a mere subset of dimensions characterizing experienced stimuli, learners can acquire categories that are broader than a Bayesian model would predict. (Kapatsinski et al., 2017)

4.7.1   Generative Models in Purely Perceptual Categorization?
Probably Not

Do we routinely build generative models of the world? Or are we usually content to merely learn contingencies among observed events and cues to what we cannot (yet) observe, discriminating among the predictors of alternative futures? Hsu and Griffiths (2009, 2010) suggest that learners can learn in either a generative or a discriminative fashion depending on what they are asked to predict and what information becomes available first and therefore can serve as the cue.

Hsu and Griffiths (2010) revisited the category variability effect. As in many previous studies, learners were exposed to categories of lines differing in length. Unlike in previous studies, participants were trained without feedback, learning purely by observation, as is typical with natural categories. On each trial, participants in the generative condition were presented with category information first and the exemplar later. Participants in the discriminative condition saw exemplars before category information on each trial. Participants in the generative condition were sensitive to within-category variability, assigning stimuli in between two categories to the more variable one, while those in the discriminative condition were not.

It is, of course, unsurprising that the generative condition (where categories are presented before exemplars) leads participants to predict exemplar characteristics from category labels. Indeed, discriminative models make the same prediction for this condition (Ramscar et al., 2010). The claim behind generative models of perception is that we automatically build generative models of observed events, even when they are not useful for predicting the future from the present. Hsu and Griffiths's (2010) discriminative condition data are not consistent with this proposal, suggesting that participants are unlikely to build generative models of categories during typical, unsupervised, observational category learning.[7] In chapter 5, we revisit this issue for observational learning of speech categories. Compared to learners of visual categories, learners of speech categories have better reason to try to model the generative process behind the categories they learn, as they may be called on to reproduce it.

4.7.2   Generative Models of Language? Perhaps

Hsu and Griffiths (2009) argued that generative models *are* routinely used to learn contingencies between verbs and syntactic constructions. This is a domain where natural language learning appears to make extensive use of entrenchment (Braine & Brooks, 1995; Brooks et al., 1999; Stefanowitsch, 2008; Theakston, 2004): otherwise frequent verbs that do not appear in

certain constructions are taken to be *ineligible* to occur in these constructions. For example, both *disappear* and *vanish* are almost never followed by
direct objects but English speakers judge *He disappeared it* as being worse
than *He vanished it* (Theakston, 2004). Since *disappear* is more frequent than
vanish, *disappeared it* has a higher *expected frequency* than *vanished it* under
the hypothesis that it can be freely followed by direct objects: $p(disappeared$
$it|disappear$ can be transitive) $> p(vanished$ $it|vanish$ can be transitive), making the implicit negative evidence against the transitivity of *disappear*
stronger than implicit evidence against the transitivity of *vanish*. Arppe et
al.'s (2014) implementation of the discriminative Rescorla-Wagner (1972)
model does not predict entrenchment: *disappear* and *vanish* are equally
predictive cues to the absence of a following direct object. Neither does
logistic regression (Hsu & Griffiths, 2009). The fact that learners of natural
languages do exhibit entrenchment effects is therefore taken to suggest that
they do use generative models in learning syntactic contingencies from perceptual input.

Hsu and Griffiths (2009) also show that participants can be made to
learn "discriminatively" (as evidenced by failing to show entrenchment)
when they are presented with grammatical and ungrammatical sentences,
asked to judge each sentence as grammatical or not, and then provided
with feedback on the accuracy of their judgments. However, given how
unnatural this learning task is, the finding does not provide evidence for
discriminative learning of syntax in the real world: real language learners do not face the task of discriminating grammatical from ungrammatical sentences, and indeed do not hear ungrammatical sentences labeled
as such.

Thus, the results of Hsu and Griffiths (2009, 2010) appear to provide
support for generative learning of syntactic constructions and discriminative learning of perceptual categories. It appears plausible to assume, as a
working hypothesis, that generative learning may play a role in domains
where the perceiver is also a producer. Under this hypothesis, when perceiving syntactic input, the listener attempts to construct a model of how this
input was generated because they themselves will need (or perhaps are currently attempting) to generate it. This is the usual case in language learning,
with the possible exception of speaker-specific variation that the listener
does not wish, for whatever sociolinguistic reasons, to emulate.

In contrast, typical nonlinguistic category learning and Pavlovian classical conditioning involve stimuli of which the perceiver is not the producer. Indeed, outside of *active learning* experiments in which the learner
can intervene to influence the stimuli presented to him (Kruschke, 2008),
the perceiver has no active control over whether the sensation will occur.

In such a situation, the perceiver may be content to learn predictive contingencies between environmental events (via error-driven *discriminative learning*). Without the ability to intervene in the world, the causal links underlying one's experience are very difficult to discover. Thus, Pavlov's dog cannot tinker with the bell to see whether the bell *causes* food to appear or is merely indicative of the food's appearance. The true generative model is not always inferable from perceptual input.

In chapter 6 I show that entrenchment *is* predicted by associative models as long as outcome absences are less salient than present outcomes, a rather sensible assumption (e.g., Wasserman et al., 1990; Levin et al., 1993; Kao & Wasserman, 1993; Tassoni, 1995) that even has a Bayesian explanation: any stimulus is present less often than it is absent, which makes presences more informative than absences (McKenzie & Mikkelsen, 2007). The Rescorla-Wagner model as implemented by Arppe et al. (2014) treats unexpectedly present and absent outcomes identically and therefore fails to predict entrenchment, but this is merely a simplifying assumption, not one inherent in discriminative learning models. Finally, the perceiver can also learn to be a producer by learning *bidirectionally*, rather than assigning one direction the privileged causal status. Therefore Hsu and Griffiths's (2009) arguments for generative learning in "*bidirectional domains*" can also be used to support bidirectional associative learning.

4.8 Conclusion

Accuracy is a good thing. Other things being equal, a learner wants to hold accurate beliefs about the world. However, accuracy of belief is desirable only if it produces adaptive behavior in a reasonable time. It is only achievable if getting there does not require one to suffer intense punishments, forgo valuable rewards, or expend great effort with no reward in sight. Learning is often not optimal or rational. However, it is *rashional*: it produces behavior that can be learned fast enough, that rewards more than it punishes (within the *foreseeable* future), and does not cost too much time or other resources to plan and execute.

The Bayesian turn in cognitive science has forced learning theory to tackle issues it paid little attention to, particularly issues having to do with confidence in belief as a possible outcome of learning. Confidence naturally falls out of generative Bayesian models and is the most obvious explanation for entrenchment effects. Nonetheless, it is always worth considering the possibility that what looks like sophisticated statistical inference can be simple associative learning. We return to the category variability effect in chapter 5 and entrenchment in chapter 6.

5   Continuous Dimensions and Distributional Learning

> The mind can always intend, and know when it intends, to think of the Same.
> —William James (1890, vol.1, p. 459)

The associationist framework conceives of learning as updating connection weights between cues and outcomes, and perhaps merging these units into larger units. Importantly, cues and outcomes are discrete. This discreteness at first appears incompatible with the fact that we live in a continuous space. A vowel token has a specific duration and specific formant trajectories that can be measured on continuous scales. Different tokens of the same vowel have different values on these dimensions, a cloud of individual exemplars that can be described with a multivariate distribution. Bayesian models—where all knowledge is knowledge of distributions, and all learning is inference about the continuous parameters defining the distributions (such as mean and variance)—seem to be a more intuitive tool for dealing with a fundamentally continuous environment. Yet in many cases continuity is only apparent. For example, the sound spectrum is discretized by the cochlea, which is well described by a set of bandpass filters (e.g., X. Yang et al., 1992). Furthermore, many categories people learn are difficult to describe with a parametric distribution (Ashby & Waldron, 1999). In this chapter, I argue that there are also insights to be gained by treating values or intervals on continua as cues, just like the other cues we have already examined. We begin by describing associationist approaches to dimensions, essentially ways to discretize a continuum into a set of cues. We then proceed to examine what we learn from distributions along continua, showing that the effects of selective attention we have encountered in chapter 3 also affect cues that appear to be points on an acoustic continuum.

5.1   Dimensions

Cues comprising a stimulus are not an unstructured set. In particular, certain cues can be thought of as being organized into *dimensions*, sets of cues that represent values of some parameter and are therefore mutually incompatible. Width and height of a rectangle, red, green, and blue values of a color, pitch, intensity, F1 and F2 of a vowel, are all examples of dimensions. Evidence for the psychological reality of dimensions comes from the finding that selective attention can target dimensions as well as cues, demonstrated by Kruschke (1996) using the design shown in figure 5.1.

In Kruschke's experiment, the participants first learned a categorization pattern that required attending to two out of the three dimensions describing the stimuli and then were asked to learn another categorization that involved paying attention to only one dimension, which could be either one of the previously relevant dimensions (relevant shift) or the previously irrelevant dimension (irrelevant shift). Irrelevant shifts were harder to learn than relevant shifts, despite the two types of shift involving the same number of cue-outcome reassignments. Kruschke concluded that irrelevant shifts are harder than relevant ones because they involve shifting attention to a dimension previously learned to be irrelevant.

Figure 5.1
Design of Kruschke's (1996) experiment providing evidence for selective attention to dimensions using stylized train car pictures. The cars differed on three dimensions: height, wheel color, and door location. Participants had to learn what cars contained gold. In Stage I, two of the dimensions (here, wheel color and door location) jointly determined whether the car had gold. The third dimension was irrelevant, as shown by gray shading. In Stage II, attention needed to be reallocated: the presence of gold was now determined by a single dimension. Relevant shifts shifted attention to a previously relevant dimension, here wheel color or door location. Irrelevant shifts required shifting attention to the previously irrelevant dimension, here car height. Note that the number of individual cue-category reassignments was constant across shift types (shown by crossing out the outcomes that are unexpected given Stage I training in the rightmost column). Nonetheless, relevant shifts were easier than irrelevant ones.

Attention to dimensions suggests that cues comprising a dimension have something in common. This could be handled by treating each cue as a combination of cues, one specifying (for example) that it is a wheel color cue, and the other specifying the exact color. In other words, a dimension can be thought of as simply a category of cues.

Stage I:

Wheel color	Door location	Car height	Has gold?
Black	Right	Low	+
Black	Left	Low	-
White	Left	Low	+
White	Right	Low	-
Black	Right	High	+
Black	Left	High	-
White	Left	High	+
White	Right	High	-

Stage II: Relevant shift

Wheel color	Door location	Car height	Has gold?
Black	Right	Low	+
Black	Left	Low	+
White	Left	Low	-
White	Right	Low	-
Black	Right	High	+
Black	Left	High	+
White	Left	High	-
White	Right	High	-

Stage II: Irrelevant shift

Wheel color	Door location	Car height	Has gold?
Black	Right	Low	+
Black	Left	Low	+
White	Left	Low	+
White	Right	Low	+
Black	Right	High	-
Black	Left	High	-
White	Left	High	-
White	Right	High	-

Treating the various cues comprising a dimension as *compound*, configural cues containing an identifier for the dimension is sufficient to deal with *nominal* dimensions, where the cues comprise an unordered set. However, it seems insufficient for representing *quantitative dimensions*. Cues comprising a quantitative dimension can be arranged in a linear sequence so that distance in the sequence corresponds inversely to similarity. We can again treat each cue as a compound cue consisting of smaller elements, making sure that similar cues share elements (as shown in figure 5.2). The challenge is that the learner often appears to be aware of nonlocal similarity structure so that, for example, knowing that cue CD in figure 5.2 maps onto outcome X and cue DE maps onto outcome Y would lead the learner to conclude that HI is more likely to map onto Y than onto X and AB is more likely to map onto X than onto Y. This is not captured by the similarity *chain* coding in figure 5.2: HI shared nothing with either DE or CD and is therefore equally dissimilar to both. It should therefore be as likely to map onto X as onto Y. Figure 5.3 illustrates a coding that is capable of supporting the required inference (called the *thermometer coding*). Thermometer coding allows true quantitative dimensions to be represented within a cue-based framework.

In language, quantitative dimensions can be found in both phonetics and semantics. Some evidence for acoustic dimensions being represented as dimensions is provided by Escudero and Boersma (2004), who report that native Spanish listeners pay attention to duration as a cue to the English tense/lax vowel distinction (e.g., *neat* vs. *knit*), but they do not always know

Outcomes:	?	X	← X	Y →	Y	?	?	?
Cues:	AB	BC	CD	DE	EF	FG	GH	HI

Figure 5.2
Inference on a quantitative dimension: chain coding.

Outcomes:	X		← X		Y →		Y		Y...
Cues:	011111		001111		000111		00011		000001

Figure 5.3
Inference on a quantitative dimension: thermometer coding.

which vowel is longer than the other. This finding suggests that Spanish listeners know to attend to the dimension of duration before knowing how duration values map onto the L2 sound categories. As a result, some exhibit a spontaneous reversal shift.

As noted above, many if not all quantitative dimensions are only seemingly continuous. The cochlea and the retina contain discrete cells tuned to respond to particular incoming signals, making a discrete, cue-based coding appropriate for modeling the *perceptual*—as opposed to physical—reality. What makes us able to discriminate fine distinctions between arbitrary points on visual or acoustic continua despite the discreteness of the detectors is (1) the large number of such detectors, and (2) the fact that each detector is partially activated by stimuli that are merely similar to the one the detector responds to most strongly. As a result, multiple detectors are activated by any one stimulus, with the ones tuned to the most similar stimuli activated most strongly. In the translation from input to intake, gradient physical similarity is transformed into patterns of continuous activation over discrete nodes. While any one node is limited in the discrminations it can perform, since it can only discriminate between the stimuli in and out of its *receptive field*, a population of nodes can jointly represent arbitrarily fine distinctions between stimuli (Georgopoulos et al., 1986).

As illustrated by figures 5.2 and 5.3, the population coding appropriate for a particular dimension can be inferred on the basis of *extrapolation* patterns in behavior. An interesting example is the in/on dimension discovered by Bowerman and Pederson (1992; see also Gentner & Bowerman, 2009, p. 469). This dimension ranges from meanings like "a cup on a table" to "a bandaid on a leg" to "a picture on a wall" to "an apple on a branch" to "a ribbon on a candle" to "an apple in a bowl." It appears that all languages use appositions to refer to continuous intervals on this dimension. For example, there are no languages in which there is a preposition that can be used to refer to a cup on a table and to a ribbon on a candle but not to a picture on a wall. An interesting question for our purposes is whether this dimension is mentally represented as a chain or as a thermometer scale. Stave and Pederson (2016) have investigated this question empirically. Native English speakers were exposed to a miniature artificial language in which the interval referred to in English by *on* was split between two spatial appositions. Participants were trained on intermediate cases (e.g., 'a picture on a wall' → *zuk*, 'a bandaid on a leg' → *kwim*) and tested on generalization to the more extreme cases varying in distance from the intermediate cases seen in training. The results were not consistent with the *in-on* cline being thermometer-coded: there was little correlation between distance on the continuum between training and test referents and probability of generalizing, with several distinct clusters of related meanings emerging.

Acoustic/auditory dimensions like F1 appear to be even more likely candidates for being represented with thermometer coding. Nonetheless, chain coding schemes have been proposed even for these clearly continuous parameters. Boersma (1998) notes that the chain scheme he favors predicts the result displayed in figure 5.2. For example, front vowel tokens with F1 much lower than that of any experienced vowel examples would be equally likely to be classified as [i] and [æ] despite being acoustically maximally far from [æ] on the F1 dimension. This prediction is disputed by K. Johnson et al. (1993), who find that [i]'s with extremely low (unpronounceably low!) F1 values are more likely to be classified as [i] than typical [i]'s. In the categorization literature, the same phenomenon is known under the name of *peak shift* because peak identification accuracy for a category is reached not at the value of the dimension experienced most often in category exemplars but at values farthest away from values experienced as examples of other categories (Holt et al., 1998; Kluender et al., 1998; Purtle, 1973; Rosch & Mervis, 1975; Spence, 1936). Peak shift appears to be fairly common when the more frequently experienced stimuli near category boundaries are likely to be misperceived as belonging to the wrong category (Livesey & McLaren, 2011). With vowel categories like [i], between-category discrimination is often relatively low because of the high degree of variability in realizations of a vowel across speakers and contexts. Thus, peak shift is expected to occur with vowel categories and other stimuli where the category boundaries are relatively fuzzy. Depending on the magnitude of the shift, thermometer coding may be required to account for the effect.

5.2 Within-Category Variability and Extrapolation

Rips (1989) asked human participants to judge whether a two-inch circular object is more similar to a US quarter coin or a pizza. They judged it to be more like a quarter. Nonetheless, they also thought it more likely to *be* a pizza. This is eminently sensible behavior: all quarters are essentially the same size, while pizzas can be any size. So, even though a two-inch object is less like a typical pizza than like a typical quarter, it *could* be a pizza but could not plausibly be a quarter.

Several studies of the *category variability effect* followed up on Rips (1989) by manipulating category exposure so that within-category variance was the only thing that differed between competing categories, and the test example was equidistant from the nearest experienced example of each category. An example of such a design is shown in figure 4.1, repeated here as figure 5.4 for convenience. A perceptual continuum is split into two normally distributed categories. The vertical line shows the test stimulus, equidistant from the nearest experienced members of the two categories.

Much of the literature on category learning has been dominated by the debate between *exemplar* and *prototype* models, both of which assume that a novel stimulus is compared to the representations of the competing categories, but differ in what category representations are thought to contain. Exemplar models represent categories as collections of individual experiences with category examples. Prototype models assume that the category is represented by its center and a measure of variability. However, according to both models, the learner should classify the test stimulus into the narrower category (Cohen et al., 2001; Sakamoto et al., 2008). At any distance from the test stimulus, there are at least as many narrow-category examples within that distance as there are broad-category examples. If these examples vote for the category the test stimulus should belong to, as exemplar models suggest (Nosofsky, 1986), the stimulus would be classified into the narrow category. The *prototype* (center) of the narrow category is also closer to the test stimulus than the center of the broad category. As discussed in chapter 4, the category variability effect appears to be inconsistent with discriminative models of categorization, which include both exemplar and prototype models. In contrast, it is predicted by generative models of categorization, which decide on the category for a stimulus by estimating the likelihood of a sample from each category matching the stimulus. Because the broad category has higher variance, sampling from it is more likely to produce an outlier value, making the category more likely to be extended beyond the range of experienced examples.

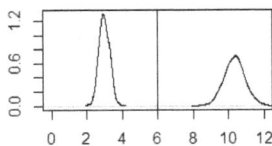

Figure 5.4
A broader category and a narrower category with a point equidistant between the two most confusable members of the two categories indicated by the vertical line. Note that the center of the narrow category is closer to the point indicated by the vertical line. Nonetheless, participants in Cohen et al. (2001) would likely assign the point to the broader category.

Interestingly, the situation for discriminative models becomes less dire if we consider that the learner represents the horizontal dimension in figure 5.4 as a set of binary cues corresponding to *receptive fields* of detectors sensitive to particular intervals on a perceptual dimension or regions in a multidimensional perceptual space (following the basic intuition behind thermometer coding). As shown in figure 5.5, there will be a relatively narrow interval containing all examples of the narrower category. Whether a stimulus falls in that interval is a highly discriminative cue. By weighting that cue highly (e.g., learning to attend to D_6 and ignore less informative intervals), a discriminative learner can avoid classifying the test stimulus into the narrower category. While there will also be an interval comprising all examples of the more diverse category (here $D_{2...4}$), it will of necessity be broader. It appears to be a basic design principle of the brain that receptors with narrower fields send activation and inhibition up to receptors with broader fields (e.g., McClelland & Elman, 1986; Mirman et al., 2006; Norris, 1994). Whenever an example of A is presented, $D_{2...4}$ will be only partially activated, as either D_2, D_3, or D_4 will fire while others will send up inhibition. In contrast, D_6 will always be activated completely by examples of B. Thus, D_6 provides a stronger signal of category identity than $D_{2...4}$.

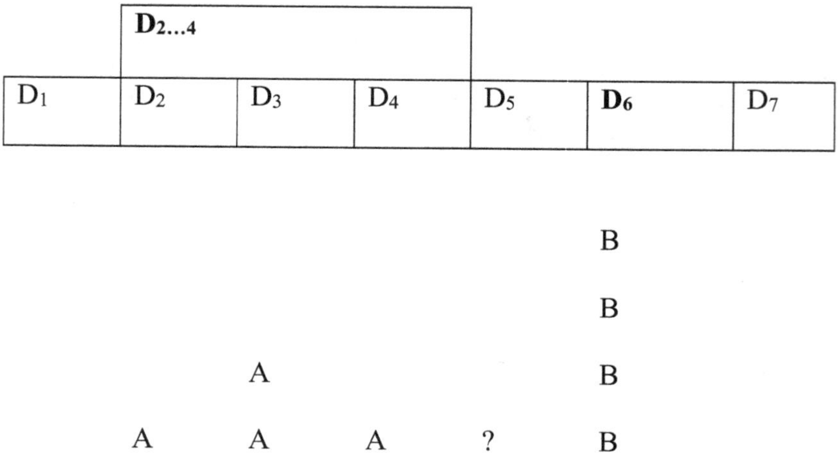

D_1	D_2	D_3	D_4	D_5	D_6	D_7
	$D_{2...4}$ (spans D_2–D_4)					
					B	
					B	
		A			B	
	A	A	A	?	B	

Figure 5.5
Two categories on a dimension (A and B) and a test stimulus (?). Representing a dimension as a set of intervals (binary dimensions $D_{1...7}$). D_6 is very informative about whether a stimulus is in B. By weighting D_6 highly, one can make D_6 (near-)necessary for belonging to B and capture the subjects' tendency to categorize "?" as an A.

Proposing that there is a detector for every interval on every perceptual dimension is clearly untenable, as there would be an infinite number of these. However, Kruschke (1992) suggested that receptive field breadth could be adapted to the discrimination tasks facing the learner, so that a single detector can be allocated to a wide region of perceptual space if the learner has no need to discriminate among points within that space. Thus, a limited number of detectors can adapt their receptive fields to the distribution of stimuli in perceptual experience through error-driven learning.

5.3   Distributions and Distributional Learning

The kind of learning observed in the studies reviewed in this chapter is often called *distributional learning* because the learner is thought to acquire knowledge of a *frequency distribution*: how often various kinds of stimuli occur in the environment.

When stimuli are represented by categorical dimensions, one has little choice but to tally how often each value or set of values occurs. One's knowledge of the distribution can then be described as knowledge of these tallied frequencies, possibly distorted by attention into knowledge of *log* frequencies. However, with continuous dimensions (and ordinal dimensions treated as continuous), one has an alternative, which is to acquire *summary statistics* describing the distribution. Equipped with a prior about the shape of the distribution, learners can then avoid having to learn the exact shape of the distribution. For example, if a learner assumes that distributions s/he is exposed to are normal, s/he can get away with learning only two numbers per distribution: the mean and the variance, as the two numbers completely describe the distribution. This considerably simplifies the learning task, if the distributions in the environment are in fact normal.

Whether one can get away with learning only summary statistics has been a topic of intense controversy in psychology, constituting the core of the debate between *prototype models*, which maintain that summary statistics are sufficient, and *exemplar models*, which maintain that they are not and that a distribution is represented by memorizing every instance it consists of (Ashby & Waldron, 1999). More recent *clustering* approaches to category learning can be seen as interpolations between the two extremes of memorizing only the center and variance of a distribution and memorizing every example on which the distribution is based. Faced with a complex distribution that cannot be easily summarized by a small set of statistics, these models attempt to decompose it into a set of simpler distributions that are more amenable to summary description (e.g., Vanpaemel &

Storms, 2008). Bayesian models often assume a distribution in practice but are also capable of inducing the most likely family of distributions that generated the data—for example, estimating how likely it is that the data have come from a normal vs. exponential vs. uniform distribution (Flannagan et al., 1986).

Identifying the distribution behind the observed data is potentially useful for extrapolating beyond the experienced values on the dimension, predicting how likely various unobserved dimension values are to be encountered in the future. For example, suppose you sampled a dictionary and did not find the most frequent word with a certain characteristic (the word with frequency above 15,000 in the top panel of figure 5.6).[1] If you then tried to estimate how frequent words of that kind could be by using a normal distribution (in the bottom panel of figure 5.6), you would never have

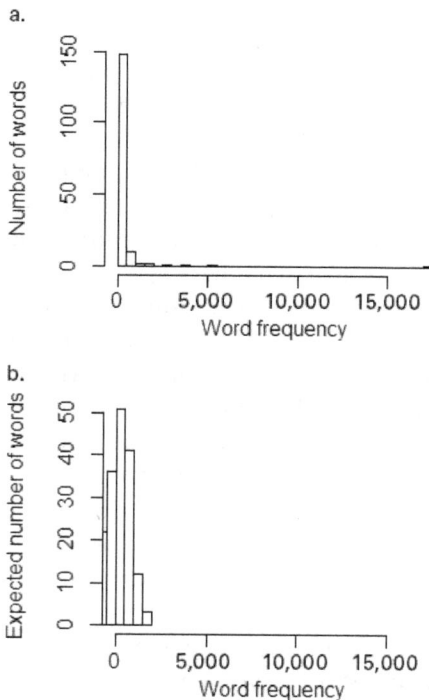

Figure 5.6
A Zipfian distribution (top): frequencies of Russian adjectives beginning with a certain prefix, and a normal distribution with the same mean and standard deviation as the distribution on the top if we excluded the most frequent word (bottom).

guessed that its frequency could be as high as its actual frequency. In fact, even if you draw 1,000,000 samples from the normal distribution on the right, you would not find one value as high as 5,000. On the other hand, you would also think that word frequencies can easily be negative, which is of course nonsensical. The same caution holds for other data with a highly skewed distribution. For example, Silver (2011) argues that the probabilities of catastrophic earthquakes in particular areas are often underestimated by underestimating the skew of the distribution of earthquake magnitudes. Unfortunately, earthquake magnitudes follow a Zipfian distribution. If one observes that earthquakes in a certain area tend not to exceed a certain modest magnitude, much larger earthquakes could still occur there.

These examples show that knowing the shape of the distribution that your sample of observations has come from is highly informative for making predictions about future events. However, identifying the distribution type is a hard task. Furthermore, a limited degree of extrapolation can also be accomplished without acquiring a *distribution*, instead using a *nonparametric* representation (much like the histograms in figure 5.6) tracking how frequently one has encountered values falling into the various intervals on the dimension in question (Ashby & Waldron, 1999). For example, in exemplar models, one extrapolates which category new stimuli belong to by comparing the new stimuli to stored examples of stimuli from each category (e.g., Nosofsky, 1986; Pierrehumbert, 2001).[2]

Ashby and Waldron (1999) argue that learners don't come to the task of learning visual categories with a strong multivariate normality assumption. They presented participants with samples from nonnormally distributed categories of lines varying in length and orientation that were too small to confidently rule out the normal distribution hypothesis. Therefore, a learner with a normality assumption should have assumed the categories to be bivariate normal. Yet participants did not infer normally distributed categories, instead appearing to extrapolate category membership to new exemplars on the basis of similar known exemplars. However, it is not known whether the same result would hold for speech sound categories, which could be argued to center on a production target, or for categories defined by single dimensions.

We know rather little about distributional learning over continuous speech dimensions. In psycholinguistics, empirical work on the issue started in earnest with the publication of May et al. (2002). Maye and colleagues noted that infants seem to acquire the sound categories (phonemes) of their native language during the first few months of life. This learning manifests itself in the infants becoming better at discriminating sounds that belong to different categories and *worse* at discriminating sounds that belong to the same category (Kuhl et al., 1992; Werker & Tees, 1984). While they learn some words really early (Bergelson & Swingley, 2012), their lexica remain quite sparse for years (Storkel, 2004). This means that they cannot discover phonemes the way linguists do, by comparing minimally different pairs of words like *cat* and *cap*, and identifying sounds as belonging to different phonemes if exchanging them changes the word meaning: there are few minimal pairs in the infant's lexicon. Maye et al. instead proposed that sound categories are first discovered by infants distributionally. Assuming that, for every category, most productions cluster around the category center, one can identify categories as "humps" on the frequency distribution. For example, the distribution in figure 5.7 suggests the existence of two categories, one centered just below zero, and another centered around 25.

Distributional learning is not just for categories of sounds. In particular, Dautriche et al. (2016) extend the idea to semantic categories, suggesting that children can identify whether a word has one abstract meaning or multiple concrete meanings by tracking the distribution of the word's referents in semantic space. Referents of a word with a single abstract meaning will be uniformly (unimodally) distributed through a region of semantic space, while those of a word with multiple concrete meanings will form distinct clusters, a bi- or multimodal distribution (see also Suttle & Goldberg, 2011). As we will see below, distributional learning can also be used to learn categories of faces and other visual stimuli varying on continuous parameters (Gureckis & Goldstone, 2008; Hendrickson et al., 2012).

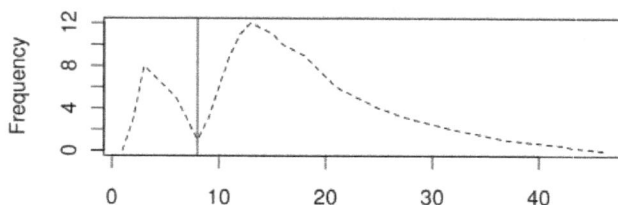

Figure 5.7
A bimodal distribution along an acoustic parameter corresponding to two sound categories. For example, if the parameter is VOT, the left hump would be voiced sounds and the right hump aspirated sounds. A learner classifying sounds on the basis of distributional learning should learn to distinguish between sounds to the right and left of the vertical line, placing a category boundary at 8. In contrast, sounds on one side of the vertical line should be treated as being the same.

Maye and colleagues tested the distributional learning hypothesis by exposing infants and adults to either a bimodal distribution or a unimodal distribution along the VOT continuum (figure 5.8). For example, Maye et al. (2008) found that infants in the bimodal condition perked up when presented with a stimulus with VOT equal to −50 ms after being bored by repeated presentation of a stimulus with VOT equal to +10 ms, whereas infants exposed to the unimodal condition were as bored by −50 following 10 as by 10 following 10. Since infants perk up when they hear something new and exciting, this finding is consistent with the unimodal-trained infants perceiving stops with −50 or +10 VOT as being the same, and bimodal infants perceiving them as being different. In English, all of the sounds with VOT less than +25 ms would be perceived as voiceless. Therefore these data provide evidence for learning in the bimodal condition— splitting the "voiceless stop" category in two but not necessarily in the unimodal condition.

5.4 The Mechanisms behind Distributional Learning

Gureckis and Goldstone (2008) showed that a bimodal distribution within an explicitly taught category is nonetheless noticed by learners, in their case adults. Participants were presented with faces forming a two-dimensional similarity space. Participants were explicitly trained to categorize along one of the two orthogonal dimensions the faces differed on. They were never told about the other dimension, or the clustering along that dimension.

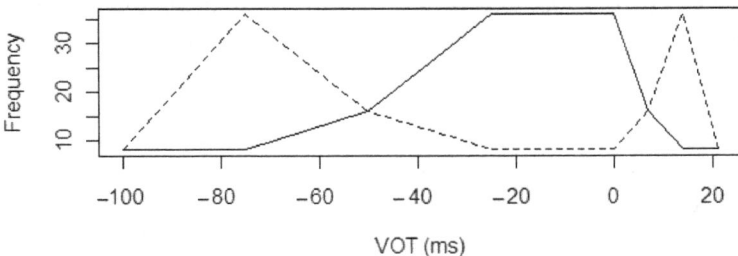

Figure 5.8
The bimodal (solid line) and unimodal (dashed line) training distributions from Maye et al. (2008, p. 125). Note that the two lines cross at VOT equal to −50 ms and +10 ms. These stimuli were therefore equally frequent during training for both groups. Thus, any differences in how they are treated cannot be attributed to the frequencies of these specific stimuli but rather to the overall VOT distribution during training.

In fact, they were trained to ignore it, assigning faces to the same category regardless of their values on the second dimension. Discrimination was tested for pairs of near-identical faces in an XAB procedure before and after training: participants would see a face, which would then be replaced by a pair of faces, one identical to what they'd just seen. They would have to judge which face was the same as the face that had just disappeared. Discrimination improved over the course of training both for pairs of faces belonging to different categories and, crucially, for faces belonging to different "humps" within a category but not for equally dissimilar faces belonging to the same hump. These results suggest that distributional learning can improve discrimination of stimuli that belong to different humps of the distribution, even when feedback indicates that the distinct humps belong to the same category. In other words, categories are inferred not only when they are predictive of labels or other attributes but also on the basis of bottom-up stimulus frequency tracking.

Another demonstration of the importance of distributional information has been provided by Harmon et al. (2017). We were interested in persuading English speakers to downweight the VOT dimension in deciding on voicing, switching attention to the secondary cue dimension, F0 of the following vowel. As discussed above, switching attention away from a previously informative dimension is an important task facing many second language learners. For example, Japanese speakers learning English need to shift attention away from F2 and onto F3 in order to learn to distinguish English [ɹ] from [l], and Spanish speakers need to switch attention away from duration and toward spectral cues to distinguish English tense and lax vowels (see Escudero, 2005, for a review). We sought to determine whether distributional learning can help effect this kind of extradimensional attention shift.

To this end, we had adult native English speakers listen to stimuli differing in VOT from a clear *bear* to a clear *pear* (5 ms to 45 ms). They used the computer mouse to click on a picture of what they thought they heard. They then were provided with feedback. Importantly, this feedback was 50% *pear* and 50% *bear* for every value of VOT, indicating that VOT is uninformative about voicing (or perhaps the semantic difference between bears and pears). Therefore, paying attention to F0 could only get them to 50% correct. On the other hand, F0 was perfectly predictive of voicing, displaying an exaggerated version of the English pattern. Thus, low F0 (180 Hz) was always *bear* and high F0 was always *pear*. Crucially, we manipulated the distribution of the stimuli along the VOT dimension, as shown in figure 5.9. Interestingly, error-driven learning models suggest that the feedback

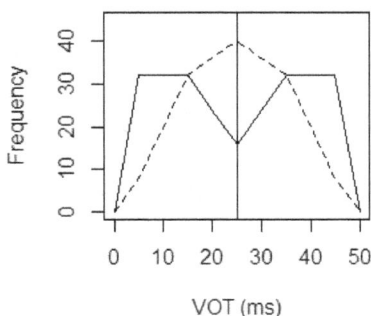

Figure 5.9
The unimodal (dashed) and bimodal (solid) VOT distributions presented to participants by Harmon et al. (2017). The vertical line shows the most ambiguous VOT value prior to training.

should be more effective with the bimodal distribution. Note that when VOT is equal to 25 ms, our English speakers tend to respond with *bear* and *pear* about half the time without training. Therefore, 50/50 feedback for the 25 ms VOT is consistent with the participants' prior beliefs and should, if anything, reinforce these beliefs. In other words, for 25 ms VOT, 50/50 feedback is perfectly consistent with VOT being informative about voicing. In contrast, when VOT is smaller or larger than 25 ms, 50/50 feedback provides evidence that VOT should be downweighted. The bimodal condition presents participants with many more trials of the latter type, compared to the unimodal condition, which often presents participants with 25 ms VOT followed by uninformative feedback. Surprisingly, we found that participants downweighted VOT and upweighted F0 only when VOT was distributed unimodally.

An intuitive way to think of these two conditions is to imagine two speakers. The first speaker produces clear [p]'s and [b]'s but has no idea which words have which sound. This is the speaker of our bimodal condition. The second speaker tends to produce sounds that are intermediate between [p] and [b] so you are not sure which sound they are trying to say half the time. This is our unimodal speaker. Which speaker would cause you to downweight the primary cue to the [p]/[b] distinction more quickly? Our results suggest that it is the second speaker, even though the first speaker provides a clearer error signal.

The results of these two studies suggest that categories can be induced purely on the basis of distributional information. We do not yet know what mechanism is responsible for this process. One candidate explanation for our data is that listeners are building a generative model of the speaker. When the speaker's productions are unimodally distributed along the VOT dimension, this suggests that the speaker has one production target along that dimension, at 25 ms. Because no one's articulation is perfect, they don't always hit the target exactly, but they are trying to always produce the same thing. In this case, variation along VOT is clearly random noise and cannot bear meaning (such as the contrast between *bear* and *pear*). In contrast, the bimodal speaker appears to have two production targets, which suggests that there may be something conditioning his choices of VOT values. This explanation appears plausible for speech sound categories because we don't usually want to only understand speech of others but also to be able to reproduce the sounds we hear, and building a generative model of the speaker would kill these two birds with one stone.

However, the results of Gureckis and Goldstone (2008) are not easily accounted for in this way, especially given that Hsu and Griffiths (2010) did not find evidence for generative model building in visual category learning (chapter 4). One plausible mechanism to account for their results is receptive field adjustment (Kruschke, 1992). When one encounters two very different stimuli—a likely situation when encountering a sample from a bimodal distribution though not an inevitable one—each stimulus is allocated a distinct receptor with a narrow receptive field (e.g., D_3 and D_6 in figure 5.5). As one continues encountering stimuli, many fall within the receptive fields of the original detectors, strengthening them, while others fall nearby, causing expansion of the receptive field. For example, a stimulus in D_2 activates D_3, which causes the detector's receptive field to expand to $D_{2...3}$. This proposal is supported by the results of Wanrooij et al. (2015), who argue that it is not bimodality per se that matters but the fact that the stimuli in the bimodal condition are more diverse. An interesting prediction of this account is that it should be possible to present a bimodal distribution in such a way as to prevent participants from forming two categories, namely by presenting the stimuli between the two modes first (cf. Sakamoto et al., 2008). This prediction remains to be tested.

Although receptive field adjustment is a plausible explanation for Gureckis and Goldstone (2008), it is difficult to imagine it being able to account for the data in Harmon et al. (2017). Gureckis and Goldstone have examined categorization involving novel dimensions, constructed by morphing two endpoint face stimuli, and consisting of a complex composite of visual features. Our stimuli, on the other hand, involved reweighting a familiar dimension (VOT), which participants have already split into categories that they use thousands of times every day to understand their native language. It is difficult to imagine that participants would be merging together receptive fields of VOT category detectors on the basis of a short laboratory training (see also Escudero, 2005). It may well be that multiple mechanisms are responsible for distributional learning effects. Later in this chapter, we will see evidence that error-driven learning may be involved as well, except at the level of predicting upcoming sounds rather than semantic or phonological interpretations. Distributional learning may not be a unique learning mechanism but rather the outcome of a number of learning mechanisms working together.

5.5 Salience of the Unexpected in Distributional Learning

While existing studies on distributional learning in speech have taught us a great deal about the circumstances that lead to category learning, they do not directly probe what participants learn from their experience with a distribution. Do participants exposed to distributions learn the distributions they are presented with veridically? For example, subjects in Gureckis and Goldstone's (2008) study are exposed to uniform distributions within the clusters: stimuli within the clusters are equally common, while stimuli outside the clusters have zero probability of occurring. Is this what the participants infer? Or do they think (for example) that the distributions are normal with a center in the middle of the cluster? If so, how do they identify this middle? Is it the mean, the median, the mode, the center of the range, or some other measure of central tendency?

A few studies in very different domains have tried elucidating the outcome of distributional learning. Lindskog et al. (2013) have probed explicit knowledge of distribution shape by asking for judgments of what proportion of the stimuli fall into various intervals on the dimension of interest. In their studies, the stimuli were revenues of companies, which were either bimodally or unimodally (normally) distributed. Participants were very good at reproducing the unimodal distribution but tended to make the bimodal distribution less bimodal. Lindskog et al. (2013) argue that this bias toward unimodality is expected if distributional learning is *lazy*: when exposed to examples varying on some dimension, they simply store the dimension values as they come in, building up a histogram much like the one in figure 5.6, rather than extracting summary statistics about the distribution. When queried about the shape of the distribution, they draw a sample of experienced examples from memory. A small sample from a bimodal distribution is quite likely to be unimodal, resulting in a bias in favor of unimodal, single-peaked distributions. A role for memory retrieval processes is also suggested by the results of Hubert-Wallander and Boynton (2015), who report that dimension values experienced first and last exert a disproportional influence on the estimated mean value for physical dimensions of visual stimuli, mirroring the primacy and recency effects observed in studies of recall.

Hubert-Wallander and Boynton (2015) is one example of a line of studies that have focused on what the learners take to be the center of the distribution. This line of work was pioneered by Spencer (1961, 1963), who examined estimates of the mean for numbers and line lengths. In auditory perception, estimates of mean tone duration were examined by Schweickert et al. (2014). In these studies, the participants experienced a series of stimuli varying on a dimension (numbers of varying magnitude, lines of varying length, tones of varying duration) and then had to estimate the mean of the experienced stimuli on that dimension. The distributions of magnitudes, lengths, or durations were either symmetrical (normal) or skewed. Participants estimated the means of symmetrical distributions well. However, estimates of the means of skewed distributions were biased toward the long tail (i.e., *away* from other measures of central tendency, the median and the mode, which are closer to the short tail than the mean). For example, the mean of the Zipfian distribution in figure 5.6 would be overestimated.

The question of how we represent skewed distributions is not merely theoretical, since many distributions in both phonetics and semantics are skewed. in semantics, Lenneberg (1957) presented English speakers with colors on a continuum and asked them to generate all possible names for each color. The resulting name frequency distributions were decidedly skewed and nonnormal (Lenneberg, 1957, p. 3). In phonetics, Koenig (2001) reported that VOT distributions for voiceless stops are typically skewed within individuals. Indeed, the VOT distributions used in the classic distributional learning studies by Maye and colleagues are also strongly skewed. Generally, when a category is bounded on only one side by another, the peaks of the frequency and typicality distributions tend to be close to the one boundary, resulting in skew. The skew is inevitable because the speaker will only make as much effort to distinguish the category from others as necessary (Lindblom, 1990), and the more extreme articulations far from the boundary tend to be articulatorily costly (see Boersma, 1998, for discussion).

Paul Olejarczuk and I have started to investigate the influence of distributional skew on the acquisition of sound categories (Olejarczuk & Kapatsinski, 2016; Olejarczuk et al., in press; see also van der Ham & de Boer, 2015). To minimize the influence of first language category boundaries, we focused on a linguistic category that was novel to our English-speaking participants, lexical tone. Participants were exposed to a set of Low-High-Low contour tones superimposed on a syllable, /ka/. They were told that these were productions of a single word from a tone language they have never heard (Komo). The individual instances of the word differed only in the magnitude of pitch excursion (the difference between the Lows and the High, in semitones). Semitones are logarithmically transformed Hertz values. A difference in one semitone is intended to have an identical perceptual effect whether the compared pitches are low or high (and indeed the semitone scale works well for perception of pitch range in intonation; Nolan, 2003). The distributions of pitch excursion magnitudes presented to different participants (depicted in the right panel of figure 5.10) always had the same mean and variance on the semitone scale. However, they differed in the direction of skew. For participants exposed to the gray distribution, the most frequent pitch excursion was a 14-semitone one, with small excursions being relatively unusual. For those exposed to the black distribution, the most frequent excursion was only 8 semitones high, with large excursions being relatively unusual.

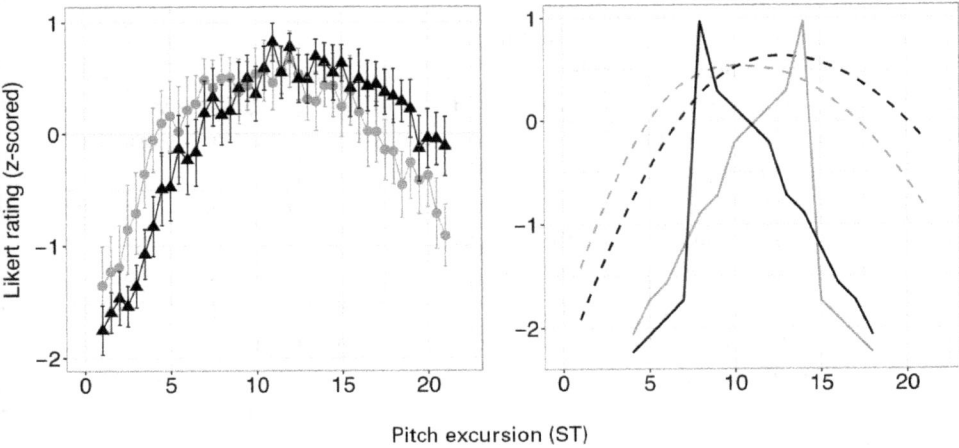

Figure 5.10
Peak typicality shifts in the direction of the long tail: peak typicality for the right-skewed distribution is further to the right than for the left-skewed distribution. Left: Mean standardized typicality ratings for individual points on the pitch excursion continuum. Right: Lowess-smoothed typicality ratings from the left panel superimposed on the frequency distributions experienced during training. The black distribution is right-skewed in training; the gray distribution is left-skewed.

After participants were exposed to 550 instances of the word, and thoroughly bored with passively listening to /ka/'s, we had them rate how typical the various pitch excursions were of Komo pronunciations. They were also asked to produce the typical Komo /ka/ (without any further training). As in studies of explicit mean estimation, peak typicality was shifted toward the long tail (away from the median and the mode); figure 5.10. In addition, the productions of participants exposed to the black distribution had significantly larger pitch excursions.

5.6   The Role of Prediction Error in Learning a Distribution

These results are, at first glance, extremely puzzling. Theories of speech perception and production have typically assumed that the center of a phonetic category corresponds to its mode. For example, Buz et al. (2016, p. 10) write that "if there are no other constraints on the target of articulation, the speaker could simply increase the target VOTs (i.e., the *mode* of the VOT distribution she is aiming for)," emphasis theirs. The mode of the pitch excursions experienced by "black" participants is lower than the mode of the pitch excursions experienced by the "gray" participants. If the mode were the target of production, the gray participants would produce larger pitch excursions than the black ones. Yet, we see the opposite pattern. What could explain this?

The likely culprit is attention to the unexpected, or—conversely—dullness of the common. Note that a distribution has two dimensions: the dimension along which the stimuli vary, and the frequency with which each of that dimension's values is observed. A combination of these two dimensions appears to determine salience.

Much work in categorization has focused on the influence of distance from some measure of central tendency as an influence on salience (e.g., Hahn et al., 2005; Tanaka et al., 1998). Unusual exemplars, which are far from the category center given the variability of the category values, draw attention. With respect to the skewed distributions in figure 5.10, observations far out on the long tail are far away from any objective measure of central tendency and may therefore draw attention, possibly having a disproportionate effect on the category representation.

Exceptionality seems to increase the likelihood of storage in memory. For stimuli varying along continuous dimensions, this effect was shown by Palmeri and Nosofsky (1995), in a study of random dot patterns (with the dimensions being locations of dots comprising the pattern). Compared to previously encountered items similar to the category prototype, previously encountered "exceptions" similar to the prototype of the *other* category were more likely to be recognized in an old/new recognition task. Sakamoto and Love (2004) further showed that the more evidence there was for a rule (as measured by type frequency, the number of distinct items obeying the rule), the better memory for exceptions was, suggesting that the more surprising an exception, the more salient it is. Similarly, Madan et al. (2014) found that people best remember outcomes of unexpectedly large or small magnitude.

Tanaka et al. (1998) proposed that unusual stimuli are not only more likely to be stored but are also likely to act as *perceptual magnets* (Kuhl, 1991), or attractor basins (Guenther & Gjaja, 1996), with stimuli similar to them erroneously perceived as being *identical* to them. They presented participants with two faces, one of which was judged to be relatively unusual, and then created a continuum of face morphs between the unusual and usual endpoints. Faces in the middle of the continuum were more likely to be classified as being the unusual face than as being the more usual one. The proposal that relatively unexpected stimuli act as perceptual attractors is also supported by the findings of Hahn et al. (2005), who studied the effect of category diversity on identification of novel stimuli falling near experienced category exemplars. Using a set of stylized flower stimuli varying in stem length and flower diameter, they showed that participants trained on a more diverse set of flowers were more likely to mistakenly identify new flowers as having been experienced. Exemplar model simulations suggested that this effect of diversity was not due to a bias to respond "old" in the diverse-exemplar condition, but rather to within-category exemplar variability reducing sensitivity to perceptual similarity between the new stimulus and experienced exemplars of the category. This result is expected if exemplar detectors in the diverse condition develop receptive fields covering larger areas of perceptual space (Kruschke, 1992). If stimuli are likely to be misperceived as salient exceptions, then exceptions would inherit the frequencies of the more typical stimuli they draw into their orbit, raising the exceptions' subjective frequencies. If exemplars far out at the end of the long tail are surprising and draw attention, they can perhaps draw closer-in, less surprising examples into their orbit and thereby leech off their frequencies.

However, there is another dimension to typicality. Recall that practicing an action (including practice at recognizing or producing a word) yields diminishing returns. The relationship between experienced frequency on the one hand and subjective familiarity or processing speed on the other is usually thought to be logarithmic (Cattell, 1885; Howes, 1957; Kreuz,

1987; Oldfield & Wingfield, 1965; see also Brysbaert & Cortese, 2010).[3] In other words, the difference between experiencing something once and experiencing it 10 times is roughly the same as the difference between experiencing something 10,000 vs. 100,000 times. The log relationship between frequency and ease of processing is a great boon to bilinguals. Assuming bilinguals don't talk twice as much as monolinguals, a bilingual experiences a word only half as often as a monolingual does. Nonetheless, the word processing speed of a bilingual is only slightly slower than that of a monolingual (Gollan et al., 2011). Knowing twice as many words does not make one twice as slow at processing any one of them. More generally, the log relationship between practice and proficiency is what makes it possible for a learner to become reasonably proficient at a multitude of skills, rather than having to commit to a single-minded pursuit of perfection in one.

Why should this logarithmic relationship between experienced frequency and its impact on behavior not hold also for frequencies with which stimuli are experienced in distributional learning? The left panel of figure 5.11 plots the consequences: the logarithmic relationship between frequency and familiarity reduces the peakiness of the distribution and increases the salience of the tails. If the distribution is symmetrical, this does not shift the center of the distribution. With an asymmetrical distribution, though, the center does shift. As the long tail becomes fatter relative to the peak, it draws the mean toward itself. As figure 5.11 shows, this can even shift the ordinal relationship between the means of a left-skewed and a right-skewed distribution, as found in our study.

If we are correct in our psychological interpretation of the log frequency effect as having to do with surprise or prediction error, then we should see the same mean shift predicted by the log frequency transformation emerge in an error-driven learning model. In collaboration with Harald Baayen (Olejarczuk et al., in press), we developed a simple error-driven model of the learning situation based on Rescorla and Wagner (1972). We conceptualized the task of the learner as predicting what pitch excursion he will experience next given the pitch excursions he has already experienced (in recent memory). Pitch excursion magnitude was treated as a nominal variable; thus, each pitch excursion value on the continuum is equidistant from all others. In other words, the learner is simply predicting particular pitch excursion magnitude values. Because our model is error-driven, connections to outcomes (in this case pitch excursion magnitude values) are strengthened to the extent that those outcomes are unexpected. If an outcome is already expected, the model's beliefs about that outcome must be correct, so the weights of connection leading to it remain unchanged.

We extracted the model's expectations in the absence of any specific preceding stimuli: how much each of the values is activated *on average*, across the possible sequences of preceding stimuli. The measure that reflects this notion best is the sum of connection weights leading to an outcome. The model's expectations are shown in the right panel of figure 5.11. It is immediately apparent that the model reproduces the mean shift predicted by the logarithmic transformation of experienced frequency. It does so because it is error-driven: the more often the model has experienced a particular pitch excursion in the past, the less surprising its future occurrences are, resulting in less prediction error and less strengthening of connection weights leading to it upon further exposure. Practicing perceiving a stimulus, like other practice, has diminishing returns.

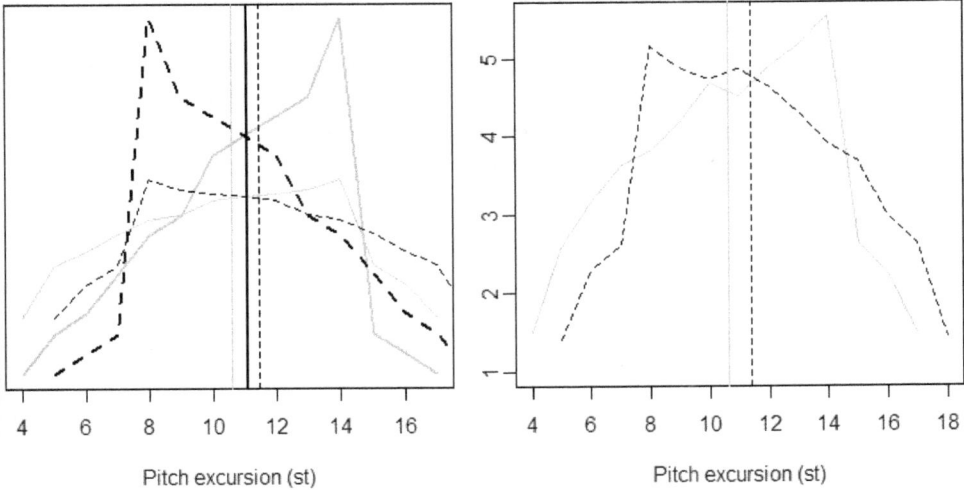

Pitch excursion (st)   Pitch excursion (st)

Figure 5.11
Left panel: Experienced frequency (dashed lines) for the left-skewed distribution (gray) and the right-skewed distribution (black) and the corresponding logarithms of experienced frequency, rescaled to have the same mean height to be visible in the graph (dashed lines). The mean continuum value for each distribution is shown by a vertical line. The mean continuum value of the sample shifts toward the long tail if value frequency is logarithmically transformed. Right panel: Expectations of the Rescorla-Wagner model (unscaled). The means of the two distributions in the model are similar to those of the log frequency distributions in the left panel.

To summarize, distributional learning is not veridical because of (1) the exceptional salience of the unusual, and (2) the fatiguing dullness of the run of the mill. As in other domains, it is log frequency and not raw frequency that is tracked by learners: experiencing something familiar and expected produces much less change in belief and behavior than experiencing something new and unexpected.

Note that, in this case, tracking log frequency is not normative and is inconsistent with Bayesian learning: probabilities of the continuum values are tracking raw frequency and not log frequency (cf. Norris, 2006; Norris & McQueen, 2008, for claims that log frequency effects in word recognition are explained by participants tracking probabilities). Indeed, as we saw in chapter 4, salience of the unexpected is behind many other nonnormative behaviors including the inverse base rate effect, highlighting, and the greater strength of forward compared to backward blocking.

5.7   Salience of the Unexpected and Regions of Perceptual Equivalence

Salience of the unexpected has major consequences for the structure of linguistic categories. Figure 5.12 shows that overestimating the typicality of the atypical results in regions of perceptual equivalence. As a fortunate side effect, such regions would allow anticipatory coarticulation on the part of

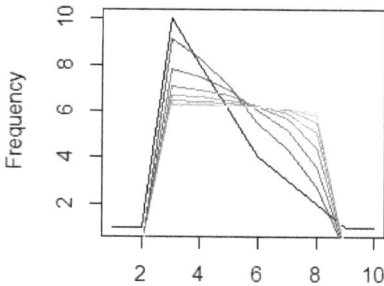

Figure 5.12
Salience of the unexpected causes an originally pointy distribution (in solid black) to become uniform within a bounded region (dotted gray) on an acoustic continuum (*x*). The original distribution depicts token frequencies of the sounds in the input. However, the learner's judgments of sound typicality/goodness tracks log(frequency) and not raw frequency: typicality = log(frequency). This makes infrequent category members more typical than their original frequency would suggest. Assuming production probability tracks judged goodness, the distribution of sounds will gradually become uniform within the original boundaries of the sound category.

the speaker to happen without major costs to the listener (Keating, 1990), allowing for speech production to be as rapid as it is.

If sounds are reproduced in proportion to their typicality, within-category sound distributions will approach the uniform distribution: all sounds within the category region should become equally acceptable (see Keating, 1990; Kapatsinski et al., 2017). If production probability tracked typicality/category goodness, the frequency distribution of sounds within categories should therefore become uniform. To the extent that this does not happen, there must be a competing pressure within the production system. I suggest that this pressure is the Zipfian pressure to reuse previously used movements. Automatization results in a rich-get-richer loop that competes with the salience-driven pressure for equality that resides in the perceptual system. Some evidence for this proposal comes from the finding that within-category articulatory variability reduces with articulatory practice, so that infants begin with uniform distributions (Kewley-Port & Preston, 1974) that gradually become less and less uniform. As one would expect from a lifelong process of practice-driven articulatory automatization, within-category variability continues to decrease well into adulthood (Baayen et al., 2017; A. Smith & Goffman, 1998; Tomaschek et al., 2013).

In grammar, the same dynamic can lead to regions of equivalence in acceptability, inflating the difference between the nonexistent and the rare compared to the difference between the rare and the ubiquitous. Thus, the difference between a structure that one has never observed and a structure one *has* observed is vastly larger than the difference between a frequent structure and an infrequent one: the rare onset in /sfik/ is more like the frequent onset in /stik/ than like the nonexistent onset in /fsik/. This is part of the explanation for why categorical models of grammaticality (e.g., Chomsky & Halle, 1968) have been so successful. Figure 5.10 suggests that, left unchecked, this process will make every structure that is ever experienced as part of one's exposure to a language equally acceptable even though the speaker will tend to *produce* the structures they have practiced producing in the past. In accordance with the prediction, speakers have been noted to produce only a limited set of structures while accepting a vastly larger array (Kapatsinski, 2012; Kempen & Harbusch, 2005).

5.8   Some Alternative Explanations for Flat Tops

There are also other reasons to suspect that distributional learning may be biased to smooth out sharp peaks, making induced distributions "flatter-topped" than the distributions in the environment. One possible reason is perceptual noise: if the most frequent dimension value is often misperceived as similar values (its neighbors on the dimension), those values will inherit some of its frequency, and the peak will flatten. For example, Palmeri and Nosofsky (1995) report that novel dot patterns similar to the exceptional dot pattern are often treated as the same pattern for the purposes of categorization and recognition. With a similar category structure, Wood (1998) reports that the influence of similarity to the exception was limited to novel stimuli that were falsely recognized as old (i.e., misrecognized as being the exception), with all other stimuli classified by "rule." In these cases, perceptual and memory noise flatten out the distribution so that it is not only the exception that is exceptionally likely to be placed in a certain category but similar stimuli are as well. However, salience of the unexpected allows regions of perceptual equivalence to grow beyond the limits set by misperception. Furthermore, misperception cannot account for our findings of the mean shifting toward the long tail. When symmetrical noise is superimposed onto the distributions, the means of the two distributions do not separate in the observed direction no matter how noisy the simulated perception is.

Another possible reason for regions of perceptual equivalence is acquisition of categorization rules like "all and only LHL pitch contours are in the category" (e.g., McKinley & Nosofsky, 1995; see Kapatsinski et al., 2017, for categories of pitch contours). Indeed, typicality decreases rapidly as pitch excursion approaches zero in figure 5.10, suggesting that participants are learning that there must be an LHL contour over a Komo /ka/. Nonetheless, participants are clearly learning something beyond this categorization rule, tracking the within-category frequency distribution, as frequency in training helps explain typicality judgments even when distance from the category boundary (an excursion of 0) is entered into the model. Frequency matters. But as frequency increases, increases in frequency matter less and less.

5.9 Conclusion

Associative learning of cue-outcome contingencies must be extended to continuous dimensions. Fortunately, it can be, if we are allowed to discretize the dimensions into sets of compound cues, with one member of the compound identifying the dimension, and others identifying location on that dimension. We saw that discrete thermometer coding preserves order within the dimension, resulting in little information loss, though not all dimensions require thermometer coding.

Representing dimensions as sets of cues predicts that attention can be selectively directed toward the dimension or to some intervals on that dimension. It also predicts that dimension value frequency will have the same effects as cue frequency for nominal cues like words. In particular, experiencing a rare dimension value should have a greater effect on behavior and belief than experiencing a frequent dimension value. Thus, speed of processing, subjective familiarity, and other reflexes of experience should track log frequency rather than raw frequency, resulting in systematic differences between exposure and representation, input and intake. Overreaction to prepare for the unexpected also results in regions of perceptual equivalence and equalizes grammatical acceptability among reasonably well-attested structures.

These predictions are strongly confirmed by the available data. Note that if dimensions are sets of cues, then integration of multiple dimensions can be reduced to the tradeoff between configural learning and selective attention, as discussed in chapter 3 (see also Escudero & Boersma, 2004). The machinery of associative learning can then be applied to continuous dimensions and multidimensional similarity spaces, rather than being restricted to relatively simple sets of cue-outcome pairings.

6 Schematic Structure, Hebbian Learning, and Semantic Change

I suppose it is tempting, if the only tool you have is a hammer, to treat everything as if it were a nail.

—Maslow (1966, p. 15)

The main part of acquiring a language is learning its system of form-meaning mappings, its *schematic structure*.[1] According to cognitive linguists and construction grammarians, both the vocabulary of a language and its grammar can be described as inventories of such mappings (Bybee, 1985, 2001; Fillmore et al., 1988; Goldberg, 1995; Langacker, 1987), often called *constructions*. Constructions are the fundamentals tools of language, allowing us to transmit information. Together, the constructions form the *constructicon*. The large constructica of human languages is what makes them such powerful communication systems. The task of learning the constructicon is truly daunting. While we rapidly acquire a few constructions of a language—giving us a foothold and a rudimentary ability to communicate—we never stop learning new constructions. No one speaker knows all the words, idioms, and semifixed expressions of a language, and vocabulary continues to grow throughout life (e.g., Keuleers et al., 2015).[2] While most animal communication systems consist of one-to-one form-meaning mappings (Skyrms, 2010), this is not true of human language: both ambiguity/homonymy and partial synonymy are rampant. One has many ways to convey the same thought, and the same sound can mean many things. Forms compete for selection and recognition. Meanings compete for expression and uptake. Because of this ever-present pool of competing constructions, the constructicon constantly changes: new words are invented while old words die or start being used in new ways. It is this last issue we focus on in this chapter: Why do meanings of forms change, and how do old words acquire new uses? We will see that when applied to the task of learning the constructicon, the simple mechanisms of associative learning shed some light on this process of semantic change.

6.1   Semantic Change in Grammaticalization

Languages are often thought to contain two kinds of items, the closed-class or grammatical, and the open-class or lexical. The grammatical items are little things, short on phonetic substance and contributing little to the meaning of the sentence. Invariably, the most frequent morphs of a language are of this type, and unsurprisingly so. A morph whose semantic content is very general can be used in a large variety of contexts. Even among grammatical items of the same class, one notices that the morphs whose meanings are more general are used more frequently. Consider two determiners, *my* and *the*. The former has some semantic specificity, and the opportunities to use it come far less often, especially in a text like this. The latter has a meaning so general and elusive that scholars continue debating what exactly we mean by it, which is why second language learners struggle with its use for much longer than its abundance in the input may lead us to expect.

Unlike lexical items, grammatical items do not spring up out of thin air, born of the whims of creative writers, scientists, and advertisers. It is easy to coin a new noun, but try coining a new determiner, say to express the meaning "something that only you have," or a new preposition. Even attempts to replace pronouns—driven by issues of personal identity and social justice—have been largely unsuccessful in achieving widespread acceptance of terms like *e* for "he or she." Where then do grammatical items come from? They develop out of lexical items, through a process called *grammaticalization*. For example, the modern suffix *-ly*, as in *manly* 'having the characteristics of a man', used to be a noun *liç* meaning "body" in Old English, with *mann-liç* meaning "having the body or appearance of a man" (Bybee, 2003, p. 148). During grammaticalization, morphs and larger constructions increase in frequency of use, reduce in size, and lose their syntactic autonomy as they are extended to new uses. Some believe that all grammar came about this way, grammaticalization turning protolanguage into language by endowing it with morphology and syntax (Givón, 1998; Heine & Kuteva, 2002; Schoenemann, 1999; Tomasello, 2003). At the very least, it is indisputable that the vast majority of affixes found in the world's languages have evolved out of separate words through grammaticalization, turning yesterday's syntax into today's morphology (Givón, 1971).

Whether or not grammaticalization gave us grammar, there is little doubt that it keeps giving us morphology.

Grammaticalization is a cluster of changes that tend to go together: increases in frequency tend to accompany phonetic reduction, which tends to accompany semantic extension, which tends to accompany loss of syntactic autonomy. However, there are also clear cases where one happens without the others. For example, a reductive sound change may spread through the lexicon without being accompanied by semantic changes in the affected words. There is no evidence that, for example, the emergence of intervocalic flapping in many varieties of English—a reductive sound change that started in frequent words (Hay & Foulkes, 2016)—was accompanied by any systematic change in the meanings of the words affected. Some have argued that such dissociations invalidate the theory that grammaticalization stems from a single cause (Joseph, 2000; Newmeyer, 2000). Ohers have countered that—while dissociable—reductive changes co-occur with each other, suggesting that there is some common force or forces that drive reduction in both form and meaning (Bybee, 2003).

What is this force? If we have to pick one, then the strongest candidate would undoubtedly be something that causes semantic extension: the grammaticalizing form is extended to new uses, which causes it to increase in frequency, leading to various kinds of reduction (e.g., Bybee, 2003; Langacker, 2011; Traugott, 2011). As a form becomes used in more contexts, its frequency of use must necessarily increase. The connection between frequency of use and phonetic reduction is also well documented (Hay & Foulkes, 2016) and appears inevitable, provided that high usage frequency results in automatization, which results in smoothing out of articulatory movements (Bybee, 2001, 2002b, 2003; see also chapter 9).

More controversially, Zipf (1949) proposed that increased frequency of use can also cause semantic extension. This sets up a positive feedback loop, where frequency of use leads to semantic extension, which leads to further increases in frequency. The positive feedback loop causes the frequency of the grammaticalizing form to skyrocket, resulting in the power-law word frequency distributions Zipf observed in natural language corpora.

How can high frequency of use lead to semantic extension? Zipf (1949) likened words to tools. Just as an artisan uses tools to accomplish various tasks, so does a speaker use words to convey various meanings. Zipf conceived of the lexicon as a workbench, where frequently used words/tools are placed closer to the artisan/speaker than others, rendering them more *accessible*.

When the artisan wishes to accomplish a task, he needs to pick a tool to use. Provided that several tools can accomplish the task—even though some may be more suited to it than others—the artisan will pick the tool that is easiest for him to access. Suppose you need to pound in a nail, and you have two hammers, a slightly better one in the closet, and a slightly inferior one next to you. Do you really want to spend an hour rummaging through the closet in search of the better hammer, or will you just use the one you can use right away? Especially under time pressure—like that faced by a speaker trying to access a word to express a meaning in real-time speech production—you are likely to settle for the more accessible tool. As a result, the more accessible tools will expand in their range of uses at the expense of the less accessible ones.

This hypothesis is supported by at least two studies of language acquisition. First, Naigles and Gelman (1995) have shown that words can be over-extended in production but not comprehension. The child may not believe that a cow is a kind of cat and yet use the word *kitty* to refer to it. When *cow* is inaccessible, *kitty* will do. Second, Gershkoff-Stowe and L. B. Smith (1997) have shown that overextensions can result from self-priming: a child is likely to reuse recently used words in inappropriate contexts, overextending them. This work suggests that overextension is driven by high accessibility of the overextended form, whatever the source of this high accessibility. In our work reported and modeled below, we have shown that accessibility-driven extensions are not limited to children and do not have to be erroneous. Rather, any instance of language production can result in an extension, seeding language change.

Zipf's hypothesis that frequency influences semantic extension through its effect on accessibility makes a unique prediction: frequency should only cause semantic extension if the more frequent form is indeed more accessible than the less frequent form. Accessibility is affected by frequency but does not reduce to it. Thus, Berg (1998) and Martin (2007) note that hard-to-pronounce words are more difficult to access than easier ones. And, as one would expect, hard-to-pronounce words seem to drop out of the language, replaced by unrelated coinages and borrowings, significantly faster than words that are easier to say. Similarly, recently used or experienced words are more accessible than words one has not used or heard for a while, and priming a form can cause that form to be selected for production over a semantic competitor, or even a semantic competitor of its homophone. For example, *none* primes production of *nun* in response to a picture of a priest (Ferreira & Griffin, 2003). These results indicate that frequency and accessibility can be experimentally dissociated, affording an opportunity to test Zipf's hypothesis.

An alternative way usage frequency can influence meaning is through the effect of repetition on reduction. According to Langacker (2011, p. 83), phonetic reduction—provided it results from a frequency increase—can lead to loss of semantic content ("bleaching"), which can result in the form being used in new contexts. While Langacker (2011) does not specify *how* phonetic reduction can lead to semantic reduction, attentional learning provides a plausible mechanism (chapter 3). Short, reduced, unstressed forms do not draw attention to themselves, which should make them less associable. Thus, a child trying to acquire the language may not associate the form with all of the semantic associations it had for her parents, who were exposed to a less reduced form of the word when learning the language (see chapter 3 on the reduced *ne* in the French *ne pas* losing its link to negation).

According to Schuchardt (1885/1972), Bybee (2003), and Haiman (1994), bleaching can also result from repetition directly.[3] Bybee (2003) suggests that the mechanism involved is *habituation*. In habituation, a repeatedly presented stimulus loses the ability to activate its associations and draws less and less attention to itself. Thus, a repeatedly experienced form is thought to lose the ability to activate its semantic associations:[4]

> Repetition itself diminishes the force of a word, phrase, or construction. Examples are legion. *Iterate* doesn't seem to mean "repeat" quite strongly enough, so we tend to add *re-*; with repetition, the strength of that fades and we say *reiterate again*. *You guys* generalizes to include females and the word *guy* now can be used in colloquial speech even for inanimate objects. In grammaticalization, the generalization or bleaching of the meaning of a construction is caused by frequency. (Bybee, 2003, p. 157)

Unlike the perceptual salience explanation, the habituation account does not require the repeated form to be phonetically reduced for frequency to effect semantic bleaching. However, both accounts are alike in attributing semantic changes to the language learner stopping to pay attention to a repeated *stimulus*. Whereas Zipf (1949) localizes the semantic change in production, habituation and attentional learning predict that the change should begin in comprehension, with the grammaticalizing form losing its ability to activate all of its semantic features as it gains frequency.

While the correlation between the frequency of a word and its number of uses/meanings is well documented in natural languages (Piantadosi et al., 2012; Zipf, 1949), studies of natural language cannot explain the correlation. Do frequency increases merely follow semantic extension, or can they also cause it? And if frequency does cause semantic extension, what is the root mechanism at work? For this, we turn to learning studies with artificial languages, where causality can be established by observing the effects of independently *manipulating* the frequency of a form in the learner's experience and its accessibility at the moment of lexical selection.

6.2   Semantic Extension vs. Entrenchment

As we saw in chapter 4, previous experimental research on the subject has suggested—counter to the tendency for frequent forms to have broader meanings—that repeatedly encountering a form with a certain meaning leads to certainty that the form should *not* be used to express other meanings. In other words, the form becomes *entrenched* in the meaning with which it is repeatedly paired in the learner's experience (Braine & Brooks, 1995; see also Ambridge et al., 2008; Stefanowitsch, 2008). As described in chapter 4, F. Xu and Tenenbaum (2007) explain this effect using a generative Bayesian model. Because of entrenchment, one might expect that the more often you encounter the word *dax* paired with Dalmatians, the *less* likely you should be to consider it acceptable to extend the word *dax* to other meanings.

While there is extensive empirical work supporting entrenchment, all of this work has controlled form accessibility, leveling the effects of frequency on accessibility. For example, F. Xu and Tenenbaum (2007) presented participants with several objects in turn and asked them whether each could be a *dax*. In this task, the form *dax* is maximally available and does not compete with any other form for selection. Studies of entrenchment in syntax have likewise usually used judgment tasks. For instance, Theakston (2004) found that participants judge *He vanished the bunny* as being better than *He disappeared the bunny*, presumably because—though neither *vanish* nor *disappear* can be used transitively—*disappear* is more frequent than *vanish*, giving participants higher confidence in its intransitivity. As in F. Xu and Tenenbaum (2007), competition for selection among alternative forms is irrelevant to this task. In the case of *vanish* and *disappear*, it is actually quite likely that judgments diverge from production probabilities and the ongoing trajectory of semantic extension. In naturalistic production as depicted by corpora, *disappear*, judged unacceptable as a transitive verb, is developing a productive transitive use:

1. "Had they killed the original child too? Or just disappeared it?"
2. "He had disappeared the dings with polymer and brought the finish back up."

3. "Curpin glanced at me and grinned, then disappeared the belly bait."
(All examples are from the *Corpus of Contemporary American English*, COCA; Davies, 2008–)

Vanish appears to be behind in its semantic extension, though some examples are attested in fantasy novels with reference to magicking something away:

4. "He drank deeply from his goblet, then vanished it when it was emptied."
(Davies, 2008–)

Brooks et al. (1999) did observe entrenchment in production, arguing—like other studies reviewed above—that frequent use of a form with a certain meaning discourages extending the form to new meanings. Children in their study extended rare, late-acquired words to unconventional uses more than frequent, early-acquired ones—for example, producing *He arrived me to school* more than *He came me to school*. However, like other studies documenting entrenchment, they did their best to eliminate accessibility differences between frequent and infrequent forms: "Because the late AOA [infrequent] verbs may not have been in the productive vocabularies of all of the children, it was necessary to provide children with a great deal of exposure to the verbs to ensure that children would use both early and late AOA verbs" (Brooks et al., 1999, p. 1328; see also Blything et al., 2014, for a similar example). If frequent forms undergo semantic extension because they are more accessible in the moment of production (Zipf, 1949), leveling accessibility differences between frequent and infrequent forms should eliminate the tendency to extend frequent forms to new uses. If Zipf's artisan places a frequently used hammer and a rarely used hammer in the same location on the workbench, and is equally proficient at using both, he has no basis for preferring the hammer he's used often. The effect of frequency on semantic extension should be mediated by the effect of frequency on accessibility. When accessibility differences between frequent and infrequent words are leveled, frequency should not favor semantic extension.

I do not wish to criticize entrenchment studies for leveling form accessibility differences. I accept that repeated exposure to a form-meaning pairing makes one more confident that the form always has the meaning with which it has been experienced. However, this increasing confidence need not prevent one from extending the experienced form to new uses under the demands of real-time production. An artisan experienced with a hammer *should* think that the hammer is not for hunting cockroaches but—when the need arises and no other tool is accessible—may nonetheless use the hammer for this purpose. A speaker may extend a frequent word to a new meaning despite being confident of never having experienced it being used that way.

In what follows, I report on an experimental study completed in my lab by Zara Harmon (Harmon & Kapatsinski, 2017), which tested the hypothesis that frequent words are likely to be used for novel purposes *because* of the effect of frequency on accessibility in production. I then show that the predicted effect of frequency on semantic extension in production falls out of any model of associative learning. However, other aspects of the results are challenging to the assumption of unidirectionality central to predictive, error-driven models (Rescorla & Wagner, 1972), providing support for the hypothesis—introduced in chapter 2—that associations are bidirectional by default.

6.3   The Experiment

Adult native English speakers were presented with one of two miniature artificial languages. Each language had the same four suffixes, *-dan*, *-sil*, *-nem*, and *-shoon*. In training, nouns bearing *-dan* and *-sil* were always paired with pictures of multiple large creatures. In contrast, each unaffixed noun co-occurred with a single large creature, while nouns suffixed with *-nem* and *-shoon* were always accompanied by a single small creature.

For each participant, one of the suffixes was three times more frequent than any of the others. For half of the participants, those presented with the Dan language, the frequent suffix was *-dan*. For the other half, those presented with the Nem language, the frequent suffix was *-nem*. The structure of the two languages is shown in figure 6.1.

Participants were never presented with a picture of multiple small creatures in training. Thus, when presented with it at test and asked to generate an appropriate form to refer to it, they needed to either extend one of the forms they learned to refer to this novel meaning, or else to combine a plural suffix with a diminutive suffix. Perhaps because they were English speakers, they seldom produced compositional suffix sequences, overwhelmingly relying on lexical extension instead.

Following Zipf (1949) and the research on grammaticalization, we expected participants to extend frequent forms to refer to the novel meaning in production. Thus, *-dan* would be more likely to be extended to the diminutive plural meaning by participants trained on the Dan language, while *-nem* would be more likely to be extended by those trained on the Nem language.

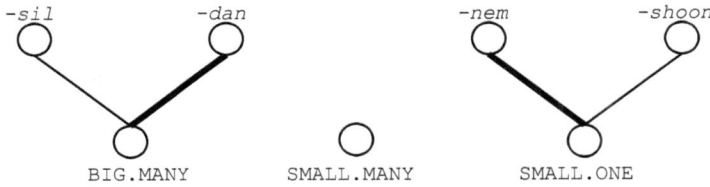

Figure 6.1
Structure of the two artificial languages Dan (where *-dan* is frequent) and Nem (where *-nem* is frequent). Thus, only one construction is the frequent one—that is, one line is the thick one in each language, either *-dan*~BIG.MANY or *-sil*~SMALL.ONE. In both languages, *-dan* and *-sil* always co-occur with multiple large creatures in training, while *-nem* and *-shoon* co-occur with a single small creature. Multiple small creatures is the novel meaning because it is never presented in training but is presented at test.

However, following experimental studies on entrenchment, we expected that the frequent forms would not be mapped onto the novel meaning in comprehension. Thus, experiencing a suffix frequently—always paired with the same meaning—should make participants less likely to map the suffix onto another meaning.

6.3.1   Entrenchment in Comprehension

Each trial of the comprehension test involved presenting the participant with a noun bearing one of the four suffixes, or no suffix at all. Four pictures then came up, one showing a single large creature, one showing a single small creature, one showing multiple large creatures, and one showing multiple small creatures. All creatures within a trial were of the same kind, as the "species" of the creature comprised the meaning of the stem. Participants were asked to click on the picture corresponding to the meaning of the word.

The right side of figure 6.2 shows that infrequent suffixes were mapped onto the novel, diminutive plural meaning quite often. This is somewhat surprising because participants had no reason to ever click on this meaning. This was particularly true of the diminutive suffix *-nem*, which was mapped onto the meaning paired with it, "diminutive singular," and the novel diminutive plural meaning about equally often. At the same time, participants almost never mapped it onto nondiminutive meanings. Participants seemed to come to the experiment expecting diminutive and plural suffixes, and not diminutive singular and plural nondiminutive ones, in

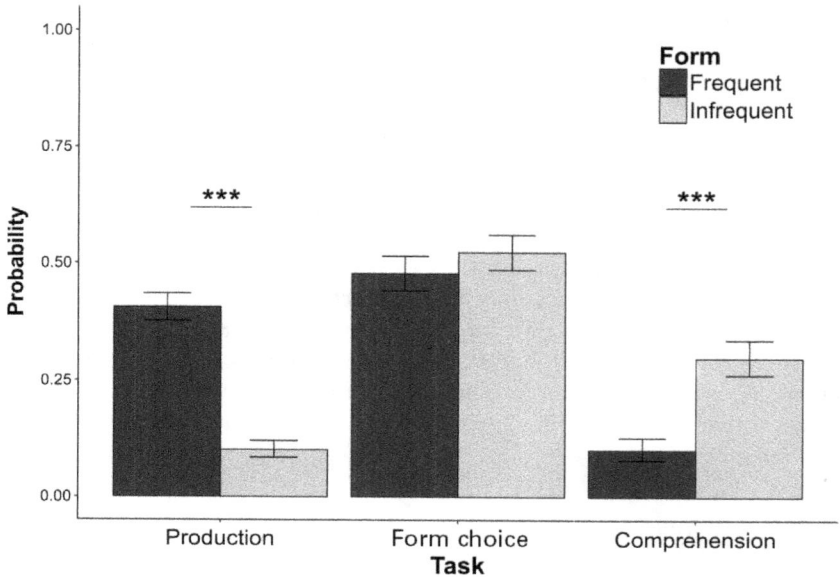

Figure 6.2
A summary of the main results of Harmon and Kapatsinski (2017, Experiment 1).
Only the results for the novel, MANY.SMALL meaning are shown. For familiar meanings, participants were close to 90% correct, overwhelmingly selecting the suffixes
that were paired with a meaning to refer to it in production and form choice and
very rarely mapping suffixes onto a familiar meaning they did not co-occur with in
comprehension. "Frequent" bars are -*dan* in the Dan language and -*nem* in the Nem
language, while "infrequent" bars are -*dan* in Nem and -*nem* in Dan.[7] Participants
tended to express the novel meaning with frequent forms (left). In other words, the
same form was chosen for production more often when it was frequent in training.
This effect of frequency disappeared in the two-alternative forced form choice task,
where the accessibility differences between frequent and infrequent forms were min-
imized (middle). Finally, even though participants chose frequent forms to express
the novel meaning in production, they tended not to click on the novel meaning
when presented with a frequent form in comprehension (right).

the same way that F. Xu and Tenenbaum's (2007) participants expected the
experimenter to refer to dogs and not Dalmatians.

With additional experience, the meanings of the suffixes became more
restricted. Thus, -*dan* is mapped onto diminutive plurals significantly less
often in the Dan language, and -*nem* is mapped onto diminutive plurals
less often in the Nem language. As -*nem* continues to always be experienced
paired with a single creature, participants become more confident that it

never refers to multiple creatures. As -*dan* continues to be paired with large creatures, participants become confident that it never refers to multiple *small* creatures. This illustrates the process of entrenchment. With experience, the meanings narrow: diminutive becomes diminutive singular, and plural becomes plural non-diminutive.

6.3.2 Semantic Extension in Production

Semantic extension was tested with the production test. On each trial of this test, participants were first presented with an unsuffixed stem form paired with a picture of a single large creature. They were then briefly shown the four pictures illustrating the space of possible meanings they could be asked to express. Subsequently, three of the pictures disappeared and one remained. Participants named the remaining picture aloud.

Because we were looking for semantic extension, we were particularly interested in the effect of suffix frequency on the likelihood of choosing that suffix to express the diminutive plural meaning. Figure 6.2 shows that high frequency favored semantic extension: -*dan* was used to refer to the diminutive plural more after exposure to the Dan language, and -*nem* was used to express the novel meaning more after exposure to the Nem language.[5]

These results strongly confirm the idea that frequently used morphs are likely to undergo semantic extension and, importantly, establish a causal relationship between frequency and semantic extension in production. Comparing the comprehension and production results in figure 6.2, you may notice that extension happens despite entrenchment. The comprehension task shows that our participants are quite sure that the frequent suffixes are not used to refer to the diminutive plural in the language they experienced. Yet these are precisely the forms they themselves are most likely to use to refer to diminutive plurals. You may be perfectly well aware that your trusty hammer is bad for hunting cockroaches, and yet its high accessibility may make it the tool you are most likely to use for this purpose.

6.3.3 Leveling Accessibility Differences Eliminates the Frequency Effect: The Forced Form Choice Task

The comprehension-production comparison establishes the causal connection between frequency and semantic extension. However, it does not establish that this connection is mediated by accessibility. To do that, we needed a task that, like production, involves selecting a form to express a meaning, but levels accessibility differences between frequent and infrequent forms. We found it in the two-alternative forced-choice task.

In this task, participants saw a picture and were then presented with two spoken words to choose between by pressing a button. On some trials, the picture was a picture of multiple small creatures (DIMPL) and the two forms were the two suffixes that differed in frequency, *-dan* and *-nem*. By presenting participants with both forms, we made them both accessible, leveling—or at least greatly reducing—accessibility differences between them. As the middle bars in figure 6.2 illustrate, participants showed no preference for using the more frequent form to express the novel diminutive plural meaning when the less frequent form was made equally accessible.[6] The effect of frequency on semantic extension is mediated by accessibility.

6.3.4   Niche Seeking in Comprehension

So far, we have discussed only the two forms whose frequencies we manipulated. We now turn to their competitors, *-sil*$_{PL}$ and *-shoon*$_{DIM}$. Figure 6.3 shows that the comprehension results provide evidence for an effect we call *"niche seeking"* (following MacWhinney, 1987, p. 292). When a frequent form co-occurs with the same meaning as an infrequent form, both forms are originally mapped onto the same, fairly general meaning (e.g., SMALL or MANY). With further experience, the frequent form is restricted to the specific meaning both forms co-occur with (e.g., MANY.BIG or ONE. SMALL) and pushes the other form out of that meaning. The infrequent form is then mapped onto whatever is left over of the original general meaning (here, MANY.SMALL). Importantly, however, we do not see niche seeking in production (figure 6.3, left).

6.4   A Hebbian Learning Model

Empirical findings are the backbone of science but any single finding could be a fluke. It is therefore reassuring to have the weight of a theory—based as it is in successfully accounting for numerous established findings—supporting a finding, lending it credence by arguing that it could not have turned out any other way. Conversely, showing that a finding does not fit into an established theory should decrease our belief in the finding—if the theory is indeed well established and buttressed by prior results—but also generate a suspicion that revision to the theory may be required.

We begin with the simplest possible model of associative learning, a (joint) frequency counter. When the model encounters a cue followed by an outcome, it simply increases the weight of the link between them by a constant number, which we set to 1 to emphasize the model's nature as a frequency counter.

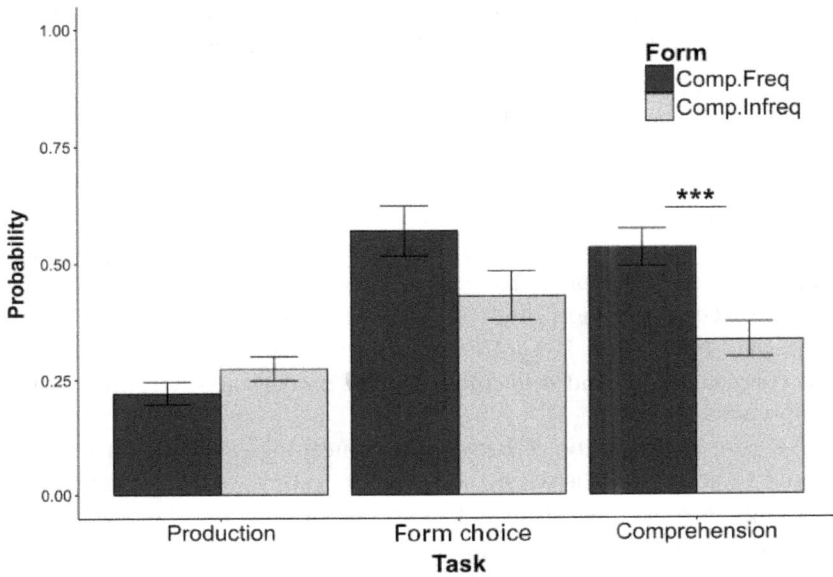

Figure 6.3
The effect of competitor frequency in Harmon and Kapatsinski (2017). "Competitor frequent" forms are $-sil_{PL}$ in Dan_{PL} Language and $-shoon_{DIM}$ in Nem_{DIM} Language. "Competitor infrequent" forms are $-sil_{PL}$ in Nem_{DIM} and $-shoon_{DIM}$ in Dan_{PL}. When a form is the synonym of the frequent form during training, it tends to be mapped onto the novel meaning in comprehension (right) but is not preferred to express this meaning in production (left). The forced form choice task patterns with comprehension numerically, but the effect of competitor form frequency is not significant in that task (middle).

To connect the model's knowledge to the experimental results, we need a set of linking hypotheses connecting the weights and activations of the model to the participants' responses in the experimental tasks. We assumed that production involves activating forms given the semantic features present on that test trial and the context cue. The activation of a form is simply the sum of connection weights from the semantic and context cues present on the test trial to that form. The choice of the form is then determined stochastically (Luce, 1959): the form is chosen in proportion to its activation value relative to the sum of all forms' activation values given the cues present. Stochastic choice implements probability matching, an empirical universal in tasks that demand repeatedly choosing between the same alternatives (Azab et al., 2016), including tests of productivity (Hayes et al., 2009; see chapter 2 for discussion).

The linking hypothesis for comprehension is more controversial. Note that the model, like the subjects, was trained only in the meaning→form direction. However, the comprehension task required participants to choose meanings given forms, reversing the cue→outcome mappings they were trained on. Participants were extremely accurate in the comprehension task, suggesting that they were able to bring the knowledge they acquired to bear on it. The model must be able to do the same. We propose that the associations that participants learn obey the Symmetry Principle: a cue→outcome association is as strong as the corresponding outcome→cue association (Asch & Ebenholtz, 1962; Kahana, 2002; Miller & Matzel, 1988). This is another way our model differs from Rescorla and Wagner (1972), and it is crucial for the model's ability to model the comprehension data.

We assume that a choice between two meanings depends on the difference in activations between the semantic features that distinguish the meanings. For example, the probability of clicking on [SMALL.MANY] rather than [BIG.MANY] when presented with -*dan* is proportional to the difference in association weights between -*dan*~SMALL (=SMALL~-*dan*) and -*dan*~BIG (=BIG~-*dan*). The bigger this difference, the more likely participants are to click on the meaning that actually *was* paired with the form cue in training. In this, we follow the basic logic of the Comparator Hypothesis by Miller and colleagues (Miller & Matzel, 1988, et seq.).

As illustrated in table 6.1, there are three other sets of connections that could potentially be updated on every trial, and alternative theories of associative learning differ in their claims about whether these connections are

Table 6.1

Outcomes Cues	Present		Absent	
Present	$p_c p_o$	+	$p_c a_o$	−
Absent	$a_c p_o$	−	$a_c a_o$	+

The four distinct sets of cue-outcome connections on every trial and whether their weights should become more positive (+) or more negative (−) in a model that is able to capture environmental contingencies veridically. We will refer to the sets with the abbreviations shown on the left sides of the table cells. A model may update all four sets or a subset of them. For example, the RW model updates the top row and can therefore be abbreviated as p_c. Other possibly reasonable subsets include $p_c p_o$ and $!a_c a_o$. It is also plausible—on neurological rather than normative grounds— to update $a_c a_o$ in the nonnormative, negative direction, since unused connections decay / undergo pruning.

indeed updated. First, there are connections from the cues present on a trial to the outcomes absent from that trial. It is usually thought that these connections' weights are reduced, so that cues that are consistently paired with the *absence* of a certain outcome develop inhibitory connections to that outcome, with the subject learning the negative contingency present in the environment. Second, there are connections from the absent cues to the present outcomes. These connections are assumed to *not* be updated by Rescorla and Wagner (1972): the RW model learns nothing about cues absent from any given trial. However, van Hamme and Wasserman (1994) and Tassoni (1995) argue that—if participants know the set of cues that *could* occur on every trial—the absence of a cue can be salient. In other words, learners may notice the consistent absence of a cue on trials containing a certain outcome and develop a negative association between that cue and the outcome. Finally, one could argue that connections from absent cues to absent outcomes may also be updated, gaining strength: when a cue and an outcome are *absent together,* the learner is in a position to learn that absence of the cue predicts absence of the outcome (Tassoni, 1995). Thus, models of learning can be arranged from the simplest (wiring together present cues and outcomes only) and the least veridical—least able to faithfully reproduce environmental contingencies—to the most complex and the most veridical (updating all connections on every trial). In what follows, we examine what kinds of updating are needed to capture the experimental results by independently varying whether each distinct set of connections undergoes updating.

Associative learning theorists are in agreement that present stimuli are more salient than absent ones (e.g., Beckmann & Young, 2007; Tassoni, 1995), for at least three good reasons. First, absent stimuli are minimally intense, and high-intensity stimuli are known to lead to faster learning (e.g., Kamin, 1965). Second, an infinite number of stimuli are absent at any one time, making it impossible to attend to every conceivable absence (Beckmann & Young, 2007; Tassoni, 1995). Finally, absences are less informative than presences, as long as the stimulus in question is absent more often than it is present (McKenzie & Mikkelsen, 2007).

Convergent evidence comes from contingency judgment / causal learning studies. In these studies, participants are asked, for every possible cue-outcome pairing, to estimate whether the cue predicts the outcome. The advantage of causal learning is that—unlike in conditioning experiments—cues and outcomes are biologically irrelevant and interchangeable. This makes it possible to compare cue and outcome salience while controlling for the identity of the stimulus. For example, a common task is to learn contingencies between diseases and test results, where experimental instructions can make participants think that the tests detect either causes of the disease or its consequences.

Several studies using causal learning have found that the frequency of $p_c p_o$ is utilized by participants most, followed by the frequency of $p_c a_o$, followed by that of $a_c p_o$, with the $a_c a_o$ frequency being used least (Kao & Wasserman, 1993; Levin et al., 1993; Wasserman et al., 1990). Their results provide empirical backing for the assumption that presences are more salient than absences. However, they also suggest that participants do—at least occasionally—learn from absences, with absent outcomes being more salient than absent cues.

6.4.1 Extension: $p_c \geq a_c$

Table 6.2 shows predicted activations of the frequent suffix, its synonym, and the two other suffixes (which are always activated equally) by the semantic features of the novel meaning (MANY and SMALL) under all logically possible models of associative learning. The left column represents the simplest model anyone believes in, a joint frequency counter (cf. Bybee, 2010). Columns 2–4 represent association sets that can be added to the frequency counter to make contingency learning more veridical, incorporating learning of connections involving absent cues and/or outcomes. Column 5 is the model that learns only from present cues (a Hebbian version of Rescorla & Wagner, 1972). Column 6 is the full model that learns even about associations between absent cues and absent outcomes (a Hebbian version of Tassoni, 1995). Extension of frequent forms to novel meanings is predicted if the activation of the frequent form exceeds that of all other forms, including the frequent form's synonym. In other words, a preference to extend the frequent form to novel meanings is predicted whenever the largest number is in the top row.

According to table 6.2, extension of the frequent form is predicted by increasing the weights of connections from present cues to present

Table 6.2

SMALL.MANY→...	$p_c p_o$	$p_c a_o$	$a_c p_o$	$a_c a_o$	p_c	all
Frequent	72	−42	−18	15	30	24
Synonym	24	−66	−6	21	−42	−12
Other	24	−66	−6	21	−42	−12

Activations of the frequent suffix, its synonym, and the other two suffixes given the novel diminutive plural meaning under alternative models.

outcomes, as well as by decreasing the weights of connections from present cues to absent outcomes. Updating connections from absent cues (in the normative direction) acts against extension.

For the simulations reported in this table, it was assumed that an absence of a cue or outcome is noticed only half the time while its presence is always noticed. One might question whether absences are missed that often, and wonder whether noticing absences more would eliminate extension. However, it turns out that, for our experiment, a_c does not overpower p_c even if absences are as salient as presences. All extant models of learning agree that absent stimuli are no more salient than stimuli that are actually present and therefore all predict Zipfian extension. Despite its controversial status among human theorists, Zipfian extension receives unanimous support from learning *theories*.

6.4.2   Absence of Outcome Competition

Note that Hebbian theories considered above are unanimous in predicting no difference in extension probability between synonyms of frequent forms and forms that have no such strong competitor. This fits with our results, where boosting -*dan* vs. -*nem* had no appreciable effect on the use of -*sil* vs. -*shoon* with diminutive plurals (figure 6.3, left).

Interestingly, predictive error-driven associative learning models instantiated by RW (Rescorla & Wagner, 1972) expect competitors of frequent forms to be used to express the novel meaning especially rarely—as long as the learning rate is fast enough for the error-driven nature of the model to manifest itself (see also section 8.13). Because these models aim to predict which form will occur given some semantic feature(s), they learn to suppress the outcome that shares cues with a frequent competitor whenever the cues to both are present. Thus, high likelihood of extending a frequent form comes along with high likelihood of *not* extending its synonym.

Unlike Hebbian models, where activations are based on joint probabilities/frequencies, reflecting cue-outcome contiguity (Arcediano et al., 2005; Miller & Matzel, 1988), activations in the RW model, at the limit, match conditional probabilities of the forms given semantic features. For example, in the Dan language, the activation of -*dan* given [MANY.SMALL] is .75 while activation of -*sil* is .25. Activations of -*nem* and -*shoon* are both .5. These numbers come from the fact that the probability of -*sil* following a plural form is 25% during training, while the probability of -*nem* or -*shoon* following a small creature is 50%. The absence of this pattern of outcome competition in our results thus constitutes support for a Hebbian rather than a (fast) error-driven learning model.

6.4.3   Comprehension Effects: $|p_o| > |a_o| > 0$

Table 6.3 reports activation differences between features that distinguish the novel meaning from the familiar meaning paired with a form in training. Because of the Symmetry Principle, the activation differences correspond to meaning→form connection weights involving the semantic features in question. For example, the activation difference between the nondiminutive and diminutive plural for -dan is the weight of the connection between -dan and BIG minus the weight of the connection between -dan and SMALL. The activation difference between the diminutive singular and diminutive plural for -nem is the weight of the connection between -nem and ONE minus the weight of the connection between -nem and MANY (cf. Miller & Matzel, 1988).

Entrenchment is observed if this difference is larger (more positive) for a frequent form compared to the "other" forms—that is, if the value in the top row in table 6.3 is larger than the value in the bottom row. If this it true, the model expects that -dan should be restricted to nondiminutive plurals in the Dan language more than in the Nem language, and that -nem should be restricted to the diminutive singular in Nem more than in Dan.

Table 6.3 shows that entrenchment is favored by strengthening $p_c p_o$ connections between present cues and present outcomes, weakening $a_c p_o$ connections between absent cues and present outcomes, and strengthening $a_c a_o$ connections between absent cues and absent outcomes. Because updating $p_c p_o$ and $p_c a_o$ weights pull in different directions, entrenchment only occurs if absent outcomes are less salient than present outcomes. In other words, the weights of connections to absent outcomes must change less than the weights of connections to present outcomes.

Table 6.3
Comprehension effects

Experienced–Not	$p_c p_o$	$p_c a_o$	$a_c p_o$	$a_c a_o$	p_c	all
Frequent	36	0	36	6	36	78
Synonym	12	−12	12	−6	0	6
Other	12	12	0	0	24	24

Each cell contains the activation difference between the meaning paired with a form in training and the novel, diminutive plural, meaning. Activations of shared features of the competing meanings cancel out. Therefore, for plural suffixes this is the difference in activations between BIG and SMALL, and for diminutive suffixes it is the difference between singular vs. plural. Entrenchment is predicted if Frequent > Other. Niche seeking is predicted if Synonym < Other.

One might wonder whether there is anything at all in the data that compels us to assume that participants are reducing the weights of connections to absent outcomes. It turns out that these adjustments are demanded by niche seeking. In table 6.3, niche seeking is predicted if the difference in activations between the meaning paired with a form in training and the novel meaning is smallest for the "synonym" forms, which have a frequent competitor. In other words, the values in the middle row in table 6.3 should be smaller than in other rows, including the bottom one.

Table 6.3 shows that this is only the case when $p_c a_o$ or $a_c a_o$ connection weights are updated in the normative direction. It turns out that niche seeking will occur as long as they are updated at all, even if the updating is rare or results in small changes. Thus, the full pattern of results can be captured only if the weights of connections leading to absent outcomes are updated but updated less than connection weights leading to present outcomes. In other words, present outcomes are significantly more salient than absent ones. This appears to be a reasonable assumption (e.g., Tassoni, 1995), though not all extant models make it. For example, the Naive Discriminative Learner (Baayen et al., 2011), which uses equilibrium equations for the RW model from Danks (2003, p. 116), does not show entrenchment because the learning rates for present and absent outcomes in Danks's equations are equal, a simplifying assumption (Danks, 2003, pp. 115–116).

6.4.4   Accessibility: $|p_o| > |a_o| > 0$

What is accessibility? The simplest possibility is to claim that it is a function of the amount of activation that the outcome node receives from the present cues. Many associative learning models, including the RW model, make this assumption, in not having a separate representation for the frequency or resting activation level of an outcome. However, this seems to provide no possibility for capturing the difference between the production task and the forced form choice task. There needs to be some mechanism for directly boosting the activation level of a node from perceptual experience, leveling accessibility differences between alternative choices (Wagner, 1981).

One's conception of accessibility needs to simultaneously account for (1) the absence of form frequency effects in the forced form choice task, whether the meaning is novel or familiar, and (2) accurate choice between forms that have been paired with a meaning and forms that have not been paired with that meaning in the same task. In other words, participants seem to choose between forms that have been paired with a meaning at random while almost never choosing forms that have not co-occurred with that meaning. I propose that choice probabilities of alternative outcomes can be equalized (pushed to the ceiling) by activation from the signal only if both outcomes' activation levels before equalization are above zero. If the cue configuration on a test trial—its pattern of cue presences and absences—"thinks" that an outcome is impossible, its choice probability cannot be boosted by perceptual activation.

Note that I have switched here to talking of choice probability rather than activation. Activation of a form obviously *can* be boosted by direct perceptual experience: the participants do perceive forms they do not select. Perhaps one way to capture this difference is to say that perceptual activation boosts a perceptual representation, but response requires a *decision* to execute whatever response corresponds to the percept (see Broadbent, 1958, pp. 187–190, for a similar proposal). As illustrated in figure 6.4, the decision is driven by the cues, which gate propagation of activation down the percept→decision link, as well as having the potential to activate the decision directly.

Bidirectionality then requires connections from the outcome percept to the PF and Decision nodes of the cue, as shown in figure 6.5. Note that these connections must emanate from the Outcome *percept* node, so as to only strengthen outcome→cue connections when the outcome is actually perceived rather than merely predicted by the cue (a concern raised by Wagner, 1981).

The difference between forms that have and *have not* been paired with a meaning appears to require outcome inhibition, and—like entrenchment—it requires absent outcomes to be relatively low in salience. Too much updating of connections to absent outcomes pushes the synonym of the frequent suffix below zero when their shared meaning is presented. Once

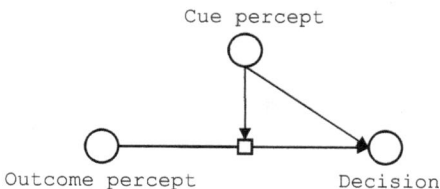

Figure 6.4
A model of associative learning that prevents perceptual activation from causing selection of activated outcomes that receive no support from the cues—for example, the wrong outcome in a binary-choice task with the choices clearly visible.

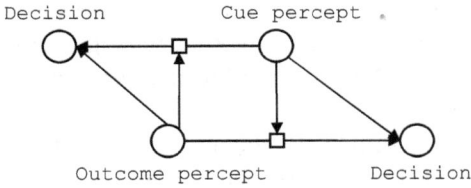

Decision   Cue percept

Outcome percept   Decision

Figure 6.5
A bidirectional architecture.

it falls below zero, the frequent suffix is predicted to always be chosen in preference to its synonym, which is not the case in the data.

Conversely, unless connections from absent cues are updated, participants are predicted to think that *-nem* and *-shoon* can be used to express nondiminutive plurals in Dan only if updating of connections to absent outcomes is really slow. To account for forms with the nonboosted meaning being chosen to express the novel meaning, present outcomes must be far more salient than their absences.

Interestingly, updating of connections between absent cues and absent outcomes makes the model far less sensitive to how much attention is paid to absent outcomes. It may be worth considering that we learn something about word-meaning pairings we do not encounter, at least in situations like this one, where the set of cues is limited, and thus cue absences are noticeable (see Tassoni, 1995; van Hamme & Wasserman, 1994; Wasserman & Castro, 2005).

6.5 Conclusion

Frequent forms expand in their range of uses as speakers extend them to new contexts and functions. In this chapter, we confirmed Zipf's (1949) hypothesis that semantic extension happens in production and that it depends on the more frequent forms being more accessible than their less frequent competitors. Extension of frequent forms happens despite entrenchment in comprehension. Frequent exposure to a form-meaning pairing increases the speakers' confidence that the form will always co-occur with that meaning in comprehension (F. Xu & Tenenbaum, 2007). Yet the frequent form becomes more likely to be chosen for expressing a novel meaning, unless accessibility differences between frequent and rare forms are neutralized. The effect of form accessibility on form choice results in a striking perception-production asymmetry: the forms that are least likely to be mapped onto a new meaning in comprehension are the most likely forms to be extended to the new meaning in production. Forms that have frequent competitors are most likely to be mapped onto a novel related meaning in comprehension but not in production.

We modeled these effects with simple Hebbian learning (Hebb, 1949), showing that all three results—*extension* of frequent forms in production, *entrenchment* of the same forms in comprehension, and frequent forms pushing their less frequent synonyms out of the shared *niche* in comprehension—can be captured with a simple learning mechanism, making a few assumptions that are typical of such models.

First, learning involves updating both weights of connections between present stimuli and—at least—weights of connections between present cues (here, semantic features) and absent outcomes. Sensibly, absent outcomes must be far less salient than present outcomes. As noted above, this assumption is uncontroversial (e.g., Beckmann & Young, 2007; Hearst, 1991; Tassoni, 1995) and supported by extensive evidence from contingency judgment studies (Kao & Wasserman, 1993; Levin et al., 1993; Wasserman et al., 1990).

One might wonder whether this implies that human learning does not result in a veridical representation of environmental contingencies. Paying too much attention to presences rather than absences can result in illusory correlations and the emergence of superstitions (Skinner, 1948). If a salient outcome follows a salient cue on a few occasions, you may learn that the cue leads to the outcome even when there is zero or negative correlation between them. However, McKenzie and Mikkelsen (2007) have pointed out that paying more attention to stimulus presences is normative whenever the stimuli are rare: the presence of a rare stimulus is more informative than its absence. In the present experiment—as in real schema learning—any given form or meaning is absent more often than it is present. Furthermore, the absence of a form in the presence of a meaning does not mean that the form cannot be used to express that meaning, whereas a form-meaning pairing means that the two *can* co-occur. Thus, one can argue that the weights of connections between present cues and absent outcomes *should* be reduced less than the weights of connections between present cues and present outcomes are strengthened on grounds of normative optimality.

Our second assumption is that learning is bidirectional by default: training on production leads to acquiring systematic form→meaning mappings that mirror the meaning→form mappings. We contend that bidirectionality is particularly important in a domain like language, where every producer wishes to be a comprehender, and every comprehender wishes to be a producer. Importantly, asymmetries between frequency effects in comprehension and production do not imply unidirectional learning. In fact, they can even fall out of a learning model that acquires bidirectional connections. As noted in chapter 4, bidirectional associative learning presents an alternative to generative models, since it can capture entrenchment effects. Given the importance of bidirectional learning, it is very fortunate that the word learning environment seems to provide plenty of opportunities for "breaking into" bidirectionality, as caretakers tend to name objects the child is looking at and continues to look at after the name is heard (Pereira et al., 2014).

Finally, learning in this experiment seems based on simple contiguity rather than prediction—a proposal that fits well with bidirectional learning (Kahana, 2002; Miller & Matzel, 1988). It is therefore consistent with Hebbian models of learning form-meaning pairings (McMurray et al., 2012, 2013; Yu & L. B. Smith, 2012). While frequent forms are especially likely to be extended to express a new meaning in production, their competitors are not particularly unlikely to be extended. This pattern of results is predicted if associations between cues and outcomes reflect joint probability of the cue-outcome pair and not conditional probability of the outcome given the cue (see also Arcediano et al., 2005; Matute et al., 1996). It is unexpected under predictive learning, at least if this learning is fast enough to result in the cue-competition effects that led learning theorists to prefer error-driven over Hebbian learning models. However, as I mentioned in chapter 1 and discuss in more detail in section 8.13, the behavior of the error-driven Rescorla-Wagner model with a slow learning rate is not appreciably different from that of a Hebbian model.

Finally, we have struggled with incorporating a notion of accessibility, as distinct from cue-driven activation, into an associative learning model. We saw that perceptual input does not boost patently incorrect outputs while equalizing choice probabilities of alternative correct outputs. This result requires rethinking the notion of an outcome. I have argued that the outcome is a decision node, distinct from a perceptual representation of the stimulus, and that cues both activate this decision node directly, thus driving whatever response is linked to it, and gate perceptual activation to the decision node.

7   Learning Paradigmatic Structure

> The strength of any particular paradigmatic response will depend on the number
> of times it has been erroneously anticipated for its stimulus.
> —McNeill (1966, p. 549)

In chapter 2, we considered the evidence for the existence of paradigmatic structure in natural languages, concluding that there are clear examples of morphological paradigms in which particular products are derived only from certain sources (Booij, 2010; Gouskova & Becker, 2013; Nesset, 2008; Pierrehumbert, 2006). If paradigmatic structure is real, then how is it learned, how is it represented, and what role does it play in language production? In this chapter, I propose that paradigmatic structure relies on (1) paradigmatic associations between segments and (2) knowledge about what parts of wordforms activated in memory should be copied into the production plan when one intends to express a particular meaning. Both of these kinds of knowledge can be represented with associations learned by generalizing over pairs of related wordforms.

7.1   Associationist Theories of Paradigm Learning

Work on paradigm learning in the lab began with McNeill (1963, 1966), who pursued an interesting hypothesis developed by Ervin (1961):

> A forward association would predict that repetition of *a cup of coffee* and *a cup of tea* would lead to the association of *coffee* with *tea* and of *tea* with *coffee*, due to their contiguity during competition of the response. A reverse, or mediated association, would be learned with practice of *front door* and *back door*. In this case, though, since *door* mediates the association of *front* and *back*, it would be the most likely response in free association. (pp. 361–362)

While Ervin (1961) developed these hypotheses to account for associations between canonical antonyms, they are clearly applicable to morphological paradigms as well. McNeill (1966), in the quote used as the epigraph above, suggests explicitly that the process involves generation of an erroneous expectation, which is then linked to what the listener perceives and therefore *should have* expected. Though McNeill considers his formulation to be a rephrasing of Ervin's hypothesis above, there are important differences that continue to distinguish alternative accounts of paradigm learning. First, Ervin's learner acquires paradigmatic associations through production practice, whereas McNeill's learns them from perceptual experience. Second, Ervin's associations are clearly bidirectional, while McNeill's are not. One might in fact question the directionality of McNeill's proposed association. It is easy to see how it is advantageous for the listener to learn an association from an incorrect output to a correct one but why would one want to learn an association from a correct output to an error? I am therefore tempted to revise McNeill's statement as "The strength of any particular paradigmatic response to a stimulus will depend on the number of times the stimulus has been erroneously anticipated when the response was contextually appropriate." In other words, a paradigmatic mapping from A to B is assumed to form whenever A is expected but B is observed. For example, a child hearing *went* in a context where she, having not yet learned a tense paradigm, expects *go* would learn a *go→went* association.

Given the dysfunctionality of Correct-Response→Wrong-Response associations, the only reason for forming such associations is that association learning is bidirectional by default (Ervin, 1961). Bidirectionality in paradigmatic learning would allow the learner to derive either of the paradigmatically connected forms from the other. While it may lead to some errors, where the wrong form is activated too much by the context-appropriate one, these errors are unlikely to be numerous. In a morphological paradigm, the context-appropriate form is supported by schematic structure: it alone allows one to express the desired meaning. This reduces the likelihood of producing a context-inappropriate form even when it is activated by the context-appropriate one. Thus, an appropriate→inappropriate association may not result in many errors, at least under normal circumstances when you have enough resources for cognitive control: a context-inappropriate form partially activated by its context-appropriate competitor is usually easily ruled out by top-down activation flow (see also Dell, 1985).

Bidirectional paradigmatic associations would allow one to account for some otherwise puzzling morphological patterns, namely morphological toggles. In a toggle, two morphological patterns are in complementary distribution within each word paradigm but form choice is not conditioned by meaning. For example, in Dinka, vowels of singulars with long vowels are shortened to form the plural, while vowels of singulars with short vowels are lengthened (Inkelas, 2015, pp. 72–74). Given bidirectional paradigmatic associations, toggles can result when schematic and contextual constraints are too weak. However, toggles are very rare, suggesting that failure to acquire semantic conditioning of form choice / top-down meaning→form associations is not a common outcome of morphological learning.

The Association-by-Anticipation hypothesis is related to the (often implicit) hypothesis that has dominated the literature on error-driven learning of paradigmatic mappings within the connectionist tradition starting with Rumelhart and McClelland (1986). For example, Plunkett and Juola (1999) write that "the child is continually taking in word tokens and comparing the words actually heard (e.g., 'went') to the tokens that the child's hypothesis generator would have been expected to produce …; when they differ, this provides evidence to the child that the hypotheses are wrong and should be modified" (p. 466). McNeill (1966) and Plunkett and Juola (1999) both propose that paradigmatic mappings are learned from perceptual experience. However, McNeill would have the child activate a known form of the same word (the base form), an expectation that is then disconfirmed. In contrast, Plunkett and Juola would have the child first hear a form produced by an adult and then predict what form they would have produced to express the same meaning given the base form. Furthermore, Plunkett and Juola's learner generates an expectation knowing what they should have expected, while McNeill's learner forms expectations and then disconfirms them. Finally, because the wrong prediction is an actual correct form appropriate in other contexts for McNeill but an incorrect form for Plunkett and Juola, McNeill's learner acquires a mapping between the wrong prediction and the correct output, while Plunkett and Juola's learns to inhibit the incorrect prediction. However, in either case, the learner acquires paradigmatic mappings from perceptual experience by generating and (dis)confirming expectations about the forms she hears.

If paradigmatic associations are acquired when the to-be-associated forms occur in similar contexts, then the more often two forms occur in the same context, the more opportunities there are for associating them together (McNeill, 1966). The importance of shared context in acquiring paradigmatic associations has been documented by Brooks et al. (1993). They contrast learning paradigmatic mappings associated with arbitrary classes of nouns and those associated with nouns marked by an additional contextual cue. In the "systematic" language illustrated in (3), each noun class was marked by a unique affix on 60% of the training trials. In the "unsystematic" language, the two affixes were randomly paired with the word classes. In both languages, each word class was associated with a distinct preposition paradigm. Thus, Class I nouns took *ast* 'at' and *eef* 'to' while Class II nouns took *tev* 'at' and *foo* 'to'. Participants exposed to the systematic language acquired the paradigmatic mappings while those exposed to the unsystematic language did not. Importantly, after exposure to the systematic language, participants did not simply learn syntagmatic affix-preposition associations: they could appropriately switch prepositions with unmarked nouns, generating *ast* for *eef* and *tev* for *foo* in the absence of a class-marking affix. Thus, with syntagmatic support, participants were able to learn paradigmatic mappings (see also Frigo & MacDonald, 1998).

(1) Class I:
      {*ast*; *eef*} N (*oik*)$_{60\%}$
      {'at';'to'} LOCATION

      Class II:
      {*tev*; *foo*} N (*oo*)$_{60\%}$
      '{at';'to'} LOCATION

Note that in Brooks et al. (1993) and Frigo and McDonald (1998), the contextual cue C shared by the to-be-associated paradigm members followed rather than preceded these members. Thus, encountering A→C and B→C led to the emergence of A←→B mappings. The mechanism behind this learning is therefore unlikely to be Association-by-Anticipation. Instead, the likely mechanism is *acquired equivalence* (Ervin's "reverse association"): the two prepositions (A~B) are associated because they are categorized together as *equivalent cues*, both signaling the same upcoming affix (see also Foss & Jenkins, 1966; Holt et al., 1998; Locke, 1968; Liljeholm & Balleine, 2010; Moreton & Pater, 2012a).

Taatgen and Anderson (2002) object to the notion that paradigmatic mappings are learned from perceptual experience and suggest that paradigmatic mappings are learned—at least in part—from production practice. They note that in earlier computational models of paradigm learning, "When the child actually has to produce a past tense, the network is used without any learning, as there is no feedback to adjust its weights. This implies language production itself has no impact at all on performance, defying the general idea that practice is an important aspect of learning" (Taatgen & Anderson, 2002, p. 129).

Assuming multiple pairs of wordforms share the same paradigmatic mapping, this mapping will keep being practiced as a speaker generates forms that are hard for her to access from forms that can be accessed more easily. A paradigmatic mapping can then be acquired through simple Hebbian learning within the production system (as also suggested by Ervin, 1961). Unfortunately, we do not have data on whether production experience is important for acquiring paradigmatic mappings. However, evidence for Hebbian learning in other domains makes this hypothesis a serious contender.

Finally, just as syntagmatic co-occurrence in speech can help one acquire pairs of canonical antonyms (see chapter 2), it can also help one acquire morphological paradigms. Morphologically related words are far more likely to co-occur within a limited window of text than any other word pairs. Because of this, computational models that seek to identify sets of words sharing a stem are found to benefit from paying attention to co-occurrence (Baroni et al., 2002; J. Xu & W. B. Croft, 1998). Paradigmatic association learning may crucially rely on experiencing paradigmatically related words in syntagmatic proximity. In fact, work by Weir (1962) suggests that children may even bring paradigmatically related words into syntagmatic proximity on their own, by spontaneously practicing morphological paradigms.

7.2 Competition in Production

When we try to produce a complex wordform, it is commonly assumed that alternative generalizations compete with each other, rooting for different outcomes. *Part* of this competition can be described as a race between *retrieving* the complete wordform from the lexicon and *constructing* the wordform using the grammar (e.g., Kapatsinski, 2010b, 2010c; O'Donnell, 2015; Pinker & Prince, 1988).

The competition between computation and retrieval explains why exceptions to productive grammatical patterns invariably occur in frequent words, which can be retrieved from memory directly (Bybee, 2001). For example, the only irregular English past tense forms that have survived the rise of *-ed* are the most frequent ones, less frequent forms having undergone "analogical change" (see also Phillips, 1984). Whereas speakers can use, and accept the use of, the innovative *weeped* in place of *wept* or *creeped* in place of *crept*, they show no inclination to use *keeped* in place of *kept* and find such uses completely unacceptable. Whenever an "exceptional" form is constructed online, it has the chance of succumbing to a more general pattern, becoming regularized and falling in line with its unexceptional peers. Since frequent forms are usually retrieved from memory directly, rather than constructed online, they are less likely to succumb to peer pressure.[1]

Bybee (2008) notes that once phonological alternations become associated with specific morphemes, they tend to lose productivity even in that specific morphological context. For example, velar palatalization in Russian has lost productivity before the verbal stem extension -*i* and no longer applies to new borrowings, despite the absence of any exceptions to velar palatalization before -*i* in Russian dictionaries (Kapatsinski, 2009b, 2010b). Competition between lexical schemas and more abstract ones helps explain this "diachronic universal." Russian speakers are able to produce existing words like *ot-srotʃ-i-tʲ* 'to delay'—cf. *srok* 'deadline'—with a [tʃ] despite producing novel borrowings like *buk-i-tʲ* 'to book' with a [k] because established words like *otsrotʃitʲ* can be retrieved from the lexicon rather than constructed on the fly. In such words, palatalization only *seems* to be applied. The word is simply retrieved from memory, [tʃ] and all. This is why—as proposed by Berko (1958)—productivity needs to be tested with novel words.

Kapatsinski (2010c) presents an interesting case in which an orthographic rule, explicitly taught to all Russian schoolchildren, remains unlearned into adulthood, and yet this lack of knowledge is never detected by teachers and testers. When a Russian is faced with an unfamiliar adjective like *bes-kreditnyj* 'creditless' containing the prefix /bez/ before a voiceless consonant, they should spell it *bes*, the way it is actually pronounced in this context. However, Russian writers are as likely to erroneously write *bez* as to correctly write *bes*—even when a grade depends on it. Nonetheless, Russians are extremely accurate at spelling adjectives they know like *bes-krylyj* 'wingless' or *bes-platnyj* 'payless/free'. Russian schoolchildren and college students are extensively tested on their knowledge of orthography using dictation tests, which involve writing down literary passages. However, because the passages contain only frequent *bes-* adjectives, the students are only ever tested on spelling words whose orthographic forms are stored and easily accessible in memory. As a result, the lack of rule knowledge remains undetected throughout the years of schooling and came as a great surprise to my mother, a Russian professor who's graded thousands of dictation tests.

7.3   Interactions between the Three Kinds of Structure in Morphology

Competition cannot be reduced to a race between the lexicon and the grammar because the grammar is itself probabilistic. Generalization over words and utterances produces competing generalizations that—in certain contexts—root for different outcomes (e.g., Albright & Hayes, 2003; Kapatsinski, 2010c, 2013).

If we know both what wordforms with a certain meaning are like and how those wordforms relate to other forms of the same word, then we have two different ways of producing a new form of a known word to express a certain meaning using the grammar. This introduces an opportunity for competition. We could use our schematic knowledge to produce a form that contains the best cues to the meaning we want to express (or epitomizes the kind of form that bears that meaning). Alternatively, we could use our paradigmatic knowledge to produce the form we don't know from the form we do know, replicating a form-form relationship we have observed or practiced. Bybee (1985, 2001) calls these two ways of producing words *product-oriented* and *source-oriented* respectively.

As we move down along the meaningfulness continuum, product-oriented schemas fade into phonotactic constraints like "a word must consist of syllables with onsets," whereas paradigmatic mappings between schemas fade into phonological rules. Of course, theories of phonology and morphology have tried to use one or the other, avoiding redundant duplication of function (e.g., Chomsky & Halle, 1968, use only rules; Prince & Smolensky, 1993/2008, use only constraints; Bybee, 2001, similarly hopes that schematic structure can capture all productive morphological patterns). However, as pointed out by Householder (1966) among others, redundancy is the norm rather than the exception in cognitive systems. Redundancy is what makes the brain robust to damage. Having multiple paths to a goal provides flexibility when one path is blocked. Furthermore, the empirical work reviewed in chapter 2 suggests that both schematic and paradigmatic mappings are learned in the course of language acquisition. Therefore, in the present book, I pursue the hypothesis that both schematic and paradigmatic mappings are applied *in parallel* as a word is being constructed.

Following a long tradition in linguistics, I assume that productive construction of a wordform is a kind of "fallback" process that takes place when lexical retrieval fails: the grammar is largely for expressing meanings you haven't expressed before (for various versions of this assumption, cf. Albright & Hayes, 2003; Aronoff, 1976; Bybee, 1985, 2001; Halle, 1973;

Nesset, 2008; O'Donnell, 2015; Pinker & Prince, 1988). In other words, the competitive processes described below drive form choice when a schema that can express the full intended meaning is inaccessible.

This is not to say that production of known words and novel words is qualitatively different, as argued by proponents of the Dual Mechanism approach (Halle, 1973; O'Donnell, 2015; Pinker & Prince, 1988). Rather, activation spreads in parallel down schematic and paradigmatic associations, resulting in competition between alternative outcomes. However, forms that can express more of the meaning the speaker intends to communicate have a competitive advantage (see also Caballero & Inkelas, 2013; Langacker, 1987; Nesset, 2008). When there is a schema that can express *all* of the meaning the speaker intends, it has the biggest advantage and usually—if frequent enough—is selected without much visible competition from other generalizations. However, Milin et al. (2009) show that competition is always there if one looks closely enough. Even when a reasonably frequent morphologically simple word is produced—a process that usually completes without error—the frequencies of other forms of the word influence processing effort.

While it is probably more usual for paradigmatic and syntagmatic structure to converge on the same output (as disagreement should be diachronically unstable), it is easy to devise an artificial language in which the two conflict, rooting for distinct products. By teaching such a language to human participants, one can then examine the sorts of experiences that are particularly helpful for acquiring the two types of structure as well as the timecourse of their acquisition.

A dramatic example of disagreement between schematic and paradigmatic structure can be seen in many cases of subtraction, where either paradigmatic or schematic structure may triumph. Dominance of paradigmatic structure is seen in across-the-board subtraction as observed in Tohono-O'odham, where perfective verbs are derived from imperfectives by deleting the final segment. In such systems, there is paradigmatic systematicity (what is deleted is always the final segment) accompanied by schematic variability (the outcome can be of any prosodic shape); see (4), from Inkelas (2015, p. 61).

(2) síkon→síko
    híwa→híw
    hi:nk→hi:n

When schematic structure plays a significant role in a subtractive process, we usually call the process *truncation*, with the idea that the form is truncated to a constant shape (Inkelas, 2015, pp. 68–70, 33–37; see also McCarthy & Prince, 1999). For example, Caballero (2008, pp. 123–126) reports that trisyllabic noun stems in Choguita Rarámuri are truncated to two syllables before the verbalizing suffix -ta. Importantly, disyllabic noun stems remain unchanged, indicating that the process is not an across-the-board subtraction.

Another example of schematic structure overriding paradigmatic structure is found in Japanese girls' nickname formation, which involves fitting the full name to a bimoraic template and suffixation with -tʃan (e.g., akira→aki-tʃan). Since most full names are longer than two morae, this means that nicknames are usually formed by subtraction. However, shorter names are lengthened to two morae (Poser, 1990, pp. 82–84; see also Inkelas, 2015, p. 34). The existence—and rarity—of lengthening suggest that, despite most nicknames being formed by subtraction, Japanese speakers learn that nicknames should be bimoraic, a product-oriented schema.

What makes one likely to learn and *use* a schema in deriving forms one has previously experienced resulting from a subtractive process? In Kapatsinski (2013), I proposed that it is crucial to know what to do in order to fill the schema: if the schema is too general, it leaves the speaker uncertain about how it should be filled. We avoid placing ourselves in situations of uncertainty by our own actions. For example, Albright (2003, 2009) shows that paradigm gaps occur precisely when two forms are equally strong competitors. Faced with uncertainty regarding whether to express "I vacuum" with *pylesosu* or *pylesošu*, Russian speakers avoid trying to produce the form altogether. This hypothesis can be considered a special case of the *uncertainty avoidance principle* in decision making (Hofstede, 1980).

In Kapatsinski (2017), I tested the uncertainty avoidance principle by presenting a large sample of native English speakers with languages that exemplified a subtractive morphological process. In paradigmatic terms, the plural was formed from the singular by deleting the final vowel. Thus, *patoki*$_{SG}$→*patok*$_{PL}$; *kalupa*$_{SG}$→*kalup*$_{PL}$; *dalumo*$_{SG}$→*dalum*$_{PL}$. However, as illustrated, all singular forms presented in training happened to fit a trisyllabic CVCVCV template. As a result, deletion resulted in plural forms fitting a disyllabic CVCVC template (much as deletion results in a bimoraic output in Japanese nicknames). Thus, learners were entitled to make the schematic generalization that plurals are CVCVC disyllables, just as Japanese speakers have apparently inferred that nicknames are bimoraic. Consider now what happens when the learner is tested on a CVCV singular like *muto*. Paradigmatic structure demands deletion of the final vowel, rooting for *mut*.

Schematic structure instead roots for a CVCVC product, demanding addition of a consonant (e.g., *mutok*).

To test uncertainty avoidance, I manipulated the speakers' uncertainty by varying whether the training favored one consonant over others for addition. If one consonant is overrepresented at the end of CVCVC plurals, the speaker knows what to add when faced with a CVCV source. If one does not know which consonant to add, one might choose to delete instead, satisfying paradigmatic structure. However, if one *does* know what consonant to add, schematic behavior should become a viable competitor (Kapatsinski, 2013).[2]

Participants ($N = 60$ per language) were presented with one of five languages. Training consisted of listening to wordforms, presented in a completely random order, while looking at pictures of referents. Training was intentionally short, concluding after only five minutes. For singular forms, the referent was a single alien creature, while for plural forms the pictures showed multiple aliens of the same kind. In all languages, plurals were formed from singulars by vowel deletion and CVCV singulars were encountered only at test. Participants were tested on both CVCV and CVCVCV singulars.

In the Baseline language (CVCVk nowhere in figure 7.1), the final consonant of the stem could be any one of {t;k;p;f;s;m;n}, with [k] occurring in three words, and every other consonant occurring in one word. Thus, if a participant decided to add a consonant, they may be quite uncertain about what *particular* consonant to add. As expected, addition was strongly dispreferred, even with CVCV singulars where schematic structure demands it.

In the DeletionBoost language (leftmost in figure 7.1), extra examples of vowel deletion with [k]-final stems were added to training. Despite the fact that these examples exemplify both deletion (paradigmatically) and "plurals are CVCVk" (schematically), they helped the schema more than they helped the rule, increasing the likelihood of consonant addition.[3]

In the ?→CVCVk ("product") and CVCVk→? ("source") languages (second panel from the left), I presented participants with additional CVCVk forms in one of the two meanings. In these languages, the additional training trials provide support for a final [k] without providing support for deletion. However, only the ?→CVCVk ("product") language provides support for the final [k] *as a cue to plurality*. The CVCVk→? ("source") language, by introducing CVCVk singulars, breaks the connection between CVCVk and the plural meaning. Thus, the CVCVk→? language favors consonant addition in a syntagmatic way—a CVCV *must* continue into a

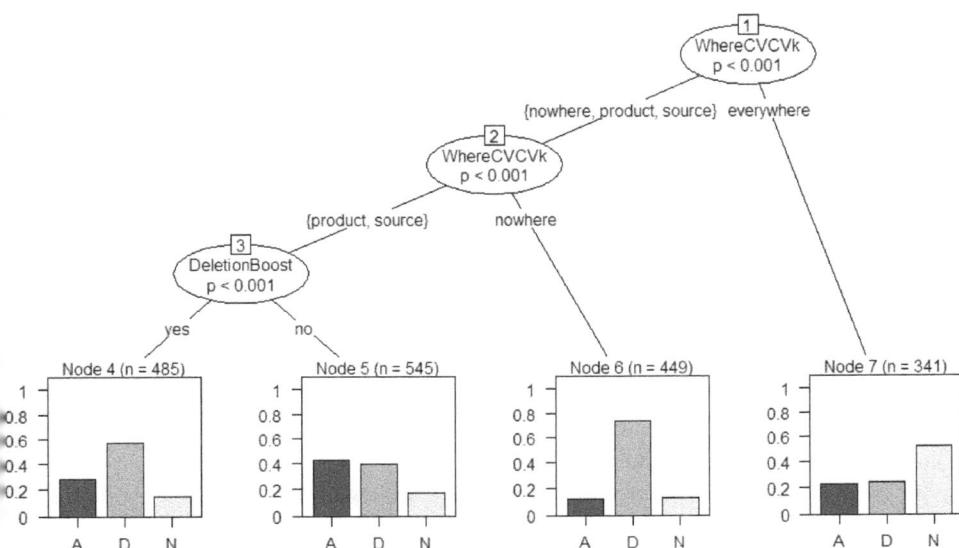

Figure 7.1
Rates of Addition (A), Deletion (D), vs. No-Change (N) operations performed on CVCV singulars. The top split is between the language in which additional CVCVk forms are added to both singulars and plurals (CVCVk everywhere) vs. others. The CVCVk-everywhere language favors not changing the base: homonymy begets homonymy. The next split separates out the language in which extra CVCVk examples are not added (Baseline), which favors deletion. Languages with additional CVCVk examples added to either the singular or the plural pattern together. However, the language in which CVCVkV singulars are also added splits off as favoring deletion (though not as much as the Baseline language).

consonant—while disfavoring it schematically: CVCVk is no longer a good cue to PLURAL. Interestingly, both languages favored addition over the baseline language and the language exemplifying deletion and did not differ from each other in the likelihood of consonant addition with CVCV singulars. Despite breaking the connection between CVCVC and plurality, the extra CVCVk~SINGULAR examples in the CVCVk→? language favored CVCV→CVCVC over CVCV→CVC. These results suggest that the favoring of addition that happened in this language—and possibly all other languages—was actually due to syntagmatic structure, not schematic structure.

Finally, the CVCVk→CVCVk language ("CVCVk everywhere," right-most panel) featured extra examples of CVCVk in both the singular and plural meaning. Thus, it doubled the number of CVCVk examples compared to either the ?→CVCVk language or the CVCVk→? language. Syntagmatic structure would therefore expect consonant addition to be most productive in this language. Interestingly, this did not happen. Instead, this language strongly favored not changing the singular form at all, favoring CVCV→CVCV over either CVCV→CVC or CVCV→CVCVC. When presented with paradigmatic mappings exemplifying no change, participants went for that (maximally easy) paradigmatic mapping.

The difference between the CVCVk→? language and the CVCVk→CVCVk language suggests that the preference for not changing the input in the CVCVk→CVCVk language is not due to CVCVC being mapped onto both singular and plural—this is true of both languages—but rather due to the presence of homophonous paradigmatically related forms. Consonant addition loses to no change in the CVCVk→CVCVk language not because CVCVC is a poor cue to plurality in this language but rather because the language provides evidence that the plural is not marked at all.

At this point, the subtraction data provide no clear evidence for a role of schematic structure in production of novel wordforms: the increase in consonant addition when trained on extra examples of CVCVCV→ CVCVk, $CVCVk_{PL}$, or $CVCVk_{SG}$ can be captured by syntagmatic structure, a hypothesis supported by the fact that it makes no difference whether the extra examples of CVCVk are paired with the right meaning. Fortunately, schemas reemerge when we examine *which* consonant is added. While participants preferred to add [k] rather than something else even in the Baseline language, [k]-addition was favored by languages that presented participants with extra examples of final [k] paired with the plural meaning. In contrast, the CVCVk→? language patterned with the baseline.[4] The fact that $CVCVk_{SG}$ examples do not favor a final [k] in the plural while $CVCVk_{PL}$ examples do suggests that this preference is schematic in nature.

Interestingly, the CVCVk→CVCVk language patterned with ?→CVCVk rather than with CVCVk→?, despite making a final [k] a bad cue to plurality. Thus, if a participant decides that the plural should be CVCVC (something they are unlikely to do when exposed to that language), the consonant they add is [k]. This is unsurprising because most CVCVC forms in this language are CVCVk. Thus, for this language, the preference for [k]—provided that some consonant is added—is favored by both syntagmatic and schematic structure.

The difference in how CVCVk→? ("source") and ?→CVCVk ("product") pattern in figures 7.1 and 7.2 suggests that participants tend to acquire

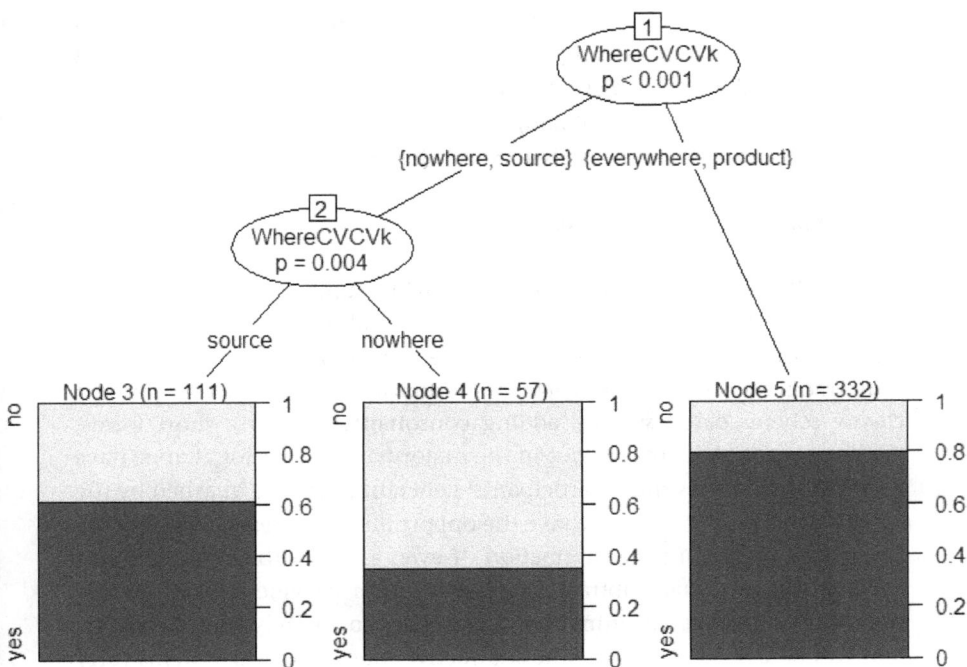

Figure 7.2
When a consonant is added, is that consonant [k]? Languages that present participants with additional CVCVk examples paired with the right meaning pattern together, favoring [k]. The language in which the CVCVk examples are always paired
with the wrong meaning patterns closer to the Baseline language, though it also
favors [k] over the Baseline.

CVCVC as a meaning-independent prosodic template while acquiring a
mapping between the specific segment k# and plurality. This reluctance
to assign meaning to the prosodic template is likely a learned irrelevance
effect that comes from experience with English. Prosodic templates *can* be
meaningful—most clearly in Semitic languages (McCarthy, 1982)—but they
are not meaningful in English. Thus, at least by the time they are undergrad-
uates, English speakers may be prepared to associate meaning with specific
segmental material but unprepared to associate meaning with a prosodic
template, paying little attention to template-meaning co-occurrences. The
dissociation of content and template also suggests that separate decisions
are made about what the template is and what it should be filled with. This
is, of course, a standard assumption in models of speech production (e.g.,

Shattuck-Hufnagel, 2015). Nonetheless, it is important to point out that an associative framework for language learning does not mean that we must necessarily eschew such mentalist notions as abstract internal representations or processing stages (Tolman, 1938; see also Bouton, 2016; McMurray et al., 2013; Rescorla, 1988; Yu & L. B. Smith, 2012).

7.4   Implications for Language Change

The results reported in this chapter provide support for a diachronic pathway from subtractive morphology to truncation; see also Kapatsinski (2017). Note that all learners in the present experiment were exposed to a subtractive system. Nonetheless, a substantial number have acquired a clearly schema-based system, adding consonants to overly short forms. While these participants are not in the majority, the seeds for change have been planted: unless these participants' generalizations are quashed by the speech community, they will have the opportunity to spread, changing the language away from pure subtraction. If even a few of the additive forms become conventional, subtraction will no longer provide a good description of the language, meaning that a path back to a purely subtractive system will be cut off. At least some subtractive morphological systems carry within them the seeds of their own destruction.

Whereas templates arise from imperfect learning of paradigmatic structure, imperfect learning of schematic structure can result in a morphological toggle. Another example is presented by the language Trique, where a stem-final /h/ is deleted to form first-person singular possessives but /h/ is added to vowel-final stems (Inkelas, 2015, pp. 72–74). I have also seen this kind of system spontaneously induced in the laboratory from exposure to a language that lacks it, suggesting that a toggle might arise *as a toggle*. For example, when I present English-speaking participants with a language in which [k]-final singulars have [tʃi]-final plurals (bluk~blutʃi), a small minority infer that [tʃ]-final singulars should have [ki]-final plurals (blutʃ~bluki), inducing a k~tʃ toggle.

If we assume that paradigmatic mappings are associations, then the emergence of toggles suggests some degree of associative symmetry (Asch & Ebenholtz, 1962). Under associative symmetry, learning k→tʃ implies learning tʃ→k. Activating one of the associated forms activates the other. Thus, toggles may be a side effect of bidirectional learning (chapter 6), in this case involving paradigmatic associations. What keeps a bidirectional paradigmatic association from leading to a toggle are the form-meaning associations of the forms it connects. If the associated forms are insufficiently associated with their meanings, then a toggle should result.

7.5   Copying: The Operation behind Creative Production

Thus far, we have been speaking of paradigmatic structure as associations between structures, whether these structures are schemas of forms, segments/gestures, or prosodic templates. However, the generalization of subtraction from trisyllables to disyllables requires something else. Mapping CVCVCV onto CVCVC and mapping CVCV onto CVC share an *operation*: the final vowel of the input is deleted, whatever the resulting outcome.

What kind of operation(s) do we need? I would like to suggest that we need only one, *copying*. Whenever a speaker tries to produce a word (or a larger structure), s/he generate a production plan, which is then executed (Lashley, 1951). Generating a production plan is of course essential for producing novel sequences that cannot simply be retrieved from memory and may also be required at the utterance level for producing an utterance in a novel way (e.g., with a novel intonation contour). The ability to plan a sequence of behaviors may be a major evolutionary prerequisite for language (Broadbent, 1958, pp. 46–47; Christiansen & Chater, 2016). Planning in speech is quite extensive and detailed. For example, speakers take bigger breaths before longer utterances, suggesting that they know how long the utterance will be before they start execution (Fuchs et al., 2013; see also Shattuck-Hufnagel, 2015, for a review). Given the need for planning, *copying* can be defined as incorporating activated units into the plan. When a form is produced in a novel context, it must have been copied, in its entirety, into the production plan.

7.5.1   What Is the Plan?

In accordance with prosody-first views of production, I assume that constructing the production plan at the word level often involves selecting and filling a prosodic template (e.g., Shattuck-Hufnagel, 2015), with the important caveat that there is nothing preventing memorized templates from being partially filled and retrieved as a whole. Following Inkelas (2015, p. 82), I consider templates to be morphological schemas constraining the prosodic shape of the product. While my participants tended not to consider the template meaningful, some templates can be associated with rather specific meanings. For example, "noise words" in Guarani all have the shape CVrVrV, with the first consonant an obstruent or [w] (Inkelas,

2015, pp. 91–92). Thus, the meaningfulness of a template—like that of other schemas—falls on a continuum of specificity.

Just as syntactic constructions are often partially filled (Goldberg, 1995, 2006), templatic constructions can be partially filled. For example, prosodic restrictions on stem shapes are often associated with specific affixes (Inkelas, 2015, pp. 88–94). In a constructionist account, the affix is part of the construction, which also has an open slot for a stem. This slot specifies a category of stem constructions, which can constrain that stem to be of a certain form or to have a certain kind of meaning. For example, the Choguita Rarámuri verbalizing template (Caballero, 2008) could be described as "verbs must have -ta preceded by a noun stem of only two syllables," or [σσ]ₙta. Like partially filled syntactic constructions such as [ ]ᴀɢᴇɴᴛ.ᵢ [ ]ᴀᴄᴛɪᴏɴ [ ]ᴀɢᴇɴᴛ.ᵢ.ᴘᴏꜱꜱ *way* [ ]ʟᴏᴄ exemplified by *I sneezed my way up the stairs*, partially filled morphological constructions can arise both by generalization over examples (Tomasello, 2003) and by fusion of co-occurring elements, segmental and prosodic (Bybee, 2002a). Indeed, it is hard to think of a theory that would *prevent* them from arising.

Some schemas are very specific about the prosodic shape of the output—for example, constraining it to be two syllables, no more and no less. Such schemas specify both boundaries of the unit they describe: [σσ]. Others merely enforce a *minimum* shape, specifying only one boundary: a *minimal word constraint* like [σσ] allows words to be arbitrarily long as long as they are long enough. Some schemas (like the ones just noted) do not specify segmental content. Others do specify segmental content without specifying the prosodic structure of the resulting word beyond what the specified segmental content requires. The affixes of concatenative morphology like plural -s] are of this kind. At the most abstract end of the specificity continuum lie schemas capturing meaning-independent phonotactic generalizations. At the most concrete end, specifying both prosodic structure and segmental content, lie wordforms. In between is morphology.

The need to learn to perform operations in production may be what makes production more paradigmatic than judgment, which is far more focused on the appropriateness of the outcome given the meaning that the speaker wants to express than on how the speaker arrived at the outcome (Kapatsinski, 2012). In language, as in many other domains, you are judged on what you accomplish, and not on how you get there. If you generate a good product in a novel, unorthodox way, you are not punished for your creativity. This means that paradigmatic conditioning of product forms is likely maintained (or even introduced) by speakers without significant normative pressure from a listener "put off" by forms with an unorthodox derivational history.

7.5.2   Why Copy?

Every new utterance is made of parts of existing utterances. Where do these parts come from? They must have been stored in and retrieved from long-term memory. However, at any given time, many linguistic units are activated in memory, to various degrees, but only some of them will be produced—and in a specific order, which may not correspond to level of activation prior to inclusion in the plan. To produce anything, the speaker must decide to incorporate it into the production plan. It is this process of decision making that I call *copying*.[5]

Copying is both necessary and sufficient to capture the attested kinds of paradigmatic mappings. That is, "no change" involves copying every element of the activated base form. Addition requires copying the base coupled with paradigmatic and/or schematic activation of the added part. Change requires copying to be outcompeted by a coalition of schematic, syntagmatic, and/or paradigmatic mappings. Subtraction requires inhibition of copying in a specific position within the template.[6]

Of course, subtractive morphology is crosslinguistically rare. Its rarity may lead one to question the need for a basic mechanism to capture its acquisition. However, crosslinguistic rarity of a pattern need not imply that it is difficult to acquire, and dissociations between crosslinguistic frequency and learnability have been reported (see Moreton & Pater, 2012b, for a review). Rather than directly reflecting learnability, crosslinguistic frequency of a pattern is also affected by usability and the frequency of diachronic pathways leading to the pattern's emergence (Blevins, 2004; Bybee, 2001; Fay & Ellison, 2013; Moreton, 2008).

Subtractive morphology is not very usable because it cannot be used bidirectionally: one knows what to subtract to form, say, the plural, but does not know what to add to form the singular when the plural is known. Low usability makes a pattern diachronically unstable. When one is faced with the task of adding something, a Zipfian rich-get-richer loop comes into play, which may eventually result in the subtractive process becoming additive. In fact, many participants excluded from the analyses in the present chapter learned an additive pattern, where [k] was added to form plurals, in accordance with a product-oriented schema with underspecified prosodic structure, k#~PLURAL.

Subtractive morphology is not only likely to go away through Zipfian accessibility pressures in production, but is also unlikely to arise. As described in chapter 6, morphology arises through grammaticalization of independent words: today's morphology is yesterday's syntax (Givón, 1971). Additive morphology arises when some word grammaticalizes enough to become an affix. Subtractive morphology, on the other hand, requires grammaticalization of at least two synonymous markers that are similar enough in sound that a single deletion rule can delete any one of them.

Fortunately, learning not to copy a particular part of the base into the production plan is useful outside of subtraction, in run-of-the-mill concatenative morphology, to take off markers added by concatenative schemas. For example, an English speaker may derive a singular form from a more accessible plural by subtracting -*s*.

Of course, subtraction, addition, and change are rarely context-independent. They usually affect only certain segments, or take place in forms with certain meanings. Thus, the strength of a tendency to copy some part of the activated base form(s) needs to vary by context. This means that the learner needs to learn *when and what to copy*. I assume that this is done by an associative learning mechanism that tries to determine when the speaker copies a segment in a certain prosodic position from another form, given surrounding segments in the output form, the content of the hypothesized base form, and the perceived meaning of the output form. In other words, copying in a certain prosodic position is an *outcome* that the learner tries to predict, given both semantic and formal cues.

7.5.3   Copying as a Paradigmatic Outcome

While many believe in some version of copying, the proposal that copying is learned (or at least upweighted), and that this learning happens by generalizing over pairs of wordforms, runs counter to many claims in the literature. For example, research in Optimality Theory argues that faithfulness—OT's version of copying—is ranked above all other constraints early in learning (e.g., Hayes, 2004). Taatgen and Anderson (2002) similarly argue that copying ("do nothing") starts out as the default morphological operation and therefore does not need to be learned. Furthermore, several researchers propose that the tendency to not change the stem (a primary function of copying) is instead due to the speaker needing to transmit the meaning of the stem to the listener. Specifically, suppose that presenting the base on a test trial results in rapid learning of schematic associations between the base form and the stem meaning (identity of the creature in our experiments). The speaker then tries to come up with a form that expresses both plurality and the stem meaning. Changing the stem would destroy cues to its meaning, resulting in avoidance of stem changes (Kenstowicz, 1996).

Crucially, if copying is a generalization made by observing lack of stem changes in training, then placing singular-plural forms sharing the stem allomorph next to each other during training should make this generalization more obvious and reduce palatalization rates. No other account of stem change avoidance makes this prediction. If copying is not learned, starting out on top to begin with, then experience with copying cannot strengthen it any further. If stem changes are avoided because the speaker wishes to express the stem meaning, then training should not matter for novel test stems, which are not encountered in training.

Fortunately for our hypothesis, the prediction was confirmed by Amy Smolek, who presented native English speakers with languages featuring palatalization of either labials or velars before -*a* and varied presentation order in training (Smolek & Kapatsinski, 2017b). In the Change Obvious condition, examples of change ($p \rightarrow t\int/\_a$ or $k \rightarrow t\int/\_a$ depending on language) were presented as pairs of corresponding singulars and plurals while examples of no change were all randomly intermixed. This condition is exemplified for the labial language—where labials change but nonlabials don't—by the trial order in (3). In the NoChange Obvious condition, the corresponding no-change singulars and plurals were next to each other as in (4). In the All Obvious condition in (5), all wordforms were randomly intermixed.

(3) ... *kwak*$_{SG}$ *snita*$_{PL}$ *blap*$_{SG}$ *blat∫a*$_{PL}$ *kwaka*$_{PL}$ *snit*$_{SG}$ *dwip*$_{SG}$ *dwit∫a*$_{PL}$ ...
(4) ... *blap*$_{SG}$ *snit*$_{SG}$ *snita*$_{PL}$ *dwit∫a*$_{PL}$ *kwak*$_{SG}$ *kwaka*$_{PL}$ *blat∫a*$_{PL}$ *dwip*$_{SG}$ ...
(5) ... *kwak*$_{SG}$ *kwaka*$_{PL}$ *blap*$_{SG}$ *blat∫a*$_{PL}$ *snit*$_{SG}$ *snita*$_{PL}$ *dwip*$_{SG}$ *dwit∫a*$_{PL}$ ...

As shown in figure 7.3, there was almost no palatalization in the NoChange Obvious condition, where temporally adjacent wordforms did not exemplify a stem change. Copying benefited greatly from being exemplified by temporally adjacent words sharing the stem, increasing in productivity in the All Obvious condition relative to NoChange Obvious (light bars in figure 7.3). However, the Change Obvious condition also differed from the All Obvious condition because participants in the Change Obvious condition tended to palatalize everything equally, including the segments they were not supposed to change. In other words, they failed to learn not to change the not-to-be-changed segments (dark bars). These results strongly support the hypothesis that both copying and changing are learned in part through paradigmatic, source-oriented generalization over morphologically related word pairs.

To be palatalized ☐ yes ■ no

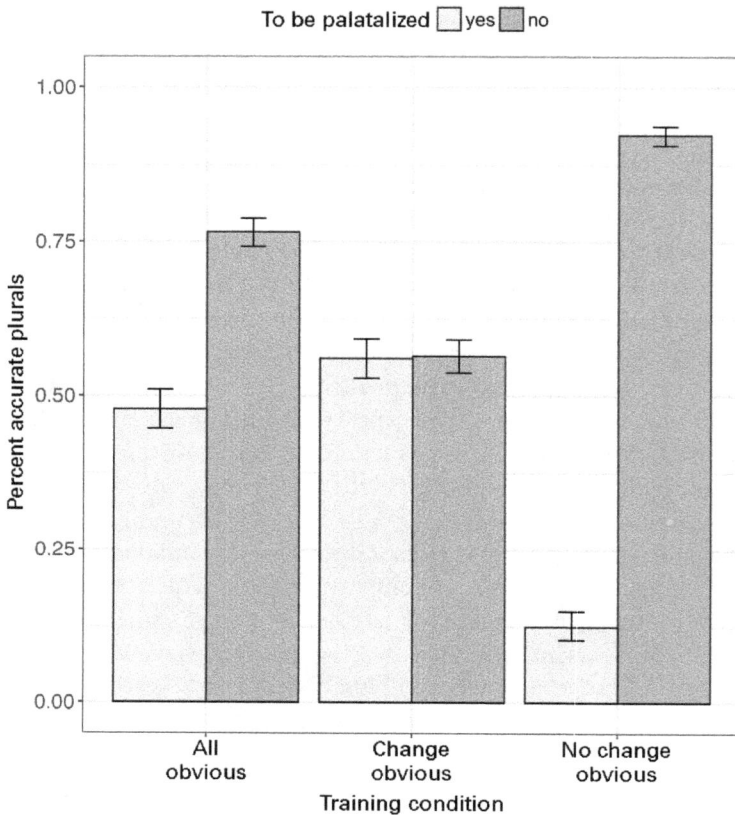

Figure 7.3
Accuracy as a function of whether a consonant was to be palatalized or not and the wordform order in training (Smolek & Kapatsinski, 2017b).

7.5.4 Copying and Learned Equivalence

While copying explains how learners can generalize deletion, how do they generalize "no change" from CVCVC→CVCVC to CVCV→CVCV? Copying seems of little use for explaining this finding because CVCV→CVCVk would copy the entire input the same way CVCV→CVCV does while also satisfying the CVCVk template abundantly exemplified in the CVCVk→CVCVk language.

One possibility is that CVCV→CVCVk does not fully copy the input because it does not retain the word finality of the second vowel (Burzio, 1997; Cho, 1998; Itô & Mester, 1996). For example, employing the bigram coding of Baayen et al. (2011), it copies C_1, C_1V_1, V_1C_2, and C_2V_2 but fails to copy V_2 (see also Wickelgren, 1969). However, it is not immediately clear that one should learn to retain V_2] by being trained to retain C_3].

However, a more likely alternative is that exposure to $CVCVk_{SG}$~$CVCVk_{PL}$ word pairs leads the learners to conclude that the singular-plural distinction makes no difference to the form of the *word*, thus teaching them to copy the entire input, rather than some part of it; copy$_{all}$. When two cues make no difference in the outcome, one learns that the cues are equivalent. Thus, when singular and plural meanings are consistently followed by exactly the same forms, learned equivalence neutralizes the number distinction. As a result, the meaning of a plural form is the same as that of a singular form. When one intends to produce a form with the exact same meaning as another form, copying that form into the production plan is the correct thing to do.

7.6 Conclusion

In this chapter, we considered possible learning mechanisms for acquiring that most elusive type of structure, paradigmatic structure. While there is little evidence available for ruling out any one of the proposed mechanisms, what I hope the reader takes away is that associative mechanisms are plausible even for acquiring paradigmatic mappings. We then saw that there is a complication: some patterns—particularly subtraction—seem to require learning to perform a particular *operation*, mutilating an accessed form in a specific way in seeming disregard of whether the outcome fits a learned schema. I then sketched an account of producing a novel form of a known word, developed further in the next chapter. This account requires (1) paradigmatic associations, (2) the notion of a speech plan built on a prosodic template, and (3) the learner being committed to learning what should and should not be put into the plan in various circumstances.

8 The Interplay of Syntagmatic, Schematic, and Paradigmatic Structure

> There are more things in heaven and Earth [...] Than are dreamt of in your philosophy
> —Shakespeare (1602/2003, p. 165)

In this chapter, we build on the ideas of chapter 7 as we approach the task of learning morphology using the error-driven learning mechanism of Rescorla and Wagner (1972); RW. While RW is often called the "standard theory" of learning (e.g., Dickinson, 2001), it does have limitations, some of which we have already discussed in this book (see also Miller et al., 1995). For example, RW is a purely predictive model and does not learn to "retrodict" cues from outcomes, an arguably routine occurrence in human learning, especially in "bidirectional" domains like language (see chapters 2 and 6). It lacks a mechanism for rapidly allocating selective attention to highly informative stimulus dimensions and a mechanism for fusing or splitting units to generate the dimensions that would afford optimal performance in a classification task (chapter 3). However, an error-driven mechanism like RW can act in tandem with Hebbian learning and chunking (Ashby et al., 2007; Caplan et al., 2014; Kahana, 2002). The argument here is therefore not that RW is *the* mechanism by which we learn all of language, or even all of morphology, but rather that the interplay of schematic, syntagmatic, and paradigmatic structure seen in morphology is amenable to a description in associationist terms. Furthermore, a predictive mechanism like RW is a good candidate for learning paradigmatic associations between forms that do not form a single chunk and are rarely close enough to fuse (chapter 7).

8.1 Paradigms and Schemas: A Review

As discussed in chapter 7, Bybee (2001) distinguishes product-oriented (i.e., schematic) and source-oriented (paradigmatic) generalizations. Schematic generalizations are made by generalizing over forms with a certain meaning. Paradigmatic generalizations are made by generalizing over pairs of morphologically related words and specify how one form can be derived from the other. While the need for paradigmatic generalizations has been questioned (Bybee, 2001), several studies have provided compelling demonstrations that they can be productive in natural languages (e.g., Gouskova & Becker, 2013; Pierrehumbert, 2006).

Nesset (2008) and Kapatsinski (2013) note that paradigmatic generalizations appear to be hard to learn, as evidenced by multiple laboratory studies (Brooks et al., 1993; Frigo & McDonald, 1998). They propose that these generalizations are second-order schemas, formed by associating schemas together. However, the data presented in chapter 7 indicate that learners can rapidly acquire paradigmatic generalizations that are not amenable to a description in terms of mappings between schemas (e.g., delete the final vowel, even if this results in an unattested product).

Thus I assume that language learners learn paradigmatic generalizations in parallel with learning schemas. However, I retain the intuition that paradigmatic mappings are difficult to learn because of the challenges they pose when the corresponding forms are nonadjacent (Kapatsinski, 2013). It appears unreasonable to suppose that, say, whenever a plural form is encountered the learner can successfully bring to mind the corresponding singular form in order to associate aspects of the two forms together (Plunkett & Juola, 1999; see Taatgen & Anderson, 2002, for similar doubts). If learners had this kind of perfect ability (and unyielding inclination) to recall morphological relatives of experienced forms and attempt to derive the experienced form from them, then arbitrary paradigms would be learned much more quickly than they are. I therefore explore the possibility that comparing morphologically related forms is a process that is available on only a minority of occasions that a particular form is encountered. The learning model should be robust enough to (eventually) learn arbitrary paradigmatic mappings even under the conditions of imperfect recall, which would slow down their acquisition relative to the acquisition of schemas.

8.2 The Data

To demonstrate the feasibility of the proposed approach, I apply the model to the data on human miniature artificial language learning reported in Kapatsinski (2009b, 2010b, 2012, 2013), Stave et al. (2013), and Smolek and Kapatsinski (2017a). While somewhat lacking in ecological validity, miniature artificial language data have the advantage of allowing the model to be trained on the input experienced by human learners whose behavior we hope to capture.

All of the modeled experiments examine the learning of miniature artificial languages with palatalization, comparing palatalization rates for different consonants. The languages presented to human learners by Kapatsinski (2009b, 2010b, 2013) are summarized in table 8.1. All languages had singular and plural nouns, two plural suffixes -*i* and -*a*, where -*i* always attached to [k]-final singulars, and a process of velar palatalization that turned /k/ into [tʃ] before [i]. They differed in whether -*i* was the dominant plural suffix for singulars ending in [t] or [p] and whether singular-plural pairings in which -*i* attached to a singular ending in [tʃ] were presented in training.

Kapatsinski (2009b, 2013) showed that a rule-based model of morphophonology (Albright & Hayes, 2003) predicts that examples of tʃ→tʃi, added to the training in Tapachi and Tipichi, should favor addition of -*i* to other consonants. Rules are changes in context. Albright and Hayes's learner takes in pairs of morphologically related forms like butʃ~butʃi and represents each word pair as a change (here, 0→i) and a context in which the change was observed (here, after [butʃ]). The learner then gradually generalizes over contexts, learning what kinds of contexts favor particular changes. Thus, butʃ→butʃi, slait→slaiti, and klop→klopi would lead to the emergence of a general rule 0→i/[-voice;-cont]__. Any additional examples of 0→i would strengthen the rule, resulting in more t→ti, p→pi, and k→ki. However, examples of tʃ→tʃi were found to consistently favor t→tʃi over t→ti. This result is unexpected under a rule-based model like Albright and Hayes (2003) since tʃ→tʃi shares a change with t→ti and not t→tʃi, and should therefore support the former over the latter.

The same problem should arise for a hybrid model proposed by Becker and Gouskova (2016). Their model splits the lexicon into sublexica defined

Table 8.1

Languages shown to human learners in Kapatsinski (2009b, 2010b, 2012, 2013)

	Tapa	Tipi	Tapachi	Tipichi
SG=...k#	PL=...tʃi#			
SG=...{t;p}#	75%	25%	75%	25%
	PL=...{t;p}a#	PL=...{t;p}a#	PL=...{t;p}a#	PL=...{t;p}a#
	25%	75%	25%	75%
	PL=...{t;p}i#	PL=...{t;p}i#	PL=...{t;p}i#	PL=...{t;p}i#
SG=...tʃ#	Not presented		PL=...tʃi#	

by the changes they exhibit. The model then learns about the characteristics of words that undergo each change, and the characteristics of words that result from each change. Because it generalizes over whole forms, the model can make generalizations that span the change/context boundary. However, its decision about which change to apply is still based only on characteristics of words that undergo the various changes. As in the case of Albright and Hayes (2003), experiencing tʃ→tʃi examples should help 0→i by expanding the range and number of forms that undergo this change.

Another difficulty presented by these data for source-oriented models is that singulars ending in [tʃ] take -i rather than -a even in the Tapa language, where -a is as common as -i and [tʃ]-final singulars are never experienced in training. Source-oriented models learn about what kinds of source forms take -a and what kinds of forms take -i. In Tapa, [k]-final sources are the only ones that take -i. As a result, [k]-final singulars should be much more likely to take -i than [tʃ]-final singulars while the opposite is true of the human data. In contrast, the fact that [tʃ]-final singulars take -i even in the Tapa language can be explained by generalization over plural forms: even in Tapa, -i follows a preceding [tʃ] 100% of the time (i.e., $p(\text{i}|\text{tʃ})=100\%$).

At the same time, a purely product-oriented model of these data is also untenable. In particular, one needs to explain how learners come to palatalize [k] more than [t] or [p], a restriction on what kinds of sources map onto [tʃi]. In addition, as we discussed in chapter 7, stem changes resulting in [tʃi] appear to be disfavored by placing singulars and plurals sharing the stem allomorph next to each other. If generalization were purely product-oriented, the contiguity between corresponding source and product forms would not matter. Based on this finding, we argued that an encounter with a word pair like butʃ_SG-butʃi_PL leads one to notice that the singular-final consonant is retained in the plural, which then boosts retention of singular-final consonants in constructing the plural form (as discussed in chapter 7).

To summarize, I designed the model to account for the following results:

1. The effect of adding examples of tʃ→tʃi:
   a. Examples of -i simply attaching to [tʃ] (tʃ→tʃi) helped t→tʃi over t→ti (Kapatsinski, 2009b, chap. 4; Kapatsinski, 2012, 2013). This result seems to provide support for schematic generalizations.
   b. However, when corresponding singulars and plurals were presented next to each other, the same examples helped k→ki over k→tʃi (Kapatsinski, 2009b, chap. 3; see also Yin & White, 2016). This result is problematic for a purely schematic theory.

c. Examples of tʃ→tʃi had no significant effect on the competition between k→ki and k→tʃi when all wordforms were presented in random order (Kapatsinski, 2009b, chap. 4).

d. There was no effect of tʃ→tʃi examples on p→tʃi vs. p→pi as [p] was almost never palatalized (Kapatsinski, 2009b, 2013).

2. Input [tʃ] favors -*i* at test, even if never encountered in training (Kapatsinski, 2009b):

Singulars ending in [tʃ] heavily favored the suffix -i over -a during test even when they were not encountered in training and -a was the more common suffix. In particular, [tʃ]-final singulars favored -*i* more than [k]-final singulars did after exposure to the Tapa language, despite the fact that [k]-final singulars were always mapped onto [tʃi] in training while [tʃ]-final singulars were never presented. This result provides support for schemas: a schema that says "plurals end in [tʃi]" should add -*i* to a [tʃ]-final singular. A rule does so only if the source is underspecified (e.g., C→tʃi rather than k→tʃi). Of course, proposing that the learner underspecifies the *sources* of source-oriented, paradigmatic generalizations, extracting C→tʃi from input that is consistent with k→tʃi, constitutes surrendering to generalizations starting out schematic and only gradually acquiring paradigmatic conditioning.

3. Simply adding -*i* to {t;p}-final singulars generalizes to [k]-final singulars (Kapatsinski, 2009b, 2010b):

Exposure to Tipi and Tipichi languages led participants to often simply add -*i* to [k]-final singulars, without changing the consonant, compared to Tapa and Tapachi. At the individual level, the more one simply attaches -*i* to {t;p} without changing the stem, the more one does the same to [k] (figure 8.1). As we noted above, the same phenomenon is observed in Russian, where velar palatalization has lost productivity before the verbal stem extension -*i* while retaining productivity before diminutive suffixes -*ok* and -*ek*. This counterphonetic development is explained by the fact that -*i* tends not to attach to velar-final stems, while -*ok* and -*ek* are favored by velar-final nouns. This result is nicely predicted by the rule-based model of Albright and Hayes (2003). When presented with the lexicon of Russian, or one of the artificial languages in table 8.1, the model learns a general rule that says "just add -*i*" after any stop, which competes with the palatalizing k→tʃi rule.

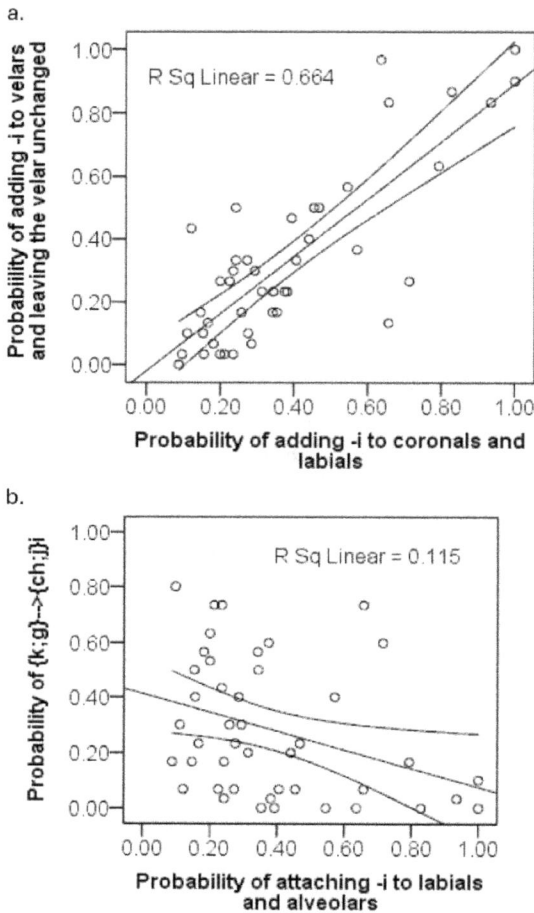

a.

b.

Figure 8.1

Participants who attach -*i* (rather than the competing suffix, -*a*) to coronals and labials are likely to also add -*i* to velars without changing the velar (top panel). There is a strong effect of the probability of {t;p}→{t;p}i on the probability of k→ki but relatively little effect on the probability of k→tʃi (bottom, from Kapatsinski, 2009b, pp. 60–61).

The more often a consonant fails to change before -*i*, the more productive the "just add -*i*" rule is, and the more likely it is to outcompete the palatalizing rule (Kapatsinski, 2010b). Generally, an alternation tends to involve a specific class of segments. A highly productive suffix like -*i* tends to attach to all kinds of segments. The segments that change are doomed to be in the minority. Unless the segments that are not eligible to change form a natural class, the model extracts a very general rule that simply attaches the productive suffix without changing the stem after a very broad class of segments that includes the segments the learner ought to change. That rule competes with the alternation-demanding rules and the alternation is therefore doomed to lose productivity. In this way, Albright and Hayes's (2003) rule-based model successfully explains why alternations lose productivity over time (Bybee, 2001) and why alternations tend to be triggered by relatively unproductive, contextually restricted affixes (e.g., Kiparsky, 1985). However, the result is also captured by a schema-based model with the assumption that schemas start out general and gradually increase in specificity over the course of learning: the schema "plurals should end in a stop followed by [i]" has greater support when -*i* often attaches to nonvelar stops that do not change (Kapatsinski, 2013).

8.3   Naive Discriminative Learner

The Naive Discriminative Learner (NDL, Arppe et al., 2014; Baayen et al., 2011; Ramscar et al., 2013) is an implementation of the RW learning theory as a fully connected two-layer connectionist network. The architecture of the network is identical to Rumelhart and McClelland's (1986) classic (and classically criticized) model of the English past tense. Each node in the network corresponds to a linguistic unit that can be associated with other units. The nodes are arranged into two layers, where one layer represents the input and the other represents the output. Learning is unidirectional, in that the network learns to predict the outputs from the inputs. Each node within the input layer is a *cue*, while each node within the output layer is called an *outcome*. Learning in the network is error-driven. Cues compete with each other to predict outcomes, so that the cues that are most predictive of an outcome become strongly and positively associated with that outcome, and cues that are predictive of the absence of an outcome acquire a strong negative association with the outcome.

A learning experience for the model consists of a pairing between a set of cues and a set of outcomes. The network has a connection from every cue to every outcome. Each connection has a weight. The sign of the weight represents whether the connection is excitatory or inhibitory. Positive weights represent excitation (the cue predicts the presence of the outcome), while negative weights represent inhibition (the cue predicts the absence of the outcome). The absolute value of the weight indicates the strength of the prediction. An outcome is expected to the extent that the present cues have strong excitatory connections to the outcome. If an outcome occurs unexpectedly, the weights of the connections from the present cues to the outcome are adjusted upward (as a result, excitatory connections are strengthened, while inhibitory ones are weakened or even change sign). If an outcome is unexpectedly absent, the present cues' connections to the outcome are adjusted downward (inhibitory connections strengthen, while excitatory ones weaken or even become inhibitory). The network learns nothing about the predictions of cues that were absent during any given learning experience.

Specifically, weight updating follows the two equations from Rescorla and Wagner (1972) below, repeated from chapter 1. To remind the reader, the weight from a cue C to a present outcome O at time $t + 1$ is increased via equation (1), while the weight from a cue C to an absent outcome is decreased using equation (2). The learning rate Λ is intended to reflect cue salience. Since the NDL weights are reflecting equilibrium weights the model settles on, Λ does not play a role in NDL. I have attempted to fit the models below using both NDL and online application of the Rescorla-Wagner learning rule, which allows for varying learning rate. If all outcomes that occur on a trial have activations equal to 1 and all absent outcomes have activations equal to 0, the model learns nothing. Otherwise, weights are adjusted so that the activation of the present outcomes given the same cue set would be closer to 1, and activations of absent outcomes would be closer to 0.

$$w_{t+1}^{C \to O} = w_t^{C \to O} + \left(1 - a_t^O\right) \times \Lambda \tag{1}$$

$$w_{t+1}^{C \to O} = w_t^{C \to O} + \left(0 - a_t^O\right) \times \Lambda \tag{2}$$

8.4   Model 1: Paradigmatic and Schematic Structure

8.4.1   Learning Task: Form Prediction

The task of the present model is *form prediction*. A learning experience consists of experiencing a wordform. We assume that when a wordform is experienced, the meaning of the wordform is activated in memory, and that—*on at least a minority of occasions*—other forms of the same word are also activated (Plunkett & Juola, 1999). The model attempts to predict the experienced wordform from other remembered forms of the same word and the meaning it thinks is being expressed. In other words, the experienced wordform is a set of outcomes (i.e., an output), and the activated memories are sets of cues (i.e., input). Alternatively, one could say that experiencing a word generates a set of predictions about features of other forms of that word, which are then confirmed or rejected when the forms are encountered (Ervin, 1961; McNeill, 1963). Again, this would only have to happen on a minority of occasions. The behavior of the model after a block of training is independent of directionality of prediction engaged in during the block.

For example, the model might experience a plural form /blaɪtʃi/, corresponding to the outcome set {$bl_{On.1}$, $aɪ_{N.1}$, $tʃ_{On.2}$, $i_{N.2}$}. This will then bring to mind the meaning of the form, crucially including the feature "PL," and the other form of the same word, /blaɪk/, encoded as a set of cues (e.g., {$bl_{On.1}$, $aɪ_{N.1}$, $k_{Cd.1}$}). If the model works perfectly, then—as a result of many such individual experiences—it will learn the outcomes that usually occur when the plural meaning is being expressed (such as $i_{N.2}$ and $tʃ_{On.2}$). It will also learn that $k_{Cd.1}$ in the singular predicts {$tʃ_{On.2}$, $i_{N.2}$} in the plural and that {$bl_{On.1}$} in the singular predicts {$bl_{On.1}$} in the plural, while {$aɪ_{N.1}$} in the singular predicts {$aɪ_{N.1}$} in the plural. The start and ideal end states of the network are illustrated in figure 8.2 (only active cues and outcomes, about which something is learned, are shown).

8.4.2   Encoding Scheme

For the languages in the present simulations, we are interested in modeling what is palatalized and when. Because of the way these languages were designed, features of the stem-final consonant are relevant for predicting the outcome, while features of other segments within the singular are not. It did not seem fair to hold the model responsible for discovering locality from a short experimental exposure: it is a strong bias that human learners bring to the experiment, rather than acquiring it from training. I therefore chose to present the model only with the task-relevant phonological features, namely those of the stem-final segment. The features used were sufficient to discriminate between the consonants presented in training, and to represent the articulatory similarity relations among them: [voiced], [voiceless], [lips], [tongue], [(tongue) blade], and [(tongue) body]. Thus, [p] would

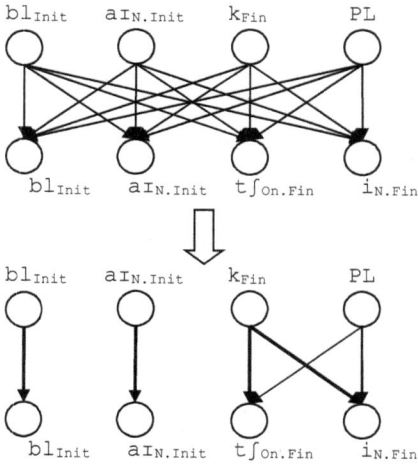
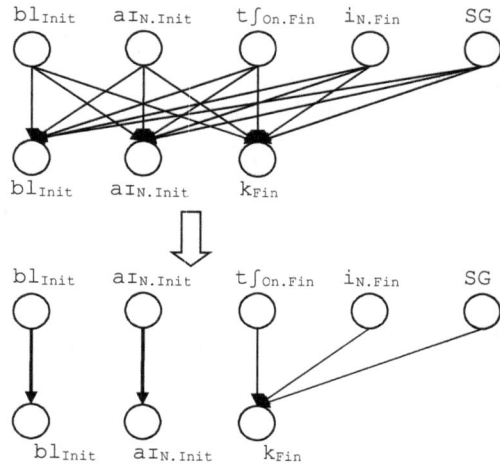

Figure 8.2

An illustration of the learning process. On the left, the network is experiencing a plural form. It activates the plural meaning and the singular form as cues (training top-to-bottom connections). On the right, the network is experiencing a singular form (training bottom-to-top connections). It activates the plural form and the singular meaning as cues. $p_c p_o$ connections from present cues to present outcomes are strengthened to the extent that the outcome was unexpected. $p_c a_o$ connections from present cues to absent outcomes are weakened to the extent that the absence of the outcome was unexpected. Connections involving cues absent on a given trial are not adjusted; neither are connections to outcomes that are absent throughout the experiment (like a [k] in the plural in the present experiments). With time (wide arrow), most connections are pruned but a few are strengthened.

be [voiceless; lips], [t]—[voiceless; tongue; blade], [k]—[voiceless; tongue; body], and [tʃ]—[voiceless; tongue; blade; body].

The onset and the vowel were treated as cues jointly identifying individual words, but were not further specified with features. Word identity is important for choosing *-i* vs. *-a* with nonvelar-final words, where the choice is otherwise unpredictable.

8.4.3 Copy Outcomes

A copy outcome is detected during training when an input unit is retained in the output (as would satisfaction of a faithfulness constraint in Optimality Theory; Prince & Smolensky, 1993/2008). We assume the existence of a copy outcome associated with each position within the template representing the source form (cf. the positional faithfulness constraints of Beckman, 1999).[1] In particular, we will need a Copy$_{Fin}$ outcome that is detected whenever the final consonant of the singular is retained in the plural output. Since this outcome is only detected when the final consonant of the singular form is retained, it will become associated with input cues that favor the retention of the base-final consonant; in particular, [place] features of the final consonant. We will also need a Copy$_{Init}$ outcome that is detected when the initial onset of the activated input is retained in the experienced output, and a Copy$_{N1}$ output that detects the retention of the stem vowel. This set of Copy outcomes is sufficient for modeling the present data but is not exhaustive.

Let us now illustrate the operation of Copy outcomes. Suppose that a learner experiencing the plural [blaɪtʃĩ] activates the singular form [blaɪk]. Again, we assume that this happens at least some of the time when [blaɪtʃĩ] is experienced. The learner will then detect the outcomes Copy$_{Init}$ and Copy$_{N1}$ but not Copy$_{Fin}$. The learning experience will then be represented as Input = {bl, a$_{IN.1}$, [stop], [voiceless], [tongue], [body]}, Output = {bl, a$_{IN.1}$, tʃĩ, Copy$_{Init}$, Copy$_{N1}$}. After a few learning experiences of this kind, and other experiences in which other final consonants *are* present in the output, the learner will associate [body] with the absence of Copy$_{Fin}$, inhibiting the copying of final velars into the plural.[2] This illustrates that copying in the trained model is input-specific—that is, conditional on meaning to be expressed and formal characteristics of activated morphologically related words, allowing the model to learn *when* and *what* to copy.[3] The erroneous output [bliki] in a language with velar palatalization, thus lacking the outcome [ki], would be predicted if Copy$_{Fin}$ has positive activation that exceeds that of [tʃĩ] or [tʃ$_{On.2}$]. The system is illustrated in figure 8.3.

8.4.4 Wordform Generation

To derive the cue-outcome weights and outcome activations in the presence of specific cue sets, I used both the NDL package in R (Arppe et al., 2014) and an online Rescorla-Wagner learning function kindly provided to me by Harald Baayen. The weights reported below are asymptotic, derived with NDL: they are what the learner would arrive at after settling into a stable equilibrium according to Danks (2003). This is perhaps unrealistic, given that we are modeling participants' behavior after a short laboratory training. Therefore, I will note if online learning with a limited learning rate makes a difference to the qualitative pattern of results throughout the discussion below.

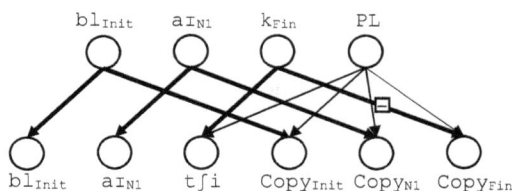

Figure 8.3
Excitatory and inhibitory links most relevant to producing the plural form of [blaɪk]
when presented with the singular after training on one of the languages in table 8.1.
The negative PF shows an inhibitory connection. All other connections are excit-
atory. Copy$_{\text{Init}}$ and Copy$_{\text{N1}}$ are activated by all input cues, while Copy$_{\text{Fin}}$ is inhibited
by the input consonants that are not retained in the plural. Plurality is associated
with [tʃi] and with copying all parts of the singular, but less so in the case of the final
consonant.

I assumed the existence of a prosodic template associated with the to-
be-expressed meaning and that the template is learned early and selected
first (chapter 7). The modeling effort reported here focuses on filling this
template with segmental material.

Some outcomes are mutually incompatible—for example, given the
input [blaɪk], final [tʃ] competes with Copy$_{\text{Fin}}$. Generally, outcomes are
incompatible if they compete for the same position in the prosodic template. To derive a product form, we therefore choose between the competing outcomes in each templatic position until every position is filled. Each
competing outcome has an activation level, which is simply the sum of
the weights of connections from the current set of cues to that outcome.
Following Luce (1959), we assume that the choice between incompatible
segmental outcomes is stochastic: the probability of the speaker choosing a segmental outcome is equal to its activation divided by the sum of
activations of the full set of competing outcomes competing for the same
position, including the Copy outcome associated with that position. Probability matching of this kind is strongly suggested by the fact that production probabilities of -*a* vs. -*i* after labials and velars—where the suffix choice
is unpredictable and neither suffix requires a stem change—match their
probabilities in training.

8.5   Evidence for Copy Outcomes

To provide an adequate simulation of human behavior in the elicited production task, the model must construct a fully specified output form. Thus,

we want the model not to merely predict the suffix and to decide whether to palatalize but rather to predict all phonological characteristics of the output (see also Albright & Hayes, 2003). Part of that task is constructing the stem allomorph and, importantly, retaining the parts of the input stem allomorph that need to be retained. In this section, we show that the notion of copying is necessary for the network to retain stem parts it has just encountered.

Pinker and Prince (1988) criticized Rumelhart and McClelland's (1986) model, which is much like the present model without copy outputs, for predicting "bizarre stem changes," such as *membled* as the past tense of the English verb *mail*. This is not a problem for NDL in the same way: even without Copy outcomes, the model performs perfectly on items that are familiar, as *mail* would be for an English speaker. In the same way that it perfectly learns which of the familiar verbs take -*a*, and which take -*i*, it also perfectly learns which input onset maps onto [bl] and which maps onto [tr].

The model also performs perfectly on novel stems as long as all cues comprising the input stem allomorph have been experienced in training. In table 8.2, every familiar input stem onset activates the corresponding output stem onset more than it activates any other onset despite the absence of Copying. The model appears close to the perfect end state illustrated in figure 8.3: familiar input stem onsets are retained in the output. This is also true of familiar stem nuclei and not-to-be-palatalized final consonants.

However, consider what happens when the model encounters a novel onset. In Smolek and Kapatsinski (2017a), all stem bodies encountered at test were novel, mostly because they had novel onsets. Table 8.3 shows that when a novel onset is encountered, the network without copy outcomes has no knowledge of whether that onset should be retained. While it has learned to retain familiar onsets, that knowledge is a set of arbitrary input-output associations specific to the experienced onsets. A novel onset activates all experienced onsets nearly equally, as seen with [bl] below. Other parts of the word can then decide on the onset to be produced. For example, the word [dræk] in table 8.3 contains the vowel [æ], which the model

Table 8.2

Activations of word-initial onsets by two test items in Kapatsinski (2013), which shared onsets and vowels with stimuli presented during training

	bl	tr	sw	v
bl_aɪp	0.98	−0.28	−0.19	−0.12
tr_up	−0.02	0.72	−0.19	−0.12

Table 8.3

Activations of experienced word-initial onsets by two test words from Smolek and Kapatsinski (2017a)

	l	gl	r	d	gw	sl	sn	p	v	g
bl_ɪt	0.06	0.05	0.05	0.06	0.05	0.06	0.05	0.05	0.06	0.05
dr_æk	0.02	0.02	0.02	0.35	0.02	0.35	0.02	0.02	0.02	0.02

has experienced in the singular-plural pairs [dæt]-[dæta] and [slæk]-[slætʃi]. Because of this, the model learned that the vowel [æ] predicts the onset [d]. With an unfamiliar input onset, the output onsets [d] and [sl] are therefore activated most highly by any word containing [æ]. This behavior is sensible but distinctly nonhumanlike.

When equipped with copy outcomes, the network successfully learns that even a novel stem onset should be copied, with activation of Copy-$_{Init}$ ranging between .71 and 1.0 across the test words. The copy outcomes are therefore able to outcompete the learned arbitrary associations between input vowels and codas and output onsets for every test word, successfully avoiding the "bizarre" stem changes of Pinker and Prince (1988) that the model otherwise produces. This result supplements chapter 7 by providing additional motivation for Copy outcomes. We will now examine whether the model, equipped with Copy outcomes, is able to account for the results of miniature artificial language learning studies of palatalization.

8.5.1   Learning What (Not) to Change

As described in Kapatsinski (2009b), the addition of tʃ→tʃi examples in Tapachi and Tipichi helps t→tʃi over t→ti (Kapatsinski, 2009b, 2013). In addition, when stem-sharing singulars and plurals are presented next to each other, these same examples help k→ki over k→tʃi. However, when singulars and plurals are not presented in pairs, the examples have no effect on k→ki vs. k→tʃi. In either case, these examples are unable to help p→tʃi over p→pi because [p] is almost never turned into [tʃ] by the participants. To simplify presentation, we focus on Tapa vs. Tapachi in presenting the model results below but the results for Tipi vs. Tipichi are exactly parallel.

Note that examples of tʃ→tʃi provide evidence for both Copy$_{Fin}$ (copying of the stem-final consonant) and the generalization that plurals end in [tʃi]. Theories separating change and context (Albright & Hayes, 2003; Chomsky & Halle, 1968; Becker & Gouskova, 2016) emphasize the former fact, and therefore have trouble capturing the finding that these examples help t→tʃi over t→ti (Kapatsinski, 2013). Network Theory (Bybee, 1985, 2001) and Clamoring for Blends (Kapatsinski, 2013) emphasize the latter fact and therefore have trouble explaining why these examples might help k→ki over k→tʃi (Kapatsinski, 2009b).

Without Copy outcomes, NDL behaves like Network Theory and C4B, predicting that tʃ→tʃi should help both t→tʃi and k→tʃi. In contrast, NDL with Copy outcomes predicts the observed difference between the effects on t→tʃi and k→tʃi. As table 8.4 shows, the model correctly predicts that there should be more palatalization of [t] in Tapachi and more palatalization of [k] in Tapa. The increased palatalization of [t] in Tapachi is driven by greater activation of [tʃi] and, crucially, reduced activation of [t] in that language. In contrast to [t], [k] never occurs in plurals during training in either language, and therefore is not an outcome the network considers learning about. As a result, tʃ→tʃi examples reduce the incidence of velar palatalization, by providing support to Copy$_{Fin}$. Thus, not learning (much) from always-absent outcomes is crucial to account for these data.

Table 8.4

a. No copy outcomes			
Singular ends in	Tapa		Tapachi
p	2%	=	1%
t	4%	<	9%
k	90%	<	100%
b. Copy outcomes			
Singular ends in	Tapa		Tapachi
p	1%	=	0%
t	3%	<	6%
k	93%	>	87%
c. Copy outcomes + imperfect recall			
Singular ends in	Tapa		Tapachi
p	4%	=	5%
t	5%	<	10%
k	89%	=	88%

Palatalization rates in NDL without copy outcomes (a), with copy outcomes for participants that always have access to the singular when perceiving the plural (b), and with copy outcomes when participants cannot recall the singular when presented with the plural half of the time in training (c).

Note that in order for a tʃ→tʃi example to provide support for Copy_Fin, the singular form must come to mind when the plural form of the same word is presented to the participant. Otherwise, repetition of the stem-final consonant across forms is not detected. As argued in Kapatsinski (2012), recalling the singular form when presented with the plural is very likely when stem-sharing singulars and plurals are presented next to each other in time, but much less likely if all wordforms are presented in random order.

To simulate the effect of presenting all wordforms in random order, I replaced half of the training trials with trials on which phonological characteristics of the singular are not recalled, and Copy outcomes are therefore also absent—that is, the input consists of the PLURAL meaning, while the outcome is the fully specified plural form (table 8.4c). With this modification, the rate of velar palatalization is virtually identical between the two languages and the productivity of nonvelar palatalization is increased. This corresponds to the pattern of results elicited when stem-sharing singulars and plurals are no longer presented next to each other in pairs, making comparison of morphologically related forms more difficult (Kapatsinski, 2012).

Limiting the learning rate does not affect the palatalization rates of labials, while increasing palatalization rates of coronals to ~20%–25% in Tapa and to ~43%–53% in Tapachi. Palatalization rates of velars reduce. For Tapa, the palatalization rate of velars can be as low as 67% with a very slow learning rate of .0001. For Tapachi, the palatalization rate at the same learning rate is 80%. Overall, reducing the learning rates makes the quantitative effects of place of articulation more realistic, but the qualitative pattern of results holds across learning rates: the additional tʃ→tʃi examples roughly double coronal palatalization rates, while having no effect on the labials and a relatively small effect on the velars. The one difference is that the effect on the velars is consistently facilitatory. However, the experimental data do not let us distinguish a small facilitatory effect on velar palatalization from a small inhibitory effect or zero. All we can really say is that the effect is smaller than that observed for the alveolars, which is predicted by the model regardless of learning rate.

8.6   Avoidance vs. Overgeneralization

Table 8.5 shows that human participants closely matched the probabilities of -a vs. -i (25% -i in Tapa vs. 75% -i in Tipi) with [t]-final and [p]-final singulars, generating -a 30% of the time in Tapa and 67% of the time in Tipi. The model successfully predicts this result, closely matching the observed probabilities. This result holds with or without copy outcomes as long as

Table 8.5

Singular ends in	Tapa language	Tipi language
{t;p}	24%	73%
k	83%	97%

Activation of -i vs. -a in the NDL model following training on Tapa vs. Tipi (with Copy and configural outcomes, but the results are qualitatively similar without these).

the learning rate is not too high. However, the model overpredicts the use of -i with [k]-final singulars in Tapa (cf. figure 8.1, top). This result holds at even the slowest learning rates where the probability of attaching -i to [k] in Tapa approaches 75% and the probability of attaching it to [k] in Tipi approaches 92%. These rates of -i use in table 8.5 are quite a bit higher than most participants' rates in figure 8.1.

There are two possible reasons for why participants might underuse -i with velar-final singulars: (1) avoidance of the stem-changing -i when it would call for a stem change, and (2) overgeneralization about where -a occurs.

The first proposal, avoidance of -i, claims that it may be no coincidence that -i is avoided by humans precisely when its addition would require a stem change. Just as children avoid adding suffixes that require stem changes in adult language (Do, 2013), or avoid selecting words that are hard to produce (Schwartz & Leonard, 1982), the experimental participants may be avoiding attaching -i when its attachment calls for a stem change. A possible scenario is as follows. Having attached -i to a [k]-final singular at test, the speaker runs into difficulty: changing the stem is hard while a plural ending in [ki] sounds wrong. The speaker then decides to avoid this situation thereafter, fleeing a difficult choice (Albright, 2003).[4] Here, choosing -i over -a as the suffix leads to the difficult choice between [ki] and [tʃi], causing participants to choose -a over -i after experiencing the difficulty in the early test trials.

The second proposal is that -a is overgeneralized from {t;p}-final singulars to [k]-final singulars because [t] and [p] do not constitute a natural class of stops that excludes [k]. Unlike the model, participants thus might associate -a with [stop], in addition to associating it with [lips] and [tongue blade], particularly since p(stop|a)=100%, while p(lips|a)=p(blade|a)=50%. The NDL model does not make this connection because learning in the model is discriminative: [stop] is not predictive of the choice between -a vs. -i. For example, in Tapa, all consonants encountered in training are stops, so knowing that a consonant is a stop reveals nothing about whether -a or

-*i* will be chosen. In contrast, knowing that the consonant is made with the tongue body makes one certain that the suffix should be -*i*. Thus, -*i* is strongly expected when the consonant is a stop made with the tongue body (i.e., [k]).

Overgeneralization to natural classes containing experienced sounds associated with an outcome is expected under a Hebbian learning mechanism. Hebbian learning states that associations form on the basis of simple co-occurrence: representations of events that tend to occur at the same time are wired together (just as neurons that fire together wire together; Hebb, 1949). Thus, in the present case, [stop] or [voiceless] should become associated with -*a* in every language, to a language-specific extent, leading to the use of -*a* with stops that are not [t] or [p].

Overgeneralization is expected in a discriminative model if the learning rate is sufficiently low for the model not to learn that place of articulation is highly predictive of suffix choice. The lower the learning rate, the more the model's affix choice depends on the affixes' relative type frequency. In other words, the slower the learning rate, the less discriminative and more Hebbian-like the model is at the end of training.

The languages studied in Kapatsinski (2009b, 2013) do not allow us to distinguish between avoidance of the palatalizing suffix with to-be-palatalized consonants and overgeneralization of the nonpalatalizing suffix beyond the not-to-be-palatalized consonants, since the palatalizing suffix is the only suffix that should be attached to the to-be-palatalized consonants.

However, the languages studied by Stave et al. (2013), described in table 8.6, do provide an opportunity to distinguish the two explanations. In

Table 8.6

	Labial palatalization	Alveolar palatalization	Velar palatalization
Singular	Plural	Plural	Plural
…ap	…a{tʃa;pi}	…apa	…apa
…ip	…itʃa	…ipa	…ipa
…at	…ata	…a{tʃa;ti}	…ata
…it	…ita	…itʃa	…ita
…ak	…aka	…aka	…a{tʃa;ki}
…ik	…ika	…ika	…itʃa

Labial, alveolar, and velar palatalization patterns presented to participants in Stave et al. (2013), two of which might be familiar from chapter 7.

these languages, palatalization is supposed to be applied before -a but not before -i. Despite the phonetic unnaturalness of the pattern, it is learned by the participants in that they almost never palatalize before -i. As shown in figure 8.4, palatalization rates before -a are little affected by the identity of the stem vowel. The *non*palatalizing suffix -i is to be used only when the to-be-palatalized consonant is not changed, and is therefore available as a way to avoid choosing between palatalizing and not palatalizing. The target rate of -i use with [a] stems ending in the to-be-palatalized consonant is 50%, affording the opportunity to see overuse of -i (avoidance) as well as overuse of -a (overgeneralization). Here, we focus on the velar palatalization group, for comparability with Kapatsinski (2009b, 2013).

Figure 8.5 shows that participants were quite accurate in where they used -i vs. -a. In particular, participants did not show avoidance of the palatalizing suffix (-a) with velars, suggesting that the underuse of the palatalizing suffix in Kapatsinski (2009b, 2013) is unlikely to be due to avoidance. Rather, it appears to be due to overgeneralization of the nonpalatalizing suffix beyond the context in which it occurred in the input.

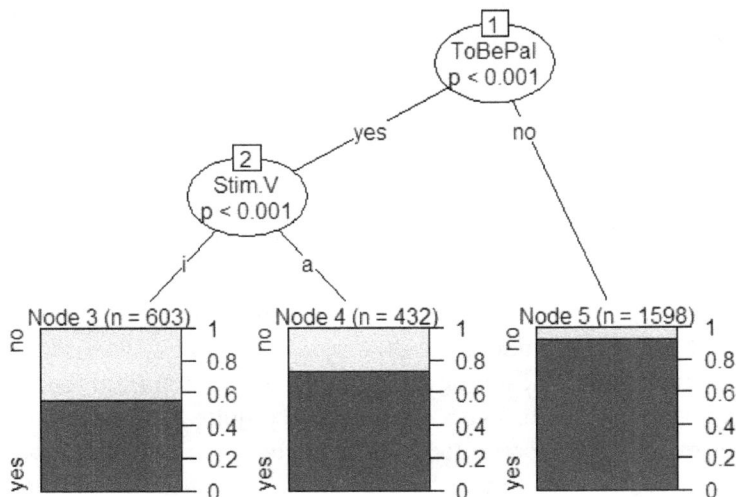

Figure 8.4
Whether the stem consonant is retained (not palatalized) before -a depending on whether the consonant is [k], which should be palatalized (ToBePal="yes"), and the identity of the stem vowel. The stem vowel [i] favored the palatalizing suffix -a when the consonant was the one to be palatalized. Participants learned this generalization quite well.

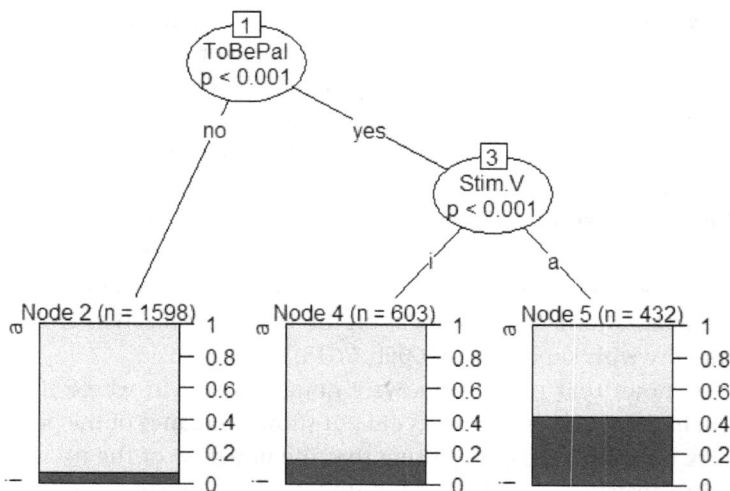

Figure 8.5
Use of -*a* vs. -*i* by participants in Stave et al. (2013) depending on whether the consonant was to be palatalized (ToBePal) and whether the stimulus stem vowel (Stim.V)
was [i] or [a]. An ideal learner would use -*i* only after to-be-palatalized consonants,
and only when the stem vowel is [a], and would use -*i* 50% of the time in this
environment.

8.7   Perseveration

The greater use of -*i* in Tipi predicted in table 8.5 does not necessarily
mean predicting increased production of k→ki, because k→tʃi also involves
activating -*i*. Unlike humans, the model feels no difficulty changing [k]
into [tʃ]. The overprediction of stem change happens even if the model is
equipped with Copy outcomes because the model successfully learns that
velar stops are not copied, acquiring an inhibitory association from [body]
to Copy$_{Fin}$. The human participants either do not acquire this association
(to the same extent), or are prevented from changing the stem at test by an
extragrammatical tendency to perseverate during production. Given that
changing the stem is judged by our participants to be more acceptable than
not changing the stem (Kapatsinski, 2012; Smolek & Kapatsinski, 2017a;
see also Zuraw, 2000, for evidence that stem changes may be preferred to
no change yet seldom produced in a natural language), we believe the association is in fact acquired during training, and participants are prevented
from manifesting this knowledge fully in production by production-internal perseveration that boosts copy outcomes (Stave et al., 2013).

If copy outcomes are boosted by a constant amount in both languages, as one would expect from a constant perseveratory tendency, the greater incidence of k→ki in Tipi compared to Tapa is successfully predicted. This is not because [tʃ] or [tʃi] is weakened in Tipi relative to Tapa, nor because Copy$_{Fin}$ is strengthened: these outcomes are unaffected by the increased use of -i. Thus the proportion of trials featuring palatalization remains unchanged between the two languages. However, [i] is strengthened relative to [a]. As a result, when one looks only at the trials where -i was attached, a lower proportion of these trials will feature palatalization: even when palatalization loses to no change, -i is still likely to win over -a. For example, adding .5 to Copy outcome activations across languages predicts that, when -i is attached to a [k]-final singular, the [k] will be retained only 38% of the time in Tapa but 58% of the time in Tipi. As in humans (figure 8.1), the difference in palatalization rates before -i comes from greater use of k→ki in Tipi rather than from reduced use of k→tʃi.

8.8   The Need for Syntagmatic Structure

The main problem faced by the proposed model is presented by [tʃ]-final singulars in Tapa and Tipi. In these languages, [tʃ]-final singulars are never presented during training. As a result, the model has no choice but to treat final [tʃ] as an unfamiliar consonant. There are good reasons to treat [tʃ] as having the place features of both coronals and dorsals: both the tongue body and the tongue blade are involved in its articulation (Yun, 2006), and alternations between [t] and [tʃ] are about as common as those between [k] and [tʃ] across languages (Bateman, 2007; Kochetov, 2011). Having place features intermediate between the dorsal [k] and the coronal [t], [tʃ] should therefore show intermediate behavior. In all languages, but especially in Tapa, [k] favors the attachment of -i while [t] favors the attachment of -a; [tʃ] is expected to be in between. In contrast, human learners attach -i to [tʃ] more than they attach it to anything else.

Furthermore, the input feature [coronal] becomes associated with the output [t], predicting that a singular-final [tʃ] will often map onto [t] in the plural. Copy outcomes barely alleviate this problem because [tʃ]'s [dorsal] feature is associated with lack of final-consonant copying. Thus, [tʃ] is expected to map onto [t] ~40%–50% of the time in Tapa and Tipi, across learning rates.

Unfaithful mapping of [tʃ] onto [t] does happen in the human data. However, it is quite rare (<10%). While it is possible to reduce the rate of tʃ→t by boosting Copy outcomes, implementing perseveration at test, a boost to Copy$_{Fin}$ that reduces the incidence of tʃ→t also reduces the incidence of t→tʃ, which is incorrectly expected to be lower than the incidence of tʃ→t even without boosting Copy outcomes (5% vs. 40% in table 8.7).[5]

I suggest that a [tʃ]-final singular should not be treated as either novel or intermediate between a [k]-final singular and a [t]-final singular. After experiencing k→tʃi, learners know what to do with a [tʃ]-final singular (namely, that it should take -*i*, becoming [tʃi]): k→tʃi is taken to imply tʃ→tʃi.

While there is agreement on this point in the field (cf. Stave et al. 2013; White 2013), there is disagreement on the underlying reason. On the one hand, this can be seen as a special case of a proposed bias against saltation. According to this proposal, if X→Y and there is a sound Z that is between X and Y, then X→Y is taken to imply Z→Y (Boersma, 1998; Hayes & White, 2015; Steriade, 2001; White, 2013). The relevant generalization is a generalization across *changes* and relies on a knowledge base about change magnitudes: a bigger change implies a smaller change, resulting in (avoidance of) the same output. Empirical support for this position is provided by White's (2013) finding that participants trained on p→v would also change [b] into [v], while those trained on b→v would not change [p] into [v]. However, we should note that participants in White's study were trained to criterion, and (given that p→v is harder to learn) participants trained on p→v received more training on changing the stem than participants trained on b→v.

Smolek and Kapatsinski (2017a) did not train participants to criterion, instead using a constant number of training trials (as in Kapatsinski, 2009b, 2013). We examined learnability of labial (p→tʃ) vs. lingual (k→tʃ or t→tʃ) palatalization. As shown in table 8.8, [t] and [k] are between [p] and [tʃ]; thus it may be expected that p→tʃ would be taken to imply t→tʃ and k→tʃ. In contrast, [t] is not between [k] and [tʃ], so k→tʃ need not imply

Table 8.7

	a	tʃ	Copy$_{Fin}$	i	p	t
p	0.58	0.05	0.79	0.25	0.74	0.05
t	0.6	0.09	0.8	0.29	0.04	0.75
k	0.15	0.78	0.1	0.74	0.04	0.07
tʃ	0.18	**0.45**	0.18	0.45	−0.24	**0.42**

Final consonant and suffix activations in Tapa (especially problematic cells are highlighted in boldface).

Table 8.8

+lips	-lips	-lips	-lips
tongue blade	+tongue blade	*tongue blade*	+tongue blade
tongue body	*tongue body*	+tongue body	+tongue body
p	t	k	tʃ

Articulatory descriptions of English stops and [tʃ]. Italics highlight similarities between [p] and other consonants.

t→tʃ. Similarly, t→tʃ need not imply k→tʃ. Thus, there should be more [t] palatalization after training on p→tʃ than on k→tʃ, and more velar palatalization after training on p→tʃ than on t→tʃ. However, there were no significant differences, contrasting with the strong preference for tʃ→tʃi after training on k→tʃi or p→tʃi. Therefore, tʃ→tʃi appears to be implied by X→tʃi more strongly than any other change resulting in [tʃi]. It is not simply a case of a smaller change resulting in the same output.

Based on these results, the knowledge acquired by the participants is probably best captured by a syntagmatic generalization: exposure to X→tʃi increases the probability of [tʃ] preceding [i] and the probability of -*i* following [tʃ]. As reviewed in chapter 2, these kinds of between-segment transitional probabilities have been shown to be automatically learned even by young infants and uncontroversially play a role in language acquisition (Aslin et al., 1998). The next section presents an NDL model designed to learn these kinds of generalizations, showing that it recovers the transitional probabilities between segments within plurals (see also Baayen et al., 2011), and discusses ways this kind of knowledge could be brought to bear on producing a novel form of a known word.

8.9   Model 2: Syntagmatic Structure

8.9.1   The Task: Syntagmatic Prediction

Unlike in the schema/paradigm model, the task for the present model is syntagmatic prediction (i.e., predicting what follows what). In this model, every time a learner encounters a word, tries/he tries to predict all segments of that word from all other segments. That is, exposure to a word can be modeled as a set of cue-outcome pairings, where each pairing is an attempt to predict a segment from all other segments comprising the word—for example, blutʃi = {bl, u, i}→tʃ; {bl, u, tʃ}→i; {bl, tʃ, i}→u; {u, tʃ, i}→bl. For the sake of simplicity, we focus on just the final CV here. As I argued earlier, this kind of bidirectional association formation supporting pattern completion may be better captured by chunking and Hebbian association formation (chapter 3), which are inherently bidirectional. However, the error-driven nature of NDL does not make a difference to the simulation results for the present data, and using the same learner for both syntagmatic and paradigmatic associations makes it easier to integrate the two.

The learned syntagmatic probabilities are cell-specific. Thus, a separate set of probabilities is kept for plurals and for singulars. As a result, the model's syntagmatic predictions are meaning-specific (i.e., the model is better described as learning syntagmatic relationships within a schema than as learning phonotactics). The crucial prediction of this proposal is that augmenting training with homophones of product forms should not help fill the prosodic templates of product forms. For example, adding examples like blutʃiₛG→blutʃiₚL should not help -i call forth a preceding [tʃ]. This prediction was confirmed in chapter 7 and Kapatsinski (2017).

8.9.2 Simulation Results

As shown in table 8.9, the model learns both forward and backward conditional probabilities. In Tapa, there is a 75% probability of -a following [p] or [t], 100% probability of -i following [tʃ], 50% [p] or [t] before -a, and 67% [tʃ] before -i. Now we turn to how these learned syntagmatic probabilities within products can be harnessed for constructing a novel product.

8.9.3 Combining Syntagmatic and Paradigmatic Knowledge

There are two ways syntagmatic probabilities within products could be brought to bear on production. One possibility is that some parts of the product are constructed first, which allows them to be used as cues in constructing the rest of the product (à la rule-based theories of language; e.g., Chomsky & Halle, 1968). For the attached -i to influence the choice of the stem-final consonant, the -i has to attach first. For the product [tʃ] to

Table 8.9

	p	t	tʃ	a	i
p	0	0	0	0.75	0.25
t	0	0	0	0.75	0.25
tʃ	0	0	0	0	1
a	0.5	0.5	0	0	0
i	0.17	0.17	0.67	0	0

Activations of outcomes (columns) from the cues (rows) that syntagmatically co-occur with them in Tapa plurals.

influence the selection of the suffix, it has to be chosen first. The alternative is to construct (or preactivate) multiple possible products and let them compete with each other on their merits (as in Optimality Theory / Harmonic Grammar; Prince & Smolensky, 1993/2008). Thus, an input [tʃ] would lead to the construction of products ending in [tʃi] and [ta] (among others), which could then be evaluated on the basis of syntagmatic generalizations.

The basic problem to be solved is that [tʃ] is all too frequently mapped onto [ta], rather than [tʃi], in Tapa. This problem cannot be solved by increasing a bias against stem changes—whether by favoring copying, disfavoring large changes, or requiring the speaker to produce all known cues to the meaning of the stem—because such a bias would also reduce the incidence of t→tʃi. The conundrum is exacerbated by the fact that [t] is coronal, while [tʃ] is also dorsal, since participants are trained to change the dorsal [k] and not to change coronals. However, note that a source [tʃ] favors product -*i* over -*a*, and product -*i* favors [tʃ] over [t]. Thus, one path toward decreasing the incidence of tʃ→ta and increasing the incidence of tʃ→tʃi would be to choose the suffix first, based on the source form, and choose what to do with the stem-final consonant later, once the suffix is available to bias the choice.

Why would the suffix become available first? One possibility, proposed by rule-based generative grammar, is that suffixes are always chosen first: morphology feeds into phonology. However, there are documented natural language systems in which this does not hold (e.g., Kapatsinski, 2010b). An intriguing alternative is that suffix and stem consonant selection actually proceed in parallel but the choice of the suffix completes earlier because it is easier than the choice of the stem-final consonant given a source [tʃ]. Choice difficulty usually does translate into longer decision time (e.g., Usher & McClelland, 2001). The choice of the product stem-final consonant given a source [tʃ] is more uncertain than the choice of the suffix even in Tapa.[6]

8.9.4   An Alternative: Generative Models

An alternative explanation for why examples like t→ta do not provide strong support for tʃ→ta whereas examples like k→tʃi do provide support for tʃ→tʃi is available in the Bayesian framework. O'Donnell (2015) argues that learners try to infer *how* a particular wordform came to be (i.e., how it was generated). In his theory (a Bayesian version of Pinker, 1999), words are either retrieved from memory or computed by rule, and a person who hears a word tries to infer which mechanism the speaker used to produce it. In the present theory, segments comprising words are either copied from a base form (which could be the same form in the case of a word retrieved completely from memory) or supplied by a schema. Following O'Donnell, we can then propose that the learner infers, for each segment of a perceived wordform, whether it came from a base or not. Segments that are inferred to be copied from the base then do not provide support for a schema that would demand the same segment; in fact, they provide evidence against it. Under this theory, examples like t→ta provide evidence against a schema that demands plurals ending in [ta]. It is then no wonder that [ta]-final plurals are seldom produced from singulars ending in other consonants.

This theory does run into trouble with the finding that examples of tʃ→tʃi help t→tʃi over t→ti (Kapatsinski, 2012, 2013). However, it may be that the existence of examples of k→tʃi in the languages provides learners with enough evidence for a PL~[tʃi] schema that examples of tʃ→tʃi are then interpreted as being generated by that PL~[tʃi] schema rather than by copying of [tʃ], especially when copying is difficult to detect in training (i.e., when corresponding singulars and plurals are not next to each other). An interesting prediction follows: if tʃ→tʃi needs to be interpreted correctly when it occurs, and this interpretation comes from observing examples of k→tʃi, then presenting such unfaithful mappings first should increase the likelihood that presenting tʃ→tʃi examples later will boost the productivity of palatalization. This prediction remains to be tested.

8.10   A Channel Bias against Large Changes

Stave et al. (2013) focused on demonstrating a learning bias against labial palatalization. Participants palatalized labials following training on labial palatalization less than they palatalized nonlabials following training on alveolar or velar palatalization. This result is argued to follow from a bias against large changes rather than against unnatural *rules* (changes in context), since it is observed both before *-i* (a natural context for palatalization) and between [a]'s, an unnatural context (see also Skoruppa et al. 2011). The bias also does not appear to be due to preferences against certain stop-vowel sequences: faithful illegal outcomes were disliked equally, whether they contained a labial, a coronal, or a velar. For example, participants exposed to labial palatalization came to dislike plurals ending in [pi] as much as those exposed to alveolar palatalization came to dislike plurals ending in [ti].

Smolek and Kapatsinski (2017a) attributed the findings to a bias against associating dissimilar units. There is good neurological motivation for such a bias in that more synaptic modification is required to associate together representations that are relatively far from each other in the brain (see also Kapatsinski, 2011; Moreton, 2008; Warker & Dell, 2006). It has also been well documented in the associative learning literature by Rescorla and Furrow (1977). Results on the difficulty of learning dependencies within vs. across perceptual dimensions reviewed by Keele et al. (2003), and the data on similarity influencing the learnability of syntagmatic dependencies in phonology (Moreton, 2008; Wayment, 2009), may also be accounted for by this same general principle.

Our model, even when equipped with copy outcomes, does not have this bias and is therefore equally good at learning labial and lingual palatalization. This failure of the model supports the existence of a *bias* against changing labials into alveopalatals. Fortunately, the bias can be implemented in the model very directly, by decreasing the learning rate on p→tʃ connections. With this addition, the model successfully predicts that, given the same number of training trials on labial vs. lingual palatalization, labials are changed into alveopalatals less than nonlabials are.

8.11   A Comparison to Clamoring for Blends

Kapatsinski (2013) used much of the data discussed here to argue for a theory of morphophonology that combines aspects of Bybee's (1985, 2001) Network Theory and Legendre and Smolensky's Harmonic Grammar (Legendre et al., 1990; Smolensky & Legendre, 2006). Network Theory donated schemas, while Harmonic Grammar donated faithfulness constraints and the overall architecture, where faithfulness constraints and schemas vote for candidate outputs (blends).

Both C4B and NDL are able to capture much of the empirical data discussed in this chapter. However, only NDL is able to predict that tʃ→tʃi examples can help t→tʃi over t→ti while helping k→ki over k→tʃi (when stem-sharing forms are presented next to each other).

The bias against large stem changes also finds a much more natural home in the current model. In NDL, this bias has to do with the learnability of a paradigmatic association linking the alternating segments. C4B does not have paradigmatic associations, so the only home for the bias is in the relative weights of "keep [p]" vs. "keep [t]" or "keep [k]." However, it is not clear that labials are *overall* less changeable than other consonants, regardless of what they are changed into. For example, White (2013, p. 145) reports that participants change labial stops into labiodental fricatives more readily than they change coronal stops into coronal fricatives. It seems that the bias is about the size of the change, not about changeability of the input gestural chunk.

8.12   Limitations and Future Directions

First, the model as formulated here has been applied to only a few datasets and a single test task. It is important to also apply the model to other datasets, including morphophonological patterns from a variety of natural languages. Baayen et al.'s (2011) results on applying NDL to learning large lexical databases suggest that this kind of scaling up should be possible. Nonetheless, the model does occasionally lead to counterintuitive results. In particular, some of the best cues to a meaning can, in specific circumstances, be cues that *never* co-occur with the meaning in question within the learner's experience. These are relatively rare cues that co-occur with strong inhibitors of the meaning (see Caballero & Kapatsinski, 2017, for an example). Note that the RW equation (2) states that weights of connections to an outcome are increased when the outcome's activation is below zero. As a result, when a cue co-occurs with another cue that strongly inhibits a meaning and drives its activation below zero, that cue will develop a strongly positive weight to compensate. The RW equations consider that activation levels below 0 are errors, even though an absent outcome is correctly inhibited: the learning rule drives activation levels to 1 and 0 and overshooting these targets is just as bad as undershooting them. Kruschke (1992) calls this the "strict teacher" approach and considers it inappropriate when the outcomes are nominal—as they often are in language. He proposes that in such cases there can be no overshooting: if an absent outcome is *really* unexpected, therefore having activation below 0, its nonoccurrence should confirm the learner's beliefs and no learning should occur, just as when the outcome's activation is equal to 0. Because the learner is not punished for outdoing the teacher, this is a "humble teacher" approach. While to the extent that the "accidental excitors" are rare, the strict teacher problem is alleviated by using the RW model with a slow learning rate—which makes strict and humble teachers indistinguishable because activations do not overshoot the target levels—the strictness of the RW teacher signal remains in principle problematic. Furthermore, one can set up a miniature artificial language in which the problem arises for any learning rate. It is worth exploring whether humble teacher signals would be more appropriate for morphological learning.

As implied by the discussion above, the behavior of the model is quite sensitive to learning rate, as it should be, given that learning rate is its one real parameter. We can distinguish between slow learning rates, which do not allow activations to approach or overshoot 0 and 1 by the end of training, and fast learning rates, which do. Slow learning rates appear to be beneficial for the task of learning morphology. When the learning rate is high, the model ends up being overly sensitive to conditional probabilities rather than joint probabilities. As a result, it becomes trapped by accidentally exceptionless generalizations (Albright & Hayes, 2006). Patterns that occur in only one word that happens to have a particular suffix or meaning are inferred to be the best cues to that suffix or meaning. Similarly, particular stem bodies are learned to be highly predictive of suffix choice on the basis of single words that have those stem bodies in training and end in [p] or [t], where the choice of suffix is really unpredictable / lexically specific. When those stem bodies then occur at test with a different final consonant, the model relies on the stem body to choose the suffix rather than relying on the final consonant. In contrast, participants rely on the final consonant. Finally, the model is also misled into considering the "accidental excitors" above to be the best cues to meaning. All of these problems disappear once the learning rate is lowered sufficiently: the model becomes sensitive only to generalizations that hold across words and becomes very sensitive to type frequency (the number of words participating in a pattern). This appears to be the right behavior for learning grammar, since type frequency has been repeatedly found to be the primary correlate of pattern productivity (see Bybee, 2001; Kapatsinski, in press, for reviews). The conclusion that slow learning rates are better for picking up on generalizations that hold across individual training items also fits well with the discussion of the benefits of slow cortical learning in McClelland et al. (1995).

On the other hand, slow learning rates are too slow to allow the model to exhibit the cue-competition effects that have been used as the primary arguments for adopting error-driven learning models over Hebbian ones. For example, highlighting refers to the fact that an unexpected outcome paired with a set of familiar cues and an unfamiliar one is rapidly associated with the unfamiliar cue (Kruschke, 1996, 2006, 2009). Accidentally exceptionless generalizations *are* highlighting in action. Capturing blocking in the RW model requires learning rates to be fast enough for activations to reach 0 and 1 by the end of the first, A→X training stage. Finally, the salience of the unexpected-exemplars effect in category learning discussed in chapter 5 also demands a fast learning rate (Olejarczuk et al., in press). The behavior of an RW model with a slow learning rate is not appreciably different from that of a Hebbian model. And, indeed, Ashby et al. (2007) suggest that the slow-learning cortical system of McClelland et al. (1995) learns in an essentially Hebbian manner. This is perhaps a welcome result as it allows us to estimate just how Hebbian learning is within the RW framework by estimating the learning rate, instead of having to decide between Hebbian and error-driven learning mechanisms. Though the neural systems implementing both types of learning appear to be distinct, both are likely involved in any language learning task, making it unrealistic to expect learning to ever be purely Hebbian or purely error-driven.[7]

What then determines the learning rate? One possibility is the complexity of the task: morphological learning involves many more cues and outcomes than simple conditioning and contingency learning paradigms where the classic cue-competition effects were documented. The complexity of the learning task may result in reduced learning rates through divided attention. In the RW model, learning rate is a function of cue and outcome salience. Unattended cues or outcomes are, of course, minimally salient. Thus, learning rates are expected to be slower when many cues and outcomes are competing for the participant's attention. It may therefore be that blocking and highlighting effects are most likely to be observed with particularly salient cues and outcomes. However, properly modeling this proposal will require integrating the RW model with an attentional learning model.

The discussion above highlights the need to elucidate the interactions between error-driven learning described by the RW model and other kinds of learning, including learning to allocate selective attention, Hebbian learning (provided that it can be distinguished from slow error-driven learning), and chunking.

The representational and processing assumptions made above also require more testing and justification. First, order of selection is an area about which little is known. For example, the structure of the model allows for biases in favor of selecting the suffix first or deciding on the shape of the stem first. It is not clear whether there is a general bias affecting order of selection (e.g., Chomsky & Halle, 1965; Caballero & Inkelas, 2013), or whether selection is driven solely by choice difficulty, and indeed whether the assumption that only a single output is constructed can be maintained.

Second, I have relied on prosodic templates to represent inputs and outputs (Vihman & W. Croft, 2007). As part of trial-by-trial learning and scaling up to natural language datasets, it will be important to grow the template as additional words with novel prosodic structure are encountered, since it is unrealistic to imagine that the template is set a priori. The primary challenge in growing the template is to do so without losing generalizations that are made about the paradigmatic mappings and likelihood of copying from various templatic positions.

Generalizing copying to a greater variety of prosodic shapes and morphological processes would require spelling out the mechanisms for preventing the input chunks from being copied into the wrong output positions, especially since the prosodic positions of the input may not match those in the output (for example, above, the coda of the singular becomes the second onset of the plural). Even if we know what we should and should not copy, how do we know where to insert what we have copied, keeping reordering to reasonably low levels? One possibility is that copy outcomes referring to earlier positions generally have higher resting activation levels, perhaps simply because they are more likely to be correctly detected in training under incremental processing conditions before attention is withdrawn. C. J. Davis (2010) shows that serial order can then be effectively maintained as earlier units outcompete later ones for, in our case, incorporation into the template, and then take themselves out of contention by self-inhibition. Another possibility is that morphological boundaries are needed after all. Unlike prosodic boundaries, they are constant across the input and the output and can therefore be used to align the source location and the target location of a copied element.

The last challenge is to describe how the prosodic specifications described in the articulatory plan, notions like coda and onset, are represented in the serially ordered execution chain (described in the next chapter). Note that this issue does not arise when a known word (qua "listeme," a stored unit) is being produced, because the articulatory representation for the word can then be retrieved directly from the lexicon (Bybee, 2001; Kapatsinski, 2010a; Ramus et al., 2010; Redford, 2015). However, for a novel word, the copied gestures need to be prosodified and then executed. Here, prosodification is enforced by the selected template, which has positions that correspond to differences in articulation. In fact, the positional tags in the template are *irrelevant* for execution except when they influence articulation in a way that cannot be described as inherent in optimal production of the gestural sequences comprising the word. Therefore, one way to view them is as cues to gestures. For example, "onset" cues the light /l/ and "coda" cues the dark /l/ in English. Execution of a newly formed word then involves traversing the template (which occupies the "form" level), with each element in the chain activated in sequence from the semantics, and in turn activating the corresponding articulatory representations. This traversal establishes contiguity between the semantics and the articulatory units activated by the template and thereby establishes direct connections between the word's semantics and the articulatory units it contains. At that point, a hierarchical articulatory representation is established and can then become automatized with repetition as described in chapter 9.

8.13   Conclusion

It has long been a major goal of linguistic theory to specify an acquisition mechanism for deriving a grammar from linguistic experience. I have argued that this goal is fruitfully approached by building on the foundation of domain-general learning mechanisms that are inherent in any neuromotor system. Here, we have focused on a specific part of the grammar, productive morphophonology, which allows speakers to generate novel forms of known words, even words they hear for the first time.

I have argued that speakers may accomplish this task by activating the meaning to be expressed as well as known forms of the word. To derive the novel form, they make use of word-sized prosodic templates, segmental form-meaning associations, meaning-specific syntagmatic dependencies, phonologized perseveration (knowing what and when to copy from the activated forms of the word), and arbitrary paradigmatic associations between phonological units. The novel form of a known word is derived by gestural chunks copied from other activated forms and chunks activated by the meaning to be expressed or by features of the activated forms racing in parallel to fill out a prosodic template. Once part of a template is filled, it may become available to bias the filling of the remaining parts of the template through syntagmatic co-occurrence relations.

With these basic building blocks in place, the acquisition mechanism for productive morphophonology can be approximated by classic theories of associative learning. The present modeling effort is able to capture both product-oriented rule conspiracies (Bybee, 2001; Kapatsinski, 2013; Kisseberth, 1970), and arbitrary paradigmatic mappings (Becker & Gouskova, 2016; Booij, 2010; Nesset, 2008; Pierrehumbert, 2006). It also (arguably) provides the simplest account of these data so far. Compared to product-oriented models, it does away with construction and evaluation of multiple candidate outputs, separate learning mechanisms for schema extraction and paradigm learning, and separate learning stages for extracting first- and second-order schemas. Compared to source-oriented models, it does away with the need to split words into changes and the contexts in which they occur, and relaxes the tacit assumption that learning phonology always proceeds by comparing two morphologically related wordforms.

More importantly, expressing the acquisition of phonology in the common vocabulary of associative learning opens up avenues for comparisons across domains, and even species, allowing work on language acquisition to inform general learning theory and vice versa. Future work should explore how error-driven discriminative learning interacts with other types of learning necessary for language acquisition, including Hebbian learning (chapter 6), chunking (chapters 1, 3), automatization (chapter 9), and learned (in)attention (chapter 3). The present chapter provides only a starting point for what I hope will be a fruitful discussion about how associative learning mechanisms work together in generating the complexity of language.

9 Automatization and Sound Change

Units used together fuse together.
—Bybee (2002a)

The change of a sound ... consists of the sum of microscopic displacements. It is therefore dependent on the number of repetitions. ... These repetitions are to be counted within individual words. ... Rarely-used words drag behind, very frequently-used ones hurry ahead.
—Schuchardt (1885/1972, p. 26)

As we do something over and over again, we get faster. We also get more accurate, reducing unwanted variability in the behavior across trials (Bryan & Harter, 1897; A. Smith & Goffman, 1998; Pierrehumbert, 2001; Tomaschek et al., 2013; Baayen et al., 2017). As one practices throwing darts at a board, one becomes more and more reliable at hitting the board, and more and more likely at hitting the bull's-eye. It also takes less and less time to *plan* an accurate throw. In the case of more complex goal-directed behaviors that require a preplanned series of actions before the goal is reached, the *execution* of the action sequence also takes less and less time as the sequence is practiced. Furthermore, the action sequence itself changes, becoming more streamlined and fluid, as unnecessary deviations from a smooth trajectory are eliminated. At the same time, execution of the sequence becomes less and less easy to disrupt or alter in novel ways. In this chapter, we explore this automatization process and its implications for language processing and language change, as well as tackling what it means for some part of a sequence of motor movements to be unnecessary. We begin by considering possible representations of familiar action sequences.

9.1 Sequence Representations: Hierarchies and Chains

The ability to learn and execute long sequences of actions may be a major evolutionary prerequisite for the development of language (Broadbent, 1958; Christiansen & Chater, 2016). Broadbent (1958, pp. 46–47; citing Hunter, 1920; Kinnaman, 1902) argues that nonhuman animals have difficulty learning to produce sequences of actions unless each action can be associated with a specific environmental cue, and that faced with the same tasks, humans seem to do relatively well. He concludes that humans "can use language because they can deal with sequences."

A number of possible representations for well-practiced sequences are possible (figure 9.1). All of these representations assume that the sequence is triggered by external input. In language production, this external input comes from semantics/conceptualization, the message the speaker wishes to express. The representations in figure 9.1 differ in how much control they allow this external input to have on how the sequence is executed. In the *chain* model, preceding units activate those that follow, with only the first unit in the chain being triggered by top-down activation from outside the chain. In his classic argument against the chain model, Lashley (1951, p. 118) noted that it disallows various observed error patterns—for example, deletion errors, in which a unit in the middle of the chain is omitted from production. However, such errors can be introduced in a chain model if activation is allowed to *cascade* through the chain (Wickelgren, 1969) or if noninitial elements of the chain can receive activation from "context" cues outside of the chain (Snyder & Logan, 2014). For example,

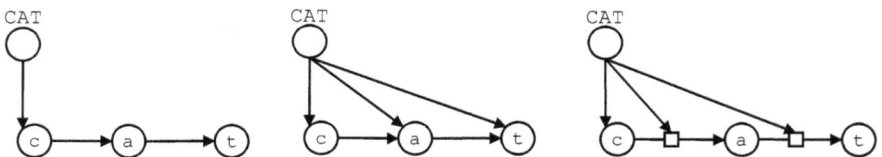

Figure 9.1
Possible representations for an action sequence involved in typing *cat*. Left: A chain, in which the meaning to be expressed activates a chain of actions, with each action activating the next action. Middle: A hierarchical control structure, where the meaning to be expressed sends activation down to each element comprising the chain. Right: A gated chain, where the meaning sends activation down to *propagation filters* (Sumida & Dyer, 1992; Sumida, 1997; see also chapter 3) on links connecting the elements, allowing or—in a cascaded activation model—facilitating activation spread down the chain.

if activation from A can flow through B to C in A→B→C→D, and C is more accessible—for reasons of frequency, priming, or attentional salience—then B may well be omitted, with C seizing control over the articulators before B had its chance (Wickelgren, 1969, p. 5). As activation of C decays—through latent or top-down inhibition (cf. Dell et al., 1997)—B then may temporarily be activated more strongly than D, resulting in a B–C exchange error. Thus, contrary to Lashley (1951), the chain model is not out of contention for representing serial order in behavior (see also Botvinick & Plaut, 2004; Snyder & Logan, 2014).

An alternative, which rose to overwhelming dominance after Lashley (1951), is the *hierarchical* control model, where top-down input can activate every unit of the sequence. The hierarchical control model allows for more flexibility than the chain, even a chain with cascading activation. In particular, the hierarchical control model allows production to start from noninitial units in the chain, affording flexible ordering and reordering of the elements of the sequence. Therein, however, lies its downfall as a model of well-practiced, automatized sequences (see also James, 1890, pp.114-116). A well-practiced sequence has presumably been repeatedly produced from the beginning as anything else would be an error. As a result, every time a sequence is practiced in its entirety, top-down connections to noninitial units in the sequence should atrophy, so as to avoid starting the sequence from the wrong place. With practice, a hierarchy should become a chain. Supporting evidence for this proposal has been provided by Caplan et al. (2014), who find that a newly learned compound noun (like *batshock*) is equally easily accessed from either component stem. However, a well-known compound like *batshit* is much more easily accessed from its first member. As the compound is practiced, its sequential organization becomes more entrenched in the practiced order.

Finally, in the *gated chain* model, top-down input allows activation to spread from preceding units to following units, instead of activating the noninitial units directly. This proposal goes back to the idea that links have *propagation filters*, which mediate the spread of activation from the head of a link to its tail (Sumida & Dyer, 1992; Sumida, 1997; see also Bouton & Nelson, 1994).

According to Local Activation Spread Theory (Kapatsinski, 2005b, 2007a; Snider, 2008), every A→B is really A→PF→B. The PF of a link receives excitation/inhibition only from outside the A→B link itself; thus, activation of A does not increase activation of the PFs of all links emanating from A. However, the resting activation level of the PF does depend on how much the A→B sequence is practiced: when both A and B are activated, the

PF is strengthened (see Kapatsinski, 2005b, 2007a, for a Hebbian spreading activation model of this process). More generally, we can say that the PF is where the weight of the A→B association is stored, regardless of how the association weight is learned.

When the PF is activated above a threshold, activation can spread through the link, so that activating A now activates B. In contrast to top-down excitatory connections to noninitial elements of a sequence, connections to propagation filters are not expected to decay as the chain is practiced because they do not result in omission errors, instead promoting rapid execution of the chain.

Importantly, the idea of a propagation filter can be reconciled with the idea of activation cascading down the chain (Wickelgren, 1969). All that is required is to allow *some* activation to spread through the link when the propagation filter is in the "off position," having not (yet) reached the activation threshold. The propagation filter is a gate obstructing the flow of activation, but it is a leaky gate.

9.2 Automatization: From Hierarchy to Chain

In speech/language production, it appears promising to consider stored production plans for variable-order constructions (e.g., argument structure constructions in languages with variable word order, or affixal templates in which some affixes can switch positions) to be hierarchical control structures, with fixed-order constructions being gated chains. Variable element order means that top-down connections to noninitial elements are useful and should be maintained, while fixed order indicates that they have atrophied to the point of irrelevancy. In addition, fixed order means pruning or top-down inhibition of backward connections from following elements to preceding ones, whereas variable order may lead to maintenance of both sets of syntagmatic connections (see also James, 1890, vol.2, pp.586–587).

A strong argument can be made against the hierarchical control representation for English words. In a series of studies, Zara Harmon and I have examined a large sample of replacement and repetition disfluencies from natural American English speech (Harmon & Kapatsinski, 2015, in press; Kapatsinski, 2005a, 2010a). These are cases like (1) and (2), where the speaker stops the flow of speech before completing the utterance and then restarts, often repeating what has just been produced. While word execution can be stopped midway, speech production always restarts from the beginning of a word. Thus, cases like (3) do not occur. Seldom can one say *always* in social science. That we can do so here suggests that restarting production from inside a word is extremely difficult. The chain models in figure 9.1 capture this fact by preventing top-down activation of non-word-initial articulatory targets in the absence of some activation flow from the beginning of the word.[1] Note that this avoidance of word-medial restarts is not expected to be a property of words as lexical units but rather a property of fixed-order sequences. In polysynthetic languages, which allow for more word-internal variability in sequencing (including noun incorporation and variable affix order), it may be possible to restart speech from the onset of a word-internal morpheme (as reported by Evans et al., 2008, for Dalabon, a polysynthetic language of Australia).

(1) *I like to listen to the newsp-, uh, radio in the morning.*
(2) *We were collecting inte-, uh, intelligibility judgments.*
(3) **We were collecting inte-, uh, -ligibility judgments.*

Convergent evidence has also been provided by a study of typing in English. Snyder and Logan (2014) document that priming word-initial letter sequences facilitates typing the words that contain them but, crucially, typing noninitial word-internal sequences does not. They interpret this finding as being consistent with chain models of serial order in typing and inconsistent with hierarchical control models. In accordance with the hierarchy-to-chain hypothesis, Snyder and Logan (2014, p. 1698) speculate that repetition of a sequence may make that sequence more and more chainlike: "Typing tasks usually present familiar words that have been typed many times before. Each repetition strengthens sequential associations between keystrokes, forming a chain. The cognitive system may prefer serial chaining for skilled typing because the sequential associations speed typing." While Snyder and Logan are wary of extending chain models to other examples of serial behavior, including speech, a chain may well be the end result of automatization for any sequence that is repeatedly executed in a fixed order. Consider James (1890):

> If an act requires for its execution a chain, A, B, C, D, E, F, G, etc., of successive nervous events, then in the first performances of the action the conscious will [i.e. top-down control structures] must choose each of these events from a number of wrong alternatives that tend to present themselves; but habit soon brings it about that *each event calls up its own appropriate successor* [emphasis mine] without any alternative offering itself, and without any reference to the conscious will, until at last the whole chain, A, B, C, D, E, F, G, rattles itself off as soon as A occurs, just as if A and the rest of the chain were fused into a continuous stream. […] The marksman sees the bird, and, before he knows it, he has aimed and shot.

A gleam in his adversary's eye, a momentary pressure from his rapier, and the fencer finds that he has instantly made the right parry and return. A glance at the musical hieroglyphics, and the pianist's fingers have ripped through a cataract of notes. And not only is it the right thing at the right time that we thus involuntarily do, but the wrong thing also, if it be an habitual thing. Who is there that has never wound up his watch on taking off his waistcoat in the daytime, or taken his latchkey out on arriving at the door-step of a friend? [...] The writer well remembers how, on revisiting Paris after ten years' absence, and, finding himself in the street in which for one winter he had attended school, he lost himself in a brown study, from which he was awakened by finding himself upon the stairs which led to the apartment in a house many streets away in which he had lived during that earlier time, and to which his steps from the school had then habitually led." (vol.1, pp. 114–115)

9.3   Automatization, Anticipatory Coarticulation, and Trajectory Optimization

Moving down the chain involves activating the future while executing the present and inhibiting the past (inhibition is necessary to prevent the same target from being executed ad infinitum once activated); Dell et al. (1997). The more a sequence is practiced, the better the producer is able to *anticipate* upcoming targets. As one gains expertise in speech production over the course of language learning, one makes fewer and fewer speech errors. Dell and his colleagues noted that as the overall rate of speech errors decreases, more and more of the remaining errors are *anticipatory*, as in (4), where an anticipated future is anticipated too much, surfacing in the present.

(4) *In less exciting news from Louisiana, Clinton currently leaders Sanders by 47 percentage points.* (http://fivethirtyeight.com/live-blog/louisiana -kansas-kentucky-maine-primaries-presidential-election-2016.)

Increasing anticipation of the future with practice results in faster execution of the action sequence: future targets become easier and easier to activate, which results in the activated targets seizing control of the motor system earlier and earlier. As a result, practice results in an increase in *anticipatory coarticulation*. This process is pervasive in speech but is perhaps more easily understood with the example of a manual action sequence. Sosnik et al. (2004) examined manual movements involved in drawing a line that has to pass through a series of dots at predetermined locations in a predetermined order but can take any path between these dots. As illustrated in figure 9.2, Sosnik et al. show that practice allows one to anticipate upcoming targets

Novice: Expert:

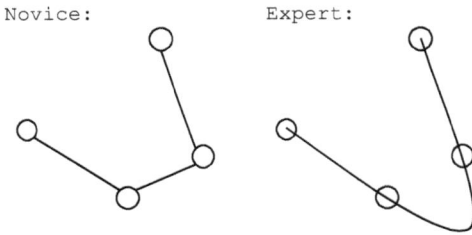

Figure 9.2
When asked to draw a line that passes through four points in a particular order, the novice participant draws four lines, slowing down at each target point. Practice turns the novice into an expert who instead draws one trajectory that passes through all four points in a single smooth movement (based on Sosnik et al., 2004).

and optimize movements so that all targets are reached with a minimum of effort and a maximum of speed by preplanning a single smooth movement trajectory toward a distal target that traverses more proximate targets on the way. Not only do movement trajectories become smoother over time, without sacrificing the ability to reach intermediate goal locations, but the velocity profiles also become smoother. An inexperienced participant slows down at each target location to plan the next movement and change movement direction. In contrast, the practiced participant rapidly passes through the intermediate targets on their way to the ultimate endpoint of the movement trajectory.

Articulation is also commonly thought of as traversal of a series of static targets (the static features of Goldsmith, 1976; and gestures of Browman & L. Goldstein, 1989), leaving the speaker free to optimize the transitions between these targets to conserve time and energy. A word is then much like the 1234 sequence in figure 9.2 (though see below for complications). If words are stored in memory in a gestural format (Bybee, 2001; Kapatsinski, 2010a; Ramus et al., 2010), their articulation is free to be optimized in the same way as the path through the four dots in Sosnik et al. (2004).

Note that the trajectory traversed by the expert participant on the right of figure 9.2 is actually longer than the trajectory traversed by the novice. This means that certain seemingly nonreductive changes can nonetheless be the result of automatizing articulation. For example, the tongue-body positions corresponding to a vowel between two consonants may be represented along the lines of figure 9.2, as illustrated in figure 9.3 for the vowel in *tag* and *tab*. As seen in figure 9.3, the optimal trajectory for the tongue body between two articulatory targets defining a vowel may actually take

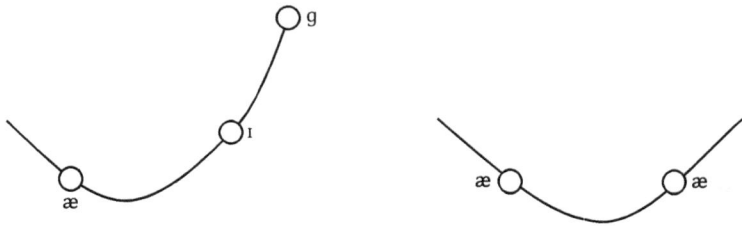

Figure 9.3
Stylized tongue-body trajectories for [æɪ] before [k] or [g] (left) and of [æ] (right).
Time flows from left to right under each trajectory.

the tongue lower than either target position. Even though vowel lowering is usually not thought of as reductive, it may result from automatization of articulator movements, as long as the vowel in question is defined by more than one articulatory target. Recent research in sociophonetics has emphasized that long, stressed vowels often do require more than one articulatory target to accurately characterize (e.g., Farrington et al., 2017; Fox & Jacewicz, 2009; Hillenbrand et al., 1995). Interestingly, the midpoints of diphthongs defined by a rising tongue-body trajectory—like the one shown in figure 9.3—have also sometimes been shown to lower (e.g., in Nevada English; Gunter et al., 2017). Figure 9.3 suggests that this kind of lowering may be motivated by automatization of articulation.

Multipoint specifications are especially likely for vowels that are either inherently or contextually long. Multiple targets are unlikely to arise or persist in short vowels because they are hard to achieve in the short time between the consonants (see Lindblom, 1963) and because they would be unlikely to be recognized as distinct by the listener. On the other hand, long monophthongal vowels can become diphthongal. For example, diphthongization of stressed vowels is a well-known feature of Southern American English, which is also characterized by longer vowel durations (Clopper et al., 2005; Jacewicz et al., 2007). In some dialects of American English, [æ] and [ɛ] have developed an [ɪ] offglide before [g]—so that the vowels of *beg* and *bag* have become more like the vowel of *bagel* (Baker et al., 2008; Carignan et al., 2016). Some modern American pop singers produce [i] offglides for high back vowels before [d], as in Selena Gomez pronouncing *good* as [gʊid] in the song "Good for You" (Gick et al., 2017; Ugwu, 2015). Importantly, the diphthongization does not usually occur before the voiceless stops, [k] and [t], where the vowel is shorter. In these cases, the optimal tongue trajectory from the vowel nucleus to the following velar or coronal stop goes through a region of acoustic space that is occupied by another vowel category (Baker et al., 2008; Carignan et al., 2016). When the vowel is long, the tongue stays in this region for a while, and therefore the listener can interpret the sound accompanying the tongue movement as having been intended by the speaker (cf. Ohala, 1981). If the listener then replicates this innovation in their own speech, the diphthongization of the vowel is on its way to being part of the community grammar.

Given that durations vary across dialects and can be phonemic, duration must itself be specified in the articulatory plan. One possible way of specifying duration would be for the speaker to plan to hold a particular gesture for a longer or shorter time period. However, holding in place appears to be articulatorily difficult, in part because it is the ultimate break in the continuity of a movement, and in part because it is simply fatiguing for the muscles involved (try holding your arms in front of you for a minute or two). Therefore, automatizing a hold may involve changing it from a hold to a dynamic movement, to the extent that the change is not noticeable to the listener. For example, the relatively long duration of the English low vowel [æ] in *cab* may be represented by two articulatory targets in the same position, but the optimal trajectory between these targets may involve lowering the tongue even further between these two targets. Accordingly, Baayen et al. (2017) show that compared to relatively inexperienced youngsters, older adults produce lower low vowels. Farrington et al. (2017) suggest that two points are sufficient to describe differences between vowel trajectories across the dialects of American English, and that listeners may not be sensitive to the trajectory between the two points, which suggests that the speaker has room to optimize this trajectory. It is worth asking whether the apparently complicated triphthongal vowels of Southern English may be the result of such optimization.

Stopping, exemplified by pronouncing *that* as *dat*, is a common process in both child language and language change, and another possible example of trajectory optimization. Producing a lingual fricative requires carefully positioning the tongue so that it is close enough to the roof of the mouth to produce turbulent airflow but not so close as to close off the flow of air. This makes fricatives difficult to produce reliably, especially when they need to be produced quickly. Accordingly, children have particular difficulty producing fricatives in nonfinal positions, which require quickly getting the tongue in and out of the target position for the fricative. In contrast, stops can be produced by a rapid ballistic movement (e.g., Drachman, 1978). Compare the task of punching a wall vs. bringing your hand within a quarter inch of it. The latter is much more difficult. As in the case of lowering an already low vowel, what looks like a strengthening can in fact be optimization of articulation.

Importantly, the targets of articulation are not single points but regions of perceptual space, within which distinct productions are perceptually equivalent (Keating, 1990; see also Kapatsinski et al., 2017). Perceptual equivalence does not mean that the productions within that region cannot be distinguished by the ear: auditorily distinguishable productions can nonetheless be equally acceptable as instances of a perceptual category (e.g., Gibson & Gibson, 1955; Kapatsinski et al., 2017; Olejarczuk & Kapatsinski, 2017; Pavlov, 1927; see also chapter 5), often because variation within that range has been uninformative in the listener's experience. The existence of perceptual equivalence regions leaves the speaker room to optimize the entire movement trajectory by shifting the targets themselves. Thus, in the left panel of figure 9.4, the gray trajectory simplifies articulation over the black trajectory while still reaching the same targets.

The target-region locations are not fixed forever: each generation of language learners has to recreate the perceptual targets from experience with the productions of the speakers around them. Labov et al. (1991) documented cases of "near-merged" speakers who produce a distinction between two vowels but do not seem to understand their own production as well as speakers from other dialect regions would. These speakers appear

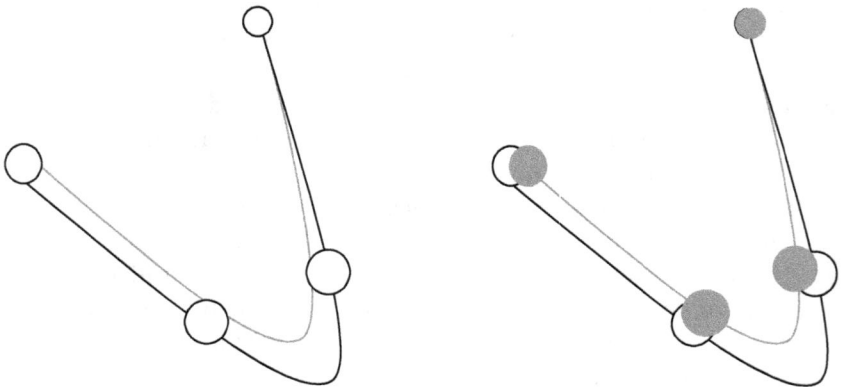

Figure 9.4
Left: The speaker optimizes production by choosing to traverse the areas of the target regions that minimize effort and maximize speed. Right: Because the targets are learned from experience with other people's productions, they will shift to center on the areas that the speakers prefer to traverse.

to invariably live in communities where most speakers do not make the distinction, leaving the distinguishing cues nonpredictive. When a distinction is nonpredictive in one's experience, perceptual learning downweights the acoustic cues distinguishing two sounds, resulting in learned equivalence among sounds distinguished by the cues.

The breadth of an equivalence region specified by one's speech community may determine whether stopping or lenition will occur. Note that an intervocalic fricative in a word like the English *butter* or the Spanish *tostada* is easier to produce than a stop, unless one needs to care about the exact acoustics produced. If the language does not specify that frication needs to occur, then the entire continuum from approximants to fricatives forms an equivalence region. Hitting a target that will produce a sound somewhere within that region is not difficult, allowing intervocalic stops to develop into fricatives and approximants in languages like English and Spanish. Importantly, phonetic studies of both processes do not find stops developing into fricatives *alone*. Rather, we see a broad continuum of articulations ranging in duration and degree of closure (e.g., Kapatsinski, 2015, for English). This suggests that the changes have involved the formation of a broad equivalence region that does not specify a precise acoustic target. It is the precision required to reliably produce frication every time one is attempting to produce [s] that is hard to achieve and requires extensive practice leading to entrenchment, the shrinking of off-target variability.

Perceptual learning / phonetic recalibration continues throughout life, allowing listeners to rapidly adapt to the changing pronunciations around them (Bertelson et al., 2003; Norris et al., 2003; see Mirman et al., 2006, for a Hebbian model of this process). Therefore, at any one point, the region of perceptual equivalence for the listener must center on the productions s/he experienced—unless some of the productions are perceived to be categorically different, perhaps because they are imbued with social meaning. As a result, even the targets of articulation are somewhat free to drift under the pressure to optimize production. For example, if every speaker chooses the more articulatorily optimal gray trajectory over the black one, the perceptual target regions will shift to center on the gray trajectory, as shown by the gray circles in the right panel of figure 9.4. The cycle of automatization in production and perceptual learning can then continue, gradually simplifying the trajectory (from [ɛɪ] to [eɪ] or from *probably* to *prolly*). Other things being equal, the more often a word is produced, the more its production will be simplified (Bybee, 2001; Hay & Foulkes, 2016; Schuchardt, 1885/1972). We now turn to a more detailed description of this process before considering the processes that keep articulatory simplification in check.

9.4   Speech: A Network of Chains

As noted above, Articulatory Phonology describes speech as consisting of sequences of *articulatory gestures* (Browman & L. Goldstein, 1989, 1990), target constrictions of the vocal tract. Like line trajectories between dots in Sosnik et al. (2004), the trajectories of articulator movements between gestures can be freely optimized to minimize time and energy expenditures. However, because there are several independent articulators involved in producing constrictions at various locations in the vocal tract (including the glottis, the body of the tongue, the tip of the tongue, and the lips), several temporally co-ordinated gesture sequences must be involved in producing any word.

Articulatory Phonology describes gestural coordination as a coupling graph, in which two gestures are coupled either in phase (and therefore activated simultaneously) or antiphase (and therefore realized in sequence); Browman & L. Goldstein (1990). A coupling graph corresponds to a network of gated chains as illustrated in figure 9.5, where each tier of the coupling graph is a gated chain of gestures, and gestures are able to send activation down their own tier and to *propagation filters* gating the flow of activation on other tiers.

Antiphase coordination between gestures could then be achieved by linking the preceding gesture to the propagation filter of the following gesture, whether the two gestures are on the same tier or not. For example, the tongue-body closure gesture of the [k] in *ducks* would allow activation of the tongue-tip gesture of [s] by activating the appropriate propagation filter on the tongue-tip tier. In this way, activation of a gesture on one tier could

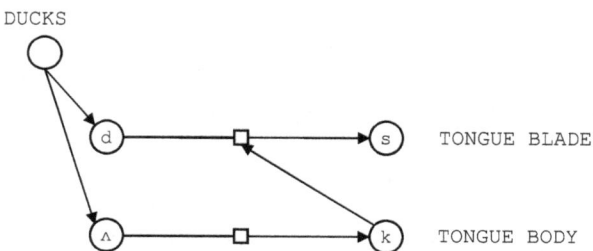

Figure 9.5
A simplified network of gated chains representing the word *ducks*. Top-down activation of the onset consonant and vowel gestures is followed by activation spreading to the gesture for [k] followed by activation of the [s] gesture.

allow activation of a gesture on another tier to occur as long as the preceding target on that tier has already been activated because it alone can send activation to the following gesture on the same tier.

Of course, nothing prevents the same node from sending activation to filters gating the spread of activation on multiple tiers, resulting in two or more gestures being activated simultaneously. Thus, gated chains also allow for in-phase coupling of gestures—for example, allowing the tongue-tip gesture of [d] and the tongue-body gesture of [ʌ] to be activated simultaneously at the onset of *duck*.

9.5   The Role of Automatization in Sound Change

Automatization of repeated sequences of motor actions has the potential to explain many sound changes, particularly ones that start in rapid speech (Browman & L. Goldstein, 1990) and in the more practiced, frequent words (Bybee, 2001, 2002b).

A sound change that results from automatization in the most obvious fashion is the emergence of anticipatory assimilation. For example, suppose you want to produce [np], as in *seven pugs*. This involves producing an alveolar closure for [n] followed by a labial closure for [p]. The alveolar closure is achieved with the tongue blade while the labial closure is achieved by lip and jaw movement. These are independent articulators, making it possible for multiple targets to be articulated at the same time. Thus, if the labial gestural target is activated early enough, it can be executed simultaneously with the alveolar closure, and before the alveolar closure has been held long enough to produce a perceptible [n], resulting in a percept of [m] (Browman & L. Goldstein, 1990, p. 22). If this kind of coarticulation happens often enough, its perceptual consequences can become conventionalized, so that the tongue blade no longer attempts to reach closure before a [p]. At that point, the perceptual target has changed to match the frequent perceptual outcome of coarticulation and coarticulation has turned into assimilation. Other examples of this process include nasalization of vowels before nasal consonants (as in English) and devoicing before voiceless obstruents (as in Russian).

In general, when upcoming gestural targets become activated earlier, the early activation can result in increased overlap with preceding gestures produced by other articulators: activation spreading down the chain can trigger the upcoming target even before the propagation filter floodgate opens if the resting activation level of the upcoming target is high enough (e.g., because it has been preactivated by the context). Aside from assimilation, anticipatory coarticulation can produce apparent deletion and insertion. Consider the phrase *perfect memory* (figure 9.6). The [t] at the end of *perfect* is often not audible. Browman and L. Goldstein (1990) show that in many cases, the inaudible [t] is still articulated. However, the acoustic cues to the [t] are not perceptible because the tongue-blade closure gesture comprising the [t] is released *after* the lips close to articulate the following [m]. The burst of the [t] is stifled by the closed lips, and thus no acoustic cue to the [t] is produced. Again, if this happens often enough, the deletion may become conventionalized, so the speaker no longer attempts the alveolar closure. In a corpus study, Cohen Goldberg (2015) shows that deletions of a word-final /r/ can occur even in a rhotic variety of English (Ohio). These deletions are favored across varieties when the word that follows the /r/ is highly predictable. The likely explanation is that predictable words are accessed and sent off to execution earlier than unpredictable ones, taking control over the articulators before the production of the preceding word is complete.

Figure 9.6 also shows that even apparent insertions can be seen as a result of anticipatory coarticulation. For example, the word *prince* is often pronounced with an excrescent [t], making it homophonous with *prints*. Where does the [t] come from? Browman and L. Goldstein (1990) point out that pronouncing *prince* without a [t] involves doing three things at exactly the same time (at the end of [n]): raising the velum to close airflow

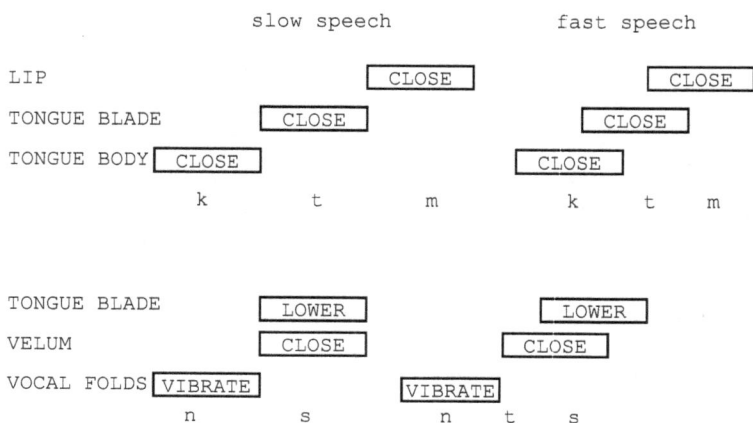

Figure 9.6
Top: How *perfect memory* can become *perfec' memory*. Bottom: How *prince* can become *prints*. Based on Browman and L. Goldstein (1990, p. 364).

into the nose, spreading the vocal folds to stop voicing, and slightly lowering the tongue blade to allow for turbulent airflow from the mouth. If the velum is closed too early, before the tongue blade is lowered, an oral stop is articulated.[2]

A variety of lenitions can be accounted for by two gestural targets tugging for control over a *single* articulator, as opposed to temporal overlap between articulations independently achieved by distinct articulators. For example, to produce a full alveolar stop closure between vowels in *butter* or *tostada*, the tongue blade needs to be raised from its low position during the preceding vowel all the way to the roof of the mouth, and held there. Instead, we find that the tongue is usually raised only partway, or the closure is not held long enough to produce a full burst, as the following vowel gains control over the tongue and pulls it back down. The outcome is a smoother trajectory like ones observed for well-practiced manual movements by Sosnik et al. (2004). Again, if reduction happens often enough (or is associated with sociolinguistic meaning), it can become conventionalized, broadening the equivalence region, which lets speakers run with it, as in American English and most varieties of Spanish.

A similar explanation can be provided for vowel shortening before consonants, a nearly universal process (with a few possible "mora-timed" exceptions like Japanese), as well as vowel raising, commonly observed in short unstressed syllables in "stress-timed" languages like English and Russian. A consonant demands a closure. Once a consonantal gestural target gains control of an articulator, it begins moving the articulator toward closure, raising the vowel first, then strangling it by reducing the airflow necessary for it to continue (and continue being a vowel).

Harmony processes are also varieties of assimilation of this kind: as temporally adjacent gestures battle for control over the lumbering tongue body or the slowly rounding and unrounding lips, sequences demanding rapid change tend to disappear. Thus, languages like Turkish, Hungarian, and Navajo require sequences of tongue-body gestures to be alike in various ways. A prediction that appears to hold crosslinguistically is that harmony processes should involve relatively slow articulatory gestures, where transitioning between disharmonic gestures would take considerable time and involve the subsequent gestures vying for control of a single articulator. An illuminating example is major-place consonant harmony, which would turn *take* into *cake* or *tate*. This appears to be a universal process in child language—nearly every child acquiring any language seems to exhibit it—but it never shows up in adult phonologies (Bybee, 2001, 2010; Vihman, 1980). This puzzle is resolved if one considers the fact that what is easy for an expert is often not what is easy for a novice. When one first learns to swim, the dogpaddle is easier than freestyle, but a proficient swimmer finds freestyle much easier than the dogpaddle. On land, all children find crawling easier than walking, but there are no communities in which everyone crawls. Whether this is due to learning alone (like the transition from the dogpaddle to freestyle) or learning and maturation working together (like the transition from crawling to walking), what is articulatorily easy for a child speaker is not necessarily what is easy for an adult. Similarly, children do not start life with fine-grained control over individual parts of the tongue. At first, the tongue gestures they make are undifferentiated (Gibbon, 1999), so that velar and alveolar gestures are vying for control over a single articulator, the tongue, and may even be the same gesture. This lack of precision in motor control results in major-place consonant harmony. By the time we are adults, alveolars and velars are distinct articulatory targets reached largely with different articulators, the tongue blade and the tongue body, and major-place consonant harmony disappears.

Articulatorily motivated sound change is expected to start in frequently used words (Bybee, 2001, 2002b; Schuchardt, 1885/1972). The best evidence for this claim comes from Hay and Foulkes (2016), who have documented—using a remarkable diachronic audio corpus—that an articulatorily motivated change in New Zealand English (flapping of /t/ between vowels) has progressed significantly faster in frequent words over the last 120 years. The reason frequent words are expected to lead articulatorily motivated sound change is that frequent words have the best chance of becoming highly automated behavioral routines (Bybee, 2001, 2002b; Kapatsinski, 2010a; Ramus et al., 2010; Snyder & Logan 2014). Automaticity is reflected in the finding that the execution of a frequent word is less interruptible (Kapatsinski, 2010a; Logan, 1982). Automatization of word-sized production units starts early, as children seem to automatize word-sized perceptual targets, resulting in "phonological idioms." Articulation of the same segment can vary widely from word to word, even within the same phonological context, and it is possible for a word to sound like the adult target without sharing any individual gestures with it (Ferguson & Falwell, 1975; Vihman & W. Croft, 2007). However, contrary to some claims in the literature, "phonological idioms" do not disappear by adulthood. Even seemingly homophonous words can differ in the specifics of articulation, with frequent words being shorter and more reduced than infrequent words (e.g., *time* vs. *thyme*, Gahl, 2008; see also Sóskuthy & Hay, 2017). Many frequent words and phrases are furthermore subject to "special reduction" (Bybee & Scheibman, 1999; Bybee et al., 2016), which has made it acceptable to produce *I don't know* as a single long nasal with a specific intonation contour. Special reduction is special because it has not diffused through the lexicon. What then keeps special reduction special? What keeps reduction in check?

9.6   Keeping Reduction in Check

Automatization of production that occurs with practice is not mere reduction (Bybee, 2002b). It is reduction of material that can be safely omitted. A well-practiced violin player does not skip the notes of a familiar piece of music. She can perform the piece faster and at the same time with more precision. As the piece is practiced, speed increases and deviation from the target decreases. With practice, Sosnik et al.'s (2004) participants smooth out their motor movements, anticipating where they will need to move after reaching the upcoming target, but they do not become worse at hitting the targets. Similarly, Baayen et al. (2017) show that stressed vowels of frequent, well-practiced words are articulated more precisely than the stressed vowels of infrequent words: the low vowels are lower, and the high vowels are higher. Older, more practiced speakers can also hit vowel targets better than younger speakers: the older one is, the lower the random, within-category variability in one's productions (Bryan & Harter, 1897; A. Smith & Goffman, 1998; Tomaschek et al., 2013; Baayen et al., 2017). Importantly, the off-target reductions of immature speakers seldom drive sound change (Bybee, 2001, 2010; Vihman, 1980): the child is shaped by both its parents and—later—its peers to reproduce the speech patterns that have social cachet in its environment (M. Goldstein et al., 2003). In contrast, older speakers are entrenched in their ways. A distribution of articulations containing millions of tokens cannot be shifted by a single experience (Pierrehumbert, 2001). Therefore, reduction is constrained in part because the speakers that are in a social position to spread changes tend to be speakers who have already learned what parts of the signal can be safely reduced or omitted.

What then can be safely reduced or omitted? The simple answer is that the reduced or omitted elements must not be highly discriminative; they must not be crucial for recovering the meaning that the speaker intends to transmit (cf. Lindblom, 1990). Even extreme reduction does no damage to comprehension in frequent and contextually predictable words because those words are recoverable from context even when highly reduced. Much work has shown that contextual predictability correlates with reduction: words are more likely to be reduced when they are predictable from context (e.g., Seyfarth, 2014). However, predictability in the current context is not all there is to it. For example, Wedel et al. (2013) show that diachronic sound mergers tend not to merge contrasts that distinguish many minimal pairs of words (i.e., contrasts with a high *functional load*). In large-scale corpus studies, Cohen Priva (2015) shows that highly informative segments tend not to be reduced in duration or deleted (see also van Son & Pols, 2003; van Son & van Santen, 2005), while Seyfarth (2014) and Sóskuthy and Hay (2017) show that speakers also tend not to reduce informative words. In all of these studies, informativity goes beyond the local context: words and segments that are *on average* highly informative disfavor reduction. This suggests that one learns that certain segments and words should not be reduced.[3]

While the studies cited above have focused on the importance of sounds and words for transmitting lexical meaning, social meaning is at least equally important. To the extent that articulatory variation has perceptible acoustic consequences, deviation from a community norm marks the speaker as different. These differences can then be associated with social meaning by becoming associated with characteristics of the deviating speakers, and thereby evolve into ways of expressing social identity. A classic example is the pronunciation of -*ing* in words like *walking* and *talking*. The suffix can be pronounced either with a velar or an alveolar nasal, -*ing* or -*in'*. This difference is socially salient enough to be used to represent dialectal, stylistic, and social class variation in writing. Accordingly, even though the development of -*in'* out of -*ing* is articulatorily motivated, the two pronunciations have been in stable variation for centuries (Labov, 1989). Once alternative pronunciation variants are associated with distinctive uses—whether social, lexical, or both—articulatory ease is no longer free to determine pronunciation. Thus, a sound change can be stopped if the innovative and/or conservative pronunciation variant becomes associated with particular lexical or semantic contexts (see also Bybee, 2008). In some cases, the direction of the change may even reverse if the social meaning with which the innovative variant has become associated is not one that speakers wish to express, or are reinforced for expressing.

As we discussed in chapter 3, one way a sound can become associated with particular contexts is via a kind of hierarchical inference: words and segments can become associated with pronunciation variants if they tend to occur in contexts that favor these variants (Bybee, 2002b; Seyfarth, 2014; Sóskuthy & Hay, 2017). The variants can then become entrenched in the contexts they occur in. According to this theory, the learner aims to replicate and predict the pronunciation variants he observes in his environment, and does so using a variety of cues of various sizes. For a change in pronunciation to generalize across words, the innovative pronunciation must not be associated with the specific words in which it first occurred. Given that the words in which reductions begin are frequent words, reduction is particularly likely to be attributed to, and therefore restricted to, the lexical context in which it started, remaining "special." Like children, frequent words may be particularly good at initiating articulatorily motivated changes but particularly bad at getting others to adopt their innovative behavior.

In addition, it is not frequency alone that determines the likelihood of reduction in a particular instance of speech production. Reduction is also influenced by the predictability of the word in the current context (Gregory et al., 1999; Jurafsky et al., 2001), and by its average predictability across contexts (Seyfarth, 2014). Controlling for frequency, unpredictable—and therefore informative—words are particularly unlikely to be reduced. Furthermore, speakers appear to be able to dynamically take into account the likelihood of being misperceived in order to adjust their pronunciation, choosing the pronunciation variant that is least likely to be misunderstood (Baese-Berk & Goldrick, 2009; Buz et al., 2016). The needs of the listener seem to constrain reduction, preventing the speaker from neutralizing distinctions the listener relies on to understand what the speaker is saying (Wedel et al., 2013). But how do the needs of the listener come to influence the behavior of the speaker?

The answer may lie in instrumental conditioning, also often called reinforcement learning or "selection by consequences" (Skinner, 1984).[4] Reducing something informative runs the risk of causing misunderstanding. As the reader must know from personal experience, not being understood is aversive. Therefore, reduction of an informative unit is likely to be punished, in the associative learning sense of the word, to the extent that it produces misunderstanding. Direct evidence for this proposal has been provided by a number of studies investigating speakers' reactions to being misunderstood. In particular, Oviatt et al. (1998), Levow (1999), and Stent et al. (2008) investigated how people talk to speech recognition systems and showed that misperceived words are hyperarticulated when repeated. Furthermore, the hyperarticulation appears to target the part of the utterance that the machine appeared to misperceive. Maniwa et al. (2009), Schertz (2013), Buz et al. (2016), and Seyfarth et al. (2016) take this a step further, showing that speakers hyperarticulate cues that distinguish the sound they intended to produce from the sound it was misperceived as. For example, they increase VOT for voiceless stops misperceived as voiced and shorten it for voiced stops misperceived as voiceless. Buz et al. (2016) show that the effect is long-lived: hyperarticulation of VOT can occur the next time the misperceived word is produced in the same context even when immediate repetition is not required or is even disallowed (see also Stent et al., 2008), suggesting that the aversive effect of misperception can affect subsequent productions. Finally, misperceptions that do not have to do with voicing do not appear to affect VOT, suggesting that the participants are able to attribute the misperception to their realization of a specific phonetic contrast (Schertz, 2013; Seyfarth et al., 2016).

How does one hyperarticulate VOT in response to aversive feedback on one's previous production? Buz et al. (2016) propose that the speaker has control over the variance of his within-category VOT distribution and can invest effort into hitting the target VOT more precisely. The prediction of this account is that VOT values should be all over the place— relatively speaking—before misperception but should cluster around the central values of the voiced and voiceless categories after the misperception. However, this is not what they actually observe: speakers do tuck in the left tail of the voiceless VOT distribution—avoiding values in danger of being misperceived—but they do not tuck in the right tail. Instead, they produce a higher proportion of extremely long VOTs when aiming for a voiceless stop.[5]

The model of phonetic categories discussed in chapter 5 suggests a possible explanation. In that model, continua like VOT are discretized into a set of intervals. Each of these intervals can serve as a cue in perception and can be selectively attended to or ignored. It is not a huge leap to suggest that each can also serve as a target of production, so that its production can be rewarded (e.g., by articulatory ease) or punished (by articulatory difficulty or misperception). When one intends to produce an aspirated $[p^h]$ and produces a relatively low VOT of, say, 35 ms, that production is rewarded—because it saves time and energy compared to a longer VOT— unless one is misperceived, in which case the production is punished. The punishment makes one less likely to produce a 35 ms VOT in the future. If VOT is represented using the two-sided thermometer scheme in figure 5.3, misperception of a 35 ms VOT in the context of intending to produce a $[p^h]$ also punishes all values below 35 ms. This mechanism allows one to tuck in the left tail of $[p^h]$'s VOT distribution when a low VOT value is misperceived as /b/.

The mechanism for extending the right tail of $[p^h]$'s VOT distribution is different. Buz et al. (2016) suggest that targeting such values is dysfunctional: why increase a VOT of 60 ms? It is unlikely to be misperceived anyway. However, this ignores the fact that high VOT values are "safe" values—they are the best, most unambiguous cues to the intended percept. As such, they are favored by a discriminative learner in perception, developing strong associations to the meaning (e.g., Boersma, 1998; see also Purtle, 1973; Rosch & Mervis, 1975). If cue→outcome mappings learned in perception can be reversed to drive production (as I argued in chapter 6), then—upon being misperceived—the learner can target the best cues to the intended meaning for production. Targeting the safe option can work together with avoiding what one has just produced to produce both the low-level hyperarticulations Buz et al. focus on and the "extreme" hyperarticulations they do not account for. It is also likely behind hyperarticulation observed when the speaker knows that they need to identify a member of a minimal pair to the listener (Baese-Berk & Goldrick, 2009; Kirov & Wilson, 2012).

It is important to note that reaching for the most discriminative cues to a category will not always produce hyperarticulation of a phonetic contrast. In the case of VOT, the more extreme positive VOT values are the best cues to the "voiceless" category in English because there is no "superhyperaspirated" stop category with an even longer VOT. If there were such a category, the mechanism of reaching for the most discriminative cues would be expected to result in shooting for the category center instead, potentially precluding hyperarticulation. Schertz (2013) argues that this is true for vowel contrasts she examined. In her experiment, when a vowel is misperceived as another vowel, the durational cues to the target vowel are enhanced but spectral cues to vowel identity are not. For vowels that do not differ in duration, no hyperarticulation results. It is easy to relate to this finding. Since the dialects of English largely differ in vowels, any English speaker must have experienced misperceiving the vowel of another speaker of English and asking for clarification. When you do this, the speaker of the other dialect typically repeats the same vowel, possibly just making it longer;[6] unless they have experience with your dialect. They cannot easily enhance the contrast because enhancing it no longer means reaching for the best cues to the vowel in one's own experience.

Together, the tendency to do what you've done before, avoidance of misperceived targets, and targeting discriminative cues, keep the system relatively stable and functional. Indeed, Skyrms (2010) shows that a very similar mechanism of "use the meaning→form mapping you've used before unless you are misunderstood, in which case try something else" would allow a community of learners who start out randomly emitting uninformative sounds to rapidly converge on a functional communication system— one that is able to unambiguously transmit useful information about the environment, allowing the users to discriminate the meanings they need to discriminate. The reinforcement learning process just described may not only *keep* language functional but may even have shaped it into functionality to begin with.

9.7 Vocalic vs. Consonantal Changes: Social Selection vs. Automatization

The discussion above may remind the reader of Lindblom's (1990) H&H framework. In Lindblom's view, speech lies on a continuum between hypospeech—which minimizes articulatory effort—and hyperspeech—which maximizes discriminability. In particular, speakers dynamically tune production by ensuring that the acoustic correlates of the articulations they produce "possess sufficient contrast, that is discriminative power that is sufficient for lexical access" and that "during speech development ... speakers develop a feel for the survival value of phonetic forms through a process not unlike natural selection" (p. 405). The theory of automatization constrained by reinforcement learning developed here can be thought of as a specific mechanistic account of this process. The acoustic consequences of articulatory variation in production can be selected for reproduction either because they make production easier or because they are reinforced by the interlocutor. Other variants may be selected against by articulatory difficulty or social feedback, including signals of incomprehension and negative affect.[7]

For articulatory variants to be differentially reinforced by one's interlocutor, they must be sufficiently perceptually distinct and attentionally salient. Imperceptibly different articulations can be selected for reproduction on articulatory grounds alone. A good case of imperceptible production differences is presented by the English [ɹ]. The acoustics of [ɹ] can be produced either by retroflexion (curling the tip of the tongue backward) or by bunching of the tongue body. As the acoustic consequences of these very distinct articulations are imperceptible, different speakers within the same speech community are free to settle on different articulations (Boyce et al., 2015). In this case, the individual preferences of the different speakers are likely determined largely by which articulation they find easier.[8]

Stressed vowels lie on the opposite end of the spectrum. Whereas [ɹ] production involves mastering one of two relatively difficult and qualitatively distinct articulations, vowels differ on a few largely continuous parameters, the most important being the position of the tongue body. While the difference between bunched and retroflex [ɹ] is imperceptible to the listener, and within-category differences between acoustically distinct consonants are often hard to detect, within-category differences between vowels are perceived relatively easily, especially so when the vowels in question are long (Pisoni, 1973). In stress-timed languages like English, stress makes vowels longer and louder, drawing the attention of the listener and making acoustic differences between stressed vowels particularly salient.

Conversely, vowel articulations vary in difficulty much less than consonant articulations. Whereas consonants vary on many different articulatory parameters and involve many different active articulators, all vowels can be described with a small set of articulatory parameters, and all involve the same active articulators, the tongue body and the lips. Stressed vowels may be particularly uniform in articulatory difficulty. While producing a low unstressed vowel may be significantly more difficult than producing a high one due to the limited time available (Lindblom, 1963), the speaker of a stress-timed language has abundant time to get their tongue body into position when the vowel is stressed. At the same time, exact positioning of the lumbering tongue body in a specific location in the airspace under the roof of the mouth may be particularly difficult, as the proprioceptive cues to tongue position are weak when the tongue is not making contact with any surface. While all locations within the space are approximately equally easy to reach, they are all difficult to keep reaching reliably, positioning the tongue body in the exact same target position time after time. Thus, vowel articulations are inherently variable, and the variants are perceptibly different and similar in articulatory difficulty. Therefore, social feedback should have a greater influence on the selection of vowel variants than on the selection of consonant variants, and stressed vowels should be especially prone to the effects of social feedback, at least in stressed-timed languages like English where these vowels are remarkably long.[9]

Importantly, social feedback is largely arbitrary: sounds that are stigmatized in one speech community are prestigious in another (e.g., Labov, 2001). Therefore, sound change driven by social feedback can proceed in many different directions, rather than having a pronounced directionality. If changes affecting stressed vowels are particularly likely to be driven by social feedback, then they should be less constrained in their direction. This does appear to be the case. Thus, the same or similar vowels can both raise and lower in different dialects, and there are even reports of reversals, where two vowels switch places in the acoustic space (e.g., the vowels in *pin* and *pen*; Labov, 1994, 2001). In contrast, consonantal change is largely unidirectional and overwhelmingly reductive. For example, [θ] can become [f], turning *with* into *wif*, but [f] never becomes [θ] (Honeybone, 2016), presumably because, though the two sounds are highly perceptually confusable, [f] is the easier articulation.

The overwhelming unidirectionality of consonantal change suggests that consonantal changes are driven largely by automatization of articulation.[10] The multidirectionality of changes in stressed vowels suggests that their variants are more likely to be selected by social feedback. Importantly, this division of labor is predictable from the acoustic and articulatory properties of the two classes of sounds. The large differences in articulation among consonants mean that articulatory pressures will have a strong influence on the choice of consonantal variants. The low variability in articulatory difficulty among vowels, coupled with the high perceptibility of differences resulting from inherent articulatory variability in positioning the tongue body in midair, leaves them particularly susceptible to social selection.

9.8   Consonant Strengthening

In their extensive survey of well-documented sound changes, Bybee and Easterday (2017) find that consonant strengthening processes are about a tenth as common as weakening processes and always involve palatal or labial articulations. These are, of course, precisely the articulations involved in producing vowels. Furthermore, the starting point of strengthening—a palatal or labiovelar glide—is not much different from a vowel. That in itself suggests that similar explanations may apply to these changes as to the vocalic changes above.

Bybee and Easterday find that the most common process involves strengthening the palatal glide [j] to [ʒ]—for example, in words like *llegar* "to arrive" [jegar] in some dialects of Spanish. In fact, these changes share a great deal with the vocalic changes driven by social selection in English. First, like the vocalic changes, they involve a change in precise midair positioning of the tongue body or the degree to which the lips are rounded. For both of these articulators, precise positioning is difficult, and the equivalence regions are often quite broad. For example, Russians do not have a categorical distinction between [w] and [v] and use them interchangeably in English; Spanish speakers often pronounce words like *joke* with a glide instead of a fricative or affricate. Change can therefore go in both directions. It is thus likely that the strengthening of glides to fricatives is seeded by the inherent articulatory variation in the precise realization of the original glide targets, causing expansion of the equivalence region.

Bybee and Easterday (2017) further note that the languages with palatal glide strengthening are precisely the languages that also have palatalization, which involves development of frication in the transition from a stop to a palatal glide. Palatalization itself is a kind of assimilation. However, it may result in further broadening of the equivalence region that involves palatal glides because some of them are now associated with contextual frication, which can become associated with the glide instead of the stop.

Second, strengthenings occur in syllable-initial position, which is associated with longer duration and a greater forcefulness of articulation. For these reasons, strengthening can also be seen as overshoot. Instead of holding the tongue in place to produce the glide for a while, the tongue is projected with greater force and overshoots the target (as in the case of low vowels in figure 9.3).

Third, as suggested by Bybee and Easterday (2017), both palatal glide strengthening and palatalization may be the result of a change in the articulatory setting of the language (Gick et al., 2004, 2017; Honikman, 1964), a drift in the "default" configuration of the vocal tract that makes articulation of most sound sequences in the language easier.

Fourth, both stressed English vowels and the syllable-initial [j] or [w] are relatively long articulations that allow the listener to easily perceive the speaker's articulatory variation: as pointed out above (see also Bybee & Easterday, 2017), the lips and the tongue body are relatively sluggish articulators. This leaves articulatory variation resulting from imprecision available to be associated with social meanings.

Finally, socially driven strengthenings may be especially likely in syllable-timed languages like Spanish. In syllable-timed languages, stressed vowels are much shorter than in stress-timed languages, while the unstressed vowels are less spectrally reduced. This means that, unlike in stress-timed languages, there are no prominent long stressed vowels to bear social meaning, leaving initial glides to be some of the longest and most salient sounds within the language. If any speech community needs to express social meaning somewhere, and long salient sounds are likely to be selected for this purpose, then [j] is a very good candidate for social selection given the sound system of Spanish. Syllable timing may also mean that spectral reduction (centralization and raising) is held in check in unstressed syllables: unstressed vowels of Spanish are not much longer but are much less spectrally reduced than unstressed vowels of English. This means that speakers of syllable-timed languages are required to achieve precision and entrench in their vowel articulators so that similar vocalic targets are reached even though little time is available to reach them.

9.9 Automaticity and Interruptibility

Echoing Hebb's "neurons that fire together wire together," Bybee (2002a) argues that "units used together fuse together" into an automatized sequence of actions. This "fusing together" is seen not only in the increased speed with which the sequence is produced, and in the ability of upcoming targets to influence behavior through anticipation, but also in the increasing inability of the speaker to interfere with execution of the sequence once started. Automatized behaviors are more *ballistic*: like a projectile, the automatized behavior cannot be (easily) stopped once launched (Logan, 1982).

An extreme example of a complex ballistic behavior is seen in the spider *Cupiennius salei* (Eibl-Eibesfeldt, 1970). Female *Cupiennius salei* spiders build cocoons for their eggs. The building process is a sequence of about 6,400 movements, which seems to be entirely ballistic. Thus, if the spider starts building a cocoon but what has been built is destroyed halfway through the process, the spider completes the (now pointless) sequence of movements as usual. If the glands producing the cocoon's threads fail to function, so there is nothing to build the cocoon out of, the entire motor sequence is still completed. In the case of the spider, the cocoon-building program is also innate: the spider need not observe cocoon building to build one. However, not all ballistic sequences are innate, or innately ballistic. Nonballistic behaviors can become ballistic as they are practiced. Anderson (1982) has called this process *proceduralization*.

Evidence that practice can make behavior ballistic comes from several distinct experimental paradigms. In operant conditioning, the controlled/ballistic distinction is the difference between an operant behavior and a respondent one (Skinner, 1938). An operant behavior is controlled by its consequences: it is not emitted if its output is not currently desired. A respondent behavior is automatically elicited by a certain stimulus. Repeated performance of a behavior can turn it from an operant into a respondent one. For example, Packard and McGaugh (1996) repeatedly placed rats in the south arm of a "+"-shaped maze and food in the west arm of the maze. The rats would thus come to the center of the "+," turn left, and find their reward. After a bit of practice, the rats were placed in the north arm, so that reaching the rewarded location now required turning right. If the test occurred early in training, the rats turned right, going toward the rewarded location. But if the test occurred late, the rats turned left, performing the rewarded motor response (see also Hicks, 1964; Ritchie et al., 1950). The left turn had become associated with being in the maze to the point of becoming ballistic.

More evidence for practice affecting this aspect of automaticity comes from stop-signal experiments (Logan, 1982; Sosnik et al., 2015). In these experiments, a participant engages in some motor behavior. However, on a small proportion of trials, they are given a signal to stop executing the behavior as soon as possible. The time it takes the participant to stop what they are doing following the stop signal is measured. Suggesting that stopping time is influenced by word frequency, Logan (1982) found that typists take longer to stop if the stop signal (a tone) is presented while they are typing the word *the*, the most frequent word in the English language. More recently, Sosnik et al. (2015) found that the curved trajectories of figure 9.2 are ballistic late in training: as participants' experience with tracing the trajectory grows, they take longer and longer to stop execution of the movement. Early in training, when the trajectory can be described as a set of straight lines, participants tend to complete the linear movement they are executing before stopping. Late in training, after some linear movements have fused into curved movements, participants are likely to complete a whole curved movement before stopping.

Levelt (1983) argued that replacement disfluencies—as in *I like to listen to the newsp-, uh, radio in the morning*—provide an opportunity to observe stopping behavior in natural speech production. Levelt suggested that a replacement involves the speaker interrupting speech production in response to an internally generated stop signal. The stop signal is sent once an error is detected, even if a repair is not yet available. This explains why the speaker often *uh*'s and *um*'s their way through an uncomfortable pause upon interrupting production, even when the interruption occurs midway through a word.

In Kapatsinski (2010a), I examined a large sample of natural replacement disfluencies and found that words varied in how likely they were to be interrupted vs. completed prior to being replaced. The completed words tended to be the more frequent words. Words interrupted partway through, as exemplified above, tended to be the rarer ones. While frequent words are shorter than rare words, this alone did not explain the results: after average duration of a word was given a chance to explain the variance in how likely the word was to be interrupted, there remained leftover variance for word frequency to account for.

Together, these findings suggest that frequent production does make a sequence of motor movements harder to interrupt: as upcoming targets become more and more anticipated, they become harder and harder to suppress. The more easily they are activated by the preceding context, the more top-down inhibition is needed to suppress them, and the more difficult this becomes. As you practice something, it becomes easier and easier to complete and harder and harder to stop partway through. As you walk from home to work over and over again, it becomes harder and harder to stop and smell the flowers.

9.10   Automatization and Entrenchment

In other words, automatization results in entrenchment. The more one has practiced a particular sequence of movements in specific ways, the more difficult it is to alter. Thus, the more automatized words and the more automatized speakers are also more entrenched. For example, Goldinger (1998) has shown that asking participants to closely shadow others, repeating what the other speaker has just said, causes the acoustics of their productions to converge with those of the speakers they shadow. Speakers unconsciously and automatically imitate speech they have just heard, down to fine, subphonemic details. However, the degree of convergence is smaller for frequent words, whose production is more automatic. Having had more experience with producing a frequent word, speakers are less affected by the recently experienced acoustics of the speech they are asked to shadow. Similarly, Ryalls and Pisoni (1997) have shown that younger children display a greater degree of convergence than older children or adults: being based on less experience, children's productions are more easily shifted by a few recent tokens.[11]

While I have just argued that automatization causes entrenchment, it is often observed that experts can be as flexible as or even more flexible than novices. For example, we noted above that frequent words are typed faster than infrequent words, and typists are slower to stop typing in response to a stop signal when they are in the midst of typing a frequent word (Logan, 1982). This suggests that automatic typing is more ballistic, and so less subject to interference. However, improvements in typing speed do not always come with increased stopping latency. Expert typists can type faster than novices, but they are not slow to stop (Logan, 1982; Cohen & Poldrack, 2008). These demonstrations do not, to my mind, contradict the proposal that automatization causes entrenchment because they constitute *practiced variation.* Bryan and Harter (1897, p. 45) wrote that "accidental variation is a somewhat accurate inverse measure of skill, while the [intentional, practiced] variation for inflection, is likely to be larger rather than smaller with increasing expertness." This point remains underappreciated in more recent work (see, for example, Vaughn et al., 2016, on speech production). An expert typist has practiced stopping in response to an error signal from their internal error monitor, and is therefore an expert at stopping typing as well as at typing itself. Similarly, an expert speaker is an expert at dealing with speech error and disfluency and in adjusting their speech on the basis of familiar fluctuations in environmental noise, the capacities of the vocal tract, and listener characteristics. More generally, we can say that an expert knows how to adjust their behavior to accomplish the same goal in response to many different cues. However, given the same constellation of task-relevant cues, the expert will be more consistent in their response than the novice.

To get an intuitive feel for the importance of practicing adjustments to a source of outcome variability, think of an expert bow hunter versus an expert dart thrower. Both experts will be less variable than novices when faced with the same exact environmental conditions (down to the conditions of their tools and motor systems). However, the expert bow hunter practices her craft outdoors, and so has to deal with variable wind conditions. Expertise will therefore involve being able to vary her motor actions in response to the direction and strength of the wind. The dart thrower practices his craft indoors, in the back of a bar, which does not tend to be a windy environment. An expert dart thrower may not be so good at adjusting for the wind and may well miss the target if the bar is suddenly windy.[12]

9.11   Automatization and (In)attention

In psycholinguistics, automatization is usually studied on the production side of things. However, there is nothing about the processes just described that prevents them from operating in perception (see also Ashby et al., 2007; Broadbent, 1958; Bryan & Harter, 1897, 1899; James, 1890; Lim et al., 2014). Just as it is hard to stop and not finish executing a well-practiced series of movements in production, it is hard to stop and not finish accessing meaning from frequently used cues in perception.

This kind of perceptual automaticity is well demonstrated by the classic Stroop task (Stroop, 1935). In the original paradigm, participants are presented with words, printed in color, and asked to name, as fast as they can, the color of the ink with which each word is printed. When the words are themselves color words, and the colors they are printed in do not match their meanings, this task is very difficult. Participants tend to automatically read the words instead of naming the ink color. This is not entirely attributable to accessing the spoken form because the participants do not tend to read noncolor words aloud in this task and interference is still present—though reduced—if responses are made using arbitrary buttons rather than by speaking (Stirling, 1979). Thus, participants seem to automatically access the meaning of a printed word. When that meaning is a color, it takes control of the motor system, since it is an input that the speaker's cognitive control system has prepared to use as a cue to the available motor responses (Cohen et al., 1990; Stirling, 1979).

A primary goal of language perception is comprehension: the main reason we listen and read is to extract meaning from the auditory and visual patterns in front of us. The waystations on the path from the retina or the eardrum to the semantics are relatively unimportant: they are only reached in service of reaching the more distal goal of extracting meaning. They are, in this way, like the places we traverse on the way to work: we need to pass through them to reach the destination, but nothing is usually gained from lingering. They may persist in memory, as we need to remember the path to take, but they do not draw lasting attention: we pass through them as fast as we can, for anticipation of the next destination on the path is always beckoning us forward (James, 1890, vol.1, p.260).

The reduced attention to form with increasing automaticity was first documented at the end of the 19th century by Bryan and Harter (1897, 1899), who studied automatization of both encoding and decoding in telegraph operators. They write: "The real expert has all the details of language with such automatic perfection that he gives them practically no attention at all" (Bryan & Harter, 1899, p. 352). Automatization of form processing appears to be necessary for the telegraph operator to divest attention from the small details of form: "In the first days one is forced to attend to letters. In the first months one is forced to attend to words. If the learner essays a freedom for which he is unfit, suddenly a letter that is unfamiliar explodes in his ears and leaves him wrecked. He has no useful freedom for higher language units which he has not earned by making the lower ones automatic" (Bryan & Harter, 1899, pp. 356–357).

What is true of Morse code may also be true of the codes we call English or Russian. Healy (1976) demonstrated that sublexical (and therefore relatively meaningless) units occurring in expected locations are difficult to detect, despite being predictable. In her experiments, participants were asked to circle all instances of the letter *t* in a paragraph. They were very likely to miss the *t* in *the*. Misses were much less likely in the rare determiner *thy*. The difference between frequent and rare words was reduced—though not eliminated—by scrambling the word order, so that words could occur in unexpected places. The error rate was also reduced when readers were forced to spend time on the frequent words because the paragraph was presented to them in four-word increments (Hadley & Healy, 1991). In normal reading, frequent words appearing in expected positions are often perceived parafoveally, without the reader focusing attention on them (Rayner & Raney, 1996). Once the meaning is accessed, the eyes move on (Greenberg et al., 2004).

Alas, you can't move your ears around a spoken sentence the way you can move your eyes around a printed one. The sounds just keep coming in the order the speaker produces them, hitting the ears in an endless stream of sound. Nonetheless, there is evidence that we do not attend to the speech stream equally at all times. Rather, we upregulate attention at points of *predictable unpredictability* and downregulate it at points of predictable predictability (Kosie & Baldwin, 2016; see also chapter 3). In other words, the listener can anticipate when new, unpredictable information will come and can plan on attending accordingly.

The notion that attention is downregulated during predictable auditory events may help explain why the same sublexical unit can be harder to detect when it occurs in a frequent spoken word or phrase than when it occurs in a rare one (Bybee & Brewer, 1980; Hay, 2001; Kapatsinski & Radicke, 2009; Sosa & MacFarlane, 2002). Practice recognizing the word prevents us from dwelling on its parts. For example, Kapatsinski and Radicke (2009) had participants monitor for the sound of *up* in spoken sentences, regardless of whether it was a morpheme or not. Sometimes *up* was inside a word. We found that the sound was harder to detect in frequent words like *cup* than in rare words like *sup*. While we suggested that this indicates that the word is a separate node at the form level (available for being associated with other units in configural patterns), the finding could also be interpreted as indicating reduced attention during the processing of frequent units, or a more rapid withdrawal of attention from the word due to faster completion of semantic access. Reduced attention may prevent or slow down the rise in the activation levels of the word's parts, preventing them from becoming activated to the level required for conscious awareness. Just as a masked prime, not being activated enough to be recognized, is able to transmit activation onward to the target (e.g., Forster & C. Davis, 1984; Kouider & Dehaene, 2009), the parts of a frequent word may transmit enough activation to semantics for the word to be recognized without being activated enough to be available to consciousness.

The automaticity of sound→meaning mapping appears to prevent selective attention to sublexical units as small as phones or features (Morais et al., 1979). Accordingly, teaching children to read involves the training of "phonemic awareness." Phonemic awareness training may be so important for learning to read because it trains selective attention (e.g., Stevens et al., 2013), since selective attention to a cue appears to make it more associable (Kruschke, 1992; Rescorla & Wagner, 1972; see Ellis, 2006, for a review of evidence from language acquisition). By drawing selective attention to the phones, we make them more associable so they can be mapped onto new outcomes, the letters of the alphabet.

9.12   Automatization vs. Unitization

According to many researchers, automatization is a sign of *unitization* (Anderson, 1986; Bryan & Harter, 1899; Bybee, 2002b; Healy, 1976, 1994; Kapatsinski & Radicke, 2009; Rosenbloom & Newell, 1986; Sosnik et al., 2015). The sequence fuses together into a larger unit. For example, for Bryan and Harter (1899), language is a "hierarchy of habits," with letters, words, prosodic patterns, frequent phrases, and syntactic constructions forming nodes in this hierarchy. Bybee (2001) points out that frequent words often undergo semantic change, becoming noncompositional in their meaning. For instance, the meaning of *blackmail* is not transparently derived from the meanings of *black* and *mail*. Bybee argues that for a frequent word to become associated with the noncompositional meaning, it must be stored in memory as a configural whole *prior* to this event, while its meaning is still compositional. Otherwise, what is it that gets associated with the unpredictable parts of the meaning?

However, Baayen et al. (2011) caution us that it is possible to model such findings by *sublexical* form-meaning associations (e.g., associating the *ckm* in *blackmail* with the meaning of *blackmail*). While this is intuitively implausible, we have just argued that automatization of the form→meaning mapping can make routinely used cues to meaning inaccessible to conscious reflection without selective attention being explicitly trained on the cues. What we use to get to meaning may not be what we think we use. Automatization of a sequence does not necessarily imply that the sequence is now a node in the associative network, available to serve as a configural cue. More work is needed to examine how the co-occurrence probabilities influence associability of the whole and the parts. For example, is *ckm* highly associable because of its great usefulness for predicting the meaning of *blackmail* (Baayen et al., 2011)? Or are such boundary-spanning sequences not even encoded as nodes in the associative network (Kapatsinski, 2009c)?

In the present framework, configural associability—the ability to easily acquire associations that are not shared with the parts (chapter 3)—and the ability to overshadow the parts are the least ambiguous sources of evidence for a complex whole being a node in the associative network (Kapatsinski, 2009c; Kapatsinski & Radicke, 2009; see also Blumenthal-Dramé, 2012; Graf Estes et al., 2007). In the absence of such evidence, automatization of a sequence may not mean the emergence of a new node but rather increased strength of part-part connections leading from the future to the past (e.g., Broadbent, 1958, p. 285; James, 1890, vol. 2, pp.586–587).

9.13 Conclusion

Automatization speeds up processing of a sequence, and it prevents you from easily tinkering with the sequence: the future is easily anticipated and inexorably draws us forward. To stop, or even to take time to reflect on what's been accomplished so far, becomes more and more difficult. Increasing anticipation of the future means that inessential intermediate steps are skipped over. In production, this means smoothing out of articulatory trajectories, resulting in sound changes that begin in frequent words whose production is highly automated. In comprehension, automatization means reduced ability to consciously attend to the parts of an automatized sequence.

While it is hard to stop in the middle of an automatized sequence of actions, it is even harder to start such a sequence from the middle. When certain actions are always executed in a certain order to achieve a particular goal (e.g., to express the meaning of a frequent word), it becomes harder and harder to execute them out of order. Top-down connections allowing excitation to flow to noninitial elements of the sequence weaken and atrophy. Thus a repeatedly executed hierarchical control structure becomes an inflexible chain. I have argued that in speech, each gestural tier within the articulatory representation of a frequent word can be thought of as such a chain, while the word itself is a network of such chains linked to each other through propagation filters, leaky floodgates that restrict the flow of activation that cascades down each chain. As variable order—which requires flexible hierarchical control—is more common at higher levels of language structure (utterances, discourse episodes, etc.), much of the constructicon can be described as a hierarchy of chain networks.

10 Bringing It All Together

The mechanisms of change ... are the only true universals of language, in the sense that they operate in all languages at all times.

—Bybee (2008, p. 108)

There are many different ways to approach language. We can focus on language structure, documenting common patterns and typological rarities. We can focus on language processing, studying how the comprehender extracts meaning from sounds and sights and how the producer plans and executes an intricate program of muscle movements that is intended to convey a message for eliciting a reaction in the comprehender. We can focus on language acquisition, studying how experience is transformed into knowledge and ability. Finally, we can investigate language change, examining how languages change over time at the level of an entire community of speakers. However, a linguistic theory—an account of why languages are the way they are—must address and connect all of these domains. Theories that ignore the diversity of structure run the risk of being specific to individual languages, failing to explain how a language learner can acquire the language of any community they are born into. Theories that ignore acquisition run the risk of proposing a processing system that could never arise in a biological learner and of failing to explain why some of the most powerful influences on processing—frequency, transitional probability, priming, age of acquisition—have the effects they do. Similarly, theories that ignore language change are in danger of generating or assuming grammatical descriptions that do not allow for grammatical diversity to arise from a common root through known diachronic processes. A theory of acquisition is, in its very essence, a theory of how and why the learner's comprehension and production abilities change over time, and must therefore make commitments to how the developing learner comprehends and produces language. Finally, a theory of change cannot hope to explain why some changes are more common than others without being informed by knowledge of the mechanisms involved in acquisition and processing and the biases inherent in those mechanisms. This book is therefore intended to argue for certain working hypotheses and theoretical commitments in all of these areas. The main aim of this chapter is to review these hypotheses and commitments.

10.1   Structure

Language *structure* refers to systematicity in the linguistic environment encountered and picked up by the language learner: in other words, what there is to learn. Some kinds of structure are there in all languages, suggesting that they are very easy to learn and/or indispensable to the functioning of language as a communication system. Other kinds of structure are rare. In these cases, it is important to determine why they are rare. Some structures may arise only under specific circumstances, as a result of a series of specific historical developments, but can nonetheless be readily transmitted from parents to children once arisen. The theory of language change must therefore explain their rarity, but the theory of language acquisition must explain how they can be learned. Other structures may be rare because they are hard to learn or use (in either comprehension or production). Much recent debate in the field has been concerned with the reasons for rarity, and the extent to which rare structures are rare because there is something wrong with them (e.g., Blevins, 2004; Bybee, 2001; Moreton, 2008; Prince & Smolensky, 1993/2008; Wedel, 2007). When is rarity due to the rare structure being difficult to acquire, process, or use, and when is it due to the rarity of its historical precursors? This is a question that probably every linguist would like to know the answer to.

10.1.1   Schematic Structure

Languages are tools for achieving communicative goals. In production, the goal is usually to affect one's interlocutor in some way, effecting some change in the world. In comprehension, it is usually to get information about the current state of the world, including the beliefs and desires— and likely future behaviors—of the speaker. From this standpoint, the core of language is the system of goal-linked schemas that allow us to accomplish these goals. Construction Grammarians call these schemas *constructions* (Goldberg, 1995). A construction connects a category of forms, which themselves connect categories of action sequences to categories of sounds, and a category of meanings/communicative goals for which the form is used. A construction's form—and its meaning—can vary in specificity. Thus, some constructions may specify segmental context, while others may specify prosodic structure. The most specific constructions, like individual wordforms, specify both. The least specific ones, like argument structure constructions, specify neither.

Schematic structure refers to the *system* of form-meaning mappings, a network of form categories connected to meaning categories in which alternative expressions compete with each other to be incorporated into the production plan. The competition between schemas is analogous to competition between tools to be selected to perform a task (Zipf, 1949). The tools most suited for the task at hand are more likely to be chosen than less suitable tools. In the case of schemas, the more suitable ones are better cues to the meaning the speaker wishes to express—either because they contain more cues to the meaning or because the probability of the meaning given the cue is relatively high (Bates & MacWhinney, 1989). However, more accessible tools may be chosen over more suitable ones by a hurried artisan. In the same way, a frequent, easily constructed, or easily pronounced/ executed schema may be selected over a more contextually appropriate but less accessible competitor. A rich-get-richer loop results: choosing to produce a form increases the likelihood of selecting it for production in the future.

The outcome of a rich-get-richer loop is *Zipf's law*, a linear relationship between log frequency of a word and the logarithm of the number of words that have that frequency (Zipf, 1949). If the slope of the relationship is 1, a corpus has one word that occurs 10,000 times, there will be about 10 words that occur 1,000 words each, and 10,000 words that occur exactly once. Zipf's law appears to be a true universal, holding in all corpora (see Baayen, 2001). Of course, as anticipated by Zipf, this universal is not only true of language. In fact, Zipf's law generalizes to any domain with rich-get-richer loops: income, spread of diseases, fads and innovations, citation numbers for scientific articles, counts of visits and links to websites (see Silver, 2011). When there is an upper limit on growth, expansion plateaus at the ceiling. For example, when two markers are competing for their share of a limited set of words, Zipfian rich-get-richer dynamics cause convergence on one marker being chosen 100% of the time (e.g., Wedel, 2007). In this way, the same rich-get-richer dynamic that produces Zipfian word frequency distributions also generates the overwhelming regularity of grammatical patterns. Like other universals, Zipf's law cannot be understood without reference to the dynamics of acquisition and change that bring it about. If using a form did not change the likelihood of reusing it, a rich-get-richer loop would not occur in language production, Zipf's law would not hold for word frequencies, and regularization would be much rarer than it is. Fortunately for Zipf, rich-get-richer loops are ubiquitous in language learning within individual speakers as well as in the spread of linguistic innovations through speech communities.

10.1.2   Syntagmatic Structure

The term *schematic structure* is intended to parallel the more traditional terms *syntagmatic structure* and *paradigmatic structure*. Syntagmatic structure is about sequencing. A language without syntagmatic structure would either have to have a distinct analog form for every meaning or would have no restrictions on what can follow what. Both of these possibilities are of course nonstarters. A language of analog forms is ruled out by limited discrimination abilities coupled with the infinity of meanings one wants to express, among other reasons (see Christiansen & Chater, 2016, pp. 129–130; von Humboldt, 1836/1999, p. 91; Nowak & Krakauer, 1999). A language of random sequences is ruled out by the fact that some sequences of forms are harder to produce than others, and—secondarily—the fact that some sequences of meaningful forms are easier to understand. In addition, it is doomed by automatization pressures, the fact that producing something in one order makes it easier to produce it in the same order the next time around.

10.1.3   Paradigmatic Structure

I define paradigmatic structure as relations between forms that occur in complementary sets of contexts. Paradigmatic structure is learned to produce one of the forms when the other is accessed but contextually inappropriate. Under this definition, paradigmatic structure is only necessary in morphology.

Synchronically, the existence of paradigmatic structure in languages is somewhat mysterious. There is little reason for having, say, classes of nouns that have distinct morphological paradigms, and many languages do perfectly well without them. It is also hard to learn. Therefore, paradigmatic structure appears dysfunctional, like the ambiguity between *can* and *can't* in most varieties of North American English (which even native listeners struggle with interpreting; Ernestus et al., 2017). I propose that just as *can/ can't* ambiguity arose through functional reductive sound change, paradigmatic structure arises through a recurrent—and functional—diachronic process, grammaticalization.

Grammaticalization is the set of historical processes by which independent words turn into grammatical morphemes in particular contexts. Grammaticalization is a *diachronic universal*, taking place in all languages at all times, and is rarely if ever reversible. As multiple morphemes grammaticalize in parallel, they can become synonymous in particular contexts. For example, *gonna* and *will* are currently competing ways to express futurity, despite coming from constructions with distinct meanings, motion and volition. Parallel grammaticalization can result in *layering* of markers that have grammaticalized from distinct sources into the same function, resulting in multiple ways to express the same meaning (e.g., Bybee et al., 1994). While all verbs in modern English can occur with both *will* and *gonna*, some verbs significantly favor *gonna* while others favor *will* (Gries & Stefanowitsch, 2004, p. 114). For example, *see* favors *will* while *say* favors *gonna*. If these verb-auxilliary co-occurrences grew stronger through a Zipfian feedback loop, it is easy to imagine *will* and *gonna* grammaticalizing further into verbal prefixes (Bybee, 2002a). At that point we would say that English has developed two distinct verbal tense paradigms.

While this future English would have paradigms, learners of future English would not yet need to learn paradigmatic associations to form the future tense, because the choice of the future marker would at this point be conditioned on the verb stem, which occurs in the future form. However, as the markers grammaticalize, marker choice would inevitably also become associated with some phonological and/or semantic features of the context, particularly features pertaining to the co-occurring verbs. For example, verbs currently favoring *will* tend to be "non-agentive or low-dynamicity actions" (Gries & Stefanowitsch, 2004, p. 114). Even if some such feature co-occurs with a marker by random chance, this correlation may be noticed and strengthened through rich-get-richer feedback loops. When you choose a marker in a particular context, it becomes easier to choose it again in that context. In addition, to the extent that speakers do maximize production accuracy (see chapter 2), whenever one of the markers is more likely in a context, it maximizes accuracy to choose it in that context over its competitors.

A feature used to choose between competing markers in one cell of a morphological paradigm—say, animacy—is also likely to be used to choose between competing markers in another cell. If a feature has become associated with a marker, it must have been salient enough to be noticed, and its salience should also make it noticed in other paradigm cells. Furthermore, if a feature has been learned to be predictive of marker choice, this in and of itself should make it more salient across paradigm cells. If multiple paradigm cells happen to have competing morphological markers (because of layering arising through parallel grammaticalization), we will become even more likely to say that the language has paradigmatic structure.

For example, suppose the English *did* and *have* also develop into verbal prefixes—which would also require a high degree of co-occurrence with particular verbs (Bybee, 2002a)—indicating simple past, a common diachronic pathway (Bybee et al., 1994). It is not too unlikely that the past tense prefix choice, like the future prefix choice, would also be conditioned by dynamicity of the action. In particular, *did*—a former emphatic past as in *I did do it!*—could become associated with agentive, dynamic actions. We would then have two conjugations, one for dynamic verbs like *say—did~gonna*—and another for more passive ones like *see—have~will*. Note that this semantic conditioning does not have to be perfect. Some verbs might be individually associated with *have*. Some verbs might disfavor a prefix because its addition would make the combination hard to pronounce, leading the speaker to avoid it once they experience the difficulty (Berg, 1998; Martin, 2007). This kind of probabilistic conditioning is typical of natural language paradigms.

Once the language has a paradigm with at least two markers in at least two cells, paradigmatic mappings are useful to extend the paradigms to new verbs that do not clearly have the feature(s) associated with marker choice (e.g., verbs of middling dynamicity). Acquisition of paradigmatic mappings helps the paradigm persist and be extended to novel words, but it can also weaken the influence of the original semantic or phonological conditioning. If one can produce *gonna* from *did* without knowing anything else about the word, one should be able to do so even when *did* is chosen in a *did~gonna*-disfavoring context. In addition, paradigms can become less systematic when the markers are associated with individual frequent words that tend to co-occur with them, likely a precondition for the loss of syntactic autonomy turning separate words into affixes. If associations with particular words block associations with features of those words (chapter 3)—particularly likely when the words are frequent and few in number— then the markers will not be extended to new words with the feature.

Paradigmatic structure is not universal. Though some languages achieve remarkable paradigmatic complexity, many do fine without complex morphology. The present account of the emergence of paradigmatic structure is admittedly speculative and may be wrong, but any plausible alternative must show how paradigmatic structure can emerge from the diachronic processes of language change. It is only when we approach language as a changing system of competing generalizations that we can hope to explain why languages have features like morphological paradigms, which lack a clear synchronic motivation (Blevins, 2004; Bybee, 2001).

10.1.4   Category Structure

A *schema* links a *category* of forms to a category of meanings. These categories are never maximally specific. Even if we assumed—counterfactually— that there is no language-independent perceptual categorization, a form that only refers to a particular view of a particular dog on a particular day would be quite useless. It would either be extended to related percepts—at least different views of the same dog—or fade from memory and die out through disuse.

Whenever a category contains more than one member, these members may differ in typicality, the degree to which they resemble other members of the category and differ from members of other categories. Perhaps the most robust finding in the study of categorization is that knowing a category implies knowing which members of the category are more typical than others (the so-called *prototype effect*; Rosch & Mervis, 1975). The prototype effect holds for categories of linguistic forms just as it holds for other categories (J. Miller, 1994). However categories are represented in the mind/brain, this representation should not quash the differences between category members out of existence, as all categories have internal structure.

What is the internal structure of a linguistic category like? In chapter 5, I have argued that there is a tension between the rich-get-richer dynamic in production (which favors very peaky within-category frequency distributions) and attention to novelty in perception (which favors uniform within-category typicality distributions). In production, the more you choose a form to express a meaning, the more likely you are to choose it in the future (Zipf, 1949). In perception, novel stimuli attract attention. The more a form is perceived, the less salient it becomes (e.g., Bybee, 2003). As a result, typicality tracks log frequency rather than raw frequency, reducing the differences between the frequent and the rare and magnifying the differences between the rare and the nonexistent. It is little wonder that theorists who focus on the difference between the acceptable and the unacceptable have downplayed frequency differences between attested forms (as in the famous dictum "those who count don't count").

Examining the relations between typicality distributions in perception and frequency distributions in production constitutes an important area for future research that can help clarify the perception/production relationship and the extent to which the same representations are involved in both.

Some form representation shared between perception and production, the gateway to meaning, is necessary to maintain the hypothesis that schemas/ constructions are bidirectional form-meaning pairings. While I have argued that bidirectional *learning* of form-meaning associations is something we routinely engage in as competent language learners, this need not imply bidirectional *associations* between forms and meanings. Approximately equal weights of parallel form→meaning and meaning→form associations are sufficient to account for associative symmetry and sensitivity to joint probabilities of form-meaning pairings.

Because linguistic forms are sequences of recombinant units, categories of linguistic forms are defined by a set of cues that must be perceived in a certain order. For example, the form of the word *kitten* expected by a native speaker of American English with little exposure to foreigners can be coarsely described as the sequence [kʰɪ(ə){t;ɾ;ʔ}(ə)n]. The speed of speech means that speech category recognition demands syntagmatic prediction as well as detection of cues to fairly large configural units of meaning. Because of noise and variation, any given cue can be missed. When a cue is missing, the listener had better be able to fill it in from context. The need to "fill in" missed or missing information is one reason for learning not only to predict the future but also to retrodict the past. This need for retrodiction— and empirical evidence for sensitivity to the conditional probability of the past, *backward* transitional probability (Pelucchi et al., 2009; Perruchet & Desaulty, 2008)—provides an argument for bidirectional learning and use of syntagmatic and schematic associations.

10.2   Processing

The brain is a massively redundant, massively parallel system. Its redundancy is what gives it resilience in the face of damage and its ability to deal with noise, both in the environment and in neural computation (e.g., Rumelhart, 1990). Massive parallelism means that there are many routes from a particular form to its meaning, and there are many ways to construct the same form to express a meaning. In other words, processing is a mess. In any instance of processing, in both perception and production, myriad mental representations representing units of various sizes become activated and compete with each other.

The primary difference between processing in production and comprehension is that comprehension is incremental (chapter 3; see also Cutler, 2012, for a more extensive review)—input is processed as it is perceived— whereas production involves some degree of planning (chapter 8) followed by execution (chapter 9). In comprehension, we do not wait until the end of some linguistic unit to start interpreting the signal and activating meanings. Instead, the signal-so-far constantly activates meanings, generates expectations about what is coming up, as well as decisions about the meaning of the utterance and the allocation of attention (including planning where to look next in reading and how much to pay attention in speech perception). Sometimes—when the most likely interpretation eventually turns out to be incorrect—incremental processing leads us into trouble. Usually, however, it allows for comprehension to proceed as fast as it possibly can. Importantly, incrementality does not mean that the listener needs to hear the beginning of a word in order to perceive the word correctly (Dahan, 2010; Salasoo & Pisoni, 1985): if something is missed, it can be retrodicted from what follows. However, like prediction, retrodiction happens online as the signal is perceived by the senses.

Production, on the other hand, is characterized by extensive preplanning. For speech parameters, planning extends at least up to the utterance level. Preplanning an utterance allows for the speech rate and intonation contour dynamics to be sensitive to how long the utterance will be (see Shattuck-Hufnagel, 2015, for review). Planning allows speech to be reasonably fluent and error-free. The utterance plan can be thought of as instantiating a high-level construction/schema, specifying the syntax and prosody of the utterance, including its intonation contour, and triggered in part by an illocutionary goal such as requesting information (Redford, 2015). Like other schemas, the utterance schema can be fully or partially specified. For a familiar utterance, the schema is specified fully and can be executed directly. However, above the word level, this is rarely the case, requiring the schema to be "filled out."

After the high-level utterance schema is selected, the filling-out process begins. However, the speaker may begin executing the high-level schema before it is fully filled out. Starting execution is a pragmatic decision driven both by expectations about when the planning process will complete and values placed on fluency vs. control of the floor. For example, if the speaker wants to be sure to claim the floor, he may actually anticipate making a disfluency but think it a reasonable price to pay for dominating the conversation. When one reaches an underspecified part of the plan, a disfluency results, triggering various time-buying strategies (see Harmon & Kapatsinski, 2015, in press).

Filling out a schema involves competition between alternative fillers, which come in a variety of sizes (chapter 8). As Caballero and Inkelas (2013) argue, units that are larger and more specific have an inherent advantage in this struggle. The competing units are activated by the meaning the speaker wishes to express. Units that can express *more* of the activated meaning are activated more strongly, and therefore usually block the less specific units. Thus, if there is a schema to express GO+PAST, that schema will block the schema that expresses only PAST and the schema that expresses only GO, allowing the speaker to appropriately produce *went* rather than *goed*. The "ultimate whole," a fully specified utterance-level schema (which could be a word in a word production task), has the ultimate advantage on these grounds. Similarly, schemas that are strongly associated with the meaning to be expressed have an advantage over less appropriate schemas. However, frequency also plays a role, with more frequent forms likely to be selected over less frequent forms (chapter 6). Thus, an irregular past tense form may lose the competition to the regular past tense schema if it is infrequent (Bybee, 2001), and especially if it is less frequent than a base form that can be plugged into a regular construction (Hay, 2001).

Constructing a production plan involves copying activated units into the production plan that is being constructed. While some of the units are activated from the meaning to be expressed, this is not the only source of activation. Some forms are activated merely because they have been recently produced or perceived, and are therefore primed (e.g., Ferreira & Griffin, 2003). Furthermore, when a fully specified, inflected wordform appropriate for the meaning to be expressed is inaccessible, the meaning of that word's stem activates other forms of the same word, which are then available to be copied into the production plan. Both of these sources of activation are usually functional, improving the rapidity of planning and retrieval, but both can also lead to error. For example, activation of other forms of the same word can lead to production of a context-inappropriate form of the stem, leveling a stem change (Smolek & Kapatsinski, 2017). Activation of an orthographic form of a related word can lead to spelling errors when that word does not have the same spelling (Kapatsinski, 2010c).

Execution of the plan (chapter 9) involves activating the future while executing the present and (optionally) inhibiting the past (Dell et al., 1997). Following Articulatory Phonology, we can think of the plan as a set of temporally aligned gesture sequences (Browman & L. Goldstein, 1989). Like any other behavior, execution can be practiced and is subject to automatization. Automatization speeds execution up and smoothes transitions between neighboring gestural targets (Bybee, 2001; Sosnik et al., 2004). This smoothing out of transitions can explain most instances of reductive sound change, and—crucially—can account for the fact that reductive sound change starts in high-frequency words (Bybee, 2001,

2002b; Hay & Foulkes, 2016; Schuchardt, 1885/1972). Frequent words are production plans that have become automatized through frequent execution. Automatization also makes it difficult to stop in the middle of the automatized sequence and makes it even more difficult to restart production from a point at which one does not normally start execution. As part of automatization, one learns where to start execution from and, importantly, where not to.

10.3   Acquisition

The brain is a redundant, massively parallel system. Just as there are many routes from form to meaning and from meaning to form, there are multiple learning mechanisms that have developed over the course of evolution to pick up and act on constantly changing environmental contingencies with sufficient accuracy and sufficient speed.

First, there is error-driven predictive learning, supported by cue-competition effects and implemented in humans in subcortical structures (chapter 1), though the same learning mechanism may also be implemented in other neural hardware in other species. This system allows the learner to acquire predictive associations from cues (predictors) to outcomes whose occurrence one wishes to predict. Learning in this system is directional (from cue to outcome), relatively rapid, and converges on a stable system of knowledge if the pattern to be learned is simple enough for the organism's predictions to be (almost) always accurate. Belief revision is driven by surprise: when an outcome is unsurprising, it must have been predicted by one's current system of beliefs (i.e., cue-outcome associations). An *expected* occurrence or nonoccurrence of an outcome leads to no change in beliefs. This system likely plays a role in acquiring relatively long-distance dependencies that afford time between cue and outcome to generate a prediction before the outcome is perceived, providing confirmation or disconfirmation.

Directional associations of error-driven predictive learning also appear important for automatization of production plans, where the activated future should inhibit the present, despite a different brain locus for this kind of learning. As emphasized by Bayesian theorists (e.g., Anderson, 1991), it is important to realize that principles of belief updating may generalize over many different neural structures that implement them because organisms with very different nervous systems still need to learn and act on similar environmental contingencies. The tasks animals have to perform are no less important in explaining the learning mechanisms that evolve to carry them out than the biological hardware that evolution has available to tinker with (see also Christiansen & Chater, 2016).

Second, the slow learning in cortical areas does not give rise to cue competition: if a cue co-occurs with an outcome—and both are attended to—they are wired together, independently of how predictive other cues are of the same outcome. When the cue occurs but the outcome does not, the association is weakened and may become inhibitory if this happens too often. Accordingly, studies that fail to find cue competition provide support for a slow-learning mechanism (e.g., Matute et al., 1996), though as we saw in chapters 6 and 8, the Rescorla-Wagner (1972) model can mimic such models when its learning rate is slow enough and therefore there is always enough error to drive learning.

Hebbian learning is also characterized by bidirectionality. Bidirectional learning is suggested by our results on construction learning (chapter 6), which are consistent with the notion of a construction as a bidirectional form-meaning pairing (see also McMurray et al., 2012, 2013). Indeed, bidirectional learning in this domain is eminently functional: a competent speaker/hearer needs to be able to both retrieve a meaning given a form and to retrieve the form given the meaning. However, I have argued that bidirectional learning is the outcome of actively forming backward associations under the guidance of cognitive control, a process that is easily disrupted by distraction (chapter 1). True Hebbian learning likely occurs on a much slower timescale than seen in miniature artificial language experiments and probably requires overnight consolidation (McClelland et al., 1995).

Third, sensory processing areas (both in and below the cortex) are tuned to pay attention to stimuli and dimensions that are informative and to ignore those that merely distract you from important information by top-down error-driven feedback (chapter 3). Salient, attended stimuli are more associable—easier to associate with other things. Learned selective attention is an important reason for the difficulties faced by second language learners. More generally, selective attention explains many ways biological learners depart from the normative criterion of Bayesian optimality (chapters 4 and 5).

The existence of multiple learning mechanisms and multiple kinds of learning raises the question of how the learning mechanisms interact as a learner achieves proficiency in a particular task. It is likely that something as complex as language acquisition is accomplished by the full team of domain-general learning mechanisms acting in concert. While there is important computational work addressing what parts the individual learning mechanisms play in this concert (e.g., McClelland et al., 1995; Ashby et al., 2007), little empirical data is yet available—particularly on specific aspects of language acquisition (though see Kachergis et al., 2012; Ramscar et al., 2010, 2013).

10.4 Change

While "mainstream" generative linguistics has been committed to a search for synchronic universals, statements that hold true of all languages, functional linguists have searched for recurring pathways of language change. While languages look very different synchronically, leaving few synchronic universals unchallenged (Evans & Levinson, 2009),[1] there are strong diachronic generalizations to be made. Language change is typically irreversible and overwhelmingly unidirectional. This is true of sound change as well as of the complex of changes characterizing grammaticalization. For example, while an intervocalic stop often reduces over time into a tap or a fricative and subsequently a glide, the reverse developments are unattested. The numeral "one" has independently developed into an indefinite article (*a/an* in English) in many languages, yet indefinite articles never develop into numerals. Similarly, a verb meaning "want" has developed into a future marker in many languages, but future markers do not become verbs of desire. Verbs meaning "finish" develop into perfect markers, but not vice versa (Bybee, 2003, 2015). The fact that some changes occur over and over while others never do demands an explanation.

A slew of such explanations is suggested by the biases inherent in the learning and processing mechanisms we just reviewed. Indeed, as a usage-based linguist, I am primarily interested in these mechanisms insofar as they can explain the patterns of language change. One could argue that representational differences that do not translate into differences in observable behavior are of no interest to the linguist, whose primary task is explaining why languages are the way they are. If two different learning mechanisms, faced with the same linguistic experience, would lead the learner to perform the same behaviors in all circumstances, then identifying the mechanism responsible for the learner's linguistic behavior is of no importance to linguistic theory. Because only observable behavior can be conventionalized, language change comes from changes in behavior, and not merely changes in mental representation. Fortunately, distinct learning mechanisms often make different predictions regarding the behavior that would result from a particular history of learning experiences.

At the highest level of generality, changes to forms that have already been *created* or *borrowed* and therefore exist in the language can be considered to involve *generalization, specialization,* and *reduction.* In addition, because forms do not exist in isolation but rather compete for expressing meanings, changes can influence each other, resulting in *chain shifts.*

Generalization involves extending a frequent form to new uses, the fundamental process behind grammaticalization (Bybee, 2003). In chapter 6, I argued that the main mechanism behind extension is that frequent forms are sometimes selected for production over their more specialized competitors (Zipf, 1949). I argued that accessibility results from Hebbian learning: extension occurs because the frequent form becomes associated with semantic features shared by its original meaning and the meaning to which the form is extended. The crucial prediction of the Hebbian account is that extending a form to a novel meaning does not make it less likely that other semantically related forms will also be extended to that meaning. For example, if *will* develops into a future marker, this does not reduce the likelihood of *want* developing into a future marker at the same time. In contrast, predictive learning—if it is fast enough to exhibit cue competition, its classic behavioral signature—also demands competition between the alternative forms for expressing the novel meaning, which should reflect their relative competitiveness in the original contexts.

A very similar example of generalization is *analogical change,* which involves grammatical patterns being extended to words that had previously been associated with a different pattern. For example, *weeped* is replacing *wept, creeped* is replacing *crept,* and *leaped* is replacing *leapt* (Bybee, 2002b). The extended pattern is usually one of high type frequency and low token/type ratio, not being associated with—and therefore restricted to— particular lexical contexts. However, irregularizations are also found (e.g., *string~stringed* changing into *string~strung*). Crucially, this kind of change starts in low-frequency verbs for which the previously correct past tense form is relatively hard to access, allowing a combination of the base and a frequent morphological construction to outcompete it in the moment of production (see Bybee, 2001, 2002b). Again, change arises when the form that *should have been* produced is not accessible enough, letting a competitor move in.

Specialization is most clearly seen in various cases of *lexicalization,* where patterns become associated with individual words, which often leads— through *entrenchment*—to these patterns being *restricted* to the words in question. However, other cases of patterns becoming associated with specific contexts (e.g., pejoration, the development of semantic prosody and linguistic stereotypes for social groups) can also be considered specialization. Like lexicalization, these kinds of specialization also lead a form to become restricted to the context with which it is associated. For example, once a particular linguistic behavior is associated with a particular social group, you should not perform it if you do not want the listener to infer that you belong to the group in question.

Lexicalization can involve *pragmatic strengthening*, whereby contextual inferences become associated with particular constructions (Traugott, 1988). Traugott (p. 411) gives the example of *instead*, which used to mean *in the location of*, as in *I have planted cacti in (the) stead of roses*, meaning "in the location where roses used to be." If you say this to me, I will invariably infer that you preferred cacti to roses. This inference of preference has become associated with the form so strongly that it is now perceived as being part of the meaning of *instead*. Note that this likely involves bidirectional learning. The listener hears the utterance and then generates the inference. Presumably I did not know you preferred cacti to roses before you told me of your gardening decisions. As a result of this perceptual experience, the listener then learns to produce *instead* after activating the "I prefer X to Y" meaning to transmit to the listener. Thus, experience of a form followed by a meaning leads to the formation of meaning→form associations.

Lexicalization can involve form as well as meaning. As proposed by Bybee (2002b), words that tend to occur in reduction-favoring contexts become associated with reduction, so that—even outside of such contexts—they are more likely to reduce than other words (Seyfarth, 2014). This can be modeled in at least two ways. First, the meaning of the word could become associated with two alternative wordforms—reduced and full—with the more frequent form being more likely to be selected for production (Bybee, 2002b). Second, words might become associated with sublexical variants of phonological structures, abstract sublexical schemas (Pierrehumbert, 2002). Again, the more frequent variants would compete with less frequent variants for production, with the variant most strongly associated with the word to be produced being more likely to win. In either case, this involves forms becoming associated with the contexts in which they tend to occur.

Paradoxically, specialization can actually result in extension, its apparent opposite: when a form becomes strongly associated with a meaning, it can be selected to express that meaning even when other features of the meaning to be expressed would not favor its selection. Thus, *instead* can now be used for preference regardless of whether the preferred and the dispreferred share location. Flapping has left its original colloquial domain borne inside words used in colloquial contexts. While lexicalization *can* be accompanied by entrenchment, entrenchment is not an inevitable outcome of lexicalization. What then determines whether entrenchment will result? In chapter 6, we showed that entrenchment is disfavored by strengthening associations between present cues and present outcomes—wiring together units when they are used together—and favored by updating connections involving absent cues and/or absent outcomes. Therefore, entrenchment should happen when absent cues or outcomes are salient. If the salience of a form's absence is related to the salience of its presence, forms that draw attention to themselves are likely to become restricted to the specific contexts in which they occur, whereas unobtrusive low-salience forms are free to spread to new contexts. In grammaticalization, a rich-get-richer loop results: grammaticalizing forms are reducing, becoming less and less salient, under pressure of automatization, and the resulting low salience makes it easier for the grammaticalizing form to spread to new contexts, increasing its frequency and driving grammaticalization on.

Unlike forms, alternations usually do become restricted to lexical contexts one finds them in (Bybee, 2008; Bybee & Brewer, 1980). This reflects the fact that productive alternations result from productive sublexical structures, whether paradigmatic—*electric*~electricity → ik~is → *symbric~symbricity*, schematic—N~*simplicity* → N~*i*[s]*ity* → N~*simbricity*, or syntagmatic—*simplicity, electricity* → [s]/*ity*. As illustrated above, sublexical structures must be extracted from experienced words and sublexical structure is always in competition with direct retrieval of a form that can express the entirety of the meaning the speaker has in mind. When an alternation is restricted to a few frequent words, then the forms of those words can be effectively retrieved via direct whole-word retrieval, blocking the acquisition of sublexical associations that would produce alternations the words exemplify. Consider an analogy. The same way pragmatic strengthening can result in extension, a specialist may be in demand as a collaborator or consultant beyond their specific discipline precisely because they are strongly associated with a specific field of study. When thinking of a discipline makes you think of Mr. or Ms. X, Mr. or Ms. X is likely to be in demand outside of that discipline, even though they are likely to be thought of as *being* the discipline because their knowledge is highly specialized. And if someone always works as part of the same team, they may be less likely to come to mind when one thinks of the major players in a field than if they work on a number of different teams or sometimes work alone. Sublexical structures are always "part of a team" because a word is the smallest possible utterance. As a result, they are always in danger of being overshadowed by the whole (chapter 3).

An alternative way of thinking about overshadowing by the whole is that all members of the whole overshadow each other. In the analogy above, does one think of the whole team, or does one think of individuals within it and become unsure about any single member's competency? Given my commitment to a redundant, multiroute processing system, my bet is that wholes can overshadow parts and parts can overshadow each other. However, much work remains to be done on establishing this hypothesis (cf. Baayen et al., 2011).

When an alternation is associated with a specific morphological trigger, there is one other reason—beyond overshadowing—for the alternation to lose productivity, and that concerns the productivity of the trigger. If the trigger occurs in many contexts, only some of which involve the alternation, the alternation is likely doomed (Kapatsinski, 2009b, 2010b). This is perhaps part of the explanation for less productive affixes being the ones most likely to productively trigger phonological alternations, the observation behind lexical phonology (Kiparsky, 1985). Suppose we have a suffix that triggers an alternation when added to stems ending in specific segments. Syntagmatically, a productive suffix is unlikely to demand that any particular segment precede it, preventing acquisition of alternations demanding that other segments must change into the segment the suffix requires. Paradigmatically, one is likely to learn that the suffix is frequently associated with copying the stem verbatim, increasing the productivity of "no change." Schematically, the schema for the suffix is likely not to specify the preceding segment in any great detail, thus being consistent with copying the entire stem without alteration (chapters 7 and 8).

In my dissertation (Kapatsinski, 2009b; see also 2010b), I documented an intriguing change in Russian. Velar palatalization, which changes velars into alveopalatals, was productive before the suffixes -ek and -ok but not before -i, despite -i being a better trigger for palatalization across languages (Guion, 1998). There were no exceptions to velar palatalization before any of the suffixes in dictionaries; thus we cannot say that the palatalization rule lost productivity before certain suffixes because it had too many exceptions in those contexts (cf. C. Yang, 2016). However, Russian suffixes that remain productive triggers for velar palatalization (–ok and –ek) tend to attach to velar-final stems while –i usually does not: being highly productive, it attaches to all sorts of stems, and most stems do not end in velars. Subsequent testing with miniature artificial languages confirmed the direction of causality. If—in addition to experiencing –i changing velars—one also experiences it *not* changing labials and alveolars, palatalization of velars is rarely acquired, despite being abundantly exemplified. The across-the-board productivity of –*i* dooms the alternation it triggers.

Most sound change, at least in the consonantal domain, involves *reduction* (Bybee, 2015). There are at least two kinds of reduction: phonetically gradual reduction brought about by automatization of execution in production (chapter 9) and phonetically abrupt loss of low-salience parts that have been left meaningless by overshadowing in perception (chapter 3). The former is far more common and is exemplified, for example, by reduction of closures between vowels (such as American English flapping in words like *butter*), as well as by shortening and centralization of unstressed vowels. The latter—while possibly playing a role in articulatorily motivated change as well—is best exemplified by loss of unstressed morphemes that are no longer meaningful. The most studied example is the French development of *ne pas* from "not a step" to a simple "not" followed by (optional) reduction to *pas*. First, *ne pas* was extended beyond "not a step" to other instances of negation. At that point, there was too little meaning left for both *ne* and *pas* to acquire distinct semantic associations, and the stressed *pas* overshadowed the unstressed *ne*, which is now no longer obligatorily triggered by activating the "not" meaning (Harmon & Kapatsinski, 2015).

The extension of *ne pas* to nonemphatic negation is a possible example of *bleaching*, or semantic reduction (chapter 6). While most extensions are likely due to the high accessibility of frequent forms, and their strong meaning→form associations, extension of emphatic forms to nonemphatic uses can happen in part through *habituation* (Bybee, 2003; Haiman, 1994). If "not a step" is used all the time, it loses its emphatic nature, just as cusswords are not so shocking when coming from someone who uses them in every other sentence. However, one still has to explain how "not a step" came to be used all the time to elicit habituation in the first place, and here accessibility of *pas* compared to other nouns that could fill that role likely played a role. Originally, many different nouns could follow *ne* in this construction. Eventually, *pas* came to dominate, an accessibility-driven positive feedback loop. Once dominant, it lost its oomph and was no longer emphatic, but being more salient than *ne*, it was in a good position to overshadow it and take over its meaning.

Finally, forms do not change in complete isolation. At the lowest level, form categories compete for dividing up phonetic space in such a way that the space is split up exhaustively, with no territory remaining unclaimed. If one category drifts off, under pressure of random variation and articulatory reduction, another category may claim the empty space separating it from its former neighbor simply because productions falling in this unclaimed space will no longer be perceived as incorrect (see also Boersma, 1998). Assuming that there is some reason for productions to fall in that space, perhaps the same reason that is pushing the other category in the same direction, a *drag chain* must result. Form categories also compete for expressing meanings. Here, if a form is no longer good at expressing a particular meaning (perhaps because it has been bleached through overuse), another form may be extended to take on that function. Again, there is nothing mysterious about the process: if speakers consider the meaning useful, they will use some form to express it. As a result, in domains where overuse is particularly deadly to a form, such as slang—which must be kept secret from outsiders—and intensifiers—whose oomph is subject to habituation—we see repeated cycles of extension and obsolescence, semantic drag chains. How many words are there that mean "very"? Or "cool"? How many of them will survive the next quarter century?

More interesting are *push chains*. In a push chain, a form extending into another form's phonetic or semantic territory pushes the other form away, causing it to undergo phonetic or semantic change. Push chains suggest some pressure that keeps competing forms distinct. In phonetics, Baese-Berk and Goldrick (2009) showed that phonetic parameters are exaggerated when members of a minimal pair (i.e., words with phonological neighbors) are produced. Furthermore, it is precisely the parameters that are necessary to use for distinguishing that word from its neighbors that are exaggerated (see also Kirov & Wilson, 2012). Wedel et al. (2013) show that mergers are least likely to level contrasts that distinguish many members of minimal pairs from each other. In semantics, Zara Harmon and I showed that synonyms of frequent, highly accessible forms skitter away from the shared meaning in comprehension: learners assume they do *not* have the same meaning as the frequent form.

What is this pressure that keeps forms apart? As described in chapter 6, Zara Harmon and I have argued that semantic push chains can result from bidirectional learning of form-meaning associations. The pressure against homophony in phonetics may also result from bidirectional learning (Boersma, 2007, 2011). Assuming that an acoustic dimension is discretized into a set of cues (chapter 5), then cues representing intermediate values on the continuum will not be strong cues to word meaning. Of the cues representing more extreme values, cues that the listener never needs to rely on in identifying a word will also not be strong cues. If weak cues are weakly associated with meaning due to their low salience, and learning is bidirectional, then cues representing intermediate values on an acoustic continuum will seldom be activated by meaning in production. Their production must therefore result from reductive articulatory pressures inherent in automatizing a repeatedly executed sequence of motions. Extreme values on a dimension will be activated more strongly when they *must* be relied on to identify the meaning from the acoustic signal, and thus will not succumb to the reductive pressures as easily. As Boersma points out, bidirectional learning and subsequent use of the learned bidirectional mappings for both production and perception can account for the effect of functional load in production without requiring the speaker to model the listener.

10.5   Explaining Rarities

As emphasized by Blevins (2004), an emphasis on the processes and mechanisms of change rather than synchronic universals allows a linguist to explain the emergence of typological rarities alongside recurrent patterns, and to predict which patterns will be rare and which will be common. Morphology and associated phonology constitute a domain particularly rich with rarities, for several good reasons.

First, morphology itself is the outcome of extensive grammaticalization that strips erstwhile words of their ability to stand on their own. Bound morphemes that cannot stand on their own are never practiced as independent production plans, losing autonomy altogether. Compared to word boundaries, the possible starting points of production, word-internal morpheme boundaries are of little use. While they can be identified by an analyst, there are good arguments for phonological material within words fusing into schemas across morphological boundaries (chapter 8). In this process, schematic and syntagmatic associations disrupt established paradigms.

For example, if a morph demands a stem change, the outcome of that change can fuse with the morph, forming a single schema linked to the morph's meaning. For instance, if you are exposed to a language in which the plural suffix –*i* tends to be preceded by [tʃ], then you may understandably extract a –*tʃi* schema. Thus, exposure to examples like blutʃ→blutʃi and snit→snitʃi may lead one to derive [bluktʃi] from [bluk], attaching a –*tʃi* schema. As schemas start general and become more specific with experience (chapter 3), avoiding such additions appears to require further learning to notice that –*i* is never preceded by a consonant cluster (Kapatsinski, 2013).

Sequences of co-occurring affixes can likewise fuse into a unified schema. For example, in Russian, the suffix –*nik* of *rabotnik* and *razbojnik*—an equivalent to the agentive –*er* of *worker* and *robber*—has fused with the verbal stem extension –*a* that follows and palatalizes it, forming a verbalizing schema, X–*nitʃatʲ* 'to behave as an X–er would'. (The [k] in –*nik* palatalizes before –*a*, a process no longer productive elsewhere.) The proof of the fusion is in the fact that such verbs do not have to have a corresponding *nik*–final noun. For instance, *razbojnitʃatʲ* 'to rob' does have one, *razbojnik* 'a robber'. However, *nervnitʃatʲ* 'to be nervous' does not: there is no noun **nervnik*; there is only *nervnyj* 'nervous' and *nerv* 'nerve'. Similarly, *kapriznitʃatʲ* 'to act capriciously' does not have a corresponding **kapriznik* but only *kapriznyj* 'capricious' and *kapriz* 'caprice'. The verb *xozʲajnitʃatʲ* 'to behave like you are the owner of the place' does have a corresponding noun, *xozʲain* 'owner', but it does not end in –*nik* (Kapatsinski, 2005b, pp. 153–154; see Booij, 2010, and Haspelmath, 1995, for more examples).

Developing schemas can also disrupt the regularity of paradigmatic mappings involving nonconcatenative morphology. In chapter 7, we saw that subtraction—deletion of a specific structure—can become truncation— deletion of whatever you need to delete in order to *produce* a specific structure—when learners acquire a prosodic schema (Inkelas, 2015). When there are also source forms that would have to undergo addition rather than subtraction for the same structure to result, the same process leads to a morphological template. As discussed in chapter 7, Japanese nickname formation documented by Poser (1990) presents a good example: nicknames suffixed with –*tyan* are normally truncated to two morae, unless they are too short, in which case they are augmented. Subtraction is clearly the more frequent process, since most names are longer than two morae, yet Japanese learners do not acquire across-the-board subtraction: they know that a nickname must sound a certain way.

Russian nicknames can also be cited in this context: usually a nickname is formed by extracting a CVC from the full name and suffixing it with –ʲ*a*, which palatalizes the last consonant. Alternatively, a nickname can be a CVCV or (more rarely) CVCVCV ending in *ʃa*, a competing schema. Some commonly used nicknames become conventionalized shortenings of the corresponding full names. As usual, labials resist palatalization. For example, my name, *Vsevolod*, has two conventional nicknames: *Volʲa*, with a palatalized [l], and *Sʲeva*, where the [v] is left unpalatalized. Similarly, *Sofija* becomes *Sofa* and not *Sofʲa*. However, in the name *Pavel*, which already has a palatalized [vʲ], the conventional shortening is *Paʃa*, with a palatal fricative, and not **Pavʲa*. Similarly, *Glafira* becomes *Glaʃa* and not **Glafʲa*. It appears that [vʲa] or [fʲa] is not a possible end for a nickname. Similarly, because [kʲ] does not exist in Russian except before front vowels, *Aleksej* becomes *Leʃa* or *Aleʃa*, while *Aleksandr*, having another CVC to extract, becomes *San'a* or *Saſa*. All nicknames end up alike, but they get there in many different ways.

Of course, the development of a nickname is a prolonged process, quite likely involving coming up with multiple alternatives and rejecting ones that do not sound right—whether because of phonotactics, avoidance of homonymy (a strong pressure in this domain), or sound symbolism. However, in chapter 7, we saw that overattestation of a structure in product forms can lead learners to derive that structure in ways they have not experienced *merely because they believe that is what the language requires*. Thus, learners exposed to a language in which subtraction often results in a CVCVk product end up learning and using a template, deleting a vowel from a CVCVCV source form but adding a [k] when the source is an overly short CVCV.

Paradigmatic associations may also sometimes trump schematic associations. In chapter 7, we argued that bidirectional paradigmatic mappings may result in morphological toggles. In a toggle, there are two forms associated with two paradigm cells but the form-cell mappings are inconsistent. All that is consistent is that the two forms of a single word must be distinct—for example, if a singular ends in –*ri*, the plural must end in –*na*, and if the singular ends in –*na*, the plural must end in –*ri*. Morphological toggles involve a bidirectional paradigmatic mapping, coupled with weak or nonexistent form-meaning associations: –*ri* activates –*na* or vice versa but neither form is associated with either number. Since form-meaning associations are usually stronger, more useful, and more easily learned than paradigmatic associations, the rarity of toggles is unsurprising. Indeed, as we discussed above, paradigmatic structure is itself a bit of a rarity, both because it is hard to learn, and because it usually requires parallel grammaticalization of synonymous affixes.

In morphophonology, one often observes another kind of rarity, a phonological process going against phonetic pressures (e.g., Bach & Harms, 1972; Blevins, 2004). A good example is the finding that velar palatalization in Russian is more productive before –*ok* and –*ek* than before –*i* and –*ik* (Kapatsinski, 2009b, 2010b). Crosslinguistically, palatalization usually arises before [i] or [j], whether because of coarticulation or because [k] and [tʃ] are perceptually confusable in that context (Guion, 1998). Furthermore, there is evidence that palatalization is more easily learnable before [i] than before [e], let alone [o]. In particular, Mitrović (2012) shows that Serbian children trained on palatalization before [e] generalize it to the pre-[i] context but not vice versa, despite palatalization in Serbian being more productive before some [e]–initial suffixes (see also Wilson, 2006).

To paraphrase Tolstoy, all phonetically natural patterns are alike; each unnatural pattern is unnatural in its own way. There is a history behind unnaturalness. How did velar palatalization come to be more productive before [o] and [e] than before [i] in Russian? Historically, palatalization arose naturally in its appropriate context, before [i] and [j], through phonetic processes: the suffixes that are so good at triggering palatalization in Russian, *–ok* and *–ek*, used to begin with [j], *–jok* and *–jek*. However, at present, there is no synchronic phonetic pressure to palatalize before *–ok*, and relatively little pressure to palatalize before *–ek*. Instead, palatalization in this context, and it turns out in pre-[i] contexts as well, is something one has to learn as part of acquiring the phonology of the language.

Acquiring phonology, like acquiring the rest of grammar, requires learning a large number of associations. Phonetically motivated associations may have an advantage in this process—for example, because they link similar units—but this advantage is often fairly weak in empirical studies (Moreton & Pater, 2012b). This makes sense: because phonology is often unnatural, the learner must be able to acquire phonetically unmotivated, arbitrary associations as well as phonetically motivated ones. Under such conditions, innate biases in favor of specific patterns are strongly disfavored in biological evolution (Christiansen & Chater, 2016; see also B. Thompson et al., 2016). In modern Russian, the competing outcomes of palatalization and faithful copying of the stem-final consonant are associated with specific suffixes. The suffixes that tend to be preceded by a palatal are the ones that continue triggering a stem change. Those that tend to be preceded by a faithful copy of a (nonvelar) consonant are associated with copying. Copying before *–i* and *–ik* is generalized, being misapplied to velar consonants, resulting in failure of palatalization when the full product form—palatalization and all—cannot be retrieved from memory.

The general point is that much synchronic phonology and morphology is learned by generalization over the lexicon (Bybee, 1985, 2001), and this means that the statistical strength of a pattern in the lexicon can override the pattern's phonetic naturalness. An important goal for learning models is to reveal the conditions for this kind of statistical override, a goal that has been approached by training learning models on realistic lexica to derive predictions for elicited production tests with novel source forms (for some work in this vein, see Becker et al., 2011; Hayes et al., 2009; Kapatsinski, 2010b; Pierrehumbert, 2006). However, we need to move beyond treating linguistic experience as a static dictionary. Some patterns—even ones with a good phonetic motivation—may be supported by many dictionary examples but nonetheless be blocked or overshadowed by other patterns as language is experienced in real time. Some patterns may also be insufficiently robust in words that the learner acquires early, failing to attract attention before error-free performance decreases learning rates (Pierrehumbert, 2001b). As large-scale longitudinal corpora of linguistic experience come online, we may get a better idea of why the learner seems to pick up on some patterns in the lexicon and ignore others (cf. Becker et al., 2011, vs. Hayes et al., 2009).

10.6 Some General Principles

It is worth reviewing a few general principles here, before previeing the future. First, in both linguistic theory—explaining why languages are the way they are—and learning theory—explaining how we learn—it is worth paying attention to both what is easy and what is needed. While change in existing forms is often reductive, there is constant renewal through creative production and borrowing. Languages do not reduce to a single easily pronounceable syllable—despite such a language being undoubtedly easiest to learn and produce—because such a language would not be functional: it would not allow us to do the things we do with language (see also Bybee, 2001; Christiansen & Chater, 2016; Lindblom, 1990). Thus every language has a sizable inventory of meaningful schemas requiring an extensive amount of practice to produce fluently and accurately. Similarly, updating only the connections between present cues and present outcomes—counting frequencies—is in some ways the easiest kind of learning, requiring no attention, no prediction, and therefore no noticing of absence. However, it would be terrible for picking up on the true environmental contingencies and reacting appropriately to novel, unexpected events. So something more complicated has been supplied by evolution. Simplicity is desirable only without a significant loss of functionality, though *some* functionality may well be sacrificed.

Second, we should not fear redundancy (see also Beekhuizen et al., 2013; Householder, 1966; Winter, 2014, among many others). Redundancy in processing means having many different ways to achieve the same goal: multiple routes from a meaning to a form, or from a form to its meaning. Processing redundancy is important. In speech perception, it allows the listener to deal with a noisy environment and lapses of attention. In production, it allows the speaker to deal with the fact that everything one wants to say does not come to mind in a fixed left-to-right order, and lapses of memory or attention can interfere with a system that is too rigid and inflexible. Redundancy in representation means robustness in the face of damage, allowing us to maintain and access knowledge for years and even decades despite fallible neural hardware. It also means greater plasticity, as learning can select from among the available connections just those that are useful or supported by the organism's experience. Redundancy in language structure provides the listener with multiple cues to seize on in trying to access meaning. It also allows for optimization of articulation as nonessential articulations are pruned by automatization. Redundant learning mechanisms ensure that one does not miss out on important contingencies, or suffer catastrophic interference from seemingly incompatible beliefs. Where Hebbian learning ensures efficient retrieval, error-driven predictive learning allows for anticipation of the future and appreciation of the causal structure of the world. Attentional learning allows for different cue-outcome relationships to be rapidly associated with the appropriate contexts, allowing us to learn that the world has changed without abandoning our beliefs about how it used to be—and may become again. The division of labor between rapid hippocampal learning and slow cortical learning similarly provides stability for long-held beliefs in the face of short-term fluctuations in the environment.

Third, at all levels of analysis, change looks like evolution. In the brain, unused or error-generating synaptic connections or even entire neurons are pruned over the course of development. Virtually every instance of learning consists of pruning associations as well as growing new ones. Changes in behavior can be effected via selection by consequences. For example, motor variability produces a pool of synchronic variants, which can then be selected for reproduction by articulatory ease or social evaluation. As well stated by William James (1880, p. 455), "New conceptions, emotions and active tendencies ... are originally produced in the shape of ... spontaneous variation in the functional activity of the excessively unstable human brain, which the outer environment simply confirms or refutes, adopts or rejects, preserves or destroys—*selects*, in short." From the level of neural connectivity to the level of social structure, change involves variation and selection. To explain change, it is therefore important to specify sources of variation and the pressures that influence variant selection.

Finally, science strives for functional simplicity. If one mechanism suffices to account for all the data, positing two systems runs afoul of Occam and his razor. Positing special learning mechanisms just for language acquisition should be dispreferred if domain-general learning mechanisms would suffice. This is especially true of a domain where generalizations that cannot be acquired by the learner will inevitably disappear. Not picking up on cues to food or tigers threatens the learner's survival. Not picking up on a linguistic structure threatens survival of the structure. Unlike the contingencies of the physical world, the contingencies of language are created and recreated by the learners. Languages that cannot be acquired must change or die. This suggests that language is much more likely to adapt to preexisting learning mechanisms than that special learning mechanisms embodying special principles of belief updating have evolved just to acquire language (see also Christiansen & Chater, 2016; Deacon, 1997; Tomasello, 2003). It also makes it important to pay attention to research on learning mechanisms involved in learning things other than language.

10.7   The Future

Where does this leave us? Much of this book has been concerned with behavioral results on learning in the lab, drawing on the experimental paradigms of miniature artificial language learning, causal learning, perceptual learning, distributional learning, and classical and instrumental conditioning. Ideally, experimental study of learning affords the linguist interested in explaining why languages are the way they are several opportunities.

First, it is often the case that historical and typological research can show that certain changes "go together," forming a recurrent pathway of change. Grammaticalization is a case in point: grammaticalizing morphemes undergo parallel changes in form, meaning, and syntactic autonomy, with changes in the opposite direction being rare or unattested (e.g., Bybee, 2003). Unfortunately, it is rarely the case that historical studies can establish causation: which of these changes, if any, cause others, and by what mechanism? Here, experimental studies are crucial because an artificial language affords us an opportunity to change it in specific ways and see if other changes follow when the language is learned and used by human learners.

For example, in chapter 6, we noted that historical linguists have found increases in frequency to correlate with semantic extension but disagree about the direction of causation and the mechanism behind the change. In particular, the notion that increases in frequency can *cause* semantic extension is highly controversial, and even those who agree that it can play a causal role disagree on whether the effect occurs due to habituation in perception or accessibility in production. By *manipulating* frequency, we saw that high frequency can indeed cause semantic extension. By testing participants on multiple tasks, we saw that frequency favors extension when the speaker tries to generate a form to express a meaning, and the alternative forms differ in accessibility. Thus, we showed that high frequency of a form favors semantic extension because the frequent form is more accessible than the less frequent form, and therefore more likely to be selected for production.

In my dissertation, I noticed that there seems to be a negative correlation between the likelihood of a suffix triggering a stem change and the likelihood of the suffix attaching to stems eligible to undergo the change. The suffixes that were best at palatalizing novel velar-final bases in Russian were the suffixes that tended to prefer attaching to velar-final bases. However, one could conceive of two reasons for this correlation. It could be that a suffix may fail to trigger an alternation *because* it often attaches to unchangeable bases (my favored hypothesis). Alternatively, speakers could really want to produce the alternation—for example, because the unaltered base is a bad cue to the meaning the speakers wants to express. They would then perhaps avoid attaching suffixes that are bad at triggering the alternation to bases that should undergo it. Experiments reported in chapter 8 (for details see Kapatsinski, 2009b, 2010b) establish the direction of causation. *Manipulating* the number of non-velar-final bases that bear a suffix that palatalizes velars changes the learners' willingness to palatalize velars. Therefore, suffixes that often attach to nonvelars are bad at palatalizing velars *because they often attach to nonvelars*. Since the statistics of an artificial language can be tightly controlled, I could devise two languages that were closely matched on everything except the potential cause of the differences in palatalization rates. For example, the number of examples of velar palatalization was the same regardless of how often the palatalizing suffix attached to nonvelars—in fact, they were the same examples. Whenever the suffix attached to a velar, the velar was always palatalized, and this happened the same number of times in both languages. The number of total training trials was also the same: when the palatalizing suffix rarely attached to nonvelar bases, its competitor suffix would attach to them. The palatalizing suffix was always the same, –*i*. The nonpalatalizing one was always –*a*. While Russian comes close, it appears well-nigh impossible to find two suffixes this closely matched in a natural language, preventing isolation of a specific causal factor.

There are also limitations to this method. In particular, the experience a learner has in the lab can never rival the experience they would have learning a natural language "in the wild." This limitation is not specific to artificial language experiments. For example, the experience an animal has learning to obtain food in the wild is vastly different from the experience it has learning to obtain food in a conditioning experiment. In both cases, the experimental paradigm is much simpler than the task faced by the learner in real life. A typical conditioning experiment has only a couple of cues, while the cues in the natural environment are legion. A miniature artificial language is far from a full-fledged language. The variety of learning experiences in the lab is also much smaller than the variety of behaviors an animal engages in while learning something naturally. For instance, some learning experiments involve only perceptual experience with language. Interestingly, Baese-Berk and Samuel (2016) show that learning new speech sound categories is harder if the learner is encouraged to repeat the sounds they experience during the experiment. Of course, in real life language learners engage in production as well as perception. What Baese-Berk and Samuel's results suggest, however, is that the limitations of the experimental situation may be a virtue for determining *what kinds of* experiences lead to specific changes in knowledge or behavior. In the same way, conditioning experiments have been undeniably informative about the kinds of experiences necessary to produce a behavioral change, such as overcoming drug addiction (Bouton, 2016). Control over the kinds of experiences a learner receives allows us to ask questions difficult to address by examining learning in the wild. For example, in chapter 7, we discussed a number of theories about how paradigmatic mappings are learned. Is experience with producing novel wordforms important, even essential (Taatgen & Anderson, 2002), or is perceptual learning enough (Ervin, 1961; Plunkett & Juola, 1999)? Manipulating availability of production practice, and whether this practice involves generating forms one has not memorized, would go a long way toward addressing the debate.

Trial-by-trial tests of knowledge using nonintrusive measurements of surprise like pupillometry and event-related potentials promise to enhance this enterprise by letting us examine both the precise timecourse of belief change and the importance of individual formative trials. For instance, how closely does surprise (e.g., as measured by pupil dilation) track log frequency (chapter 5)? Is it affected by distance of the sound from the center of the distribution, and if so which measure of central tendency is most predictive? Is it affected by distance from the sound just experienced? To the extent that learning is driven by surprise, as error-driven learning mechanisms lead us to expect, measuring surprise on a trial-by-trial basis in a way that does not interfere with learning is critically important.

The limited nature of laboratory linguistic experience does mean that caution is needed in extrapolating from the biases of laboratory learning to recurrent patterns in language change. First, the contingencies of miniature artificial languages may differ in crucial ways from those of natural languages. For example, the Zipfian frequency distributions universal to natural languages may be crucial to how broadly learners generalize from their learning experience (Goldberg et al., 2004; Madlener, 2016) but frequency distributions in miniature artificial languages are usually uniform. This may well encourage overgeneralization in miniature languages with many distinct forms and a low token/type ratio, and encourage undergeneralization in miniature languages with few forms and a high token/type ratio, with neither pattern reflecting the balance of generalization and lexically specific knowledge seen in natural languages. This, however, is more of a flaw of practice than a limitation of the methodology: the great strength of the miniature artificial language paradigm is precisely in endowing the linguist with the ability to manipulate the contingencies characterizing the language.

Second, we must keep in mind the limited amount of experience the learner has in the lab. For example, would more extensive experience with the subtraction languages of chapter 7 encourage all learners to converge on pure subtraction, or on a schema-based system with source forms flexibly adjusted to fit an inflexible prosodic template? Or would they converge on individual CVCVk and CVC wordforms without settling on either subtraction or addition?

The *kind* of experience learners receive may matter even more than the *amount* of experience. Even a short training can reveal the biases of the learning system as long as it is representative (e.g., Kalish et al., 2007). However, if crucial experiences are omitted from training, the biases of real-world learning may remain undiscovered. For example, if—unlike in laboratory experiments—paradigmatic mappings are usually learned "in the wild" from experience producing novel wordforms (Taatgen & Anderson, 2002), laboratory research to date may have underestimated the likelihood of a language developing and maintaining paradigmatic structure.

The way key experiences are distributed over time may be crucial. If some generalizations tend to be learned before others, one expects blocking and occasion setting. Furthermore, overnight integration of new hippocampal knowledge with long-term cortical associations (McClelland et al., 1995) may be important. Would overnight consolidation of memories result in a different pattern of behavior in the morning? Would some generalizations be particularly subject to decay? For instance, Peperkamp and Martin (2016) suggest that knowledge of vowel harmony does not diminish after the participants have had a good night's sleep, while knowledge of vowel disharmony—a less phonetically natural generalization—does. Perhaps the most likely explanation is that vowel harmony is consistent with long-term knowledge about coarticulation while disharmony is not.

As new knowledge is integrated with old knowledge during sleep, knowledge that is inconsistent with long-held beliefs is likely to suffer from interference: integration of new knowledge into the cortical system is likely to have a confirmation bias. This confirmation bias can alleviate the effects of salience of the unexpected seen in rapid learning (chapter 5), allowing the learner to maintain a stable system of long-held beliefs while rapidly adjusting to a changing world.

Finally, the goals learners have when learning language in the lab may differ from the goals they have in learning and using languages in real life. For example, Kirby et al. (2008) showed that, without a communicative motivation to keep forms with different meanings distinct, training participants on an artificial lexicon caused them to collapse all meanings onto a few forms, resulting in massive homonymy. Homonymy avoidance may also occur in natural languages because it results in a failure of communication. K. Smith et al. (2013) demonstrated that requiring learners to communicate with each other using an artificial language greatly increased the likelihood of regularization / synonymy avoidance. Similarly, when there is no need to transmit one's excitement or certainty to the listener, there is little motivation to augment forms that have been bleached through habituation.

These cautions are not to suggest that looking for learning biases driving change in language learning experiments is worthless. As we have seen throughout the book, this approach has been extremely fruitful in both evaluating hypotheses proposed within historical linguistics and generating new ones. Rather, as in other domains where experiments strip away the full glorious complexity of the system, care is needed in considering additional influences present outside of the experimental situation. Large-scale longitudinal multimodal databases are beginning to provide a great source of data on what the important influences might be (Roy et al., 2015; L. B. Smith et al., 2011). For example, L. B. Smith et al. (2011) collected a corpus of mother-child interactions with both interlocutors wearing cameras on their heads. Using this corpus, Pereira et al. (2014) show that whenever the parent labels an object for a child, the child is usually in the midst of looking at the object, affording the child an opportunity for bidirectional association formation. This fact must be taken into account in designing word learning experiments intended to mirror real-world word learning.

It is also worth considering ways of bridging the chasm between the lab and the outside world. One possible way forward is to systematically manipulate various contingencies in real-world language learning experiences. Madlener (2016) forged the path from laboratory experimentation to the second language classroom, investigating the effects of type frequency, token frequency, and the distribution of token frequency over types in teaching syntactic constructions to second language learners. However, there are limits to the applicability of this method. It is difficult to see how one could apply it in first language learning, and one of course would not want to change the contingencies of the language the learners are trying to acquire in a way that would systematically mislead them about the language's grammar. Therefore, we must also continue infusing laboratory experimentation with the characteristics and complexities of real-life language learning, particularly augmenting the learning experience with interactive, communicative tasks (Buz et al., 2016; K. Smith et al., 2013).

Aside from connecting lab learning to "real-world learning," we need to see more integration among different kinds of lab learning. For example, Wasserman et al. (2015) point out that the number of cue-outcome mappings learned in parallel during word learning is vastly larger than the number of cue-outcome mappings in a typical conditioning study, and they develop a conditioning paradigm that more closely approximates word learning in this respect. This allows them to be more confident in cross-species comparisons designed to investigate whether word learning requires specialized, species-specific learning mechanisms (it still doesn't). Apfelbaum and Sloutsky (2016), Kapatsinski et al. (2017), and Moreton et al. (2017) note parallels between visual category learning and phonological learning. Moreton et al. argue that phonotactic constraints can be seen as generalizations about what kinds of forms belong to language. Kapatsinski et al. argue that intonation contours can be seen as categories of pitch patterns associated with meanings. In both cases, there are clear parallels between results in visual category learning and phonological category learning when the same contingency structures are examined. In particular, perceptual learning in both domains is strongly constrained by selective attention, which favors categories defined by individual cues and disfavors categories defined by cue configurations (chapter 3).

Behavioral study of lab learning also needs to connect to the neural mechanisms of learning. This involves both looking for behavioral signatures of Hebbian learning, chunking, and error-driven learning and incorporating the methods of cognitive neuroscience. Neuroimaging can be used to examine areas of neural activity associated with specific outcomes of learning. Recent developments in statistical analysis of neuroimaging data give me hope that we can start examining the neural correlates of specific generalizations, such as particular schemas (Allen et al., 2012). For example, do participants who add [k] to a CVCV at test show the same kinds of neural changes over the course of training as participants who delete the final vowel? Are there neural assemblies used to carry out subtraction regardless of the resulting product? Are there others that light up whenever a CVCVk product is being constructed regardless of whether it is constructed by subtraction or addition? Do behavioral patterns suggesting bidirectional learning correspond to hippocampal activity while those suggesting predictive, directional error-driven learning correspond to activity in the basal ganglia (Ashby et al., 2007; Lim et al., 2014)? While there is important computational work suggesting they do, little empirical work on language learning is there to assess these predictions.

Neuroimaging should of course be complemented by studies of atypical populations, development, aging, and individual differences with known neural correlates, as well as studies of other animals whose brains can be examined with more invasive methods. A person's position on the autism spectrum correlates with breadth of generalization after exposure to a novel syntactic construction or a novel pronunciation of a sound (M. Johnson, 2013; Mielke et al., 2013). Individuals with amnesia appear to learn in a more Hebbian fashion than nonamnesiac individuals (McClelland, 2001). Maturation of the auditory cortex around age 12 (J. K. Moore, 2002) may be associated with changes in auditory category learning that occur around the same time. The slow development of frontal executive control areas may also change language learning—for example, by making attention more selective (Ramscar & Gitcho, 2007). At the same time, changes in learning abilities and biases that are associated with age, whether that of the growing child or the aging adult, can often be attributed to either maturation or learning—including learning to learn and changes in knowledge available to bootstrap and interfere with new learning (e.g., Ramscar et al., 2014). We must keep in mind that the brain is not a static structure. Learning itself changes the learning system.

Finally, we need better descriptions characterizing what is learned by a native speaker of a language and what there is to learn. It is important for description to proceed in a fairly objective fashion, allowing for discovery of generalizations that the analyst does not expect (W. Croft, 2001). Computational models that automatically extract rules, constraints, or schemas from linguistic data are an important tool in this regard (e.g., Albright & Hayes, 2003; Hayes & Wilson, 2008). While no such model is unbiased, the biases of a model are objectively identifiable, and its analysis is easily reproducible. Computational models are particularly useful for identifying probabilistic patterns and specific contexts in which a generalization does or does not hold. In many cases, a human analyst is in danger of coming up with a generalization that is broader than the generalizations that are actually most reliable given the data. For example, Albright and Hayes (2003) use their computational rule-extracting model to show that the classic "add –*ed* to form the past tense" rule of English is not equally productive with all verbs. In particular, verbs ending in voiceless fricatives are particularly likely to form the past tense using the regular suffix. The model picks up on this, extracting an "add –*ed* to voiceless fricatives" rule that is assigned a higher reliability than the more general "add –*ed*" rule.

Importantly, any generalizations one extracts from a corpus or a dictionary—whether by hand or with the help of a model—are merely tentative (Berko, 1958). A description needs to go beyond providing a concise summary of someone's words and utterances (Chomsky & Halle, 1965; cf. Chater et al., 2015, chap. 3; Householder, 1966). The generalizations reified in the grammar need to be tested for productivity to ensure that the learner does need to be held responsible for their acquisition. Just because a generalization is obvious to a linguist does not mean it is learned by all, most, or—indeed—any native speakers of the language (e.g., Becker et al., 2011; Dąbrowska, 2012; Kapatsinski, 2010b; Zimmer, 1969). Even explicitly teaching a rule does not guarantee that it will be internalized (Kapatsinski, 2010c). Thus the only reason Albright and Hayes's (2003) model should be commended for discovering the "add –*ed* to voiceless fricatives rule" is because English speakers seem to discover it too, being particularly wary of forming past tense forms using irregular schemas when faced with a form ending in a voiceless fricative. For a descriptive grammar to be seen as describing the knowledge that a learner of the language needs or is likely to acquire, that grammar needs to be psychologically real.

10.8 Conclusion

Language is hard and full of structure. It must be, to allow us to communicate an infinite set of ideas, some of which we have never expressed or even heard before. This incredible complexity has led generative linguists to posit stores of specialized knowledge about what languages are like ("Universal Grammar") and specialized learning mechanisms to take advantage of this innate knowledge. *Learning*, with its implication of domain generality, became a dirty word, replaced with *acquisition* and *development*.

More recently, learning has returned (Bates & Elman, 1996; Holt et al., 1998). Experimental studies of learning have shown remarkable, though importantly constrained, ability to rapidly soak up statistical regularities in the linguistic input—even in tiny infants (Maye et al., 2002; Saffran et al., 1996; Yu & L. B. Smith, 2007). At the same time, associationist theories based on conditioning paradigms and the characteristics of learning in simple neural systems have made significant progress in showing how much could be learned from limited data (e.g., Baayen et al., 2011; Holt et al., 1998; McMurray et al., 2012, 2013; Moreton et al., 2017).

Beginning in the 1980s, alongside the connectionist revolution in cognitive science, functional and cognitive linguists developed constructionist theories of adult grammatical knowledge whose acquisition does not require Universal Grammar (Bybee, 1985; W. Croft, 2001; Fillmore et al., 1988; Goldberg, 1995, 2006). These theories drew on increasing awareness of the fact that a grammar of any language cannot be described by a small set of innate principles and parameters, and that the search for arbitrary synchronic universals has not been fruitful (Blevins, 2004; Bybee, 2001; W. Croft, 2001; Evans & Levinson, 2009). When knowledge of language is reduced largely to knowledge of form–meaning mappings, and most of these mappings are specific to particular languages, little is to be gained by positing that a few of these mappings are innately known to exist. To the extent that synchronic universals are found, they are rather straightforwardly explained by the uses to which every language is put, the universal dynamics of language learning and processing, and the fact that any act of production involves planning and executing an intricate sequence of muscle movements.

Historical linguists have shown language change to be incompatible with a parametric view of language as well; and that changes usually diffuse through the language gradually, construction by construction, instead of the language undergoing massive restructuring as a parameter is switched (e.g., Bybee, 2001). The very notion of the grammar as distinct from the lexicon has fallen out of favor, as it has become clear that lexical constructions grow more and more "grammatical" through a gradual process of grammaticalization (Bybee, 2003; Bybee et al., 1994). While the search for synchronic universals foundered, a veritable bounty of diachronic universals—recurrent paths of change—has been discovered (e.g., Bybee, 2001; Bybee et al., 1994). The field has therefore shifted from explaining why all languages have certain properties to why they change in predictable directions. To this new question, the theory that languages are different settings of a fixed collection of innate switches offered no solution.

Instead, usage-based linguists—lately joined by computational modelers with an interest in cultural evolution (e.g., Christiansen & Chater, 2016; Kirby et al., 2008)—have come to see recurrent paths of change as arising from constant pressures inherent in the mechanisms of language processing and language learning. For example, most sound change could be seen as the inevitable result of motion sequences becoming more streamlined with repeated execution. Semantic extension of frequently used words—the very basis of grammaticalization—is an inevitable outcome of associating forms with compositional meanings and the difficulties inherent in selecting one of myriad known forms to express an intended meaning under time pressure. Languages change in predictable directions across societies and language families because we all use and learn language in essentially the same ways. Being human, we are all equipped with similar machinery for basic associative learning and motor performance, wherever we grow up.

The main aim of the present book has been to provide theoretical linguists with a deeper understanding of this machinery. Another aim has been to show how experimental and computational research on learning and processing, a constructionist understanding of language structure, and a usage-based approach to language change fit together in explaining why languages are the way they are. The concepts and models of learning theory, of computational cognitive neuroscience, of Bayesian inference, of constructionist approaches to grammar, of grammaticalization theory, of usage-based linguistics, and of cultural evolution all fit together, and all drive toward the same conclusion. The remarkable diversity of language should not make us despair of finding what all languages share. It is just that what they share—and what makes us human—is not innate knowledge but rather innate capacities to learn and to act, to predict and to remember, capacities that are both powerful and powerfully constrained. Do simple associative models suffice to characterize these capacities? The tools of neuroscience, psychology, and linguistics are a powerful arsenal to either shoot this hypothesis down or to help confirm it. Whatever the outcome, it should be interesting. Keep in touch.

Notes

Chapter 1

1. In linguistic theory, blocking (also known as statistical pre-emption; Goldberg, 1995) refers to an interaction between two rules or linguistic structures differing in the breadth of contexts in which they are used. For example, *went* is used only to express the past tense of *go*, while *-ed* can be used to express the past tense of any verb (*walked*, *clapped*). If an English speaker is told to form the past tense of a novel verb like *to wug*, they usually form it by adding *-ed* (e.g. Albright & Hayes, 2003; Berko, 1958; O'Donnell, 2015; Pinker, 1999). Nonetheless, *-ed* is not used to form the past tense of *go*, and so is said to be blocked by *went*. This sense of blocking is different from associative blocking because the blocked form need not co-occur with the blocker to be blocked. Instead, statistical pre-emption closely resembles associative interference (see Miller & Escobar, 2002). First, the pre-emptor is usually more frequent and learned earlier than the pre-empted form. Infrequent forms are inferior blockers, and are likely to be regularized, falling prey to *-ed* instead of blocking it (Bybee, 1985, 2001). Second, the pre-emptor is also usually more context-specific and is therefore associated with a greater number of cues present in the pre-emption context: *went* can block the *-ed* in the context of going because it is associated with both the meaning of past and the meaning of locomotion.

2. In addition, Mackintosh and colleagues (e.g., Mackintosh, 1975) have proposed that AB→X trials teach participants not to attend to B because it makes no difference in the outcome. In support of this hypothesis, Mackintosh and Turner (1971) and Kruschke and Blair (2000) report that B is harder to associate with outcomes other than X following AB→X training, again suggesting that something *is* learned about B during AB→X trials. See chapter 3 on *associability*.

3. This is clearly not all the hippocampus does: there appear to be complementary learning systems even inside the hippocampus itself (Schapiro et al., 2017). However, it may be one thing that it does (via the trisynaptic pathway). Learning in the other pathway looks much more like striatal learning.

4. Ramscar et al. (2013) report that this result does not hold for adults, but it may be that adults' attention wanes more slowly and that adults too would demonstrate this effect with extended training.

5. The ability to associate cues from the visual and auditory modalities, which enables the use of visual cues to perceive speech (e.g., McGurk & MacDonald, 1976), is a pleasant side effect.

Chapter 2

1. Christian and Griffiths (2016, pp. 303–305), following Thompson (1933), argue that maximizing on a single trial and probability matching on multiple trials is optimal in solving the explore/exploit dilemma (provided that mistakes are not deadly).

2. Nickerson (2002, p. 248) argues that people are poor at generating truly random response sequences "not because they have poor memories but simply because they have memories. The way to produce a truly random sequence is to completely forget each item that is produced, as soon as it is produced. But people cannot do that." Similarly, the way to avoid producing a locally representative response sequence or to match probabilities in general is to not remember what one has produced.

Another possibility is that children do not expect the test to be as long as the adults do, which would make it rational for children to maximize and for adults to probability match.

3. This prediction is also made by Ramscar and Gitcho's (2007) proposal that probability matching requires effortful and distraction-prone cognitive control.

4. In addition, when the learner is *taught* two responses, they often assume there is some reason to produce both (Perfors, 2016). However, in real language use, the form a speaker prefers to use usually becomes the form they think is best: a form we choose often for a particular function becomes the *right* form to express that function. Even if we are aware of alternatives, we may discount them as inferior or erroneous: by the time we are adults, we are in control of our language variety.

5. To those familiar with my previous work, the architecture is retained from Local Activation Spread Theory (LAST, Kapatsinski, 2005b; Snider, 2008). I remain committed to the notion that associations are formed between categories, and that the category-category connection network is best seen as fully connected in its initial state. However, whereas LAST assumed exemplar-based categorization, this assumption is dropped here in favor of a more elemental, cue-based approach (see chapter 5).

6. This is part of the reason preparedness (Seligman, 1970) is no challenge to associative learning. Even if all associations we can ever form are present innately, the

task of pruning them requires a lot of learning and is the main task associative learning is designed to accomplish.

7. This should not be too surprising to a linguist, given the important role lexical fields have played in structuralist and, more recently, cognitive semantics (Trier, 1934, et seq.; see also Clark, 1987, p. 11).

8. We could also call them *constructions*, in the sense of usage-based Construction Grammar (Goldberg, 2006; see also Bryan & Harter, 1899, p. 366). However, the term *construction* unfortunately suggests that the form is *constructed* online, as in "constructivist" theories of morphology. I prefer *schema* to connect the term to motor schemas (e.g., Broadbent, 1958, p. 65): "Schemas are ... instances of partial preservation of information from sequences." Foreshadowing current debates, Broadbent notes that schemas can be extracted from both perceptual and production experience and suggests that production schemas are more stable and less malleable by recent experience. He also introduces the term *schematic behavior* to refer to behavior that can be described by, and suggests, the existence of schemas.

9. Bryan and Harter (1899, p. 366) write: "A grammatical construction often used to express a certain feeling (or plurality, futurity, doubt or the like) comes to be automatically associated with that feeling, apart from any particular sentence, so that either instantly and effortlessly suggests the other, to serve as one of many elements in the reading or making of a new sentence." Further, "the dissociation of language elements from the specific wholes in which they have occurred, and their use in the construction or understanding of new sentences, are ... perhaps the most remarkable task of which men are capable" (p. 365).

10. There are schemas that do not seem to have a slot but yet are not filled, particularly *phonaesthemes* like [gl...]_Word ~ LIGHT exemplified by *glow, glisten, glint*, etc. However, these schemas can still be viewed as form categories linked to meaning categories. Despite appearances, we can think of this kind of schema as *being* an open form slot that specifies that the form must begin with /gl/, a classical category defined by the presence of a set of necessary features.

11. Speakers do often imperfectly recall forms in a way that looks like response generalization. For example, in Harmon & Kapatsinski (2017), we reported an experiment that involved participants learning a language with the suffixes *-dan, -nem, -shoon*, and *-sil* (see chapter 6). Several of our participants consistently used *-dem* for the suffix *-nem* or *-soon* for *-shoon*, despite repeating forms correctly during training. However, this likely represents memory interference rather than response generalization—that is, it is unlikely that someone *knowingly* uses *-dem* for *-nem* because she thinks the choice of the initial consonant does not matter.

Chapter 3

1. Some support for fusion of co-occurring units is also provided by Graf Estes et al. (2007) and J. F. Hay et al. (2011), who exposed infants to a nonsense stream of syllables in which some syllables reliably co-occurred (à la Saffran et al., 1996). Then the experimenters paired either statistically cohesive or noncohesive sequences with meanings. They found that the former were easier to associate with meanings than the latter. However, the form-meaning training did not involve configural patterns. Therefore, it is possible to explain the results by the hypothesis that *parts* of the cohesive sequences were easier to associate with meanings than parts of the noncohesive sequences. In particular, the initial syllable of a cohesive sequence might be easier to associate with a meaning than the initial syllable of a noncohesive sequence because the former occurred (relatively unexpectedly) after low-probability transitions and would therefore draw attention, whereas the latter never occurred unexpectedly and may therefore be expected to have lost associability.

2. Though in languages that have words of fairly equal length, like Mandarin (where they are either mono- or disyllabic), this is much less of an issue.

3. Crossover interactions may also be difficult to maintain in production: witness the example of the English possessive, which is spelled *'s* in most places, in contrast to the plural *-s*, which is spelled closed (*my cat's claws are sharp* but *my cats claw me often*). However, after *it*, the possessive is spelled closed *(its claws are sharp)*. It is reasonable to suggest that the possessive meaning usually inhibits the more common closed spelling as well as activating the apostrophe. However, after *it*, the reverse pattern of activation is required (inhibit *'s*; activate the closed spelling), a crossover interaction. As a result, spelling mistakes abound in this context even after years and years of experience.

4. If VOT and F0 are both cues to voicing, the predictions depend on whether voicing can be dissociated from VOT, the primary cue—in other words, on whether a *beer/pier* contrast cued primarily by F0 is still cued by [voice]. Escudero and Boersma (2004) suggest that the primary cue is learned first, as a cue to the phonological contrast, and secondary cues are learned later as cues to the primary cue. For them, therefore, [voice] *is* VOT for an English speaker.

5. One interesting difference from classic occasion-setting experiments is that in this case the occasion setter itself is not at all predictive of voicing: it is unlikely that people tend to refer to bears and beers when they talk slowly and to pears and piers when they talk fast. However, this makes it only more likely that mediation should occur: the input provides no evidence for a direct rate-voicing relationship.

6. Hullinger et al. (2015) argue that environmental patterns that call for occasion-setting is in fact crucial for the evolution of selective attention in biological

organisms. Hullinger et al. allow natural selection to tinker with learning algorithms of simulated learners, so that learners that fail to learn, or learn too slowly to adapt to a changing world face extinction. They then vary the environmental contingencies of the simulated environment and test whether the organisms that evolve in this environment display the tell-tale behavioral signs of selective attention (the highlighting effect). The learners have no processing limitations, and are in principle able to pay attention to everything at once. Under these assumptions, selective attention emerges only in environments where environmental contingencies can change and where this change can be detected based on a specific occasion-setter. In such environments, learning to switch attention based on a cue really pays off, despite the non-normative behaviors that result from it.

Chapter 4

1. Stahl and Feigenson (2017) have recently found that children exhibit better word learning for words that refer to objects that have just violated the child's expectations (e.g., an object that seemed solid but passed through walls). They argue that this result indicates that surprise increases willingness to learn and does so only for the surprising object. However, these results can be explained as surprise increasing the object's salience and do not require updating confidence values of specific associations.

2. The same effect can be seen within individuals: the *fan effect* refers to the finding that the more you know about something, the harder it is to retrieve any single individual fact about it, especially if these facts are unrelated to each other (Anderson, 1974; Anderson & Reder, 1999; E. Smith et al., 1978). The fan effect can also be seen with priming: the more associations a prime has, the less it is able to prime any one of its associates (Thomsen et al., 1996; Perea & Rosa, 2000). Furthermore, the stronger the competing associations, the less priming there is (Anaki & Henik, 2003). Assuming that priming is learning examined closely (F. Chang et al., 2000; Kapatsinski, 2005b), these findings suggest that paired associate learning would also be harder for words that already have many strong associations (Kapatsinski, 2005b), a prediction that (as far as I know) remains untested within subjects.

3. Christian and Griffiths (2016, pp. 55–58) note that entrenchment in old age also maximizes rewards: the older you are, the less you can benefit from exploration— exploring can pay off only if you have time to exploit the knowledge you gain from it afterward. Conversely, the older you are, the better your knowledge of the opportunities the world affords, the consequences of alternative decisions, and your own likes and dislikes. Therefore, the older you are, the more likely the actions you entrench on are to be the best actions for you to take.

4. Kruschke (2006) models learning as a system of two Bayesian learners, where the first learns what cues to attend to, while the second learns how the attended cues

map onto outputs. While the proposed model succeeds in capturing many effects of selective attention, it is not an ideal learner of the cue-outcome mappings. An ideal learner would avoid being "trapped" by its selective attention into not attending to potentially informative cues. While it consists of Bayesian learners, the full model is therefore not itself *globally* Bayesian.

5. This distinguishes highlighting with the canonical design from the *inverse base rate effect* (IBRE, Gluck & Bower, 1988; Shanks, 1992). In IBRE, I.PE→E and I.PL→L trials are intermixed in one stage but I.PE→E trials are more frequent than I.PL→L. As in canonical highlighting, participants choose L when cued with PE.PL despite the lower base rate (and so prior probability) of L. Kruschke (1996, 2006) argues that the IBRE arises because participants learn about the cues to the frequent L before they learn about the cues to the rare E. Thus, under this account, IBRE is a special case of highlighting.

6. This example raises a general issue with generative models: it is not clear how the learner intuits the generative process, and why they would need to do so to generate the desired behavior. In other words, why should the learner aim to generate the behavior they wish to produce *in the same way*? Why should they try to determine whether to compute or retrieve any given word instead of trying to do both in parallel and letting the faster route win? Furthermore, if one does remember words one hears (an uncontroversial assumption), how does one prevent oneself from retrieving them from memory if one has decided other people produce them using the grammar?

7. See also Perlman et al. (2012) and L. Yang and Wu (2014) for failures to replicate the category variability effect.

Chapter 5

1. The sample in figure 5.5 is the set of adjectives with the prefix *bez-* '-less' in Russian studied in Kapatsinski (2010c). The most frequent adjective is literally *priceless*, which means "free."

2. Some degree of extrapolation also comes for free, from being unable to distinguish between old stimuli and similar new stimuli: if a new stimulus is similar to an old one, and one's memory of the old stimulus is imperfect or tolerantly underspecified, the new stimulus will be treated like the familiar old one.

3. It is uncontroversial that continued exposure, like continuing practice with a skill, yields diminishing returns, which makes processing ease a decelerating function of frequency. What is still a matter of debate is how sharply decelerating the function is. For example, Keuleers et al. (2015) suggest that the logarithmic function underestimates the degree of deceleration. For our purposes, the magnitude of deceleration predicted by the logarithmic function is sufficient.

Chapter 6

1. The project reported in this chapter has been led by my graduate student Zara Harmon. For a full description of the experiments summarized here, see Harmon & Kapatsinski (2017).

2. Check out your own knowledge at http://vocabulary.ugent.be/ to join the hundreds of thousands of English speakers who have already participated in their study!

3. In this, Bybee and Haiman follow Schuchardt (1885/1972, p. 27), who likewise proposes that repetition can by itself lead to semantic bleaching: "If I say *g'Morgen* for *guten Morgen*, the adjective is deprived almost completely of its meaning, but only in consequence of the incessant repetitions."

4. One might question habituation as a possible mechanism for bleaching because habituation rapidly diminishes with delays between the repeated presentations (R. Thompson & Spencer, 1966), while—except perhaps for the most frequent forms, like *the*—a grammaticalizing form is typically not repeated in rapid succession. A plausible alternative is the CS-preexposure effect. However, unlike habituation it is highly context-specific (Hall & Channell, 1985; Hall & Honey, 1989), and therefore may not be expected to lead to bleaching of a form across contexts.

5. Unsurprisingly, frequency also favored the frequent suffix being selected to express the meaning with which it was paired in training: *-dan* was favored over *-sil* to express PL in the Dan language, while *-nem* was favored over *-shoon* to express DIM in the Nem language.

6. Note that the lack of preference for the frequent form was not due simply to performance in this task being more random than performance in production: participants were accurately choosing *-dan* to refer to the nondiminutive plural and *-nem* to refer to the diminutive singular.

7. Restricting analysis to only *-dan* and *-nem* allowed us to control for any preferences for particular meanings or forms participants may have.

Chapter 7

1. I have phrased this difference here in terms of retrieval vs. computation, but constructionist approaches to language suggest that there is no qualitative difference between the two (Bates & Goodman, 1997; Bybee, 1985; Goldberg, 1995; Langacker, 1987). From that perspective, one could also say that filling out of a frequent lexical schema is so automatized as to always complete before more general schemas can manage to impose their demands; perhaps, because the lexical schema is more specific and therefore consistent with a greater number of semantic cues comprising the meaning the speaker intends to express.

2. The term *schematic behavior* was first proposed by Broadbent (1958, p. 65) to refer to behavior that suggests the use of a schema.

3. This parallels the previous finding, described and modeled in detail in chapter 8, that [tʃ]~[tʃi] examples favor [t]~[tʃi] over [t]~[ti] (Kapatsinski, 2009b, 2013).

4. This is also the pattern of data in judgment data, where the participant must necessarily judge both the template and the filling (Kapatsinski, 2017).

5. It is not, of course, literal copying—one does not take a part of the brain representing a pattern and move it elsewhere. Nonetheless, the term *copying* gives an intuitive sense of the process.

6. This notion of copying is closely related to the base identity constraints of Benua (1997) and Kenstowicz (1996), and arguments in favor of such constraints can be used to support copying as well. In particular, like base identity, copying predicts that the crosslinguistic tendency to preserve the stem is really a tendency to preserve the whole base form (see also Inkelas, 2015, pp. 29, 247–250).

Chapter 8

1. Sometimes—perhaps usually—multiple sources compete for influencing the product. The effects of this competition can be seen, for instance, when the product is driven by how the majority of other forms of the same word behave (McCarthy, 2005). There would need to be a separate copy outcome for each position of each source form, as long as copying from that position has been experienced (i.e., the source form was activated in the course of perceiving or generating the product form).

2. If $Copy_{Fin}$ is never obeyed, it will be absent from the set of outcomes and so will never be obeyed in any environment.

3. By separating the position-specific faithfulness constraint from its conditioning environment, the present approach is more flexible than positional faithfulness constraints, which are specific to both a particular position and a particular input feature (Beckman, 1999). Thus, the activation of a copy outcome may vary across morphological environments and generalize across input segments, allowing the model to learn generalizations like "the initial syllable should be preserved" (Becker et al., 2012) or "don't retain the final /z/ of a plural form when deriving a singular." This appears crucial for implementing *morpho*phonology, where changes affect only segments in specific positions and specific semantic contexts (such as PLURAL or SINGULAR).

4. Note that it is the difficulty of choosing rather than the goodness of the produced outcome that drives avoidance under this account: "phew, that was hard," not "ew,

that was bad," since [ka] is rated as being no better than [ki] (Kapatsinski, 2009b, p. 79; see also Albright, 2003; cf. Martin, 2007).

5. This comparison also underscores the fact that the problem cannot be solved by assuming that the model maximizes accuracy in choosing the output, always picking the most activated outcome from the set of competitors. While this would eliminate tʃ→t, it would also eliminate t→tʃ as well as preventing the model from matching the probabilities of -i vs. -a after {p;t}.

6. Without copy outcomes, the entropy of the suffix choice for a source [tʃ] is 0.65 bits in table 8.4a, while the entropy of the final consonant choice is 1 bit. If Copy outcomes are indeed independent outcomes (i.e., copying is a choice distinct from applying an arbitrary source-product mapping that results in the same product), they do not greatly reduce the uncertainty of the final consonant choice for a [tʃ]-final input: entropy of the final consonant choice reduces to only 0.86 bits. Thus, the relative uncertainty of consonant choice compared to final vowel choice is a viable explanation for why the suffix would be chosen first, with or without copy outcomes.

7. The benefits are entirely parallel to those of estimating the w parameter to gauge the magnitude and direction of the belief updating bias of a learner over a ternary decision between confirmation bias, disconfirmation bias, and normative inference (see also Kruschke, 2015, chap. 10, for the benefits of parameter estimation over model comparison more generally).

Chapter 9

1. Existence of word-medial *interruption* can be captured by top-down inhibitory links to propagation filters and/or to nodes representing the content of the sequence. Alternatively, top-down inhibition (and top-down excitation of "that felt good, do it again" kind) may not be link-based at all, instead flooding all parts of the sequencing network directly. As the relevant neural mechanisms are largely based on release of neurotransmitters, this is a rather attractive alternative.

2. This stop is usually [t] rather than [d] because the vocal folds have also been prematurely pulled apart in anticipation of the voiceless [s]. Since English, like most languages, has no contrast between voiced and voiceless nasals, there is no cost to stopping vocal-fold vibration early in this case, which may make premature glottis opening more frequent than premature velum closing. Thus, [t] and not [d] is the usual outcome.

3. Stressed segments are a special case of segments one should not reduce, for many different reasons: the increased duration and loudness associated with stress inherently draw attention; stress and prosodic prominence more generally are cued by the less expected and therefore more salient pitch values (Kakouros & Räsänen,

2016); increased duration also makes it easier to reach a distant articulatory target in time (Lindblom, 1963); and listeners learn to pay attention to stressed segments because the lack of reduction in stressed syllables makes stress a cue to informative locations in the signal. Thus, de Jong (1995) calls stress "conventionalized hyperarticulation" and Aylett and Turk (2004) consider prosody to mediate the effects of informativity on reduction. However, the effects of predictability in recent studies cannot in general be reduced to the effects of stress or even prosodic prominence.

4. In her popular textbook on language acquisition, Hoff (2013, p. 130) states that "the behaviorist account of phonological development ... ignores the evidence that it is not sheer frequency of sounds, but less obvious factors such as functional load and phonotactic probability that influence sound production." I contend that not only are functional load effects compatible with behaviorism, they are difficult to explain without that workhorse of behaviorism, instrumental conditioning.

5. Buz et al. (2016) find that the effect on the right edge is not significantly different from zero; however, they excluded "highly hyperarticulated" articulations with very long VOTs and participants that tended to produce them from analysis (p. 6).

6. Increasing duration and/or loudness and inserting pauses usually help with misperceptions as well as making it easier to reach the more extreme and less practiced articulatory targets of clear speech. It is therefore not an accident that this is what speakers tend to do, even when it is unhelpful in a particular situation.

7. Imitating sounds appears to be self-reinforcing in humans. The strongest evidence for an innate propensity to imitate is provided by Mampe et al. (2009), who documented that the first cry of a newborn raised in a German-speaking environment differs from that of a newborn raised in a French-speaking environment, in a way that reflects the differences in prosody between the two languages. While there is reason for fetuses to pay attention to speech signals—these are perhaps the best signals for what will happen to their environment next—there is no particular reinforcement for learning to reproduce these signals prior to birth (cf. Oudeyer & L. B. Smith, 2016).

8. These differences are in part due to innate differences in the physiology of the vocal tract and the motor control system, and in part due to individual differences in learning history. Linguistic experience changes the inherent difficulty of a sound by forcing speakers to adapt to their linguistic environment. Nonetheless, the experience-independent component of articulatory difficulty appears to be strong enough for there to be recurrent pathways of articulatorily motivated sound change.

9. Consonantal differences are much more socially marked in syllable-timed Spanish, where even stressed vowels are relatively short.

10. The unidirectionality of consonantal change suggests that articulation was less streamlined in the past than it is today. Part of the explanation may lie in the fact

that streamlining of articulation is especially important for rapid speech. It appears likely that speech rates have been increasing over historical time. The increases in speech rate could then drive increased streamlining of articulation. This hypothesis is of course extremely speculative as speech rate does not show up in historical records, but it is at least somewhat plausible given the present-day existence of dialectal variations in speech rate (Kendall, 2013) and the apparent—but poorly documented—correlation between speech rate and community size / urbanization (Hewlett & Rendall, 1998).

11. These results closely parallel Ramscar et al.'s (2014) argument that paired associate learning of novel word-word associations like *cat-eagle* is harder for older adults because older speakers have learned that these words do not co-occur. The word-word association weights of older speakers are built on a lifetime of experience and not easily shifted by a short laboratory training.

12. However, an *expert* dart thrower is likely to miss only once, because they should be expert at adjusting for the dart flying off course due to not being perfectly symmetrical.

Chapter 10

1. A few seem safe. In all languages, there is schematic structure. All languages feature Zipfian frequency distributions. Acceptability tracks log frequency rather than raw frequency. Category structure is universally gradient. However, these surviving universals are extremely general, to the extent that they are not really universals of *language,* and are consequently rather few in number.

References

Ackerman, F., Blevins, J. P., & Malouf, R. (2009). Parts and wholes: Implicative patterns in inflectional paradigms. In J. P. Blevins & J. Blevins (Eds.), *Analogy in grammar: Form and acquisition* (pp. 54–82). Oxford: Oxford University Press.

Albright, A. (2009). Lexical and morphological conditioning of paradigm gaps. In C. Rice & S. Blaho (Eds.), *Modeling ungrammaticality in Optimality Theory* (pp. 117–164). London: Equinox Press.

Albright, A. (2003). A quantitative study of Spanish paradigm gaps. In *Proceedings of the 22nd West Coast Conference on Formal Linguistics*, 1–14.

Albright, A., & Hayes, B. (2006). Modeling productivity with the gradual learning algorithm: The problem of accidentally exceptionless generalizations. In G. Fanselow (Ed.), *Gradience in grammar: Generative perspectives* (pp. 185–204). Oxford: Oxford University Press.

Albright, A., & Hayes, B. (2003). Rules vs. analogy in English past tenses: A computational/experimental study. *Cognition, 90*(2), 119–161.

Allen, K., Pereira, F., Botvinick, M., & Goldberg, A. E. (2012). Distinguishing grammatical constructions with fMRI pattern analysis. *Brain and Language, 123*(3), 174–182.

Allopenna, P. D., Magnuson, J. S., & Tanenhaus, M. K. (1998). Tracking the time course of spoken word recognition using eye movements: Evidence for continuous mapping models. *Journal of Memory and Language, 38*(4), 419–439.

Altmann, G., & Mirković, J. (2009). Incrementality and prediction in human sentence processing. *Cognitive Science, 33*(4), 583–609.

Ambridge, B., & Lieven, E. V. (2011). *Child language acquisition: Contrasting theoretical approaches*. Cambridge: Cambridge University Press.

Ambridge, B., Pine, J. M., Rowland, C. F., & Young, C. R. (2008). The effect of verb semantic class and verb frequency (entrenchment) on children's and adults' graded judgements of argument-structure overgeneralization errors. *Cognition, 106*(1), 87–129.

Anaki, D., & Henik, A. (2003). Is there a "strength effect" in automatic semantic priming? *Memory & Cognition, 31*(2), 262–272.

Anderson, J. R. (1991). The adaptive nature of human categorization. *Psychological Review, 98*(3), 409–429.

Anderson, J. R. (1986). Knowledge compilation: The general learning mechanism. In R. S. Michalski, J. G. Carbonell, & T. M. Mitchell (Eds.), *Machine learning: An artificial intelligence approach* (Vol. 2, pp. 289–310). Palo Alto, CA: Morgan Kaufmann.

Anderson, J. R. (1982). Acquisition of cognitive skill. *Psychological Review, 89,* 369–406.

Anderson, J. R. (1974). Retrieval of propositional information from long-term memory. *Cognitive Psychology, 6*(4), 451–474.

Anderson, J. R., & Reder, L. M. (1999). The fan effect: New results and new theories. *Journal of Experimental Psychology: General, 128*(2), 186–197.

Apfelbaum, K. S., & Sloutsky, V. (2016). Allocation of attention during auditory word learning. *Proceedings of the Annual Conference of the Cognitive Science Society, 38,* 2195–2200.

Arcediano, F., Escobar, M., & Miller, R. R. (2005). Bidirectional associations in humans and rats. *Journal of Experimental Psychology: Animal Behavior Processes, 31*(3), 301–318.

Arcediano, F., Escobar, M., & Miller, R. R. (2003). Temporal integration and temporal backward associations in human and nonhuman subjects. *Animal Learning & Behavior, 31*(3), 242–256.

Arnon, I., & Ramscar, M. (2012). Granularity and the acquisition of grammatical gender: How order-of-acquisition affects what gets learned. *Cognition, 122*(3), 292–305.

Arnon, I., & Snider, N. (2010). More than words: Frequency effects for multi-word phrases. *Journal of Memory and Language, 62*(1), 67–82.

Aronoff, M. (1976). *Word formation in generative grammar.* Cambridge, MA: MIT Press.

Arppe, A., Hendrix, P., Milin, P., Baayen, R. H., & Shaoul, C. (2014). ndl: Naive Discriminative Learning. R package version 0.2.16. http://CRAN.R-project.org/package=ndl.

Asch, S. E., & Ebenholtz, S. M. (1962). The principle of associative symmetry. *Proceedings of the American Philosophical Society, 106*(2), 135–163.

Ashby, F. G., Ennis, J. M., & Spiering, B. J. (2007). A neurobiological theory of automaticity in perceptual categorization. *Psychological Review, 114,* 632–656.

Ashby, F. G., & Waldron, E. M. (1999). On the nature of implicit categorization. *Psychonomic Bulletin & Review, 6*(3), 363–378.

Aslin, R. N., Saffran, J. R., & Newport, E. L. (1998). Computation of conditional probability statistics by 8-month-old infants. *Psychological Science, 9*(4), 321–324.

Astheimer, L. B., & Sanders, L. D. (2009). Listeners modulate temporally selective attention during natural speech processing. *Biological Psychology, 80*(1), 23–34.

Aston-Jones, G., & Cohen, J. D. (2005). An integrative theory of locus coeruleus-norepinephrine function: Adaptive gain and optimal performance. *Annual Review of Neuroscience, 28,* 403–450.

Atkinson, R. C., & Estes, W. K. (1962). *Stimulus sampling theory* (Technical Report No. 48). Stanford, CA: Institute for Mathematical Studies in the Social Sciences, Applied Mathematics and Statistics Laboratories, Stanford University.

Avillac, M., Hamed, S. B., & Duhamel, J. R. (2007). Multisensory integration in the ventral intraparietal area of the macaque monkey. *Journal of Neuroscience, 27*(8), 1922–1932.

Aylett, M., & Turk, A. (2004). The smooth signal redundancy hypothesis: A functional explanation for relationships between redundancy, prosodic prominence, and duration in spontaneous speech. *Language and Speech, 47*(1), 31–56.

Azab, H., Ruskin, D., & Kidd, C. (2016). Adults' guesses on probabilistic tasks reveal incremental representativeness biases. *Proceedings of the Annual Conference of the Cognitive Science Society, 38,* 2831–2836.

Baayen, R. H. (2001). *Word frequency distributions.* Dordrecht: Springer.

Baayen, R. H., Dijkstra, T., & Schreuder, R. (1997). Singulars and plurals in Dutch: Evidence for a parallel dual-route model. *Journal of Memory and Language, 37*(1), 94–117.

Baayen, R. H., Hendrix, P., & Ramscar, M. (2013). Sidestepping the combinatorial explosion: An explanation of *n*-gram frequency effects based on naive discriminative learning. *Language and Speech, 56*(3), 329–347.

Baayen, R. H., Milin, P., Đurđević, D. F., Hendrix, P., & Marelli, M. (2011). An amorphous model for morphological processing in visual comprehension based on naive discriminative learning. *Psychological Review, 118*(3), 438–481.

Baayen, R. H., Tomaschek, F., Gahl, S., & Ramscar, M. (2017). The Ecclesiastes principle in language change. In M. Hundt, S. Mollin & S. E. Pfenninger (Eds.), *The changing English language: Psycholinguistic perspectives* (pp. 21–48). Cambridge: Cambridge University Press.

Bach, E., & Harms, R. T. (1972). *How do languages get crazy rules?* Bloomington: Indiana University Linguistics Club.

Bacon, F. (1620/1939). Novum organum. In E. A. Burtt (Ed.), *The English philosophers from Bacon to Mill* (pp. 24–123). New York: Random House.

Baese-Berk, M., & Goldrick, M. (2009). Mechanisms of interaction in speech production. *Language and Cognitive Processes, 24*(4), 527–554.

Baese-Berk, M., & Samuel, A. G. (2016). Listeners beware: Speech production may be bad for learning speech sounds. *Journal of Memory and Language, 89*(1), 23–36.

Baker, A., Mielke, J., & Archangeli, D. (2008). More velar than /g/: Consonant coarticulation as a cause of diphthongization. In C. B. Chang and H. J. Haynie (Eds.), *Proceedings of the 26th West Coast Conference on Formal Linguistics*, 60–68. Somerville, MA: Cascadilla Proceedings Project.

Baldwin, D. (2016). Riding the wave: Characterizing fluency in event processing. UO Linguistics Colloquium.

Barnet, R. C., Cole, R. P., & Miller, R. R. (1997). Temporal integration in second-order conditioning and sensory preconditioning. *Animal Learning & Behavior, 25*(2), 221–233.

Baroni, M., Matiasek, J., & Trost, H. (2002). Unsupervised discovery of morphologically related words based on orthographic and semantic similarity. In *Proceedings of the Workshop on Morphological and Phonological Learning of ACL/SIGPHON-2002*, 48–57, Philadelphia. Association for Computational Linguistics.

Barr, R., Vieira, A., & Rovee-Collier, C. (2002). Bidirectional priming in infants. *Memory & Cognition, 30*(2), 246–255.

Bateman, N. (2007). *A crosslinguistic investigation of palatalization* (doctoral dissertation, UCSD).

Bates, E., & Elman, J. (1996). Learning rediscovered. *Science, 274*(5294), 1849.

Bates, E., & Goodman, J. C. (1997). On the inseparability of grammar and the lexicon: Evidence from acquisition, aphasia and real-time processing. *Language & Cognitive Processes, 12*(5–6), 507–584.

Bates, E., & MacWhinney, B. (1989). Functionalism and the Competition Model. In B. MacWhinney & E. Bates (Eds.), *The crosslinguistic study of sentence processing* (pp. 3–73). Cambridge: Cambridge University Press.

Bates, E., Reilly, J., Wulfeck, B., Dronkers, N., Opie, M., Fenson, J., ... & Herbst, K. (2001). Differential effects of unilateral lesions on language production in children and adults. *Brain and Language, 79*(2), 223–265.

Bayes, T. (1763). An essay towards solving a problem in the doctrine of chances. *Philosophical Transactions of the Royal Society of London, 53*, 370–418.

Beach, L. R., & Scopp, T. S. (1968). Intuitive statistical inferences about variances. *Organizational Behavior and Human Performance, 3*(2), 109–123.

Becker, M., & Gouskova, M. (2016). Source-oriented generalizations as grammar inference in Russian vowel deletion. *Linguistic Inquiry, 47*(3), 391–425.

Becker, M., Ketrez, N., & Nevins, A. (2011). The surfeit of the stimulus: Analytic biases filter lexical statistics in Turkish laryngeal alternations. *Language, 87*(1), 84–125.

Becker, M., Nevins, A., & Levine, J. (2012). Asymmetries in generalizing alternations to and from initial syllables. *Language, 88*(2), 231–268.

Beckman, J. N. (1999). *Positional faithfulness: An Optimality Theoretic treatment of phonological asymmetries*. London: Routledge.

Beckmann, J. S., & Young, M. E. (2007). The feature positive effect in the face of variability: Novelty as a feature. *Journal of Experimental Psychology: Animal Behavior Processes, 33*(1), 72–77.

Beekhuizen, B., Bod, R., & Zuidema, W. (2013). Three design principles of language: The search for parsimony in redundancy. *Language and Speech, 56*(3), 265–290.

Bengio, Y., Courville, A., and Vincent, P. (2012). Representation learning: A review and new perspectives. *arXiv, 1206*(5538), 1–34.

Benguerel, A. P., & Cowan, H. A. (1974). Coarticulation of upper lip protrusion in French. *Phonetica, 30*(1), 41–55.

Bennett, W. G., & Braver, A. (2015). Phonology or morphology: Inter-speaker differences in Xhosa labial palatalization. Paper presented at the Annual Meeting of the Linguistic Society of America, Portland, OR.

Benua, L. (1997). *Transderivational identity: Phonological relations between words* (doctoral dissertation, University of Massachusetts, Amherst).

Berg, T. (1998). *Linguistic structure and change: An explanation from language processing*. Oxford: Oxford University Press.

Bergelson, E., & Swingley, D. (2012). At 6–9 months, human infants know the meanings of many common nouns. *Proceedings of the National Academy of Sciences, 109*(9), 3253–3258.

Bergen, B. K. (2004). The psychological reality of phonaesthemes. *Language, 80*(2), 290–311.

Berko, J. (1958). The child's learning of English morphology. *Word, 14*, 150–177.

Bertelson, P., Vroomen, J., & De Gelder, B. (2003). Visual recalibration of auditory speech identification: A McGurk aftereffect. *Psychological Science, 14*(6), 592–597.

Best, C. A., Yim, H., & Sloutsky, V. M. (2013). The cost of selective attention in category learning: Developmental differences between adults and infants. *Journal of Experimental Child Psychology, 116*(2), 105–119.

Bever, T. G., & Poeppel, D. (2010). Analysis by synthesis: A (re-) emerging program of research for language and vision. *Biolinguistics, 4*(2–3), 174–200.

Binder, J. R., Desai, R. H., Graves, W. W., & Conant, L. L. (2009). Where is the semantic system? A critical review and meta-analysis of 120 functional neuroimaging studies. *Cerebral Cortex, 19*(12), 2767–2796.

Blair, M. R., Walshe, C., Barnes, J. I., & Chen, L. (2011). Rethinking the role of error in attentional learning. *Proceedings of the Annual Conference of the Cognitive Science Society* (Vol. 33, pp. 1649–1655).

Blaisdell, A. P., Gunther, L. M., & Miller, R. R. (1999). Recovery from blocking achieved by extinguishing the blocking CS. *Animal Learning & Behavior, 27*(1), 63–76.

Blevins, J. (2004). *Evolutionary phonology: The emergence of sound patterns*. Cambridge: Cambridge University Press.

Blough, D. S. (1967). Stimulus generalization as signal detection in pigeons. *Science, 158*(3803), 940–941.

Blumenthal-Dramé, A. (2012). *Entrenchment in usage-based theories: What corpus data do and do not reveal about the mind*. Berlin: Walter de Gruyter.

Blything, R. P., Ambridge, B., & Lieven, E. V. (2014). Children use statistics and semantics in the retreat from overgeneralization. *PloS One, 9*(10), e110009.

Boersma, P. (2011). A program for bidirectional phonology and phonetics and their acquisition and evolution. In A. Benz & J. Mattausch (Eds.), *Bidirectional Optimality Theory*, 33–72. Amsterdam: John Benjamins.

Boersma, P. (2007). Some listener-oriented accounts of h-aspiré in French. *Lingua, 117*(12), 1989–2054.

Boersma, P. (1998). *Functional phonology: Formalizing the interactions between articulatory and perceptual drives* (doctoral dissertation, University of Amsterdam).

Bolles, R. C. (1970). Species-specific defense reactions and avoidance learning. *Psychological Review, 77*(1), 32–48.

Bonardi, C. (1989). Inhibitory discriminative control is specific to both the response and the reinforcer. *Quarterly Journal of Experimental Psychology, 41*(3), 225–242.

Bonardi, C., & Jennings, D. (2009). Learning about associations: Evidence for a hierarchical account of occasion setting. *Journal of Experimental Psychology: Animal Behavior Processes, 35*(3), 440–445.

Booij, G. (2010). *Construction morphology*. Cambridge: Cambridge University Press.

Booij, G. (1996). Inherent versus contextual inflection and the split morphology hypothesis. In G. Booij & J. van Marle (Eds.), *Yearbook of morphology 1995* (pp. 1–16). Dordrecht: Kluwer.

Botvinick, M., & Plaut, D. C. (2004). Doing without schema hierarchies: A recurrent connectionist approach to normal and impaired routine sequential action. *Psychological Review*, *111*(2), 395–429.

Bouton, M. E. (2016). *Learning and behavior: A contemporary synthesis* (2nd ed.). Sunderland, MA: Sinauer Associates.

Bouton, M. E., & Nelson, J. B. (1994). Context-specificity of target versus feature inhibition in a feature-negative discrimination. *Journal of Experimental Psychology: Animal Behavior Processes*, *20*(1), 51–65.

Bowerman, M., & Pederson, E. (1992, November). Crosslinguistic perspectives on topological spatial relationships. Paper presented at the 87th Annual Meeting of the American Anthropological Association, San Francisco.

Boyce, S. E., Tiede, M., Espy-Wilson, C. Y., & Groves-Wright, K. (2015). Diversity of tongue shapes for the American English rhotic liquid. In The Scottish Consortium for ICPhS 2015 (Ed.), *Proceedings of the International Congress of Phonetic Sciences*. London: International Phonetic Association.

Boyd, R., & Richerson, P. J. (1987). The evolution of ethnic markers. *Cultural Anthropology*, *2*, 65–79.

Braine, M. D. S. (1963). The ontogeny of English phrase structure. *Language*, *39*, 1–14.

Braine, M. D. S., & Brooks, P. J. (1995). Verb argument structure and the problem of avoiding an overgeneral grammar. In M. Tomasello & W. E. Merriman (Eds.), *Beyond names for things: Young children's acquisition of verbs* (pp. 353–376). Hillsdale, NJ: Erlbaum.

Breland, K., & Breland, M. (1961). The misbehavior of organisms. *American Psychologist*, *16*(11), 681–684.

Broadbent, D. E. (1967). Word-frequency effect and response bias. *Psychological Review*, *74*(1), 1–15.

Broadbent, D. E. (1958). *Perception and communication*. Oxford: Pergamon Press.

Brooks, D. C., & Bouton, M. E. (1993). A retrieval cue for extinction attenuates spontaneous recovery. *Journal of Experimental Psychology: Animal Behavior Processes*, *19*(1), 77–89.

Brooks, P. J., Braine, M. D. S., Catalano, L., Brody, R. E., & Sudhalter, V. (1993). Acquisition of gender-like noun subclasses in an artificial language: The contribution of phonological markers to learning. *Journal of Memory and Language*, *32*, 79–95.

Brooks, P. J., Tomasello, M., Dodson, K., & Lewis, L. B. (1999). Young children's overgeneralizations with fixed transitivity verbs. *Child Development*, *70*(6), 1325–1337.

Browman, C. P., & Goldstein, L. (1990). Tiers in articulatory phonology, with some implications for casual speech. In J. Kingston & M. E. Beckman (Eds.), *Papers in laboratory phonology I: Between the grammar and physics of speech* (pp. 341–376). Cambridge: Cambridge University Press.

Browman, C. P., & Goldstein, L. (1989). Articulatory gestures as phonological units. *Phonology, 6*(2), 201–251.

Brown, R., & Berko, J. (1960). Word association and the acquisition of grammar. *Child Development, 31*(1), 1–14.

Bryan, W. L., & Harter, N. (1899). Studies on the telegraphic language: The acquisition of a hierarchy of habits. *Psychological Review, 6*(4), 345–375.

Bryan, W. L., & Harter, N. (1897). Studies in the physiology and psychology of the telegraphic language. *Psychological Review, 4*(1), 27–53.

Brysbaert, M., & Cortese, M. J. (2010). Do the effects of subjective frequency and age of acquisition survive better word frequency norms? *Quarterly Journal of Experimental Psychology, 64*(3), 545–559.

Bunsey, M., & Eichenbaum, H. (1995). Selective damage to the hippocampal region blocks long-term retention of a natural and nonspatial stimulus-stimulus association. *Hippocampus, 5*(6), 546–556.

Burkhardt, P. E., & Ayres, J. J. (1978). CS and US duration effects in one-trial simultaneous fear conditioning as assessed by conditioned suppression of licking in rats. *Animal Learning & Behavior, 6*(2), 225–230.

Burzio, L. (1997). Cycles, non-derived environment blocking and correspondence. In J. Dekkers, F. van der Leeuw, & J. van de Weijer (Eds.), *The pointing finger: Conceptual studies in Optimality Theory* (pp. 47–87). Oxford: Oxford University Press.

Bush, N. (2001). Frequency effects and word-boundary palatalization in English. In J. Bybee & P. Hopper (Eds.), *Frequency and the emergence of linguistic structure* (pp. 255–280). Amsterdam: Benjamins.

Bush, R. R., & Mosteller, F. (1951). A mathematical model for simple learning. *Psychological Review, 58*(5), 313–323.

Buz, E., Tanenhaus, M. K., & Jaeger, T. F. (2016). Dynamically adapted context-specific hyper-articulation: Feedback from interlocutors affects speakers' subsequent pronunciations. *Journal of Memory and Language, 89*, 68–86.

Bybee, J. (2015). *Language change.* Cambridge: Cambridge University Press.

Bybee, J. (2010). *Language, usage and cognition.* Cambridge: Cambridge University Press.

Bybee, J. (2008). Formal universals as emergent phenomena: The origins of structure preservation. In J. Good (Ed.), *Linguistic universals and language change* (pp. 108–121). Oxford: Oxford University Press.

Bybee, J. (2003). Cognitive processes in grammaticalization. In Michael Tomasello (Ed.), *The new psychology of language: Cognitive and functional approaches to language structure* (Vol. 2, pp. 145–167). Mahwah, NJ: Erlbaum.

Bybee, J. (2002a). Sequentiality as the basis of constituent structure. In T. Givón & B. F. Malle (Eds.), *The evolution of language out of pre-language* (pp. 109–134). Amsterdam: John Benjamins.

Bybee, J. (2002b). Word frequency and context of use in the lexical diffusion of phonetically conditioned sound change. *Language Variation and Change, 14*(3), 261–290.

Bybee, J. (2001). *Phonology and language use.* New York: Cambridge University Press.

Bybee, J. (1985). *Morphology: A study of the relation between meaning and form.* Amsterdam: John Benjamins.

Bybee, J., & Brewer, M. A. (1980). Explanation in morphophonemics: Changes in Provençal and Spanish preterite forms. *Lingua, 52*(3), 201–242.

Bybee, J., & Easterday, S. (2017). *The prominence of palatal articulation: A crosslinguistic study of assimilation and strengthening.* Ms., University of New Mexico.

Bybee, J., File-Muriel, R. J., & De Souza, R. N. (2016). Special reduction: A usage-based approach. *Language and Cognition, 8*(3), 421–446.

Bybee, J., Perkins, R., & Pagliuca, W. (1994). *The evolution of grammar: Tense, aspect, and modality in the languages of the world.* Chicago: University of Chicago Press.

Bybee, J., & Scheibman, J. (1999). The effect of usage on degrees of constituency: The reduction of *don't* in English. *Linguistics, 37*(4), 575–596.

Caballero, G. (2008) *Choguita Rarámuri (Tarahumara) phonology and morphology* (doctoral dissertation, University of California, Berkeley).

Caballero, G., & Inkelas, S. (2013). Word construction: Tracing an optimal path through the lexicon. *Morphology, 23*(2), 103–143.

Caballero, G., & Kapatsinski, V. (2017). *How agglutinative? Searching for cues to meaning in Choguita Rarámuri (Tarahumara) using an amorphous model.* Ms. University of California San Diego and University of Oregon.

Calvert, G. A., Campbell, R., & Brammer, M. J. (2000). Evidence from functional magnetic resonance imaging of crossmodal binding in the human heteromodal cortex. *Current Biology, 10*(11), 649–657.

Caplan, J. B., Boulton, K. L., & Gagné, C. L. (2014). Associative asymmetry of compound words. *Journal of Experimental Psychology: Learning, Memory, and Cognition, 40,* 1163–1171.

Cappelle, B. (2006). Particle placement and the case for "allostructions." *Constructions, SV1*(7), 1–28.

Carignan, C., Mielke, J., & Dodsworth, R. (2016). Tongue trajectories in North American English/æ/tensing. *Methods in Dialectology, 15,* 313–320.

Castles, A., Davis, C., Cavalot, P., & Forster, K. (2007). Tracking the acquisition of orthographic skills in developing readers: Masked priming effects. *Journal of Experimental Child Psychology, 97*(3), 165–182.

Cattell, J. M. (1885). Über die Zeit der Erkennung und Benennung von Schriftzeichen, Bildern und Farben [On the time to recognize and name letters, pictures and colors]. *Philosophische Studien, 2,* 635–650.

Chang, C. B. (2013). A novelty effect in phonetic drift of the native language. *Journal of Phonetics, 41*(6), 520–533.

Chang, F., Dell, G. S., Bock, K., & Griffin, Z. M. (2000). Structural priming as implicit learning: A comparison of models of sentence production. *Journal of Psycholinguistic Research, 29*(2), 217–230.

Chapman, G. B. (1991). Trial order affects cue interaction in contingency judgment. *Journal of Experimental Psychology: Learning, Memory, and Cognition, 17*(5), 837–854.

Chater, N., Clark, A., Goldsmith, J., & Perfors, A. (2015). *Empiricism and language learnability.* Oxford: Oxford University Press.

Cho, T. (1998). Intergestural timing and overlap in Korean palatalization: An Optimality-Theoretic account. *Japanese/Korean Linguistics, 8,* 261–276.

Chomsky, N. (1995). *The Minimalist Program.* Cambridge, MA: MIT Press.

Chomsky, N. (1981). Principles and parameters in syntactic theory. In N. Hornstein & D. Lightfoot (Eds.), *Explanation in linguistics: The logical problem of language acquisition* (pp. 32–75). London: Longman.

Chomsky, N. (1966). *Cartesian linguistics: A chapter in the history of rationalist thought.* New York: Harper & Row.

Chomsky, N. (1959). A review of B. F. Skinner's *Verbal Behavior. Language, 35*(1), 26–58.

Chomsky, N. (1957). *Syntactic structures.* Berlin: Mouton de Gruyter.

Chomsky, N., & Halle, M. (1968). *The sound pattern of English.* New York: Harper & Row.

Chomsky, N., & Halle, M. (1965). Some controversial questions in phonological theory. *Journal of Linguistics, 1*(2), 97–138.

Chomsky, N., & Lasnik, H. (1993). Principles and Parameters Theory. In J. Jacobs, A. von Stechow, W. Sternefeld, & T. Vennemann (Eds.), *Syntax: An International Handbook of Contemporary Research* (pp. 506–569). Berlin: Walter de Gruyter.

Christian, B., & Griffiths, T. (2016). *Algorithms to live by*. New York: Holt.

Christiansen, M. H., & Chater, N. (2016). *Creating language: Integrating evolution, acquisition, and processing*. Cambridge, MA: MIT Press.

Clark, E. V. (1987). The principle of contrast: A constraint on language acquisition. In B. MacWhinney (Ed.), *Mechanisms of language acquisition* (pp. 1–33). Hillsdale, NJ: Erlbaum.

Clark, E. V. (1973). What's in a word? On the child's acquisition of semantics in his first language. In T. E. Moore (Ed.), *Cognitive development and the acquisition of language* (pp. 65–110). New York: Academic.

Clopper, C., Pisoni, D., & de Jong, K. (2005). Acoustic characteristics of the vowel systems of six regional varieties of American English. *Journal of the Acoustical Society of America, 118*, 1661–1676.

Cohen, A. L., Nosofsky, R. M., & Zaki, S. R. (2001). Category variability, exemplar similarity, and perceptual classification. *Memory & Cognition, 29*(8), 1165–1175.

Cohen, J. D., Dunbar, K., & McClelland, J. L. (1990). On the control of automatic processes: A parallel distributed processing account of the Stroop effect. *Psychological Review, 97*(3), 332–361.

Cohen, J. R., & Poldrack, R. A. (2008). Automaticity in motor sequence learning does not impair response inhibition. *Psychonomic Bulletin & Review, 15*(1), 108–115.

Cohen Goldberg, A. M. (2015). Abstract and lexically specific information in sound patterns: Evidence from /r/-sandhi in rhotic and non-rhotic varieties of English. *Language and Speech, 58*(4), 522–548.

Cohen Priva, U. (2015). Informativity affects consonant duration and deletion rates. *Laboratory Phonology, 6*(2), 243–278.

Conway, C. M., & Christiansen, M. H. (2006). Statistical learning within and between modalities: Pitting abstract against stimulus-specific representations. *Psychological Science, 17*(10), 905–912.

Conway, C. M., & Pisoni, D. B. (2008). Neurocognitive basis of implicit learning of sequential structure and its relation to language processing. *Annals of the New York Academy of Sciences, 1145*(1), 113–131.

Courville, A. C., Daw, N. D., & Touretzky, D. S. (2006). Bayesian theories of conditioning in a changing world. *Trends in Cognitive Sciences, 10*(7), 294–300.

Cowan, N. (2001). Metatheory of storage capacity limits. *Behavioral and Brain Sciences, 24*(1), 154–176.

Crain, S., Goro, T., & Thornoton, R. (2006). Language acquisition is language change. *Journal of Psycholinguistic Research, 35,* 31–49.

Croft, W. (2001). *Radical Construction Grammar: Syntactic theory in typological perspective.* Oxford: Oxford University Press.

Culbertson, J., Smolensky, P., & Legendre, G. (2012). Learning biases predict a word order universal. *Cognition, 122*(3), 306–329.

Cutler, A. (2012). *Native listening: Language experience and the recognition of spoken words.* Cambridge, MA: MIT Press.

Cutler, A., & Norris, D. (1988). The role of strong syllables in segmentation for lexical access. *Journal of Experimental Psychology: Human Perception and Performance, 14*(1), 113–121.

Dąbrowska, E. (2012). Different speakers, different grammars: Individual differences in native language attainment. *Linguistic Approaches to Bilingualism, 2*(3), 219–253.

Dahan, D. (2010). The time course of interpretation in speech comprehension. *Current Directions in Psychological Science, 19*(2), 121–126.

Daniloff, R., & Moll, K. (1968). Coarticulation of lip rounding. *Journal of Speech, Language, and Hearing Research, 11*(4), 707–721.

Danks, D. (2003). Equilibria of the Rescorla-Wagner model. *Journal of Mathematical Psychology, 47*(2), 109–121.

Dautriche, I., Chemla, E., & Christophe, A. (2016). Word learning: Homophony and the distribution of learning exemplars. *Language Learning and Development, 12*(3), 231–251.

Davies, M. (2008–) *The Corpus of Contemporary American English: 520 million words, 1990–present.* http://corpus.byu.edu/coca.

Davis, C. J. (2010). The spatial coding model of visual word identification. *Psychological Review, 117*(3), 713–758.

Daw, N. D., Courville, A. C., & Dayan, P. (2008). Semi-rational models of conditioning: The case of trial order. In N. Chater & M. Oaksford (Eds.), *The probabilistic mind: Prospects for Bayesian cognitive science* (pp. 431–452). Oxford: Oxford University Press.

Dayan, P., Kakade, S., & Montague, P. R. (2000). Learning and selective attention. *Nature Neuroscience, 3,* 1218–1223.

Deacon, T. W. (1997). *The symbolic species: The co-evolution of language and the brain.* New York: Norton.

Deese, J. (1962). Form class and the determinants of association. *Journal of Verbal Learning & Verbal Behavior, 1*, 79–84.

De Houwer, J., & Beckers, T. (2003). Secondary task difficulty modulates forward blocking in human contingency learning. *Quarterly Journal of Experimental Psychology, 56B*(4), 345–357.

de Jong, K. J. (1995). The supraglottal articulation of prominence in English: Linguistic stress as localized hyperarticulation. *Journal of the Acoustical Society of America, 97*(1), 491–504.

DeLancey, S. (2014). Sociolinguistic typology in North East India: A tale of two branches. *Journal of South Asian Languages and Linguistics, 1*(1), 59–82.

Dell, G. S. (1985). Positive feedback in hierarchical connectionist models: Applications to language production. *Cognitive Science, 9*(1), 3–23.

Dell, G. S., Burger, L. K., & Svec, W. R. (1997). Language production and serial order: A functional analysis and a model. *Psychological Review, 104*(1), 123–147.

Dell, G. S., Reed, K. D., Adams, D. R., & Meyer, A. S. (2000). Speech errors, phonotactic constraints, and implicit learning: A study of the role of experience in language production. *Journal of Experimental Psychology: Learning, Memory, and Cognition, 26*(6), 1355–1367.

Desrosiers, G., & Ivison, D. (1986). Paired associate learning: Normative data for differences between high and low associate word pairs. *Journal of Clinical and Experimental Neuropsychology, 8*(6), 637–642.

Dickinson, A. (2001). Causal learning: An associative analysis. *Quarterly Journal of Experimental Psychology, 54B*(1), 3–25.

Dickinson, A. (1996). Within compound associations mediate the retrospective revaluation of causality judgements. *Quarterly Journal of Experimental Psychology, 49B*(1), 60–80.

Do, Y. A. (2013). *Biased learning of phonological alternations* (doctoral dissertation, MIT).

Doll, B. B., Jacobs, W. J., Sanfey, A. G., & Frank, M. J. (2009). Instructional control of reinforcement learning: A behavioral and neurocomputational investigation. *Brain Research, 1299*, 74–94.

Domjan, M. (1983). Biological constraints on instrumental and classical conditioning: Implications for general process theory. *Psychology of Learning and Motivation, 17*, 215–277.

Doya, K. (1999). What are the computations of the cerebellum, the basal ganglia and the cerebral cortex? *Neural Networks, 12*(7), 961–974.

Doyle, A. C. (1890). *The sign of four*. London: Spencer Blackett.

Drachman, G. (1978). Child language and language change: A conjecture and some refutations. In J. Fisiak (Ed.), *Recent developments in historical phonology* (pp. 123–144). Berlin: Mouton de Gruyter.

Dufour, S., & Frauenfelder, U. H. (2016). Inhibitory phonetic priming: Where does the effect come from? *Quarterly Journal of Experimental Psychology, 69*(1), 180–196.

Durvasula, K., & Liter, A. (2016). Generalizing from ambiguous data. Poster presented at the Annual Meeting of the Linguistic Society of America, Washington, DC.

Edelman, G. M. (1987). *Neural Darwinism: The theory of neuronal group selection*. New York: Basic Books.

Edgell, S. E. (1983). Delayed exposure to configural information in nonmetric multiple-cue probability learning. *Organizational Behavior and Human Performance, 32*(1), 55–65.

Edgell, S. E., & Morrissey, J. M. (1987). Delayed exposure to additional relevant information in nonmetric multiple-cue probability learning. *Organizational Behavior and Human Decision Processes, 40*(1), 22–38.

Efron, B. (1975). The efficiency of logistic regression compared to normal discriminant analysis. *Journal of the American Statistical Association, 70*, 892–898.

Eghbalzad, L., Deocampo, J., Smith, G., Na, S., King, T., & Conway, C. (2017). Neural correlates associated with learning adjacent and non-adjacent regularities during statistical learning: An fMRI study. Paper presented at the International Conference on Interdisciplinary Advances in Statistical Learning, Bilbao, Spain, June 28–30.

Eibl-Eibesfeldt, I. (1970). *Ethology: The biology of behavior*. New York: Holt, Rinehart, & Winston.

Ellis, N. C. (2006). Selective attention and transfer phenomena in L2 acquisition: Contingency, cue competition, salience, interference, overshadowing, blocking, and perceptual learning. *Applied Linguistics, 27*(2), 164–194.

Emberson, L. L., Liu, R., & Zevin, J. D. (2013). Is statistical learning constrained by lower level perceptual organization? *Cognition, 128*(1), 82–102.

Endresen, A. (2015). *Non-standard allomorphy in Russian prefixes: Corpus, experimental, and statistical exploration*. (doctoral dissertation, University of Tromsø.)

Ernestus, M., Kouwenhoven, H., & Van Mulken, M. (2017). The direct and indirect effects of the phonotactic constraints in the listener's native language on the comprehension of reduced and unreduced word pronunciation variants in a foreign language. *Journal of Phonetics, 62*, 50–64.

Ervin, S. M. (1961). Changes with age in the verbal determinants of word-association. *American Journal of Psychology, 74*, 361–372.

Escudero, P. (2005). *Linguistic perception and second language acquisition: Explaining the attainment of optimal phonological categorization.* (doctoral dissertation, Utrecht University).

Escudero, P., & Boersma, P. (2004). Bridging the gap between L2 speech perception research and phonological theory. *Studies in Second Language Acquisition, 26*(4), 551–585.

Estes, W. K. (1950). Toward a statistical theory of learning. *Psychological Review, 57*(2), 94–107.

Evans, N., Fletcher, J., & Ross, B. (2008). Big words, small phrases: Mismatches between pause units and the polysynthetic word in Dalabon. *Linguistics, 46*(1), 89–129.

Evans, N., & Levinson, S. C. (2009). The myth of language universals: Language diversity and its importance for cognitive science. *Behavioral and Brain Sciences, 32*(5), 429–448.

Farrington, C., Kendall, T., & Fridland, V. (2017). *Vowel dynamics in the Southern Vowel Shift.* Ms., University of Oregon.

Fay, N., & Ellison, T. M. (2013). The cultural evolution of human communication systems in different sized populations: Usability trumps learnability. *PloS One, 8*(8), e71781.

Feldman, J. (2009). Bayes and the simplicity principle in perception. *Psychological Review, 116*(4), 875–887.

Fellbaum, C. (1996). Co-occurrence and antonymy. *International Journal of Lexicography, 8*(4), 281–303.

Fennell, C. T., & Werker, J. F. (2003). Early word learners' ability to access phonetic detail in well-known words. *Language and Speech, 46*(2–3), 245–264.

Ferdinand, V., Thompson, B., Kirby, S., & Smith, K. (2013). Regularization behavior in a non-linguistic domain. *Proceedings of the Annual Conference of the Cognitive Science Society, 36*, 436–441.

Ferguson, C. A., & Farwell, C. B. (1975). Words and sounds in early language acquisition. *Language, 51*(2), 419–439.

Fernandino, L., Binder, J. R., Desai, R. H., Pendl, S. L., Humphries, C. J., Gross, W. L., … & Seidenberg, M. S. (2015). Concept representation reflects multimodal abstraction: A framework for embodied semantics. *Cerebral Cortex, 76*, 17–26.

Ferreira, V. S., & Griffin, Z. M. (2003). Phonological influences on lexical (mis)selection. *Psychological Science, 14*(1), 86–90.

Fillmore, C. J., Kay, P., & O'Connor, M. C. (1988). Regularity and idiomaticity in grammatical constructions: The case of *let alone*. *Language, 64*(3), 501–538.

Flannagan, M. J., Fried, L. S., & Holyoak, K. J. (1986). Distributional expectations and the induction of category structure. *Journal of Experimental Psychology: Learning, Memory, and Cognition, 12*(2), 241–256.

Fodor, J. A., & Bever, T. G. (1965). The psychological reality of linguistic segments. *Journal of Verbal Learning and Verbal Behavior, 4*(5), 414–420.

Forster, K. I., & Davis, C. (1984). Repetition priming and frequency attenuation in lexical access. *Journal of Experimental Psychology: Learning, Memory, and Cognition, 10*, 680–698.

Foss, D. J., & Jenkins, J. J. (1966). Mediated stimulus equivalence as a function of the number of converging stimulus items. *Journal of Experimental Psychology, 71*(5), 738–745.

Fowler, C. A. (1986). An event approach to the study of speech perception from a direct realist perspective. *Journal of Phonetics, 14*(1), 3–28.

Fox, R. A., & Jacewicz, E. (2009). Cross-dialectal variation in formant dynamics of American English vowels. *Journal of the Acoustical Society of America, 126*, 2603–2618.

Francis, A. L., & Nusbaum, H. C. (2002). Selective attention and the acquisition of new phonetic categories. *Journal of Experimental Psychology: Human Perception and Performance, 28*(2), 349–366.

French, R. M., Addyman, C., & Mareschal, D. (2011). TRACX: A recognition-based connectionist framework for sequence segmentation and chunk extraction. *Psychological Review, 118*, 614–636.

Fried, L. S., & Holyoak, K. J. (1984). Induction of category distributions: A framework for classification learning. *Journal of Experimental Psychology: Learning, Memory, and Cognition, 10*(2), 234–257.

Friedman, M. P. (1966). Transfer effects and response strategies in pattern-versus-component discrimination learning. *Journal of Experimental Psychology, 71*(3), 420–428.

Frigo, L., & McDonald, J. L. (1998). Properties of phonological markers that affect the acquisition of gender-like subclasses. *Journal of Memory and Language, 39*(2), 218–245.

Fuchs, S., Petrone, C., Krivokapić, J., & Hoole, P. (2013). Acoustic and respiratory evidence for utterance planning in German. *Journal of Phonetics, 41*(1), 29–47.

Gagliardi, A., & Lidz, J. (2014). Statistical insensitivity in the acquisition of Tsez noun classes. *Language, 90*(1), 58–89.

Gahl, S. (2008). Time and thyme are not homophones: The effect of lemma frequency on word durations in spontaneous speech. *Language, 84*(3), 474–496.

Gallistel, C. R. (2012). Extinction from a rationalist perspective. *Behavioral Processes, 90*(1), 66–80.

Gallistel, C. R., Fairhurst, S., & Balsam, P. (2004). The learning curve: Implications of a quantitative analysis. *Proceedings of the National Academy of Sciences of the United States of America, 101*(36), 13124–13131.

Ganong, W. F. (1980). Phonetic categorization in auditory word perception. *Journal of Experimental Psychology: Human Perception and Performance, 6*(1), 110–125.

Garcia, J., & Koelling, R. A. (1966). Relation of cue to consequence in avoidance learning. *Psychonomic Science, 4*(1), 123–124.

Gemberling, G. A., & Domjan, M. (1982). Selective associations in one-day-old rats: Taste-toxicosis and texture-shock aversion learning. *Journal of Comparative and Physiological Psychology, 96*(1), 105–124.

Gentner, D., & Bowerman, M. (2009). Why some spatial semantic categories are harder to learn than others: The typological prevalence hypothesis. In J. Guo, E. Lieven, N. Budwig, S. Ervin-Tripp, K. Nakamura, & S. Ozcaliskan (Eds.), *Crosslinguistic approaches to the psychology of language: Research in the tradition of Dan Isaac Slobin* (pp. 465–480). New York: Psychology Press.

Georgopoulos, A. P., Schwartz, A. B., & Kettner, R. E. (1986). Neuronal population coding of movement direction. *Science, 233*(4771), 1416–1419.

Gershkoff-Stowe, L., & Smith, L. B. (1997). A curvilinear trend in naming errors as a function of early vocabulary growth. *Cognitive Psychology, 34*(1), 37–71.

Ghazanfar, A. A., & Schroeder, C. E. (2006). Is neocortex essentially multisensory? *Trends in Cognitive Sciences, 10*(6), 278–285.

Ghirlanda, S. (2005). Retrospective revaluation as simple associative learning. *Journal of Experimental Psychology: Animal Behavior Processes, 31*(1), 107–111.

Gibbon, F. E. (1999). Undifferentiated lingual gestures in children with articulation/phonological disorders. *Journal of Speech, Language, and Hearing Research, 42*(2), 382–397.

Gibson, J. J., & Gibson, E. J. (1955). Perceptual learning: Differentiation or enrichment? *Psychological Review, 62*(1), 32–41.

Gick, B., Jones, C., & Schellenberg, M. (2017) Indie-pop voice: Pharyngealization and an emerging pop dialect. Paper presented at NoWPhon 3, Vancouver, BC, May 19.

Gick, B., Wilson, I., Koch, K., & Cook, C. (2004). Language-specific articulatory settings: Evidence from inter-utterance rest position. *Phonetica, 61*(4), 220–233.

Gigerenzer, G., & Selten, R. (2002). *Bounded rationality: The adaptive toolbox.* Cambridge, MA: MIT Press.

Gittins, J. C. (1979). Bandit problems and dynamic allocation indices. *Journal of the Royal Statistical Society B, 41*, 148–177.

Givón, T. (1998). On the co-evolution of language, mind and brain. *Evolution of Communication, 2*, 45–116.

Givón, T. (1979). *On understanding grammar.* New York: Academic Press

Givón, T. (1971). Historical syntax and synchronic morphology: An archaeologist's field trip. *Chicago Linguistic Society, 7*(1), 394–415.

Glezer, L. S., Jiang, X., & Riesenhuber, M. (2009). Evidence for highly selective neuronal tuning to whole words in the "visual word form area." *Neuron, 62*(2), 199–204.

Gluck, M. A., & Bower, G. H. (1988). From conditioning to category learning: An adaptive network model. *Journal of Experimental Psychology: General, 117*(3), 227–247.

Goldberg, A. E. (2006). *Constructions at work: The nature of generalization in language.* Oxford: Oxford University Press.

Goldberg, A. E. (2002). Surface generalizations: An alternative to alternations. *Cognitive Linguistics, 13*(4), 327–356.

Goldberg, A. E. (1995). *Constructions: A Construction Grammar approach to argument structure.* Chicago: University of Chicago Press.

Goldberg, A. E., Casenhiser, D. M., & Sethuraman, N. (2004). Learning argument structure generalizations. *Cognitive Linguistics, 15*, 289–316.

Goldiamond, I., & Hawkins, W. F. (1958). Vexierversuch: The log relationship between word-frequency and recognition obtained in the absence of stimulus words. *Journal of Experimental Psychology, 56*(6), 457–463.

Goldinger, S. D. (1998). Echoes of echoes? An episodic theory of lexical access. *Psychological Review, 105*(2), 251–279.

Goldinger, S. D., Luce, P. A., & Pisoni, D. B. (1989). Priming lexical neighbors of spoken words: Effects of competition and inhibition. *Journal of Memory and Language, 28*(5), 501–518.

Goldsmith, J. A. (1976). *Autosegmental phonology.* Bloomington: Indiana University Linguistics Club.

Goldstein, M. H., King, A. P., & West, M. J. (2003). Social interaction shapes babbling: Testing parallels between birdsong and speech. *Proceedings of the National Academy of Sciences, 100*(13), 8030–8035.

Goldstein, M. H., & West, M. J. (1999). Consistent responses of human mothers to prelinguistic infants: The effect of prelinguistic repertoire size. *Journal of Comparative Psychology, 113*(1), 52–58.

Goldstone, R. L. (2003). Learning to perceive while perceiving to learn. In R. Kimchi, M. Behrmann, & C. R. Olson (Eds.), *Perceptual organization in vision: Behavioral and neural perspectives* (pp. 233–278). Mahwah, NJ: Erlbaum.

Gollan, T. H., Slattery, T. J., Goldenberg, D., Van Assche, E., Duyck, W., & Rayner, K. (2011). Frequency drives lexical access in reading but not in speaking: The frequency-lag hypothesis. *Journal of Experimental Psychology: General, 140*(2), 186–209.

Gómez, R. L. (2002). Variability and detection of invariant structure. *Psychological Science, 13*(5), 431–436.

Gopnik, A., Glymour, C., Sobel, D. M., Schulz, L. E., Kushnir, T., & Danks, D. (2004). A theory of causal learning in children: Causal maps and Bayes nets. *Psychological Review, 111*(1), 3–32.

Gopnik, A., Griffiths, T. L., & Lucas, C. G. (2015). When younger learners can be better (or at least more open-minded) than older ones. *Current Directions in Psychological Science, 24*(2), 87–92.

Gopnik, A., Meltzoff, A. N., & Kuhl, P. K. (1999). *The scientist in the crib.* New York: Morrow.

Goudbeek, M., Swingley, D., & Smits, R. (2009). Supervised and unsupervised learning of multidimensional acoustic categories. *Journal of Experimental Psychology: Human Perception and Performance, 35*(6), 1913–1933.

Gould, S. J. (2007). *Punctuated equilibrium.* Cambridge, MA: Harvard University Press.

Gouskova, M., & Becker, M. (2013). Nonce words show that Russian *yer* alternations are governed by the grammar. *Natural Language & Linguistic Theory, 31*(3), 735–765.

Graf Estes, K., Evans, J. L., Alibali, M. W., & Saffran, J. R. (2007). Can infants map meaning to newly segmented words? Statistical segmentation and word learning. *Psychological Science, 18*(3), 254–260.

Greenberg, S. N., Healy, A. F., Koriat, A., & Kreiner, H. (2004). The GO model: A reconsideration of the role of structural units in guiding and organizing text on line. *Psychonomic Bulletin & Review, 11*(3), 428–433.

Gregory, M. L., Raymond, W. D., Bell, A., Fosler-Lussier, E., & Jurafsky, D. (1999). The effects of collocational strength and contextual predictability in lexical production. *Chicago Linguistic Society, 35*, 151–166.

Gries, S. T. (2005). Syntactic priming: A corpus-based approach. *Journal of Psycholinguistic Research, 34*(4), 365–399.

Gries, S. T., & Stefanowitsch, A. (2004). Extending collostructional analysis: A corpus-based perspective on "alternations." *International Journal of Corpus Linguistics, 9*(1), 97–129.

Grosjean, F. (1980). Spoken word recognition processes and the gating paradigm. *Perception & Psychophysics, 28*(4), 267–283.

Grosvald, M. (2009). Interspeaker variation in the extent and perception of long-distance vowel-to-vowel coarticulation. *Journal of Phonetics, 37*(2), 173–188.

Guenther, F. H., & Gjaja, M. N. (1996). The perceptual magnet effect as an emergent property of neural map formation. *Journal of the Acoustical Society of America, 100*(2), 1111–1121.

Guenther, F. H., Hampson, M., & Johnson, D. (1998). A theoretical investigation of reference frames for the planning of speech movements. *Psychological Review, 105*(4), 611–633.

Guion, S. G. (1998). The role of perception in the sound change of velar palatalization. *Phonetica, 55*(1–2), 18–52.

Guion, S. G., & Pederson, E. (2007). Investigating the role of attention in phonetic learning. In O.-S. Bohn & M. J. Munro (Eds.), *Language experience in second language speech learning* (pp. 57–77). Amsterdam: John Benjamins.

Gunter, K., Clayron, I., & Fridland, V. (2017). Pre-velar raising and categorization in Nevada. Paper presented at NoWPhon 3, Vancouver, BC, May 20.

Gureckis, T. M., & Goldstone, R. L. (2008). The effect of the internal structure of categories on perception. In *Proceedings of the 30th Annual Conference of the Cognitive Science Society* (pp. 1876–1881). Austin, TX: Cognitive Science Society.

Gwilliams, L., Linzen, T., Neophytou, K., Poeppel, D., & Marantz, A. (2016). Tracking lexical garden-path resolution with MEG: Phonological commitment and sensitivity to subphonemic detail are independent. Paper presented at the 22nd AMLaP conference, Architectures and Mechanisms for Language Processing, Bilbao, Spain, September 1–3.

Hadley, J. A., & Healy, A. F. (1991). When are reading units larger than the letter? Refinement of the unitization reading model. *Journal of Experimental Psychology: Learning, Memory, and Cognition, 17*(6), 1062–1073.

Hahn, U., Bailey, T. M., & Elvin, L. B. (2005). Effects of category diversity on learning, memory, and generalization. *Memory & Cognition, 33*(2), 289–302.

Haiman, J. (1994). Ritualization and the development of language. In W. Pagliuca (Ed.), *Perspectives on grammaticalization* (pp. 3–28). Amsterdam: John Benjamins.

Hall, G., & Channell, S. (1985). Differential effects of contextual change on latent inhibition and on the habituation of an orienting response. *Journal of Experimental Psychology: Animal Behavior Processes, 11*(3), 470–481.

Hall, G., & Honey, R. C. (1989). Contextual effects in conditioning, latent inhibition, and habituation: Associative and retrieval functions of contextual cues. *Journal of Experimental Psychology: Animal Behavior Processes, 15*, 232–241.

Halle, M. (1973). Prolegomena to a theory of word formation. *Linguistic Inquiry, 4*(1), 3–16.

Halle, M., & Marantz, A. (1993). Distributed morphology and the pieces of inflection. In K. Hale & S. J. Keyser (Eds.), *The View from Building 20: Essays in Linguistics in Honor of Sylvain Bromberger* (pp. 111–176). Cambridge, MA: MIT Press.

Harmon, Z., Idemaru, K., & Kapatsinski, V. (2017). The power of a unimodal distribution in cue reweighting: Unimodality vs prediction error as signs of cue irrelevance. *Journal of the Acoustical Society of America, 141*(5), 3520.

Harmon, Z., & Kapatsinski, V. (in press). Determinants of lengths of repetition disfluencies: Probabilistic syntactic constituency in speech production. *Chicago Linguistic Society, 50.*

Harmon, Z., & Kapatsinski, V. (2017). Putting old tools to novel uses: The role of form accessibility in semantic extension. *Cognitive Psychology, 98*, 22–44.

Harmon, Z., & Kapatsinski, V. (2016). Fuse to be used: A weak cue's guide to attracting attention. *Proceedings of the Annual Conference of the Cognitive Science Society, 38*, 520–525.

Harmon, Z., & Kapatsinski, V. (2015). Studying the dynamics of lexical access using disfluencies. In R. Lickley (Ed.), *Proceedings of the Workshop on Disfluencies in Spontaneous Speech* http://www.disfluency.org/DiSS_2015/Programme_files/Harmon-DISS2015.pdf.

Harrington, J., Palethorpe, S., & Watson, C. (2000). Monophthongal vowel changes in Received Pronunciation: An acoustic analysis of the Queen's Christmas broadcasts. *Journal of the International Phonetic Association, 30*(1–2), 63–78.

Haspelmath, M. (1995). The growth of affixes in morphological reanalysis. In G. Booij (Ed.), *Yearbook of morphology 1994* (pp. 1–29). Springer.

Hauser, M. D., Newport, E. L., & Aslin, R. N. (2001). Segmentation of the speech stream in a non-human primate: Statistical learning in cotton-top tamarins. *Cognition, 78*(3), B53–B64.

Hay, J. (2001). Lexical frequency in morphology: Is everything relative? *Linguistics, 39*(6), 1041–1070.

Hay, J., & Foulkes, P. (2016). The evolution of medial /t/ over real and remembered time. *Language, 92*(2), 298–330.

Hay, J. B., Pierrehumbert, J. B., Walker, A. J., & LaShell, P. (2015). Tracking word frequency effects through 130 years of sound change. *Cognition, 139*, 83–91.

Hay, J. F., Pelucchi, B., Estes, K. G., & Saffran, J. R. (2011). Linking sounds to meanings: Infant statistical learning in a natural language. *Cognitive Psychology, 63*(2), 93–106.

Hayes, B. (2004). Phonological acquisition in Optimality Theory: The early stages. In R. Kager, J. Pater, & W. Zonneveld (Eds.), *Constraints in phonological acquisition* (pp. 158–203). Cambridge: Cambridge University Press.

Hayes, B., Siptár, P., Zuraw, K., & Londe, Z. (2009). Natural and unnatural constraints in Hungarian vowel harmony. *Language, 85*(4), 822–863.

Hayes, B., & White, J. (2015). Saltation and the P-map. *Phonology, 32*(2), 1–36.

Hayes, B., & Wilson, C. (2008). A maximum entropy model of phonotactics and phonotactic learning. *Linguistic Inquiry, 39*(3), 379–440.

Head, H. (1920). *Studies in neurology*. Oxford: Oxford University Press.

Healy, A. F. (1994). Letter detection: A window to unitization and other cognitive processes in reading text. *Psychonomic Bulletin & Review, 1*(3), 333–344.

Healy, A. F. (1976). Detection errors on the word *the*: Evidence for reading units larger than letters. *Journal of Experimental Psychology: Human Perception and Performance, 2*(2), 235–242.

Hearst, E. (1991). Psychology and nothing. *American Scientist, 79*, 432–443.

Hebb, D. O. (1949). *The organization of behavior: A neuropsychological theory*. New York: Wiley.

Heine, B., & Kuteva, T. (2002). On the evolution of grammatical forms. In A. Wray (Ed.), *The transition to language* (pp. 376–397). Oxford: Oxford University Press.

Hendrickson, A. T., Carvalho, P. F., & Goldstone, R. L. (2012). Going to extremes: The influence of unsupervised categories on the mental caricaturization of faces and asymmetries in perceptual discrimination. *Proceedings of the Annual Conference of the Cognitive Science Society, 34*, 1662–1667.

Herd, W., Jongman, A., & Sereno, J. (2010). An acoustic and perceptual analysis of /t/ and /d/ flaps in American English. *Journal of Phonetics*, *38*(4), 504–516.

Hertwig, R., Barron, G., Weber, E. U., & Erev, I. (2004). Decisions from experience and the effect of rare events in risky choice. *Psychological Science*, *15*(8), 534–539.

Hewlett, N., & Rendall, M. (1998). Rural versus urban accent as an influence on the rate of speech. *Journal of the International Phonetic Association*, *28*(1–2), 63–71.

Hicks, L. H. (1964). Effects of overtraining on acquisition and reversal of place and response learning. *Psychological Reports*, *15*(2), 459–462.

Hillenbrand, J., Getty, L. A., Clark, M. J., & Wheeler, K. (1995). Acoustic characteristics of American English vowels. *Journal of the Acoustical Society of America*, *97*, 3099–3111.

Hilpert, M. (2008). *Germanic future constructions: A usage-based approach to language change*. Amsterdam: John Benjamins.

Hockett, C. D. (1960). The origin of speech. *Scientific American*, *203*, 88–96.

Hoff, E. (2013). *Language development*. Boston: Cengage Learning.

Hofstede, G. H. (1980) *Culture's consequences*. Beverly Hills, CA: Sage.

Holland, P. C. (1992). Occasion setting in Pavlovian conditioning. In D. L. Medin (Ed.), *The Psychology of Learning and Motivation*, *28*, 69–125. San Diego: Academic Press.

Holland, P. C. (1989). Occasion setting with simultaneous compounds in rats. *Journal of Experimental Psychology: Animal Behavior Processes*, *15*(3), 183–193.

Holland, P. C. (1984). Differential effects of reinforcement of an inhibitory feature after serial and simultaneous feature negative discrimination training. *Journal of Experimental Psychology: Animal Behavior Processes*, *10*, 461–475.

Holland, P. C. (1983). Occasion-setting in Pavlovian feature positive discriminations. *Quantitative Analyses of Behavior*, *4*, 183–206.

Holt, L. L., Lotto, A. J., & Kluender, K. R. (1998). Incorporating principles of general learning in theories of language acquisition. *Chicago Linguistic Society*, *34*, 253–268.

Holyoak, K. J., & Cheng, P. W. (2011). Causal learning and inference as a rational process: The new synthesis. *Annual Review of Psychology*, *62*, 135–163.

Honeybone, P. (2016). Are there impossible changes? θ > f but f ≯ θ. *Papers in Historical Phonology*, *1*, 316–358.

Honikman, B. (1964). Articulatory settings. In D. Abercrombie, D. B. Fry, P. A. D. MacCarthy, N. C. Scott, and J. L. M. Trim (Eds.), *In honour of Daniel Jones* (pp. 73–84). London: Longman.

Horst, J. S., & Samuelson, L. K. (2008). Fast mapping but poor retention by 24-month-old infants. *Infancy, 13*(2), 128–157.

Householder, F. W. (1966). Phonological theory: A brief comment. *Journal of Linguistics, 2*(1), 99–100.

Houston, D. M., & Jusczyk, P. W. (2003). Infants' long-term memory for the sound patterns of words and voices. *Journal of Experimental Psychology: Human Perception and Performance, 29*(6), 1143–1154.

Howes, D. (1957). On the relation between the intelligibility and frequency of occurrence of English words. *Journal of the Acoustical Society of America, 29*(2), 296–305.

Howes, D., & R. L. Solomon. (1951). Visual duration threshold as a function of word-probability. *Journal of Experimental Psychology, 41,* 401–410.

Hsu, A., & Griffiths, T. (2010). Effects of generative and discriminative learning on use of category variability. *Proceedings of the Annual Conference of the Cognitive Science Society, 32,* 242–247.

Hsu, A., & Griffiths, T. (2009). Differential use of implicit negative evidence in generative and discriminative language learning. *Advances in Neural Information Processing Systems, 22,* 754–762.

Hubert-Wallander, B., & Boynton, G. M. (2015). Not all summary statistics are made equal: Evidence from extracting summaries across time. *Journal of Vision, 15*(4), 5.

Hudson Kam, C. L., & Newport, E. L. (2005). Regularizing unpredictable variation: The roles of adult and child learners in language formation and change. *Language Learning and Development, 1*(2), 151–195.

Hullinger, R. A., Kruschke, J. K., & Todd, P. M. (2015). An evolutionary analysis of learned attention. *Cognitive Science, 39*(6), 1172–1215.

Hunter, W. S. (1920). The temporal maze and kinesthetic sensory processes in the white rat. *Psychobiology, 2,* 1–17.

Idemaru, K., & Holt, L. L. (2014). Specificity of dimension-based statistical learning in word recognition. *Journal of Experimental Psychology: Human Perception and Performance, 40*(3), 1009–1021.

Idemaru, K., & Holt, L. L. (2013). The developmental trajectory of children's perception and production of English /r/-/l/. *Journal of the Acoustical Society of America, 133*(6), 4232–4246.

Idemaru, K., & Holt, L. L. (2012). Examining talker and phoneme generalization of dimension-based statistical learning in speech perception. In F. Cox, K. Demuth, S. Lin, K. Miles, S. Palethrope, J. Shaw, & I. Yuen (Ed.), *Proceedings of the 14th Australasian International Conference on Speech Science and Technology,* 165–168. Sydney: ASSTA.

Idemaru, K., & Holt, L. L. (2011). Word recognition reflects dimension-based statistical learning. *Journal of Experimental Psychology: Human Perception and Performance*, *37*(6), 1939–1956.

Idemaru, K., Holt, L. L., & Seltman, H. (2012). Individual differences in cue weights are stable across time: The case of Japanese stop lengths. *Journal of the Acoustical Society of America*, *132*(6), 3950–3964.

Inkelas, S. (2015). *The interplay of morphology and phonology*. Oxford: Oxford University Press.

Itô, J., & Mester, A. (1996). Stem and word in Sino-Japanese. In T. Otake & A. Cutler (Eds.), *Phonological structure and language processing: Cross-linguistic studies* (pp. 13–44). Berlin: Mouton de Gruyter.

Jacewicz, E., Fox, R., and Salmons, J. (2007). Vowel duration in three American English dialects. *American Speech*, *82*, 367–385.

James, C. T., & Greeno, J. G. (1967). Stimulus selection at different stages of paired-associate learning. *Journal of Experimental Psychology*, *74*(1), 75–83.

James, W. (1890). *The principles of psychology*. New York: Henry Holt.

James, W. (1880). Great men, great thoughts, and the environment. *Atlantic Monthly*, *46*, 441–459.

Jenkins, H. M. (1985). Conditioned inhibition of key pecking in the pigeon. In R. R. Miller & N. E. Spear (Eds.), *Information processing in animals—conditioned inhibition* (pp. 327–353). Mahwah, NJ: Erlbaum.

Johnson, E. K., & Jusczyk, P. W. (2001). Word segmentation by 8-month-olds: When speech cues count more than statistics. *Journal of Memory and Language*, *44*(4), 548–567.

Johnson, K. (2005). Speaker normalization in speech perception. In D. B. Pisoni & R. E. Remez (Eds.), *The handbook of speech perception* (pp. 363–389). Malden, MA: Blackwell.

Johnson, K., Flemming, E., & Wright, R. (1993). The hyperspace effect: Phonetic targets are hyperarticulated. *Language*, *69*(3), 505–528.

Johnson, M. A. (2013). *The cognitive and neural basis of language learning: Investigations in typical and autistic populations* (doctoral dissertation, Princeton University).

Johnston, L. H., & Kapatsinski, V. (2011). In the beginning there were the weird: A phonotactic novelty preference in adult word learning. *Proceedings of the International Congress of Phonetic Sciences*, *17*, 978–981.

Jones, S. (2002). *Antonymy: A corpus-based approach*. London: Routledge.

Jones, S., Paradis, C., Murphy, M. L., & Willners, C. (2007). Googling for "opposites": A web-based study of antonym canonicity. *Corpora, 2*(2), 129–154.

Joseph, B. D. (2000). Is there such a thing as "grammaticalization"? *Language Sciences, 23*(2), 163–186.

Jurafsky, D., Bell, A., Gregory, M., & Raymond, W. D. (2001). Probabilistic relations between words: Evidence from reduction in lexical production. In J. L. Bybee & P. J. Hopper (Eds.), *Frequency and the emergence of linguistic structure* (pp. 229–245). Amsterdam: John Benjamins.

Jusczyk, P. W., Cutler, A., & Redanz, N. J. (1993). Infants' preference for the predominant stress patterns of English words. *Child Development, 64*(3), 675–687.

Justeson, J. S., & Katz, S. M. (1991). Co-occurrences of antonymous adjectives and their contexts. *Computational Linguistics, 17*, 1–19.

Kachergis, G., Yu, C., & Shiffrin, R. M. (2012). Cross-situational word learning is better modeled by associations than hypotheses. In *Proceedings of the 2012 IEEE International Conference on Development and Learning and Epigenetic Robotics (ICDL)* (pp. 1–6). Piscataway, NJ: IEEE.

Kaelbling, L. P., Littman, M. L., & Moore, A. W. (1996). Reinforcement learning: A survey. *Journal of Artificial Intelligence Research, 4*, 237–285.

Kahana, M. J. (2002). Associative symmetry and memory theory. *Memory & Cognition, 30*, 823–840.

Kahneman, D. (2011). *Thinking, fast and slow*. New York: Farrar, Straus and Giroux.

Kahneman, D., & Tversky, A. (1972). Subjective probability: A judgment of representativeness. *Cognitive Psychology, 3*, 430–454.

Kakouros, S., & Räsänen, O. (2016). Perception of sentence stress in speech correlates with the temporal unpredictability of prosodic features. *Cognitive Science, 40*(7), 1739–1774.

Kalish, M. L., Griffiths, T. L., & Lewandowsky, S. (2007). Iterated learning: Intergenerational knowledge transmission reveals inductive biases. *Psychonomic Bulletin & Review, 14*(2), 288–294.

Kalish, M. L., & Kruschke, J. K. (2000). The role of attention shifts in the categorization of continuous dimensioned stimuli. *Psychological Research, 64*(2), 105–116.

Kamin, L. J. (1969). Predictability, surprise, attention, and conditioning. In B. A. Campbell & R. M. Church (Eds.), *Punishment and aversive behavior* (pp. 279–296). New York: Appleton-Century-Crofts.

Kamin, L. J. (1965). Temporal and intensity characteristics of the conditioned stimulus. In W. F. Prokasy (Ed.), *Classical conditioning* (pp. 118–147). New York: Appleton-Century-Crofts.

Kao, S. F., & Wasserman, E. A. (1993). Assessment of an information integration account of contingency judgment with examination of subjective cell importance and method of information presentation. *Journal of Experimental Psychology: Learning, Memory, and Cognition, 19*(6), 1363–1386.

Kapatsinski, V. (in press). Learning morphological constructions. In G. Booij (Ed.), *The construction of words: Advances in Construction Morphology*. Springer.

Kapatsinski, V. (2017). Learning a subtractive morphological system: Statistics and representations. *Proceedings of the Boston University Conference on Language Development, 41*(1), 357–372.

Kapatsinski, V. (2015). *Sound change and hierarchical inference: What is being inferred? Effects of words, phones, and frequency.* Ms., University of Oregon.

Kapatsinski, V. (2013). Conspiring to mean: Experimental and computational evidence for a usage-based harmonic approach to morphophonology. *Language, 89*(1), 110–148.

Kapatsinski, V. (2012). What statistics do learners track? Rules, constraints and schemas in (artificial) grammar learning. In S. Th. Gries & D. Divjak (Eds.), *Frequency effects in language learning and processing* (pp. 53–73). Berlin: Walter de Gruyter.

Kapatsinski, V. (2011). Modularity in the channel: The link between separability of features and learnability of dependencies between them. *Proceedings of the International Congress of Phonetic Sciences, 17*, 1022–1025.

Kapatsinski, V. (2010a). Frequency of use leads to automaticity of production: Evidence from repair in conversation. *Language and Speech, 53*(1), 71–105.

Kapatsinski, V. (2010b). Velar palatalization in Russian and artificial grammar: Constraints on models of morphophonology. *Laboratory Phonology, 1*(2), 361–393.

Kapatsinski, V. (2010c). What is it I am writing? Lexical frequency effects in spelling Russian prefixes: Uncertainty and competition in an apparently regular system. *Corpus Linguistics and Linguistic Theory, 6*(2), 157–215.

Kapatsinski, V. (2009a). Adversative conjunction choice in Russian (*no, da, odnako*): Semantic and syntactic influences on lexical selection. *Language Variation and Change, 21*(2), 157–173.

Kapatsinski, V. (2009b). *The architecture of grammar in artificial grammar learning: Formal biases in the acquisition of morphophonology and the nature of the learning task* (doctoral dissertation, Indiana University).

Kapatsinski, V. (2009c). Testing theories of linguistic constituency with configural learning: The case of the English syllable. *Language, 85*(2), 248–277.

Kapatsinski, V. M. (2007a). Frequency, neighborhood density, age-of-acquisition, and lexicon size effects in priming, recognition, and associative learning: Towards a single-mechanism account. *Proceedings of the Sixth Annual High Desert Linguistics Society Conference, 6,* 101–120.

Kapatsinski, V. (2007b). Implementing and testing theories of linguistic constituency I: English syllable structure. *Research on Spoken Language Processing Progress Report, 28,* 242–276.

Kapatsinski, V. (2006). Having something common in common is not the same as sharing something special: Sublexical frequency effects constrain theories of similarity. Paper presented at the Annual Meeting of the Linguistic Society of America. http://pages.uoregon.edu/vkapatsi/LSA.pdf.

Kapatsinski, V. (2005a). Measuring the relationship of structure to use: Determinants of the extent of recycle in repetition repair. In M. Ettlinger, N. Fleisher, & M. Park-Doob (Eds.), *Proceedings of the Annual Meeting of the Berkeley Linguistics Society* (Vol. 30, No. 1, pp. 481–492). Berkeley: Berkeley Linguistics Society, University of California.

Kapatsinski, V. M. (2005b). *Productivity of Russian stem extensions: Evidence for and a formalization of Network Theory* (MA thesis, University of New Mexico).

Kapatsinski, V., Olejarczuk, P., & Redford, M. A. (2017). Perceptual learning of intonation contour categories in adults and 9- to 11-year-old children: Adults are more narrow-minded. *Cognitive Science, 41*(2), 383–415.

Kapatsinski, V., & Radicke, J. (2009). Frequency and the emergence of prefabs: Evidence from monitoring. In R. Corrigan, E. A. Moravcsik, H. Ouali, & K. Wheatley (Eds.), *Formulaic Language: Vol. 2. Acquisition, loss, psychological reality, and functional explanations* (pp. 499–520). Amsterdam: John Benjamins.

Karmiloff-Smith, A. (1995). *Beyond modularity: A developmental perspective on cognitive science.* Cambridge, MA: MIT Press.

Keating, P. A. (1990). The window model of coarticulation: Articulatory evidence. In J. Kingston & M. E. Beckman (Eds.), *Papers in laboratory phonology I: Between the grammar and physics of speech* (pp. 451–470). Cambridge: Cambridge University Press.

Keele, S. W., Ivry, R., Mayr, U., Hazeltine, E., & Heuer, H. (2003). The cognitive and neural architecture of sequence representation. *Psychological Review, 110*(2), 316–339.

Kempen, G., & Harbusch, K. (2005). The relationship between grammaticality ratings and corpus frequencies: A case study into word order variability in the midfield of German clauses. In S. Kepser & M. Reis (Eds.), *Linguistic evidence: Empirical, theoretical, and computational perspectives* (pp. 329–349). Berlin: Mouton de Gruyter.

Kendall, T. (2013). *Speech rate, pause, and sociolinguistic variation: Studies in corpus sociophonetics.* New York: Palgrave Macmillan.

Kenstowicz, M. (1996). Base identity and uniform exponence: Alternatives to cyclicity. In J. Durand & B. Laks (Eds.), *Current trends in phonology: Models and methods* (Vol. 1, pp. 363–393). Salford, UK: University of Salford.

Kerswill, P. (1996). Children, adolescents, and language change. *Language Variation and Change, 8*(2), 177–202.

Kerswill, P., & Williams, A. (2000). Creating a New Town koine: Children and language change in Milton Keynes. *Language in Society, 29*(1), 65–115.

Keuleers, E., Stevens, M., Mandera, P., & Brysbaert, M. (2015). Word knowledge in the crowd: Measuring vocabulary size and word prevalence in a massive online experiment. *Quarterly Journal of Experimental Psychology, 68*(8), 1665–1692.

Kewley-Port, D., & Preston, M. S. (1974). Early apical stop production: A voice onset time analysis. *Journal of Phonetics, 1*(2), 195–210.

King, A. P., Freeberg, T. M., & West, M. J. (1996). Social experience affects the process and outcome of vocal ontogeny in two populations of cowbirds (*Molothrus ater*). *Journal of Comparative Psychology, 110*(3), 276–285.

King, A. P., West, M. J., & Goldstein, M. H. (2005). Non-vocal shaping of avian song development: Parallels to human speech development. *Ethology, 111*(1), 101–117.

Kinnaman, A. J. (1902). Mental life of two macacus rhesus monkeys in captivity. *American Journal of Psychology, 13*, 98–148, 173–218.

Kiparsky, P. (1985). Some consequences of lexical phonology. *Phonology, 2*(1), 85–138.

Kirby, S., Cornish, H., & Smith, K. (2008). Cumulative cultural evolution in the laboratory: An experimental approach to the origins of structure in human language. *Proceedings of the National Academy of Sciences, 105*(31), 10681–10686.

Kirkpatrick, S., Gelatt, C. D., & Vecchi, M. P. (1983). Optimization by simulated annealing. *Science, 220*(4598), 671–680.

Kirov, C., & Wilson, C. (2012). The specificity of online variation in speech production. *Proceedings of the Annual Meeting of the Cognitive Science Society, 34*, 587–592.

Kisseberth, C. W. (1970). On the functional unity of phonological rules. *Linguistic Inquiry, 1*(3), 291–306.

Klatt, D. H. (1979). Speech perception: A model of acoustic-phonetic analysis and lexical access. *Journal of Phonetics, 7*(3), 279–312.

Kluender, K. R., Lotto, A. J., Holt, L. L., & Bloedel, S. L. (1998). Role of experience for language-specific functional mappings of vowel sounds. *Journal of the Acoustical Society of America, 104*(6), 3568–3582.

Kochetov, A. (2011). Palatalisation. In C. Ewen, B. Hume, M. van Oostendorp, & K. Rice (Eds.), *Blackwell Companion to Phonology* (pp. 1666–1690). Hoboken, NJ: Wiley-Blackwell.

Koenig, L. L. (2001). Distributional characteristics of VOT in children's voiceless aspirated stops and interpretation of developmental trends. *Journal of Speech, Language, and Hearing Research, 44*(5), 1058–1068.

Köpcke, K.-M., & Wecker, V. (2017). Source- and product-oriented strategies in L2 acquisition of plural marking in German. *Morphology, 21*, 77–103.

Kosie, J. E., & Baldwin, D. (2016). A twist on event processing: Reorganizing attention to cope with novelty in dynamic activity sequences. *Proceedings of the Annual Conference of the Cognitive Science Society, 38*, 1337–1342.

Kouider, S., & Dehaene, S. (2009). Subliminal number priming within and across the visual and auditory modalities. *Experimental Psychology, 56*(6), 418–433.

Kreuz, R. J. (1987). The subjective familiarity of English homophones. *Memory & Cognition, 15*(2), 154–168.

Krishnan, A., Xu, Y., Gandour, J., & Cariani, P. (2005). Encoding of pitch in the human brainstem is sensitive to language experience. *Cognitive Brain Research, 25*(1), 161–168.

Kruschke, J. K. (2015). *Doing Bayesian data analysis: A tutorial with R, JAGS, and Stan* (2nd ed.). London: Academic Press.

Kruschke, J. K. (2009). Highlighting: A canonical experiment. *Psychology of Learning and Motivation, 51*, 153–185.

Kruschke, J. K. (2008). Bayesian approaches to associative learning: From passive to active learning. *Learning & Behavior, 36*(3), 210–226.

Kruschke, J. K. (2006). Locally Bayesian learning with applications to retrospective revaluation and highlighting. *Psychological Review, 113*(4), 677–699.

Kruschke, J. K. (1996). Dimensional relevance shifts in category learning. *Connection Science, 8*(2), 225–248.

Kruschke, J. K. (1992). ALCOVE: An exemplar-based connectionist model of category learning. *Psychological Review, 99*(1), 22–44.

Kruschke, J. K., & Blair, N. J. (2000). Blocking and backward blocking involve learned inattention. *Psychonomic Bulletin & Review, 7*(4), 636–645.

Kruschke, J. K., & Johansen, M. K. (1999). A model of probabilistic category learning. *Journal of Experimental Psychology: Learning, Memory, and Cognition, 25*(5), 1083–1119.

Kruschke, J. K., Kappenman, E. S., & Hetrick, W. P. (2005). Eye gaze and individual differences consistent with learned attention in associative blocking and highlighting. *Journal of Experimental Psychology: Learning, Memory, and Cognition, 31*(5), 830–845.

Kuczaj, S. A. (1977). The acquisition of regular and irregular past tense forms. *Journal of Verbal Learning and Verbal Behavior, 16*(5), 589–600.

Kuhl, P. K. (1991). Human adults and human infants show a "perceptual magnet effect" for the prototypes of speech categories, monkeys do not. *Attention, Perception, & Psychophysics, 50*(2), 93–107.

Kuhl, P. K., Williams, K. A., Lacerda, F., Stevens, K. N., & Lindblom, B. (1992). Linguistic experience alters phonetic perception in infants by 6 months of age. *Science, 255*(5044), 606–608.

Kuo, L. J., & Anderson, R. C. (2006). Morphological awareness and learning to read: A cross-language perspective. *Educational Psychologist, 41*(3), 161–180.

Kwon, N., & Round, E. R. (2015). Phonaesthemes in morphological theory. *Morphology, 25*(1), 1–27.

Labov, W. (2001). *Principles of linguistic change: Vol. 2. Social factors.* Oxford: Blackwell.

Labov, W. (1996). When intuitions fail. *Chicago Linguistic Society, 32*, 76–106.

Labov, W. (1994). *Principles of linguistic change: Vol. 1. Internal factors.* Oxford: Blackwell.

Labov, W. (1989). The child as linguistic historian. *Language Variation & Change, 1*(1), 85–97.

Labov, W., Karen, M., & Miller, C. (1991). Near-mergers and the suspension of phonemic contrast. *Language Variation & Change, 3*(1), 33–74.

Landauer, T. K., & Dumais, S. T. (1997). A solution to Plato's problem: The latent semantic analysis theory of acquisition, induction, and representation of knowledge. *Psychological Review, 104*(2), 211–240.

Langacker, R. (2011). Grammaticalization and Cognitive Grammar. In B. Heine & H. Narrog (Eds.), *The Oxford handbook of grammaticalization* (pp. 79–91). Oxford: Oxford University Press.

Langacker, R. (1987). *Foundations of Cognitive Grammar: Vol. 1. Theoretical prerequisites.* Stanford, CA: Stanford University Press.

LaPlace, P.-S. (1812). *Théorie analitique des probabilities.* Paris: Mme Ve Courcier.

Lashley, K. S. (1951). The problem of serial order in behavior. In A. L. Jeffress (Ed.), *Cerebral processes in behavior* (pp. 112–136). New York: Wiley.

Lawrence, D. H. (1950). Acquired distinctiveness of cues: II. Selective association in a constant stimulus situation. *Journal of Experimental Psychology, 40*(2), 175–188.

Lawrence, D. H. (1949). Acquired distinctiveness of cues: I. Transfer between discriminations on the basis of familiarity with the stimulus. *Journal of Experimental Psychology, 39*(6), 770–784.

Lea, S. E. G. (1979). Foraging and reinforcement schedules in the pigeon: Optimal and non-optimal aspects of choice. *Animal Behaviour, 27*, 875–886.

Legendre, G., Miyata, Y., & Smolensky, P. (1990). *Can connectionism contribute to syntax?: Harmonic Grammar, with an application.* Boulder: Department of Computer Science, University of Colorado.

Lenneberg, E. H. (1957). A probabilistic approach to language learning. *Behavioral Science, 2*(1), 1–12.

Le Pelley, M. E., & McLaren, I. P. L. (2003). Learned associability and associative change in human causal learning. *Quarterly Journal of Experimental Psychology, 56B*, 68–79.

Levelt, W. J. (1983). Monitoring and self-repair in speech. *Cognition, 14*(1), 41–104.

Levin, I. P., Wasserman, E. A., & Kao, S.-F. (1993). Multiple methods for examining the contributions of specific cell information to contingency judgments. *Organizational Behavior and Human Decision Processes, 55*, 228–250.

Levow, G. A. (1999). Understanding recognition failures in spoken corrections in human-computer dialogue. In *ESCA Tutorial and Research Workshop (ETRW) on Dialogue and Prosody* (pp.193–198). International Speech Communication Association. http://isca-speech.org/archive_open/dia_pros/index.html.

Liberman, A. M., Cooper, F. S., Shankweiler, D. P., & Studdert-Kennedy, M. (1967). Perception of the speech code. *Psychological Review, 74*(6), 431–461.

Liberman, A. M., & Mattingly, I. G. (1985). The motor theory of speech perception. *Cognition, 21*(1), 1–36.

Lidz, J., & Gagliardi, A. (2015). How nature meets nurture: Universal Grammar and statistical learning. *Annual Review of Linguistics, 1*(1), 333–353.

Lieder, F., Hsu, M., & Griffiths, T. L. (2014). The high availability of extreme events serves resource-rational decision-making. *Proceedings of the Annual Conference of the Cognitive Science Society, 36*, 2567–2572.

Liljeholm, M., & Balleine, B. W. (2010). Extracting functional equivalence from reversing contingencies. *Journal of Experimental Psychology: Animal Behavior Processes, 36*(2), 165–172.

Lim, S. J., Fiez, J. A., & Holt, L. L. (2014). How may the basal ganglia contribute to auditory categorization and speech perception? *Frontiers in Neuroscience, 8*, 230.

Lindblom, B. (1990). Explaining phonetic variation: A sketch of the H&H theory. In W. J. Hardcastle & A. Marchal (Eds.), *Speech production and speech modelling* (pp. 403–439). Dordrecht: Kluwer.

Lindblom, B. (1963). Spectrographic study of vowel reduction. *Journal of the Acoustical society of America, 35*(11), 1773–1781.

Lindskog, M., Winman, A., & Juslin, P. (2013). Calculate or wait: Is man an eager or a lazy intuitive statistician? *Journal of Cognitive Psychology, 25*(8), 994–1014.

Linzen, T., & Gallagher, G. (2014, March). The timecourse of generalization in phonotactic learning. In J. Kingston, C. Moore-Cantwell, J. Pater, & R. Staubs (Eds.), *Proceedings of the Annual Meetings on Phonology* (Vol. 1). https://journals .linguisticsociety.org/proceedings/index.php/amphonology/issue/view/1

Lionello-DeNolf, K. M. (2009). The search for symmetry: 25 years in review. *Learning & Behavior, 37*(2), 188–203.

Lisker, L. (1986). "Voicing" in English: A catalogue of acoustic features signaling /b/ versus /p/ in trochees. *Language and Speech, 29*(1), 3–11.

Livesey, E. J., & McLaren, I. P. L. (2011). An elemental model of associative learning and memory. In E. M. Pothos & A. J. Wills (Eds.), *Formal approaches in categorization* (pp. 153–172). Cambridge: Cambridge University Press.

Locke, J. L. (1968). Discriminative learning in children's acquisition of phonology. *Journal of Speech, Language, and Hearing Research, 11*(2), 428–434.

Logan, G. D. (1982). On the ability to inhibit complex movements: A stop-signal study of typewriting. *Journal of Experimental Psychology: Human Perception and Performance, 8*(6), 778–792.

Lovibond, P. F., Preston, G. C., & Mackintosh, N. J. (1984). Context specificity of conditioning, extinction, and latent inhibition. *Journal of Experimental Psychology: Animal Behavior Processes, 10*(3), 360–375.

Lubow, R. E., & Moore, A. U. (1959). Latent inhibition: The effect of non-reinforced pre-exposure to the conditioned stimulus. *Journal of Comparative and Physiological Psychology, 52*, 416–419.

Łubowicz, A. (2007). Paradigmatic contrast in Polish. *Journal of Slavic Linguistics, 15*, 229–262.

Luce, R. D. (1959). *Individual choice behavior.* New York: Wiley.

MacDonald, M. C. (1994). Probabilistic constraints and syntactic ambiguity resolution. *Language and Cognitive Processes, 9*(2), 157–201.

Mackintosh, N. J. (1976). Overshadowing and stimulus intensity. *Animal Learning & Behavior, 4*(2), 186–192.

Mackintosh, N. J. (1975). A theory of attention: Variations in the associability of stimuli with reinforcement. *Psychological Review, 82*(4), 276–298.

Mackintosh, N. J., & Turner, C. (1971). Blocking as a function of novelty of CS and predictability of UCS. *Quarterly Journal of Experimental Psychology, 23*(4), 359–366.

MacWhinney, B. (1987). The Competition Model. In B. MacWhinney (Ed.), *Mechanisms of language acquisition* (pp. 249–308). Hillsdale, NJ: Erlbaum.

MacWhinney, B., Pleh, C., & Bates, E. (1985). The development of sentence interpretation in Hungarian. *Cognitive Psychology, 17*(2), 178–209.

Madan, C. R., Ludvig, E. A., & Spetch, M. L. (2014). Remembering the best and worst of times: Memories for extreme outcomes bias risky decisions. *Psychonomic Bulletin & Review, 21*(3), 629–636.

Madlener, K. (2016). Input optimization: Effects of type and token frequency manipulations in instructed second language learning. In H. Behrens & S. Pfänder (Eds.), *Experience counts: Frequency effects in language* (pp. 133–174). Berlin: Walter de Gruyter.

Magnuson, J. S., Tanenhaus, M. K., Aslin, R. N., & Dahan, D. (2003). The time course of spoken word learning and recognition: Studies with artificial lexicons. *Journal of Experimental Psychology: General, 132*(2), 202–227.

Mahoney, W. J., & Ayres, J. J. (1976). One-trial simultaneous and backward fear conditioning as reflected in conditioned suppression of licking in rats. *Animal Learning & Behavior, 4*(4), 357–362.

Mampe, B., Friederici, A. D., Christophe, A., & Wermke, K. (2009). Newborns' cry melody is shaped by their native language. *Current Biology, 19*(23), 1994–1997.

Maniwa, K., Jongman, A., & Wade, T. (2009). Acoustic characteristics of clearly spoken English fricatives. *Journal of the Acoustical Society of America, 125*(6), 3962–3973.

Marcus, G. F., Pinker, S., Ullman, M., Hollander, M., Rosen, T. J., & Xu, F. (1992). Overregularization in language acquisition. *Monographs of the Society for Research in Child Development, 57*(4), 1–182.

Mareschal, D., Johnson, M. H., Sirois, S., Spratling, M. W., Thomas, M. S. C., & Westermann, G. (2007). *Neuroconstructivism: How the brain constructs cognition* (Vol. 1). Oxford: Oxford University Press.

Markman, A. B. (1989). LMS rules and the inverse base-rate effect: Comment on Gluck and Bower (1988). *Journal of Experimental Psychology: General, 118*(4), 417–421.

Marslen-Wilson, W. D., & Welsh, A. (1978). Processing interactions and lexical access during word recognition in continuous speech. *Cognitive Psychology, 10*(1), 29–63.

Marsolek, C. J. (2008). What antipriming reveals about priming. *Trends in Cognitive Sciences, 12*(5), 176–181.

Martin, A. T. (2007). *The evolving lexicon* (doctoral dissertation, UCLA).

Maslow, A. H. (1966). *The psychology of science: A reconnaissance.* New York: Harper.

Massaro, D. W., & Cohen, M. M. (1983). Categorical or continuous speech perception: A new test. *Speech Communication, 2*(1), 15–35.

Matthews, P. H. (1972). *Inflectional morphology: A theoretical study based on aspects of Latin verb conjugation.* Cambridge: Cambridge University Press.

Matute, H., Arcediano, F., & Miller, R. R. (1996). Test question modulates cue competition between causes and between effects. *Journal of Experimental Psychology: Learning, Memory, and Cognition, 22*(1), 182–196.

Matzel, L. D., Held, F. P., & Miller, R. R. (1988). Information and expression of simultaneous and backward associations: Implications for contiguity theory. *Learning & Motivation, 19,* 317–344.

Matzel, L. D., Schachtman, T. R., & Miller, R. R. (1985). Recovery of an overshadowed association achieved by extinction of the overshadowing stimulus. *Learning and Motivation, 16*(4), 398–412.

Maye, J., & Gerken, L. (2000). Learning phonemes without minimal pairs. *Proceedings of the Annual Boston University Conference on Language Development, 24*(2), 522–533.

Maye, J., Weiss, D. J., & Aslin, R. N. (2008). Statistical phonetic learning in infants: Facilitation and feature generalization. *Developmental Science, 11*(1), 122–134.

Maye, J., Werker, J. F., & Gerken, L. (2002). Infant sensitivity to distributional information can affect phonetic discrimination. *Cognition, 82*(3), B101–B111.

Mayr, E. (1974). Behavior Programs and Evolutionary Strategies: Natural selection sometimes favors a genetically "closed" behavior program, sometimes an "open" one. *American Scientist, 62*(6), 650–659.

McCarthy, J. J. (2005). Optimal paradigms. In L. Downing, T. A. Hall, & R. Raffelsiefen (Eds.), *Paradigms in phonological theory.* Oxford: Oxford University Press.

McCarthy, J. J. (1982). Prosodic templates, morphemic templates and morphemic tiers. In H. van der Hulst & N. Smith (Eds.), *The structure of phonological representations* (Pt. 1, pp. 191–223). Dordrecht: Foris.

McCarthy, J. J., & Prince, A. (1999) Prosodic morphology (1986). In J. Goldsmith (Ed.), *Phonological theory: The essential readings* (pp. 238–288). Malden, MA: Blackwell.

McClelland, J. L. (2001). Failures to learn and their remediation: A Hebbian account. In James L. McClelland & Robert S. Siegler (Eds.), *Mechanisms of cognitive development: Behavioral and neural perspectives* (pp. 97–121). Mahwah, NJ: Erlbaum.

McClelland, J. L., & Elman, J. L. (1986). The TRACE model of speech perception. *Cognitive Psychology, 18*(1), 1–86.

McClelland, J. L., McNaughton, B. L., & O'Reilly, R. C. (1995). Why there are complementary learning systems in the hippocampus and neocortex: Insights from the successes and failures of connectionist models of learning and memory. *Psychological Review, 102*(3), 419–457.

McGurk, H., & MacDonald, J. (1976). Hearing lips and seeing voices. *Nature, 264,* 746–748.

McKenzie, C. R., & Mikkelsen, L. A. (2007). A Bayesian view of covariation assessment. *Cognitive Psychology, 54*(1), 33–61.

McKinley, S. C., & Nosofsky, R. M. (1995). Investigations of exemplar and decision bound models in large, ill-defined category structures. *Journal of Experimental Psychology: Human Perception and Performance, 21*(1), 128–148.

McMurray, B. (2007). Defusing the childhood vocabulary explosion. *Science, 317*(5838), 631–631.

McMurray, B., Clayards, M. A., Tanenhaus, M. K., & Aslin, R. N. (2008). Tracking the time course of phonetic cue integration during spoken word recognition. *Psychonomic Bulletin & Review, 15*(6), 1064–1071.

McMurray, B., Horst, J. S., & Samuelson, L. K. (2012). Word learning emerges from the interaction of online referent selection and slow associative learning. *Psychological Review, 119*(4), 831–877.

McMurray, B., Kucker, S. C., Zhao, L., & Samuelson, L. K. (2013). Pushing the envelope of associative learning: Internal representations and dynamic competition transform association into development. In L. Gogate & G. Hollich (Eds.), *Theoretical and computational models of word learning* (pp. 49–80). Hershey, PA: IGI Global.

McMurray, B., Tanenhaus, M. K., & Aslin, R. N. (2009). Within-category VOT affects recovery from "lexical" garden-paths: Evidence against phoneme-level inhibition. *Journal of Memory & Language, 60*(1), 65–91.

McNeill, D. (1966). A study of word association. *Journal of Verbal Learning & Verbal Behavior, 5,* 548–557.

McNeill, D. (1963). The origin of associations within the same grammatical class. *Journal of Verbal Learning & Verbal Behavior, 3,* 250–262.

Medin, D. L., & Edelson, S. M. (1988). Problem structure and the use of base-rate information from experience. *Journal of Experimental Psychology: General, 117*(1), 68–85.

Mehler, J., Bertoncini, J., Barrière, M., & Jassik-Gerschenfeld, D. (1978). Infant recognition of mother's voice. *Perception, 7*(5), 491–497.

Mielke, J., Nielsen, K., and Magloughlin, L. V. (2013). Phonetic imitation by individuals with Autism Spectrum Disorders: Investigating the role of procedural and declarative memory. *Proceedings of Meetings on Acoustics, 19*, 060142.

Milin, P., Kuperman, V., Kostic, A., & Baayen, R. H. (2009). Paradigms bit by bit: An information theoretic approach to the processing of paradigmatic structure in inflection and derivation. In J. P. Blevins & J. Blevins (Eds.), *Analogy in grammar: Form and acquisition* (pp. 214–252). Oxford: Oxford University Press.

Miller, J. L. (1994). On the internal structure of phonetic categories: A progress report. *Cognition, 50*(1), 271–285.

Miller, R. R., Barnet, R. C., & Grahame, N. J. (1995). Assessment of the Rescorla-Wagner model. *Psychological Bulletin, 117*, 363–386.

Miller, R. R., & Escobar, M. (2002). Associative interference between cues and between outcomes presented together and presented apart: An integration. *Behavioural Processes, 57*(2), 163–185.

Miller, R. R., & Matzel, L. D. (1988). The comparator hypothesis: A response rule for the expression of associations. *Psychology of Learning and Motivation, 22*, 51–92.

Mirman, D., McClelland, J. L., & Holt, L. L. (2006). An interactive Hebbian account of lexically guided tuning of speech perception. *Psychonomic Bulletin & Review, 13*(6), 958–965.

Misyak, J. B., & Christiansen, M. H. (2012). Statistical learning and language: An individual differences study. *Language Learning, 62*(1), 302–331.

Misyak, J. B., & Christiansen, M. H. (2010). When "more" in statistical learning means "less" in language: Individual differences in predictive processing of adjacent dependencies. *Proceedings of the Annual Conference of the Cognitive Science Society, 32*, 2686–2691.

Mitchell, C. J., De Houwer, J., & Lovibond, P. F. (2009). The propositional nature of human associative learning. *Behavioral and Brain Sciences, 32*(2), 183–198.

Mitrović, I. (2012). A phonetically natural vs. native language pattern: An experimental study of velar palatalization in Serbian. *Journal of Slavic Linguistics, 20*(2), 229–268.

Miyawaki, K., Jenkins, J. J., Strange, W., Liberman, A. M., Verbrugge, R., & Fujimura, O. (1975). An effect of linguistic experience: The discrimination of [r] and [l] by native speakers of Japanese and English. *Perception & Psychophysics, 18*(5), 331–340.

Molina, J. C., Hoffmann, H., Serwatka, J., & Spear, N. E. (1991). Establishing intermodal equivalence in preweanling and adult rats. *Journal of Experimental Psychology: Animal Behavior Processes, 17*(4), 433–447.

Moore, J. K. (2002). Maturation of human auditory cortex: Implications for speech perception. *Annals of Otology, Rhinology & Laryngology [Supplement], 189*, 7–10.

Moore, J. W., Newman, F. L., & Glasgow, B. (1969). Intertrial cues as discriminative stimuli in human eyelid conditioning. *Journal of Experimental Psychology, 79*, 319–326.

Morais, J., Cary, L., Alegria, J., & Bertelson, P. (1979). Does awareness of speech as a sequence of phones arise spontaneously? *Cognition, 7*(4), 323–331.

Moreton, E. (2012). Inter- and intra-dimensional dependencies in implicit phonotactic learning. *Journal of Memory and Language, 67*(1), 165–183.

Moreton, E. (2008). Analytic bias and phonological typology. *Phonology, 25*(1), 83–127.

Moreton, E., & Pater, J. (2012a). Structure and substance in artificial-phonology learning: Part I. Structure. *Language and Linguistics Compass, 6*(11), 686–701.

Moreton, E., & Pater, J. (2012b). Structure and substance in artificial-phonology learning: Part II. Substance. *Language and Linguistics Compass, 6*(11), 702–718.

Moreton, E., Pater, J., & Pertsova, K. (2017). Phonological concept learning. *Cognitive Science*. doi: 10.1111/cogs.12319.

Morton, J. (1969). Interaction of information in word recognition. *Psychological Review, 76*(2), 165–178.

Mowrey, R., & Pagliuca, W. (1995). The reductive character of articulatory evolution. *Rivista di Linguistica, 7*, 37–124.

Murphy, M. L. (2006). Antonyms as lexical constructions: or, why *paradigmatic construction* is not an oxymoron. *Constructions, SV1*(8), 1–37.

Naigles, L. G., & Gelman, S. A. (1995). Overextensions in comprehension and production revisited: Preferential-looking in a study of *dog, cat,* and *cow. Journal of Child Language, 22*(1), 19–46.

Navarro, D. J., & Perfors, A. (2009). Learning time-varying categories. *Proceedings of the Annual Conference of the Cognitive Science Society, 31*, 419–424.

Nelson, J. D. (2005). Finding useful questions: on Bayesian diagnosticity, probability, impact, and information gain. *Psychological Review, 112*(4), 979–999.

Nesset, T. (2008). *Abstract phonology in a concrete model: Cognitive linguistics and the morphology-phonology interface*. Berlin: Mouton de Gruyter.

Newmeyer, F. J. (2000). Deconstructing grammaticalization. *Language Sciences, 23*(2), 187–229.

Newport, E. L., & Aslin, R. N. (2004). Learning at a distance: I. Statistical learning of non-adjacent dependencies. *Cognitive Psychology, 48*(2), 127–162.

Newport, E. L., Hauser, M. D., Spaepen, G., & Aslin, R. N. (2004). Learning at a distance: II. Statistical learning of non-adjacent dependencies in a non-human primate. *Cognitive Psychology, 49*(2), 85–117.

Nickerson, R. S. (2002). The production and perception of randomness. *Psychological Review, 109*(2), 330–357.

Nickerson, R. S. (1998). Confirmation bias: A ubiquitous phenomenon in many guises. *Review of General Psychology, 2*(2), 175–220.

Nolan, F. (2003). Intonational equivalence: An experimental evaluation of pitch scales. In *Proceedings of the International Congress of Phonetic Sciences, 15*, 771–774.

Norris, D. (2006). The Bayesian reader: Explaining word recognition as an optimal Bayesian decision process. *Psychological Review, 113*(2), 327–357.

Norris, D. (1994). Shortlist: A connectionist model of continuous speech recognition. *Cognition, 52*(3), 189–234.

Norris, D., & McQueen, J. M. (2008). Shortlist B: A Bayesian model of continuous speech recognition. *Psychological Review, 115*(2), 357–395.

Norris, D., McQueen, J. M., & Cutler, A. (2003). Perceptual learning in speech. *Cognitive Psychology, 47*(2), 204–238.

Nosofsky, R. M. (1986). Attention, similarity, and the identification-categorization relationship. *Journal of Experimental Psychology: General, 115*(1), 39–57.

Nowak, M. A., & Krakauer, D. C. (1999). The evolution of language. *Proceedings of the National Academy of Sciences, 96*, 8028–8033.

Occhino, C. (2016). *A cognitive approach to phonology: Evidence from signed languages* (doctoral dissertation, The University of New Mexico).

O'Donnell, T. J. (2015). *Productivity and reuse in language: A theory of linguistic computation and storage*. Cambridge, MA: MIT Press.

Ohala, J. J. (1981). The listener as a source of sound change. In C. S. Masek, R. A. Hendrick & M. F. Miller (Eds.), *Papers from the Parasession on Language and Behavior* (pp. 178–203). Chicago: Chicago Linguistic Society.

Oldfield, R. C., & Wingfield, A. (1965). Response latencies in naming objects. *Quarterly Journal of Experimental Psychology, 17*, 273–281.

Oldfield, R. C., & Zangwill, O. L. (1942). Head's concept of schema and its application in contemporary British psychology. *British Journal of Psychology, 32*, 267–286; *33*, 58–64, 113–129, 143–149.

Olejarczuk, P., & Kapatsinski, V. (2017). *The role of surprisal in phonological learning: The case of weight-sensitive stress.* Ms., University of Oregon.

Olejarczuk, P., & V. Kapatsinski. (2016). Attention allocation in phonetic category learning. *Proceedings of the International Conference on Cognitive Modeling in Linguistics, 14*, 148–156.

Olejarczuk, P., & Kapatsinski, V. (2015, March). Learnability of weight-sensitive stress by English speaking adults. Paper presented at the 37th Annual Meeting of the German Linguistics Society, Leipzig, Germany, March 4–6.

Olejarczuk, P., Kapatsinski, V., & Baayen, R. H. (in press). Distributional learning is error-driven: The role of surprise in the acquisition of phonetic categories. *Linguistics Vanguard.*

Onishi, K. H., Chambers, K. E., & Fisher, C. (2002). Learning phonotactic constraints from brief auditory experience. *Cognition, 83*(1), B13–B23.

Onnis, L., & Thiessen, E. (2013). Language experience changes subsequent learning. *Cognition, 126*(2), 268–284.

Oppenheim, G. M., Dell, G. S., & Schwartz, M. F. (2010). The dark side of incremental learning: A model of cumulative semantic interference during lexical access in speech production. *Cognition, 114*(2), 227–252.

O'Reilly, R. C. (1996). *The Leabra model of neural interactions and learning in the neocortex* (doctoral dissertation, Carnegie Mellon University, Pittsburgh).

Oudeyer, P. Y., & Smith, L. B. (2016). How evolution may work through curiosity-driven developmental process. *Topics in Cognitive Science, 8*(2), 492–502.

Oviatt, S., Levow, G.-A., Moreton, E., & MacEachern, M. (1998). Modeling global and focal hyperarticulation during human-computer error resolution. *Journal of the Acoustical Society of America, 104*, 3080–3098.

Packard, M. G., & McGaugh, J. L. (1996). Inactivation of hippocampus or caudate nucleus with lidocaine differentially affects expression of place and response learning. *Neurobiology of Learning and Memory, 65*(1), 65–72.

Palmeri, T. J., & Nosofsky, R. M. (1995). Recognition memory for exceptions to the category rule. *Journal of Experimental Psychology: Learning, Memory, and Cognition, 21*(3), 548–568.

Palmeri, T. J., Wong, A. C., & Gauthier, I. (2004). Computational approaches to the development of perceptual expertise. *Trends in Cognitive Sciences, 8*(8), 378–386.

Pavlov, I. P. (1927). *Conditioned reflexes: An Investigation of the physiological activity of the cerebral cortex*. Mineola, NY: Dover.

Pearce, J. M. (1994). Similarity and discrimination: A selective review and a connectionist model. *Psychological Review, 101*(4), 587–607.

Pelucchi, B., Hay, J. F., & Saffran, J. R. (2009). Learning in reverse: Eight-month-old infants track backward transitional probabilities. *Cognition, 113*(2), 244–247.

Peperkamp, S., & Martin, A. (2016). Sleep-dependent consolidation in the learning of natural vs. unnatural phonological rules. Paper presented at Laboratory Phonology 15, Ithaca, NY.

Perea, M., & Rosa, E. (2000). Repetition and form priming interact with neighborhood density at a brief stimulus onset asynchrony. *Psychonomic Bulletin & Review, 7*(4), 668–677.

Pereira, A. F., Smith, L. B., & Yu, C. (2014). A bottom-up view of toddler word learning. *Psychonomic Bulletin & Review, 21*(1), 178–185.

Perek, F. (2012). Alternation-based generalizations are stored in the mental grammar: Evidence from a sorting task experiment. *Cognitive Linguistics, 23*(3), 601–635.

Perfors, A. (2016). Adult regularization of inconsistent input depends on pragmatic factors. *Language Learning and Development, 12*(2), 138–155.

Perfors, A. (2011). Memory limitations alone do not lead to over-regularization: An experimental and computational investigation. *Proceedings of the Annual Conference of the Cognitive Science Society, 33*, 3274–3279.

Perlman, A., Hahn, U., Edwards, D. J., & Pothos, E. M. (2012). Further attempts to clarify the importance of category variability for categorisation. *Journal of Cognitive Psychology, 24*(2), 203–220.

Perruchet, P., & Desaulty, S. (2008). A role for backward transitional probabilities in word segmentation? *Memory & Cognition, 36*(7), 1299–1305.

Perruchet, P., & Vinter, A. (1998). PARSER: A model for word segmentation. *Journal of Memory and Language, 39*(2), 246–263.

Phillips, B. S. (1984). Word frequency and the actuation of sound change. *Language, 60*(2), 320–342.

Piantadosi, S. T., Tily, H., & Gibson, E. (2012). The communicative function of ambiguity in language. *Cognition, 122*(3), 280–291.

Piantadosi, S. T., Tily, H., & Gibson, E. (2009). The communicative lexicon hypothesis. In *Proceedings of the Annual Conference of the Cognitive Science Society, 31*, 2582–2587.

Pica, T. 1983. Adult acquisition of English as a second language under different conditions of exposure. *Language Learning, 33*, 465–497.

Pierrehumbert, J. (2006). The statistical basis of an unnatural alternation. In L. Goldstein, D. H. Whalen, & C. T. Best (Eds.), *Laboratory Phonology 8* (pp. 81–107). Berlin: Mouton de Gruyter.

Pierrehumbert, J. (2002). Word-specific phonetics. In C. Gussenhoven & N. Warner (Eds.), *Laboratory Phonology 7* (pp. 101–139). Berlin: Mouton de Gruyter.

Pierrehumbert, J. (2001a). Word frequency, lenition and contrast. In J. L. Bybee & P. J. Hopper (Eds.), *Frequency and the emergence of linguistic structure* (pp. 137–158). Amsterdam: John Benjamins.

Pierrehumbert, J. (2001b). Why phonological constraints are so coarse-grained. *Language and Cognitive Processes, 16*(5–6), 691–698.

Pinker, S. (1999). *Words and rules: The ingredients of language.* New York: Basic Books.

Pinker, S., & Prince, A. (1988). On language and connectionism: Analysis of a parallel distributed processing model of language acquisition. *Cognition, 28*(1), 73–193.

Pirog Revill, K., Aslin, R. N., Tanenhaus, M. K., & Bavelier, D. (2008). Neural correlates of partial lexical activation. *Proceedings of the National Academy of Sciences, 105*(35), 13111–13115.

Pisoni, D. B. (1973). Auditory and phonetic memory codes in the discrimination of consonants and vowels. *Attention, Perception, & Psychophysics, 13*(2), 253–260.

Plunkett, K., & Juola, P. (1999). A connectionist model of English past tense and plural morphology. *Cognitive Science, 23*, 463–490.

Port, R. F., & Leary, A. P. (2005). Against formal phonology. *Language, 81*(4), 927–964.

Poser, W. J. (1990). Evidence for foot structure in Japanese. *Language, 66*(1), 78–105.

Poulton, E. C. (1956). Listening to overlapping calls. *Journal of Experimental Psychology, 52*(5), 334–339.

Prince, A., & Smolensky, P. (1993/2008). *Optimality Theory: Constraint interaction in generative grammar.* Hoboken, NJ: Wiley.

Purtle, R. B. (1973). Peak shift: A review. *Psychological Bulletin, 80*(5), 408–421.

Quine, W. (1960). *Word and object.* Cambridge, MA: MIT Press.

Radeau, M., Morais, J., & Segui, J. (1995). Phonological priming between monosyllabic spoken words. *Journal of Experimental Psychology: Human Perception and Performance, 21*(6), 1297–1311.

Ragland, J. D., Cools, R., Frank, M., Pizzagalli, D. A., Preston, A., Ranganath, C., & Wagner, A. D. (2008). CNTRICS final task selection: Long-term memory. *Schizophrenia Bulletin, 35*(1), 197–212.

Ramscar, M., Dye, M., & Klein, J. (2013). Children value informativity over logic in word learning. *Psychological Science, 24*(6), 1017–1023.

Ramscar, M., & Gitcho, N. (2007). Developmental change and the nature of learning in childhood. *Trends in Cognitive Sciences, 11*(7), 274–279.

Ramscar, M., Hendrix, P., Shaoul, C., Milin, P., & Baayen, H. (2014). The myth of cognitive decline: Non-linear dynamics of lifelong learning. *Topics in Cognitive Science, 6*(1), 5–42.

Ramscar, M., Yarlett, D., Dye, M., Denny, K., & Thorpe, K. (2010). The effects of feature-label-order and their implications for symbolic learning. *Cognitive Science, 34*(6), 909–957.

Ramus, F., Peperkamp, S., Christophe, A., Jacquemot, C., Kouider, S., & Dupoux, E. (2010). A psycholinguistic perspective on the acquisition of phonology. *Laboratory Phonology, 10*, 311–340.

Rasolofo, A. (2006). *Malagasy transitive clause types and their functions* (doctoral dissertation, University of Oregon).

Raymond, W. D., & Brown, E. L. (2012). Are effects of word frequency effects of context of use? An analysis of initial fricative reduction in Spanish. In S. Th. Gries & D. Divjak (Eds.), *Frequency effects in language learning and processing* (pp. 35–52). Berlin: Mouton de Gruyter.

Rayner, K., & Raney, G. E. (1996). Eye movement control in reading and visual search: Effects of word frequency. *Psychonomic Bulletin & Review, 3*(2), 245–248.

Reali, F., & Christiansen, M. H. (2007). Processing of relative clauses is made easier by frequency of occurrence. *Journal of Memory and Language, 57*(1), 1–23.

Reali, F., & Griffiths, T. L. (2009). The evolution of frequency distributions: Relating regularization to inductive biases through iterated learning. *Cognition, 111*(3), 317–328.

Recasens, D. (1989). Long range coarticulation effects for tongue dorsum contact in VCVCV sequences. *Speech Communication, 8*(4), 293–307.

Redford, M. A. (2015). Unifying speech and language in a developmentally sensitive model of production. *Journal of Phonetics, 53*, 141–152.

Regier, T., & Gahl, S. (2004). Learning the unlearnable: The role of missing evidence. *Cognition, 93*(2), 147–155.

Rehder, B., & Hoffman, A. B. (2005). Eyetracking and selective attention in category learning. *Cognitive Psychology, 51*(1), 1–41.

Reinisch, E., & Sjerps, M. J. (2013). The uptake of spectral and temporal cues in vowel perception is rapidly influenced by context. *Journal of Phonetics, 41*(1), 101–116.

Rescorla, R. A. (1988). Pavlovian conditioning: It's not what you think it is. *American Psychologist, 43*(3), 151–160.

Rescorla, R. A. (1986). Extinction of facilitation. *Journal of Experimental Psychology: Animal Behavior Processes, 12,* 16–24.

Rescorla, R. A. (1985). Conditioned inhibition and facilitation. In R. R. Miller & N. E. Spear (Eds.), *Information processing in animals—conditioned inhibition* (pp. 299–326). Mahwah, NJ: Erlbaum.

Rescorla, R. A. (1973). Evidence for "unique stimulus" account of configural conditioning. *Journal of Comparative and Physiological Psychology, 85*(2), 331.

Rescorla, R. A., & Furrow, D. R. (1977). Stimulus similarity as a determinant of Pavlovian conditioning. *Journal of Experimental Psychology: Animal Behavior Processes, 3*(3), 203–215.

Rescorla, R. A., & Wagner, A. R. (1972). A theory of Pavlovian conditioning: Variations in the effectiveness of reinforcement and nonreinforcement. In A. H. Black & W. F. Prokasy (Eds.), *Classical conditioning: II. Current research and theory* (pp. 64–99). New York: Appleton-Century-Crofts.

Rips, L. J. (1989). Similarity, typicality, and categorization. In S. Vosniadou & A. Ortony (Eds.), *Similarity and analogical reasoning* (pp. 21–59). Cambridge: Cambridge University Press.

Rissanen, J. (1983). A universal prior for integers and estimation by minimum description length. *Annals of Statistics, 11,* 416–431.

Ritchie, B. F., Aeschliman, B., & Pierce, P. (1950). Studies in spatial learning: VIII. Place performance and the acquisition of place dispositions. *Journal of Comparative and Physiological Psychology, 43*(2), 73–85.

Rizzuto, D. S., & Kahana, M. J. (2001). An autoassociative neural network model of paired-associate learning. *Neural Computation, 13*(9), 2075–2092.

Rogers, T. T., & McClelland, J. L. (2004). *Semantic cognition: A parallel distributed processing approach.* Cambridge, MA: MIT Press.

Rosch, E., & Mervis, C. B. (1975). Family resemblances: Studies in the internal structure of categories. *Cognitive Psychology, 7*(4), 573–605.

Rosenbloom, P. S., & Newell, A. (1986). The chunking of goal hierarchies: A generalized model of practice. In R. S. Michalski, J. G. Carbonell, & T. M. Mitchell (Eds.),

Machine learning: An artificial intelligence approach (Vol. 2, pp. 247–288). Palo Alto, CA: Morgan Kaufmann.

Ross, R. T., & Holland, P. C. (1981). Conditioning of simultaneous and serial feature-positive discriminations. *Animal Learning & Behavior, 9*(3), 293–303.

Roy, B. C., Frank, M. C., DeCamp, P., Miller, M., & Roy, D. (2015). Predicting the birth of a spoken word. *Proceedings of the National Academy of Sciences, 112*(41), 12663–12668.

Rozin, P., & Kalat, J. W. (1971). Specific hungers and poison avoidance as adaptive specializations of learning. *Psychological Review, 78*(6), 459–486.

Rudy, J. W., & Cheatle, M. D. (1977). Odor-aversion learning in neonatal rats. *Science, 198*, 845–846.

Rumelhart, D. E. (1990). Brain style computation: Learning and generalization. In F. Zornetzer, J. L. Davis, C. Lau, & T. McKenna (Eds.), *An introduction to neural and electronic networks* (pp. 405–420). San Diego, CA: Academic Press.

Rumelhart, D. E., & McClelland, J. L. (1986). On learning the past tenses of English verbs. In J. L. McClelland, D. E. Rumelhart, & PDP Research Group. *Parallel distributed processing* (Vol. 2). Cambridge, MA: MIT Press.

Ryalls, B. O., & Pisoni, D. B. (1997). The effect of talker variability on word recognition in preschool children. *Developmental Psychology, 33*(3), 441–452.

Ryan, K. M. (2010). Variable affix order: Grammar and learning. *Language, 86*(4), 758–791.

Saffran, J. R., Aslin, R. N., & Newport, E. L. (1996). Statistical learning by 8-month-old infants. *Science, 274*(5294), 1926–1928.

Sakamoto, Y., Jones, M., & Love, B. C. (2008). Putting the psychology back into psychological models: Mechanistic versus rational approaches. *Memory & Cognition, 36*(6), 1057–1065.

Sakamoto, Y., & Love, B. C. (2004). Schematic influences on category learning and recognition memory. *Journal of Experimental Psychology: General, 133*(4), 534–553.

Salasoo, A., & Pisoni, D. B. (1985). Interaction of knowledge sources in spoken word identification. *Journal of Memory and Language, 24*(2), 210–231.

Samuelson, L. K., & Smith, L. B. (1998). Memory and attention make smart word learning: An alternative account of Akhtar, Carpenter, and Tomasello. *Child Development, 69*(1), 94–104.

Sanders, L. D., Newport, E. L., & Neville, H. J. (2002). Segmenting nonsense: an event-related potential index of perceived onsets in continuous speech. *Nature Neuroscience, 5*(7), 700–703.

Sandler, W., Meir, I., Padden, C., & Aronoff, M. (2005). The emergence of grammar: Systematic structure in a new language. *Proceedings of the National Academy of Sciences of the United States of America, 102*(7), 2661–2665.

Sapir, E. (1921). *Language*. New York: Harcourt, Brace & World.

Schapiro, A. C., Turk-Browne, N. B., Botvinick, M. M., & Norman, K. A. (2017). Complementary learning systems within the hippocampus: A neural network modelling approach to reconciling episodic memory with statistical learning. *Philosophical Transactions of the Royal Society B, 372*(1711), 20160049.

Schertz, J. (2013). Exaggeration of featural contrasts in clarifications of misheard speech in English. *Journal of Phonetics, 41*(3), 249–263.

Schmidt, R. (2001). Attention. In P. Robinson (Ed.), *Cognition and Second Language Instruction* (pp. 3–32). Cambridge: Cambridge University Press.

Schoenemann, P. T. (1999) Syntax as an emergent characteristic of the evolution of semantic complexity. *Minds and Machines, 9*, 309–346.

Schönefeld, D. (2012). Things going unnoticed—A usage-based analysis of go-constructions. In D. Divjak & S. Th. Gries (Eds.), *Frequency effects in language representation* (pp. 11–49). Berlin: Mouton de Gruyter.

Schover, L. R., & Newsom, C. D. (1976). Overselectivity, developmental level, and overtraining in autistic and normal children. *Journal of Abnormal Child Psychology, 4*(3), 289–298.

Schuchardt, H. (1885/1972). *Ueber die Lautgesetze: Gegen die Junggrammatiker*. Berlin: Oppenheim, 1972. Translation by T. Vennemann & T. H. Wilbur as "On sound laws: Against the Neogrammarians." In T. Vennemann & T. H. Wilbur (Eds.), *Schuchardt, the Neogrammarians, and the Transformational Theory of phonological change: Four essays* (pp. 39–72). Frankfurt: Athenäum. Pages quoted based on the original as identified by Vennemann & Wilbur.

Schwarz, C. (2016). Recency as a factor of phonological variation. In H. Behrens & S. Pfänder (Eds.), *Experience counts: Frequency effects in language* (pp. 91–110). Berlin: Walter de Gruyter.

Schwartz, R. G., & Leonard, L. B. (1982). Do children pick and choose? An examination of phonological selection and avoidance in early lexical acquisition. *Journal of Child Language, 9*(2), 319–336.

Schweickert, R., Han, H. J., Yamaguchi, M., & Fortin, C. (2014). Estimating averages from distributions of tone durations. *Attention, Perception, & Psychophysics, 76*(2), 605–620.

Seger, C. A., Dennison, C. S., Lopez-Paniagua, D., Peterson, E. J., & Roark, A. A. (2011). Dissociating hippocampal and basal ganglia contributions to category learning using stimulus novelty and subjective judgments. *Neuroimage, 55*(4), 1739–1753.

Selfridge, O. G. (1959). Pandemonium: A paradigm for learning. In *Mechanization of thought processes* (pp. 511–526). London: Her Majesty's Stationery Office.

Seligman, M. E. (1970). On the generality of the laws of learning. *Psychological Review, 77*(5), 406–418.

Seyfarth, S. (2014). Word informativity influences acoustic duration: Effects of contextual predictability on lexical representation. *Cognition, 133*(1), 140–155.

Seyfarth, S., Buz, E., & Jaeger, T. F. (2016). Dynamic hyperarticulation of coda voicing contrasts. *Journal of the Acoustical Society of America, 139*(2), EL31–EL37.

Shakespeare, W. (1602/2003). *Hamlet, prince of Denmark.* Cambridge: Cambridge University Press.

Shanks, D. R. (2006). Bayesian associative learning. *Trends in Cognitive Sciences, 10*(11), 477–478.

Shanks, D. R. (1995). Is human learning rational? *Quarterly Journal of Experimental Psychology, 48*(2), 257–279.

Shanks, D. R. (1992). Connectionist accounts of the inverse base-rate effect in categorization. *Connection Science, 4*(1), 3–18.

Shanks, D. R. (1985). Forward and backward blocking in human contingency judgement. *Quarterly Journal of Experimental Psychology, 37*(1), 1–21.

Shattuck-Hufnagel, S. (2015). Prosodic frames in speech production. In M. A. Redford (Ed.), *The handbook of speech production* (pp. 419–444). Malden, MA: Wiley.

Siegelman, N., & Frost, R. (2015). Statistical learning as an individual ability: Theoretical perspectives and empirical evidence. *Journal of Memory and Language, 81,* 105–120.

Silver, N. (2011). *The signal and the noise: Why so many predictions fail—but some don't.* New York: Penguin.

Silvetti, M., & Verguts, T. (2012). *Reinforcement learning, high-level cognition, and the human brain.* Rijeka, Croatia: INTECH. http://cdn.intechopen.com/pdfs-wm/36854.pdf.

Simons, D. J. (2000). Current approaches to change blindness. *Visual Cognition, 7*(1–3), 1–15.

Singh, L., Morgan, J. L., & White, K. S. (2004). Preference and processing: The role of speech affect in early spoken word recognition. *Journal of Memory and Language, 51*(2), 173–189.

Singleton, J. L., & Newport, E. L. (2004). When learners surpass their models: The acquisition of American Sign Language from inconsistent input. *Cognitive Psychology, 49*(4), 370–407.

Skinner, B. F. (1984). Selection by consequences. *Behavioral and Brain Sciences, 7*(4), 477–481.

Skinner, B. F. (1981). Selection by consequences. *Science, 213*(4507), 501–504.

Skinner, B. F. (1957). *Verbal behavior.* East Norwalk, CT: Appleton-Century-Crofts.

Skinner, B. F. (1948). "Superstition" in the pigeon. *Journal of Experimental Psychology, 38*(2), 168–172.

Skinner, B. F. (1938). *The behavior of organisms: An experimental analysis.* New York: Appleton-Century-Crofts.

Skoruppa, K., Lambrechts, A., & Peperkamp, S. (2011). The role of phonetic distance in the acquisition of phonological alternations. *Proceedings of the North-East Linguistics Society, 39*, 464–475.

Skyrms, B. (2010). *Signals: Evolution, learning, and information.* Oxford: Oxford University Press.

Smith, A., & Goffman, L. (1998). Stability and patterning of speech movement sequences in children and adults. *Journal of Speech, Language, and Hearing Research, 41*(1), 18–30.

Smith, E. E., Adams, N., & Schorr, D. (1978). Fact retrieval and the paradox of interference. *Cognitive Psychology, 10*(4), 438–464.

Smith, K., Fehér, O., & Ritt, N. (2013). Eliminating unpredictable linguistic variation through interaction. *Proceedings of the Annual Conference of the Cognitive Science Society, 35*, 1461–1466.

Smith, K., & Wonnacott, E. (2010). Eliminating unpredictable variation through iterated learning. *Cognition, 116*(3), 444–449.

Smith, L. B., Thelen, E., Titzer, R., & McLin, D. (1999). Knowing in the context of acting: The task dynamics of the A-not-B error. *Psychological Review, 106*(2), 235–260.

Smith, L. B., Yu, C., & Pereira, A. F. (2011). Not your mother's view: The dynamics of toddler visual experience. *Developmental Science, 14*(1), 9–17.

Smolek, A., & Kapatsinski, V. (2017a). *Why not to change (the stem): A production-internal account of paradigm uniformity.* Ms., University of Oregon.

Smolek, A., & Kapatsinski, V. (2017b). *Syntagmatic paradigms: Learning correspondence from contiguity.* Ms., University of Oregon.

Smolensky, P., & Legendre, G. (2006). *The harmonic mind: From neural computation to Optimality-Theoretic grammar.* Cambridge, MA: MIT Press.

Snider, N. (2008). *An exemplar model of syntactic priming* (doctoral dissertation, Stanford University).

Snyder, K. M., & Logan, G. D. (2014). The problem of serial order in skilled typing. *Journal of Experimental Psychology: Human Perception and Performance, 40*(4), 1697–1717.

Sobel, D. M., Tenenbaum, J. B., & Gopnik, A. (2004). Children's causal inferences from indirect evidence: Backwards blocking and Bayesian reasoning in preschoolers. *Cognitive Science, 28*(3), 303–333.

Sosa, A. V., & MacFarlane, J. (2002). Evidence for frequency-based constituents in the mental lexicon: Collocations involving the word *of. Brain and Language, 83*(2), 227–236.

Sóskuthy, M., & Hay, J. (2017). Changing word usage predicts changing word durations in New Zealand English. *Cognition, 166,* 298–313.

Sosnik, R., Chaim, E., & Flash, T. (2015). Stopping is not an option: The evolution of unstoppable motion elements (primitives). *Journal of Neurophysiology, 114*(2), 846–856.

Sosnik, R., Hauptmann, B., Karni, A., & Flash, T. (2004). When practice leads to co-articulation: The evolution of geometrically defined movement primitives. *Experimental Brain Research, 156*(4), 422–438.

Spence, K. W. (1936). The nature of discrimination learning in animals. *Psychological Review, 43,* 427–449.

Spencer, J. (1963). A further study of estimating averages. *Ergonomics, 6*(3), 255–265.

Spencer, J. (1961). Estimating averages. *Ergonomics, 4*(4), 317–328.

Stahl, A. E., & Feigenson, L. (2017). Expectancy violations promote learning in young children. *Cognition, 163,* 1–14.

Stahl, A. E., & Feigenson, L. (2015). Observing the unexpected enhances infants' learning and exploration. *Science, 348*(6230), 91–94.

Stave, M., & Pederson, E. (2016, August). The ON/IN scale of semantic extensions of adpositions: Testing through artificial language learning. Poster presented at the 38th Annual Conference of the Cognitive Science Society, Philadelphia.

Stave, M., Smolek, A., & Kapatsinski, V. (2013). Inductive bias against stem changes as perseveration: Experimental evidence for an articulatory approach to output-output faithfulness. In M. Knauff, M. Pauen, N. Sebanz & I. Wachsmuth (Eds.),

Proceedings of the Annual Conference of the Cognitive Science Society, 35, 3454–3459. Austin, TX: Cognitive Science Society.

Stefanowitsch, A. (2008). Negative entrenchment: A usage-based approach to negative evidence. *Cognitive Linguistics, 19*(3), 513–531.

Stent, A. J., Huffman, M. K., & Brennan, S. E. (2008). Adapting speaking after evidence of misrecognition: Local and global hyperarticulation. *Speech Communication, 50*(3), 163–178.

Steriade, D. (2001). *The phonology of perceptibility effects: The P-map and its consequences for constraint organization.* Ms., UCLA.

Sternberg, D., & McClelland, J. L. (2009). When should we expect indirect effects in human contingency learning? *Proceedings of the Annual Conference of the Cognitive Science Society, 31,* 206–211.

Stevens, C., Harn, B., Chard, D. J., Currin, J., Parisi, D., & Neville, H. (2013). Examining the role of attention and instruction in at-risk kindergarteners: Electrophysiological measures of selective auditory attention before and after an early literacy intervention. *Journal of Learning Disabilities, 46*(1), 73–86.

Stevens, K. N., & Halle, M. (1967). Remarks on analysis by synthesis and distinctive features. In W. Walthen-Dunn (Ed.), *Models for the perception of speech and visual form* (pp. 88–102). Cambridge, MA: MIT Press.

Stirling, N. (1979). Stroop interference: An input and an output phenomenon. *Quarterly Journal of Experimental Psychology, 31*(1), 121–132.

Stockall, L., & Marantz, A. (2006). A single route, full decomposition model of morphological complexity: MEG evidence. *The Mental Lexicon, 1*(1), 85–123.

Storkel, H. L. (2004). Do children acquire dense neighborhoods? An investigation of similarity neighborhoods in lexical acquisition. *Applied Psycholinguistics, 25*(2), 201–221.

Stout, S. C., & Miller, R. R. (2007). Sometimes-competing retrieval (SOCR): A formalization of the comparator hypothesis. *Psychological Review, 114*(3), 759–783.

Stroop, J. R. (1935). Studies of interference in serial verbal reactions. *Journal of Experimental Psychology, 18*(6), 643–662.

Sumby, W. H., & Pollack, I. (1954). Visual contribution to speech intelligibility in noise. *Journal of the Acoustical Society of America, 26*(2), 212–215.

Sumida, R. A. (1997). *Parallel distributed semantic networks for natural language processing* (doctoral dissertation, UCLA).

Sumida, R. A., & Dyer, M. G. (1992). Propagation filters in PDS networks for sequencing and ambiguity resolution. In S. J. Hanson, J. D. Cowan & C. L. Giles

(Eds.), *Advances in neural information processing systems* (pp. 233–240). Neural Information Processing Systems, Inc. https://papers.nips.cc/book/advances-in-neural -information-processing-systems-5-1992.

Suthana, N., & Fried, I. (2012). Percepts to recollections: Insights from single neuron recordings in the human brain. *Trends in Cognitive Sciences, 16*(8), 427–436.

Sutherland, N. S., & Holgate, V. (1966). Two-cue discrimination learning in rats. *Journal of Comparative and Physiological Psychology, 61*(2), 198–207.

Suttle, L., & Goldberg, A. E. (2011). The partial productivity of constructions as induction. *Linguistics, 49*(6), 1237–1269.

Swartzentruber, D., & Bouton, M. E. (1986). Contextual control of negative transfer produced by prior CS-US pairings. *Learning and Motivation, 17*(4), 366–385.

Swinney, D. A. (1979). Lexical access during sentence comprehension: (Re)consideration of context effects. *Journal of Verbal Learning and Verbal Behavior, 18*(6), 645–659.

Szmrecsanyi, B. (2005). Language users as creatures of habit: A corpus-based analysis of persistence in spoken English. *Corpus Linguistics and Linguistic Theory, 1*(1), 113–150.

Taatgen, N. A., & Anderson, J. R. (2002). Why do children learn to say "broke"? A model of learning the past tense without feedback. *Cognition, 86*(2), 123–155.

Tabossi, P. (1988). Accessing lexical ambiguity in different types of sentential contexts. *Journal of Memory & Language, 27*(3), 324–340.

Tanaka, J., Giles, M., Kremen, S., & Simon, V. (1998). Mapping attractor fields in face space: The atypicality bias in face recognition. *Cognition, 68*(3), 199–220.

Tanenhaus, M. K., & Brown-Schmidt, S. (2008). Language processing in the natural world. *Philosophical Transactions of the Royal Society of London B: Biological Sciences, 363*(1493), 1105–1122.

Tanenhaus, M. K., Spivey-Knowlton, M. J., Eberhard, K. M., & Sedivy, J. C. (1995). Integration of visual and linguistic information in spoken language comprehension. *Science, 268*(5217), 1632–1634.

Tassoni, C. J. (1995). The least mean squares network with information coding: A model of cue learning. *Journal of Experimental Psychology: Learning, Memory, and Cognition, 21*(1), 193–204.

Terrell, T. (1991). The role of grammar instruction in a communicative approach. *Modern Language Journal, 75,* 52–63.

Theakston, A. L. (2004). The role of entrenchment in children's and adults' performance on grammaticality judgment tasks. *Cognitive Development, 19*(1), 15–34.

Thompson, B., Kirby, S., & Smith, K. (2016). Culture shapes the evolution of cognition. *Proceedings of the National Academy of Sciences, 113*(16), 4530–4535.

Thompson, L. A. (1994). Dimensional strategies dominate perceptual classification. *Child Development, 65*(6), 1627–1645.

Thompson, R. F., & Spencer, W. A. (1966). Habituation: A model phenomenon for the study of neuronal substrates of behavior. *Psychological Review, 73*(1), 16–43.

Thompson, W. R. (1933). On the likelihood that one unknown probability exceeds another in view of the evidence of two samples. *Biometrika, 25*, 285–294.

Thomsen, C. J., Lavine, H., & Kounios, J. (1996). Social value and attitude concepts in semantic memory: Relational structure, concept strength, and the fan effect. *Social Cognition, 14*(3), 191–225.

Thothathiri, M., & Snedeker, J. (2008). Syntactic priming during language comprehension in three- and four-year-old children. *Journal of Memory and Language, 58*(2), 188–213.

Tolman, E. C. (1938). The determiners of behavior at a choice point. *Psychological Review, 45*(1), 1–41.

Tomaschek, F., Wieling, M., Arnold, D., & Baayen, R. H. (2013). Word frequency, vowel length and vowel quality in speech production: An EMA study of the importance of experience. In F. Bimbot, C. Cerisara, C. Fougeron, G. Gravier, L. Lamel, F. Pellegrino, and P. Perrier (Eds.), *INTERSPEECH 2013* (pp. 1302–1306). International Speech Communication Association. http://www.isca-speech.org/archive/interspeech_2013.

Tomasello, M. (2003). *Constructing a language: A usage-based theory of language acquisition.* Cambridge, MA: Harvard University Press.

Tomlin, R. S. (1995). Focal attention, voice, and word order: An experimental, cross-linguistic study. In P. A. Downing & M. Noonan (Eds.), *Word order in discourse* (pp. 515–554). Amsterdam: John Benjamins.

Toscano, J. C., & McMurray, B. (2015). The time-course of speaking rate compensation: Effects of sentential rate and vowel length on voicing judgments. *Language, Cognition and Neuroscience, 30*(5), 529–543.

Trabasso, T., & Bower, G. H. (1968). *Attention in learning: Theory and research.* New York: Wiley.

Traugott, E. C. (2011). Grammaticalization and mechanisms of change. In B. Heine & H. Narrog (Eds.), *The Oxford handbook of grammaticalization* (pp. 19–30). Oxford: Oxford University Press.

Traugott, E. C. (1988). Pragmatic strengthening and grammaticalization. In S. Axmaker & H. Singmaster (Eds.), *Proceedings of the Annual Meeting of the Berkeley*

Linguistics Society (Vol. 14, pp. 406–416). Berkeley: Berkeley Linguistics Society, University of California.

Trier, J. (1934). Das sprachliche Feld: eine Auseinandersetzung. *Neue Jahrbücher für Wissenschaft und Jugendbildung, 10,* 428–449.

Trudgill, P. (2011). *Sociolinguistic typology: Social determinants of linguistic complexity.* Oxford: Oxford University Press.

Trueswell, J. C., Tanenhaus, M. K., & Kello, C. (1993). Verb-specific constraints in sentence processing: Separating effects of lexical preference from garden-paths. *Journal of Experimental Psychology: Learning, Memory, and Cognition, 19*(3), 528–553.

Tversky, A., & Kahneman, D. (1974). Judgment under uncertainty: Heuristics and biases. *Science, 185*(4157), 1124–1131.

Ugwu, R. (2015). Selena Gomez's "Good for You" and the rise of "Indie pop voice": How a phenomenon called "vowel breaking" became an epidemic in pop music. https://www.buzzfeed.com/reggieugwu/what-is-indie-pop-voice?utm_term =.qgJwRmoKLw#.hy7ZX5MpyZ.

Uhrig, P. (2015). Why the Principle of No Synonymy is overrated. *Zeitschrift für Anglistik und Amerikanistik, 63*(3), 323–337.

Usher, M., & McClelland, J. L. (2001). The time course of perceptual choice: The leaky, competing accumulator model. *Psychological Review, 108*(3), 550–592.

Vadillo, M. A., & Matute, H. (2010). Augmentation in contingency learning under time pressure. *British Journal of Psychology, 101*(3), 579–589.

van der Ham, S., & de Boer, B. (2015). Cognitive bias for learning speech sounds from a continuous signal space seems nonlinguistic. *i-Perception, 6,* 5.

van Hamme, L. J., & Wasserman, E. A. (1994). Cue competition in causality judgments: The role of nonpresentation of compound stimulus elements. *Learning and Motivation, 25*(2), 127–151.

Vanpaemel, W., & Storms, G. (2008). In search of abstraction: The varying abstraction model of categorization. *Psychonomic Bulletin & Review, 15*(4), 732–749.

van Son, R. J., & van Santen, J. P. (2005). Duration and spectral balance of intervocalic consonants: A case for efficient communication. *Speech Communication, 47*(1), 100–123.

van Son, R. J. J. H., & Pols, L. C. W. (2003). How efficient is speech? *Proceedings (Instituut voor Fonetische Wetenschappen, Universiteit van Amsterdam), 25,* 171–184.

Vaughn, C., Baese-Berk, M., & Idemaru, K. (2016). Variability and stability in native and non-native Japanese speech. *Journal of the Acoustical Society of America, 139*(4), 2162–2162.

Vihman, M. (1980). Sound change and child language. In *Papers from the 4th International Conference on Historical Linguistics* (Vol. 14, pp. 303–320). Amsterdam: John Benjamins.

Vihman, M., & Croft, W. (2007). Phonological development: Toward a "radical" templatic phonology. *Linguistics, 45*(4), 683–725.

Vong, W., Hendrickson, A., Perfors, A., & Navarro, D. (2013). The role of sampling assumptions in generalization with multiple categories. *Proceedings of the Annual Meeting of the Cognitive Science Society, 35,* 3699–3704.

Vroomen, J., Tuomainen, J., & de Gelder, B. (1998). The roles of word stress and vowel harmony in speech segmentation. *Journal of Memory and Language, 38*(2), 133–149.

von Humboldt, W. (1836/1999). *On language: On the diversity of human language construction and its influence on the mental development of the human species.* Cambridge: Cambridge University Press.

Vouloumanos, A., & Werker, J. F. (2007). Listening to language at birth: Evidence for a bias for speech in neonates. *Developmental Science, 10*(2), 159–164.

Wagner, A. R. (1981). SOP: A model of automatic memory processing in animal behavior. In N. E. Spear & R. R. Miller (Eds.), *Information processing in animals: Memory mechanisms* (pp. 5–47). Hillsdale, NJ: Erlbaum.

Waldmann, M. R. (2000). Competition among causes but not effects in predictive and diagnostic learning. *Journal of Experimental Psychology: Learning, Memory, and Cognition, 26*(1), 53–76.

Waldmann, M. R., & Holyoak, K. J. (1992). Predictive and diagnostic learning within causal models: Asymmetries in cue competition. *Journal of Experimental Psychology: General, 121*(2), 222–236.

Waldmann, M. R., & Walker, J. M. (2005). Competence and performance in causal learning. *Learning & Behavior, 33*(2), 211–229.

Wanrooij, K., Boersma, P., & Benders, T. (2015). Observed effects of "distributional learning" may not relate to the number of peaks: A test of "dispersion" as a confounding factor. *Frontiers in Psychology, 6.*

Wanrooij, K., Escudero, P., & Raijmakers, M. E. (2013). What do listeners learn from exposure to a vowel distribution? An analysis of listening strategies in distributional learning. *Journal of Phonetics, 41*(5), 307–319.

Ward, T. B., Vela, E., & Hass, S. D. (1990). Children and adults learn family-resemblance categories analytically. *Child Development, 61*(3), 593–605.

Warker, J. A., & Dell, G. S. (2006). Speech errors reflect newly learned phonotactic constraints. *Journal of Experimental Psychology: Learning, Memory, and Cognition, 32*(2), 387–398.

Warren, D. E., & Duff, M. C. (2014). Not so fast: Hippocampal amnesia slows word learning despite successful fast mapping. *Hippocampus, 24*(8), 920–933.

Warren, R. M., & Obusek, C. J. (1971). Speech perception and phonemic restorations. *Attention, Perception, & Psychophysics, 9*(3), 358–362.

Wasserman, E. A., Brooks, D. I., & McMurray, B. (2015). Pigeons acquire multiple categories in parallel via associative learning: A parallel to human word learning? *Cognition, 136*, 99–122.

Wasserman, E. A., & Castro, L. (2005). Surprise and change: Variations in the strength of present and absent cues in causal learning. *Learning & Behavior, 33*(2), 131–146.

Wasserman, E. A., Dorner, W. W., & Kao, S.-F. (1990). Contributions of specific cell information to judgments of interevent contingency. *Journal of Experimental Psychology: Learning, Memory, and Cognition, 16*, 509–521.

Wayment, A. (2009). *Assimilation as attraction: Computing distance, similarity, and locality in phonology* (doctoral dissertation, Johns Hopkins University).

Wedel, A. B. (2007). Feedback and regularity in the lexicon. *Phonology, 24*(1), 147–185.

Wedel, A., Jackson, S., & Kaplan, A. (2013). Functional load and the lexicon: Evidence that syntactic category and frequency relationships in minimal lemma pairs predict the loss of phoneme contrasts in language change. *Language and Speech, 56*(3), 395–417.

Weinreich, U., Labov, W., & Herzog, M. (1968). Empirical foundations for a theory of language change. In W. P. Lehmann & Y. Malkiel (Eds.), *Directions for historical linguistics: A symposium* (pp. 95–195). Austin: University of Texas Press.

Weir, R. H. (1962). *Language in the crib.* The Hague: Mouton.

Werker, J. F., & Tees, R. C. (1984). Cross-language speech perception: Evidence for perceptual reorganization during the first year of life. *Infant Behavior and Development, 7*(1), 49–63.

West, M. J., & King, A. P. (2008). Deconstructing innate illusions: Reflections on nature-nurture-niche from an unlikely source. *Philosophical Psychology, 21*(3), 383–395.

West, M. J., White, D. J., & King, A. P. (2003). Female brown headed cowbirds' (*Molothrus ater*) organization and behavior reflect male social dynamics. *Animal Behavior, 64*, 377–385.

White, J. (2013). *Bias in phonological learning: Evidence from saltation* (doctoral dissertation, UCLA).

White, K. S., Yee, E., Blumstein, S. E., & Morgan, J. L. (2013). Adults show less sensitivity to phonetic detail in unfamiliar words, too. *Journal of Memory and Language, 68*(4), 362–378.

Wickelgren, W. A. (1969). Context-sensitive coding, associative memory, and serial order in (speech) behavior. *Psychological Review, 76*(1), 1–15.

Wills, A. J., Milton, F., Longmore, C. A., Hester, S., & Robinson, J. (2013). Is overall similarity classification less effortful than single-dimension classification? *Quarterly Journal of Experimental Psychology, 66*(2), 299–318.

Wilson, C. (2006). Learning phonology with substantive bias: An experimental and computational study of velar palatalization. *Cognitive Science, 30*(5), 945–982.

Winter, B. (2014). Spoken language achieves robustness and evolvability by exploiting degeneracy and neutrality. *BioEssays, 36*(10), 960–967.

Wood, T. J. (1998). *On the rules-to-episodes transition in classification: Generalization of similarity and rules with practice* (doctoral dissertation, McMaster University).

Woodbury, C. B. (1943). The learning of stimulus patterns by dogs. *Journal of Comparative Psychology, 35*(1), 29–40.

Xu, F., & Tenenbaum, J. B. (2007). Word learning as Bayesian inference. *Psychological Review, 114*(2), 245–272.

Xu, J., & Croft, W. B. (1998). Corpus-based stemming using co-occurrence of word variants. *ACM Transactions on Information Systems, 16*(1), 61–81.

Yang, C. (2016). *The price of linguistic productivity: How children learn to break the rules of language.* Cambridge, MA: MIT Press.

Yang, C. (2004). Universal Grammar, statistics or both? *Trends in Cognitive Sciences, 8*(10), 451–456.

Yang, L. X., & Wu, Y. H. (2014). Category variability effect in category learning with auditory stimuli. *Frontiers in Psychology, 5*, 1122.

Yang, X., Wang, K., & Shamma, S. A. (1992). Auditory representations of acoustic signals. *IEEE Transactions on Information Theory, 38*(2), 824–839.

Yin, H., & White, J. (2016). Neutralization avoidance and naturalness in artificial language learning. Paper presented at the Linguistic Society of America Annual Meeting, Washington, DC, January 7–10.

Yoshida, H., & Burling, J. M. (2012). Highlighting: A mechanism relevant for word learning. *Frontiers in Psychology, 3*, 262.

Yoshida, H., & Hanania, R. (2007). Attentional highlighting as a mechanism behind early word learning. In D. S. McNamara & J. G. Trafton (Eds.), *Proceedings of the 29th Annual Cognitive Science Society* (pp. 719–724). Austin, TX: Cognitive Science Society.

Yu, C., & Smith, L. B. (2012). Modeling cross-situational word-referent learning: Prior questions. *Psychological Review, 119*(1), 21–39.

Yu, C., & Smith, L. B. (2007). Rapid word learning under uncertainty via cross-situational statistics. *Psychological Science, 18*(5), 414–420.

Yum, K. S. (1931). An experimental test of the law of assimilation. *Journal of Experimental Psychology, 14*(1), 68–82.

Yun, G. H. (2006). *The interaction between palatalization and coarticulation in Korean and English* (doctoral dissertation, University of Arizona).

Yurovsky, D., Fricker, D. C., Yu, C., & Smith, L. B. (2014). The role of partial knowledge in statistical word learning. *Psychonomic Bulletin & Review, 21*(1), 1–22.

Yurovsky, D., Yu, C., & Smith, L. B. (2013). Competitive processes in cross-situational word learning. *Cognitive Science, 37*(5), 891–921.

Zeithamova, D., Dominick, A. L., & Preston, A. R. (2012). Hippocampal and ventral medial prefrontal activation during retrieval-mediated learning supports novel inference. *Neuron, 75*(1), 168–179.

Zentall, T. R. (2016). When humans and other animals behave irrationally. *Comparative Cognition & Behavior Reviews, 11*, 25–48.

Zimmer, K. E. (1969). Psychological correlates of some Turkish morpheme structure conditions. *Language, 45*(2), 309–321.

Zipf, G. K. (1949). *Human behavior and the principle of least effort: An introduction to human ecology*. Cambridge, MA: Addison-Wesley.

Zipf, G. K. (1935). *The psycho-biology of language*. Boston: Houghton Mifflin.

Zipf, G. K. (1929). Relative frequency as a determinant of phonetic change. *Harvard Studies in Classical Philology, 40*, 1–95.

Zorzi, M., Testolin, A., & Stoianov, I. P. (2013). Modeling language and cognition with deep unsupervised learning: A tutorial overview. *Frontiers in Psychology, 4*(515), 65–78.

Zuraw, K. (2000). *Patterned exceptions in phonology* (doctoral dissertation, UCLA).

Index